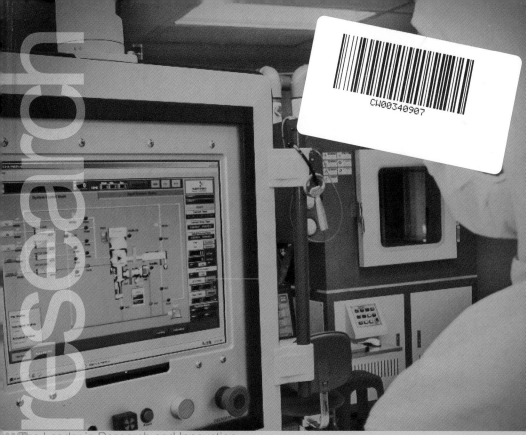

research

www.um.edu.my

The Leader in Research and Innovation

The Leader in Research and Innovation
The Leader in Research and Innovation
The Leader in Research and Innovation
The Leader in Research and Innovation
The Leader in Research and Innovation

UNIVERSITY
OF MALAYA

THE UNIVERSITY OF NEW SOUTH WALES
SYDNEY • CANBERRA • AUSTRALIA

Global Education + Global Networks = Global Opportunities

Students celebrate their graduation at the Sir John Clancy Auditorium, UNSW Sydney Campus. Graduation ceremonies are held throughout Asia and are the most moving and exciting ceremonies held to mark the successful completion of a student's academic program.

The University of New South Wales (UNSW) is Australia's first international university.

- Ranked 45th in the world in the 2008 *Times Higher Education Report of World University Rankings*
- Ranked 1st in Australia and 39th in the world for the UNSW AGSM MBA in the 2008 *Financial Times (UK) of MBA Program Rankings*
- Ranked 1st in the world for accounting research in the June 2007 edition of the international journal *Accounting and Finance*
- Consistently ranked as the leading Engineering Faculty in Australia
- A comprehensive teaching and research university offering over 400 degree programs across nine faculties

A MEMBER OF

Group of Eight
AUSTRALIA'S LEADING UNIVERSITIES

www.unsw.edu.au
UNSW International Office: Tel. +61 2 9385 6996 ■ internationaloffice@unsw.edu.au

UNIVERSITAS
The Network for
International Higher Education

3rd revised and updated edition *exclusively* featuring the latest

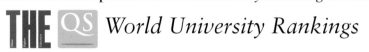 THE QS *World University Rankings*

T⬤P
UNIVERSITIES
GUIDE

John O'Leary   Nunzio Quacquarelli   Martin Ince

In association with

Published by Quacquarelli Symonds Limited

Authors

Top Universities Guide 2009 is co-authored by
John O'Leary, Nunzio Quacquarelli and Martin Ince

John O'Leary is former editor of the Times Higher Education Supplement
(now Times Higher Education) and author of
The Times Good University Guide, UK.
Previously, John was education editor at The Times.
John has a degree from Sheffield University.

Nunzio Quacquarelli is managing director of QS.
Nunzio is director of research of the THE-QS World University Rankings, assisted by
Ben Sowter, QS head of research.
Nunzio is editor in chief of TopUniversities.com, TopMBA.com and
TopGraduate.com, and writes regularly on education
and careers topics for The Times, The Times of India,
Die Zeit, South China Morning Post, and other newspapers worldwide.
Nunzio has an MA from Cambridge University and
an MBA from The Wharton School, University of Pennsylvania.

Martin Ince is a contributing editor of Times Higher Education and editor of the
THE-QS World University Rankings. Martin works as a freelance journalist and media
adviser and is author of ten books, most recently the Rough Guide to the Earth (2007).

*

Additional specialist editorial contributions by
Ann Graham and Tim Rogers

Ann Graham is a freelance education writer from New Zealand

Tim Rogers is an international education consultant and writer

*

Edited by Emma Simmons

Discover more about the world's top 500 universities and
the THE-QS World University Rankings at
www.topuniversities.com

Top Universities Guide
Published by QS Quacquarelli Symonds Limited
3rd revised and updated edition, February 2009
First published in 2006 as Guide to the World's Top Universities

QS Quacquarelli Symonds Limited
1 Tranley Mews, Fleet Road
London NW3 2DG
United Kingdom
www.qs.com

ISBN: 978-0-9558157-1-3

Acknowledgements
Sponsors: ETS-TOEFL®, ETS-GRE®, Dubai International Academic City, IELTS™
The authors would like to thank the many individuals who have contributed to this edition:
Ben Sowter, QS head of research, who compiled the data behind the THE-QS World University
Rankings assisted by Baerbel Eckelmann and Susan Gatuguta; Jason Newman, QS head
TopUniversities portfolio, project leader Top Universities Guide. Other contributing QS colleagues
include Oliver Beckett, Simona Bizzozero, Genevieve Lee, Tony Martin, Tariro Masukume,
Mandy Mok, David Nelkin, Maddalena Schiavon, Ed Winder. Thanks to Ann Graham and
Tim Rogers, and to Sarah Hudson, Emma Simmons, Simon Yeo. Additional international reporting
Jon Marcus, and contributors to previous editions: Michael Chan, Philip Fine, Michael Leidig,
Jane Marshall, Anna Martin, Geoff Maslen, and Tom McGrenery.

The authors would also like to thank Ann Mroz, editor of Times Higher Education.

Special thanks are owed to Scopus™ for the provision of the citation data used in the compilation
of the THE-QS World University Rankings 2008.

The authors would also like to thank all the universities that provided data and the numerous
governmental and research agencies worldwide that supplied information. Contact details for
many of these universities and agencies can be found in chapter six.
Thanks to the advertisers in this edition are also due.

Editorial and project coordinator: Emma Simmons
Design and cover: Sarah Hudson at Room 13 Ltd
Print management: Spixel Design Communications, Singapore
Printed on: 100gsm GoldEast Matt Artpaper
Printed by: Times Printers Pte Ltd, Singapore
Distribution: QS, OCS

Important note
Every effort has been made to ensure that all information contained in this book is accurate.
However, with the huge volume of data involved, the authors cannot offer a complete guarantee of
accuracy. The publisher regrets any inaccuracies and is most grateful for them to be brought to its
attention. Necessary corrections will be published on **www.topuniversities.com**. Please write to
Ben Sowter, QS head of research **ben@qsnetwork.com.**

WHERE HOW IT'S TAUGHT IS AS IMPORTANT AS WHAT IS TAUGHT.

INVEST TO EDUCATE.

DIAC

DUBAI
INTERNATIONAL
ACADEMIC CITY

A member of
TECOM INVESTMENTS

START

FIND YOUR WAY IN LIFE, START AT POLYU.

In the maze of choices you face in choosing the right university to chart your successful career, no university is more respected than PolyU when it comes to delivering 'real world' solutions by some of the best academic minds. Go with PolyU, and go far.

THE HONG KONG
POLYTECHNIC UNIVERSITY
香港理工大學

www.polyu.edu.hk

Contents

Introduction 13

1 How to select a university 17

THE-QS World University Rankings 2008:
Top 200 21
Masters programs 29
PhD programs 30
Top 100 profiles 33

2 What subject, what program? 137

Social sciences 139
Arts and humanities 145
Science 151
Biomedicine 156
Technology 161

3 Study abroad 167

Your career 168
Graduate study 169
Country profiles 170
Australia 173 Canada 177 France 179 Germany 181
Japan 183 Netherlands 187 Nordic countries 189
Singapore 193 UK 197 US 199 New Zealand 203
South Korea 205 Switzerland 207
Information 209

4 Fees, finance and scholarships 211

Study costs 212
Scholarships 229
Masters and PhD funding 233

5 How to apply to university 235

6 Information and resources 243

About rankings 243
Top 200 data table 247
Methodology 257
Higher education data sources 263
Top 500: Directory 267

Index 353

Universities, topics, advertisers

THE-QS World University Rankings:
Worldwide media reaction and debate

"... there are nearly 10,000 universities worldwide, so even to be included on the THE-QS list... is a remarkable achievement." *The Canadian Press*

"According to the THE-QS World University Rankings, Britain has more top-rated universities than any other country outside the United States. But other nations are catching up." *The Daily Telegraph*

"It is good to see that Australian universities continue to punch above their weight." *The Age*

"Universities in the USA and the UK continue to dominate an annual table ranking the world's top higher education institutions. Among the top 10 institutions in the Times Higher Education QS list, six are in the USA and four are in the UK." *BBC*

"The figures sparked a fierce debate about university funding on both sides of the Atlantic." *The Guardian*

"The ranking, produced by QS and Times Higher Education magazine... was based on interviews with academics and employers and on other yardsticks including staff-student ratios." *Bloomberg.com*

"The world's most comprehensive international university rankings." *Scoop, New Zealand*

"Just two institutions make annual attempts to compare universities round the world... both these indices... are closely watched by participants in a fickle and fast-expanding global education market." *The Economist, UK*

".... the ranking was a testament to a university's standing in the international community, identifying... 'an elite group of world-class universities.'" *Academica, Russia*

"The increasing internationalization of universities is one of the emerging themes in recent years." *The Nation, Thailand*

Indian institutions "... have been ranked ... in a list topped by Harvard University of US." *Indian Express*

"The world ranking of both Trinity and UCD has improved dramatically according to the most prestigious international review." *Irish Times*

"'International rankings are becoming increasingly important in a global education market...'" *UCT Daily News, South Africa*

"The latest trends show an increasing profile of technology-based universities..." *The Malaysian Bar*

"The idea of the knowledge economy requires a strong higher education sector." *The Times*

THE AUSTRALIAN NATIONAL UNIVERSITY

Great environment, **exceptional supervisors**, **international** connections. At **ANU**, you're in **good company**.

The Australian National University is Australia's top ranking university and among the world's best.

ANU is ranked 1st in Australia and 16th in the world by *The Times* Higher Education Supplement (UK) October 2008. Choose to study with us, and you'll enjoy unparalleled access to leading thinkers and first-rate facilities on a vibrant, spacious parkland campus.

ANU students enjoy all the benefits of living in Australia's capital city. Canberra has a buzzing social life and is home to many of the nation's cultural icons. But if you feel like getting away, it's not too far to magnificent beaches and alpine areas.

Don't bury your talent. Give yourself space to think, learn and have fun. Find your way at ANU.

Introduction

Welcome to this new, completely revised and updated, third edition of best-selling Top Universities Guide. It provides essential information on selecting and gaining admission to the right university; identifying not only the most highly ranked universities in the world, but also the best performing in almost 50 countries, including those universities most targeted by employers, producing the best research and teaching, and with the most international profile. With the number of young people attending university outside their home country set to grow from 3.2 million to more than 5 million by 2010, and record numbers seeking university education in their home countries, competition for the best university places worldwide is growing.

Who is Top Universities Guide for?

With more than 3 million visitors per year to **www.topuniversities.com**, thousands of students, parents, employers and academics have already found Top Universities Guide to be an indispensable handbook. Feedback on the book and rankings has been excellent. The Economist discusses "A new sort of higher education guide"...The THE-QS World University Rankings "broaden its inquiry by taking opinions from academics and employers... in the fickle and fast expanding higher education market." This customer-focused approach to evaluating universities has gained widespread approval and ensures the relevance to anyone concerned that their university studies should result in good career prospects.

This book will be an invaluable tool for you if you are bright, well educated, and aiming for a successful career after university? Or, if you are a parent wanting to give your son or daughter an edge in his or her choice of university study? Are you taking your first degree and considering a masters, PhD, or study abroad program? This edition exclusively includes the latest THE-QS World University Rankings, so, if you are an employer or researcher refining your choice of universities to target for recruitment, or an academic looking to change institution, there is almost certainly something in Top Universities Guide for you, too. Academics worldwide are referring to Top Universities Guide to benchmark the performance of their universities and departments against international peers.

Authored by acknowledged experts in the field, Top Universities Guide is born out of the recognition that employers, governments and parents want young people to select the universities and courses that will equip them with the knowledge to make a real contribution to our global society. Around the world, governments are one-by-one ending the free provision of local university education and, instead, are encouraging students to seek out the best university education, at home or abroad. Many are providing grants for international student mobility. In the US, recent Abraham Lincoln Study Abroad legislation aims to encourage one million students to study overseas, annually by 2016. Europe's Bologna Accord will make room for over 500,000 first-degree graduates to study in other EU nations for a masters degree, by 2010. Over three million Asians are expected to study outside their home country by 2020. The majority of all these students will aim to study at one of the 500 top universities featured in Top Universities Guide.

Employers put a premium on internationally educated graduates because of the greater maturity and cultural understanding gained from a period of study overseas, either as an undergraduate or postgraduate. Stephanie Ahrens, head of graduate recruiting at Morgan Stanley says, "Changes in the economy as well as today's globalization are leading to a growing need for pipeline talent with international skills, fluency in a number of foreign languages, as well as willingness to be mobile and consider a career path anywhere in the world."

Top Universities Guide offers advice on graduate career opportunities and salaries. A report for the United Nations identified that while 80 per cent of the world's 18-24 year olds were unemployed, only 10 per cent of the world's graduates were. But for many high-flyers, it is no longer enough to have a first degree from a local university. Research by QS, (publisher of this book and the researchers behind the THE-QS World University Rankings), confirms that graduates of these top universities are consistently among the most highly paid young professionals in every country in the world, and leaders, the world over, come consistently from these same universities. From knowledge based industries like consulting and banking, to global concerns such as the automotive and technology industries, and governments seeking to establish a globally minded cadre of young administrators, employers are increasingly focused internationally on the best universities to recruit graduates and, increasingly, willing to pay a premium for those with higher degrees.

Rankings

You can read this book through from start to finish or use it as a reference work, dipping in at points relevant to where you are in your university search. When reviewing rankings tables, do not rely on them out of context. A university should not be selected purely based on its worldwide ranking, when relatively small variations in data can account for large positional movements. You should cross reference the overall ranking position of each university with its strength in the subject area ranking relevant to your study interests, and follow thoroughly the guidance for researching each university. There can be some major differences, because universities are never equally good at everything. Additional information on the THE-QS World University Rankings can also be obtained at **www.timeshighereducation.co.uk**.

Career goals

Your university selection should be strongly influenced by your career goals. Various sections of the book include employer attitudes and suggest different career paths possible after studying different subjects. Aim to identify universities and study destination countries that measure up to your study and career goals and provide a feasible option in terms of cost and financial aid. Once you have drawn up a list of top universities that meet your basic criteria, you can further investigate entry requirements, culture and specific subjects offered, through the profiles of the top 100 in this book, visiting university websites and using the contact details for the top 500 in the directory (chapter six), and by exploring **www.topuniversities.com.**

In addition to making fascinating reading, we hope this guide will help change your life for the better, and the lives of tens of thousands of other high achievers, worldwide. We hope it will direct you to the top performing universities in the world, help you identify the best subject and destination, assist you in finding funding, and guide you into career paths which will allow you to achieve your full potential.

What's in the book?

As you begin your investigation into one of the most important and exciting decisions of your life, Top Universities Guide represents an ideal starting point for finding a top university at home or abroad.

Chapter one, **How to select a university** helps you through the process of choosing a university. Where do you start? What information do you need? What about rankings? How high should you aim and should you study near home or further afield? What special considerations are there at undergraduate, masters and PhD levels? And to give you a flavour of what life is really like at the Top 100 universities in the world, according to the latest THE-QS World University Rankings, there is a profile of each including student comments and a list of the top 200.

Chapter two, **What subject, what program?** investigates what you should study. It surveys five major subject areas: social sciences, arts and humanities, science, biomedicine and technology, and identifies the best 100 universities in each, worldwide. But also, it opens your eyes to the multitude of career options available, depending on which program you choose to follow. You never know; you may get quite new ideas.

Chapter three is your guide to **Study abroad**. It shows you the advantages international study can bring to your career, what employers think, and profiles, with pros and cons, the ten most popular study abroad destinations, and three up-and-coming ones. This chapter concludes with the international contacts to start your study abroad search.

Now, you've found your ideal study destination, university and program, you need to know how much it is going to cost and how you might pay for it.

Chapter four, **Fees, finance and scholarships**, runs you through the costs of study worldwide, including average tuition fees in each country and at the top 200 universities for undergraduates and postgraduates, domestic and international students. The second part of the chapter discusses funding options and points you in the direction of scholarship providers worldwide, including contact websites.

Chapter five **How to apply to university** guides you whether you are an undergraduate, masters or PhD applicant, anywhere in the world. Written by an expert on international university applications, it examines all the tasks you will be faced with, including language issues, and, with a practical approach, points you in the direction of success.

Chapter six contains your **Information and resources**. It includes the comprehensive full data tables to analyze the top 200 universities worldwide according to the THE-QS World University Rankings. It helps you understand rankings methodology and lists data sources worldwide for higher education. Finally, it includes a directory of the world's top 500 universities with their overall rank and subject area strengths, and, their web addresses. These are also available as direct links with program details, and much additional information at **www.topuniversities.com**, a QS website.

In a year marked by economic turmoil around the world, choosing the right university will be more important than ever: make the right choice. Good luck!

1

How to select a university

This chapter begins with an overview of important factors in university selection, why you should aim high and includes specific advice for choosing a masters or PhD destination. This is followed by a list of the current top 200 universities in the world (THE-QS World University Rankings 2008) and a profile of the top 100 worldwide, including student comments.

Reaching a decision on university study is one of the most important of your life. Balancing where and what to study involves many elements and a significant amount of time, so the amount of research you carry out and the sources of information you consult can make the difference between a good decision and the best decision.

So, what are the most important elements to consider when choosing a university or an academic program? Is it which country you want to study in? Or, the facilities a university has to offer? Perhaps you are focused on the academic program you wish to pursue, or the quality of research at the university. Whatever your priorities, you will have to consider a range of factors and consult a number of different sources to ensure that your decision is the best one possible. The university profiles and the rankings featured in this book are two important sources of information, but they are not the only ones. Almost every aspect of the university experience needs to be considered before choosing a university and a program and advice can come from a range of informed sources.

Before you start

Before you read any further, you might want to grab pen and paper, then read this paragraph and close the book. Why? Choosing a university and a program can be very personal. The advice touches on some of the factors that you must consider, but they may not accurately reflect what is important to you as an individual. Your rationale for applying to university is likely to be completely different from that of your best friend, your brother or sister, or a parent's opinion; but, the crucial thing is to be clear on your precise reasons. Many prospective students will be intent on an undergraduate degree as the first step towards a career that they are already sure about: this is often the case with medicine or engineering. Others will want to go back to university, after a period working, to take a masters or PhD to give them the additional skills to progress in their career, or change direction. An increasing number of students worldwide choose a university abroad, perhaps as the first step towards permanently moving after graduation. Whatever your reasons, take the opportunity, now, to note down your top ten reasons for studying and organize them into academic, career and personal categories, so that you can easily see where your priorities lie. Once you have done that, choosing a university and a program will be a great deal more straightforward.

Choosing a university location

Even if you are not considering studying abroad, the location of a potential university in your home country needs careful consideration. Many of the issues international students consider are as relevant for domestic students: do you want a city or rural location: a conveniently arranged campus-type university, or one that has multiple venues in a town or city? If your budget for living and accommodation is limited, would you consider attending a university nearby, or in your home town so that you can remain at home? What about the feasibility of earning some money while you study? If you are uncertain about being on your own, or you believe that studying with friends would be something positive, then finding out about where your friends are considering going to university may be a very helpful step.

However, the age of international education is most certainly upon us and the idea of studying for your first or an advanced degree away from your home country is now commonplace. According to the OECD, more than 75 countries have upwards of 1,000 international students enrolled in university-level courses. The country profiles in chapter three of this book (Study abroad) are a useful introduction to some of the most popular destinations for international students: they weigh up the positives and negatives of each country and provide a snapshot of each higher education system. So, what kind of country do you want to live in? The differences between European, North American and Australasian cultures, for example, are enormous and impact uniquely on your international student experience. The pace of life at an east coast US university, such as New York, is going to be significantly different from Victoria University, Wellington in New Zealand, and only you can decide what is likely to suit you better.

Although the US is the most popular country for international students, the countries of the European Union host more international students than any other world region. You may wish to choose a country where there are many international students and a significant infrastructure exists to cater for those from abroad. Or, you may be one of those students interested in being the only student from your country on campus, choosing one of the emerging country destinations for your university degree program. China, Estonia, Malaysia and Turkey are all attracting international students wanting to enjoy a less familiar culture and education system. This decision will be entirely dependent on your expectations and, to a certain extent, how good the rest of your research is in locating a university you believe to be of the right quality for your chosen degree program: chapter two (What subject, what program?) looks at subject strengths around the world.

Language

The majority of universities that welcome international students teach many degree programs in English, whether or not they are English-speaking countries. Or, you may be interested in a location where you will need to learn a new language outside of the classroom and adapt to a completely different culture. Increasingly popular destinations for international students like China, Denmark, Sweden and The Netherlands offer much of their teaching and study support in English, but encourage students to learn the local language to get the most out of the experience. Conversely, you may want to choose to study in a country where English is the official language, allowing you to integrate more quickly on and off of campus: the choice is yours.

Working while you study

All countries have different attitudes towards international students working while they study, and immediately after graduation. If you need to work while you study, this may be one of the most crucial aspects in deciding which country makes it to your shortlist, or, which university location at home (eg city or country campus). The most popular countries for international students, US, UK, Australia, Germany and France, allow students to work during study. Details vary, including what kind of work you may do, whether you are permitted to work on or off of campus and how many hours a week you can legally work, but further research will enable you to pinpoint where you are likely to be better off. The picture is not as clear for those students interested in staying on to work after the completion of their course. Many countries are aware of the advanced skills international students possess after graduation, but have yet to change their immigration legislation to allow students to remain and work indefinitely. The recently launched UK initiative to make it easier for UK-educated international students to work after studying is not available in all countries and you may have to return home, or go to another country, when you graduate.

Rankings and a top degree

Aim high: it makes sense to try to study at the best university you have the potential to get into, once all other factors have been considered. Therefore, independent rankings and league tables are an increasingly important part of choosing a university and an academic program. The THE-QS World University Rankings, included in this book, are one of the most exhaustive and well-researched ways of helping you choose a quality university, whether comparing top universities in your own country or worldwide. The evaluation criteria reflect some of the most important aspects of university-level education: the quality of the overall academic experience (as measured by the academic peer review), citations for research, employer review, staff/student ratio and an institution's commitment to internationalization (through the number of international staff and students). This data provides you with valuable information on how well a university does in the specific categories and overall. The top 200 universities worldwide in 2008 are listed in this chapter and the full table of data on the top 200 is included in chapter six (Information and resources), which also includes a directory of the top 500 universities worldwide.

Rankings, however, never provide the whole picture and should always be used in conjunction with other methods of research. Always be aware of the methodology that has been employed and what it actually measures. Rankings can prove most effective in bringing together a shortlist of potential universities and their academic departments for you to investigate further. What rankings never do is replace the more 'human' element of the university experience: how much fun it is to study in one particular university versus another, or what connections you will make there for the rest of your life. Whether looking to study at home or abroad, you should always seek the views of friends, parents, current and former students (alumni) in tandem with a university's ranking performance, in order to make a more complete decision on where might be the best place for you to study.

Global Leader in the 21st Century

KAIST

"Education for the World, Research for the Future"
Korea Advanced Institute of Science and Technology

Education for Future Leaders:
- Advanced Curriculum
- World-Class Faculty
- Solid, Balanced Infrastructure

Research on Global Issues:
- Energy
- Environment
- Water
- Sustainability

Specialized KAIST Institutes:
- BioCentury
- IT Convergence
- Design of Complex System
- Entertainment Engineering
- NanoCentury
- Eco-Energy
- Urban Space & Systems
- Optical Science & Technology

Diverse Areas of Study:
- Natural Science
- IT & Engineering
- Interdisciplinary Studies
- Business & Management
- Cultural Technology

2009 International Presidential Forum on Global Research Universities
21 September, 2009   Westin Chosun Hotel in Seoul
http://forum.kaist.ac.kr

KAIST
www.kaist.ac.kr
www.kaist.edu

For more information, please contact:
Office of External Affairs
373-1, Guseong-dong, Yuseong-gu, Daejeon 305 701, Republic of Korea
Tel: +82 42 350 2441-3 Fax: +82 42 350 4930 E-mail: irt@kaist.ac.kr

The world's top 200 universities*

Rank Institution Country

1	Harvard University US	
2	Yale University US	
3	University of Cambridge UK	
4	University of Oxford UK	
5	California Institute of Technology (Caltech) US	
6	Imperial College London UK	
7	UCL (University College London) UK	
8	University of Chicago US	
9	Massachusetts Institute of Technology (MIT) US	
10	Columbia University US	
11	University of Pennsylvania US	
12	Princeton University US	
13=	Duke University US	
13=	Johns Hopkins University US	
15	Cornell University US	
16	Australian National University AU	
17	Stanford University US	
18	University of Michigan US	
19	University of Tokyo JP	
20	McGill University CA	
21	Carnegie Mellon University US	
22	King's College London UK	
23	University of Edinburgh UK	
24	ETH Zurich CH	
25	Kyoto University JP	
26	University of Hong Kong HK	
27	Brown University US	
28	École Normale Supérieure Paris FR	
29	University of Manchester UK	
30=	University of California Los Angeles (UCLA) US	
30=	National University of Singapore SG	
32	University of Bristol UK	
33	Northwestern University US	
34=	University of British Columbia CA	
34=	École Polytechnique FR	
36	University of California Berkeley US	
37	University of Sydney AU	
38	University of Melbourne AU	
39	Hong Kong University of Science & Tech HK	
40	New York University (NYU) US	
41	University of Toronto CA	
42	Chinese University of Hong Kong HK	
43	University of Queensland AU	
44	Osaka University JP	
45	University of New South Wales AU	
46	Boston University US	
47	Monash University AU	
48	University of Copenhagen DK	
49	Trinity College Dublin IE	

50=	Ecole Polytechnique Fédérale de Lausanne CH	
50=	Peking University CN	
50=	Seoul National University KR	
53	University of Amsterdam NL	
54	Dartmouth College US	
55	University of Wisconsin-Madison US	
56	Tsinghua University CN	
57	Heidelberg Universität DE	
58	University of California San Diego US	
59	University of Washington US	
60	Washington University in St Louis US	
61	Tokyo Institute of Technology JP	
62	Emory University US	
63	Uppsala University SE	
64	Leiden University NL	
65	University of Auckland NZ	
66	London School of Economics & Political Science UK	
67	Utrecht University NL	
68	University of Geneva CH	
69	University of Warwick UK	
70	University of Texas at Austin US	
71	University of Illinois US	
72	Katholieke Universiteit Leuven BE	
73	University of Glasgow UK	
74	University of Alberta CA	
75	University of Birmingham UK	
76	University of Sheffield UK	
77	Nanyang Technological University SG	
78=	Delft University of Technology NL	
78=	Technische Universität München DE	
78=	Rice University US	
81=	University of Aarhus DK	
81=	University of York UK	
83=	Georgia Institute of Technology US	
83=	University of St Andrews UK	
83=	University of Western Australia AU	
86	University of Nottingham UK	
87	University of Minnesota US	
88	Lund University SE	
89	University of California Davis US	
90	Case Western Reserve University US	
91=	University of Helsinki FI	
91=	Université de Montréal CA	
93=	Hebrew University of Jerusalem IR	
93=	Ludwig-Maximilians-Universität München DE	
95	Korea Adv Inst of Sch and Tech (KAIST) KR	
96	University of Virginia US	
97	University of Pittsburgh US	
98	University of California Santa Barbara US	

*according to THE-QS World University Rankings

The world's top 200 universities continued

Rank Institution Country

99= Purdue University *US*
99= University of Southampton *UK*
101 Vanderbilt University *US*
102= University of North Carolina *US*
102= University of Southern California *US*
104 University of Leeds *UK*
105 Pennsylvania State University *US*
106= University of Adelaide *AU*
106= University of Zurich *CH*
108 University College Dublin *IE*
109 Technion Israel Institute of Technology *IR*
110 Georgetown University *US*
111 Maastricht University *NL*
112 Tohoku University *JP*
113 Fudan University *CN*
114 Tel Aviv University *IR*
115 University of Vienna *AT*
116 Université Catholique de Louvain (UCL) *BE*
117= McMaster University *CA*
117= Queen's University *CA*
119 University of Rochester *US*
120 Nagoya University *JP*
121 Ohio State University *US*
122= Durham University *UK*
122= University of Maryland *US*
124= University of Otago *NZ*
124= National Taiwan University *TW*
126 Erasmus University Rotterdam *NL*
127 Stony Brook University *US*
128 Eindhoven University of Technology *NL*
129 University of Waterloo *CA*
130 University of Sussex *UK*
131 University of Basel *CH*
132 University of California Irvine *US*
133= Cardiff University *UK*
133= Technical University of Denmark *DK*
133= University of Liverpool *UK*
136 University of Ghent *BE*
137= Freie Universität Berlin *DE*
137= Texas A&M University *US*
139 Humboldt-Universität zu Berlin *DE*
140 École Normale Supérieure de Lyon *FR*
141 University of Science & Technology of China *CN*
142 Wageningen University *NL*
143 Nanjing University *CN*
144= University of Groningen *NL*
144= Shanghai Jiao Tong University *CN*
146 University of Arizona *US*
147= City University of Hong Kong *HK*
147= Universität Freiburg *DE*
149 Université Pierre-et-Marie-Curie Paris VI *FR*

150 Universidad Nacional Autónoma de México *MX*
151 Rutgers The State University of New Jersey *US*
152 University of Bath *UK*
153 University of Aberdeen *UK*
154 Indian Institute of Technology Delhi (IITD) *IN*
155= VU University Amsterdam *NL*
155= Eberhard Karls Universität Tübingen *DE*
157 Tufts University *US*
158 Kyushu University *JP*
159 University of Western Ontario *CA*
160 Queen Mary University of London *UK*
161 University of Lausanne *CH*
162= Chalmers University of Technology *SE*
162= Newcastle University Newcastle Upon Tyne *UK*
164 Simon Fraser University *CA*
165 University of Florida *US*
166= Chulalongkorn University *TH*
166= Universität Göttingen *DE*
168 University of Notre Dame *US*
169 Universität Frankfurt am Main *DE*
170= University of Calgary *CA*
170= Indiana University Bloomington *US*
170= University of Lancaster *UK*
173 KTH Royal Institute of Technology *SE*
174= Hokkaido University *JP*
174= Indian Institute of Technology Bombay *IN*
174= Rensselaer Polytechnic Institute *US*
177= University of Leicester *UK*
177= University of Oslo *NO*
179 University of Cape Town *ZA*
180= University of Colorado at Boulder *US*
180= Waseda University *JP*
182 Macquarie University *AU*
183= Université Libre de Bruxelles (ULB) *BE*
183= Lomonosov Moscow State University *RU*
185 Brandeis University *US*
186= University of Barcelona *ES*
186= University of Canterbury *NZ*
188= Technische Universität Berlin *DE*
188= Pohand University of Science and Technology *KR*
190 Universität Stuttgart *DE*
191 University of Massachusetts Amherst *US*
192= University of Bern *CH*
192= University of Bologna *IT*
194 University of Reading *UK*
195 University of Antwerp *BE*
196 University of São Paulo *BR*
197= University of Buenos Aires *AR*
197= Dalhousie University *CA*
199 Kobe University *JP*
200= University of Athens *GR*
200= University of Twente *NL*

Universiti Teknologi Malaysia
Malaysia's Premier University
in Engineering, Science and Technology

Universiti Teknologi Malaysia (UTM)

Universiti Teknologi Malaysia (UTM) is located at the southern tip of Peninsular Malaysia. It is renowned for being at the forefront of engineering and technological knowledge and expertise, with a mission to be a world class centre of academic and technological excellence. UTM has also established a reputation for innovative education and leading-edge research, with a vision to educating technologists and professionals toward the development of creative human capital and advanced technological innovations. UTM is committed to providing an enriching and versatile teaching and learning environment to enhance individual creativity and potential.

In addition to providing quality and excellent academic programmes at both undergraduate and postgraduate levels in various disciplines, UTM has more than 20 specialist institutes and research centres which provide a conducive and stimulating environment for scholarly research and innovation. There are more than 15,000 full time undergraduate students at its main campus in Johor, more than 4,000 at its Kuala Lumpur campus, and more than 4,500 enrolled on distance learning programmes as part-time students. In addition, there are more than 3,000 postgraduate students in various fields of specialization.

Faculties/Schools in UTM

- Faculty of Built Environment
- Faculty of Chemical and Natural Resources Engineering
- Faculty of Civil Engineering
- Faculty of Computer Science and Information System
- Faculty of Education
- Faculty of Electrical Engineering
- Faculty of Geoinformation Science and Engineering
- Faculty of Management and Human Resource Development
- Faculty of Mechanical Engineering
- Faculty of Science
- Faculty of Biomedical Engineering and Health Science
- Faculty of Bioscience and Bioengineering
- School of Graduate Studies
- International Business School
- Business and Advanced Technology Centre

Excellence through **creativity** *and* **innovation**

www.utm.my

The world speaks IELTS

Your ticket to a world of opportunity

If you're applying to study anywhere in the world, IELTS may be the only English language test you need.

Most universities in Australia, Canada, New Zealand and the UK accept IELTS scores. In the USA, it is accepted by over 2,000 institutions including Ivy League schools.

It's also recognised for immigration to Australia, Canada, New Zealand and the UK.

IELTS – the test that proves your English skills wherever you go.

www.ielts.org

IELTS™
English for International Opportunity

Gathering information

Whether looking to study near or far away from home, it has never been easier to gather information on prospective universities, their programs and life there through the internet. All universities, and their academic departments, have websites that offer an enormous amount of detail on what makes their specific educational experience one that you should consider. These websites should always be your first port of call to gather all the basic data. However, the 'official' presentation of many university websites leaves out a lot of the information you might actually want to consider, so it is critical that you consult a far wider range of information sources than you might have initially thought.

Independent websites, printed directories and other kinds of guides can offer you a more complete picture of what a university is really like. The more independent a publication, the more objective it will be and the more useful the advice is to you. QS (the publisher of this book) hosts **www.topuniversities.com**, another useful place to start, among other more general websites. Additionally, social networking sites host active student groups from almost every university in the world, adding the dimension of the current student or fellow applicant to your research process. Student forums and chat rooms are a common feature of such sites and tend to offer an anecdotal view of what it is really like to be a student enrolled on a particular program or at a specific university. Of course, such 'advice' should always be taken in context, but it can offer you some of the flavour of the university you would otherwise never taste.

Face-to-face: fairs and alumni

The opportunity to meet a representative of a university is also an excellent way of finding out about it. Education fairs, university open days or seminars are now a common feature of student recruitment and applications, and allow you to meet people face-to-face, often in an informal setting. You may not be able to visit all universities you are interested in, and this option can be the next best thing, particularly if you are well prepared and know exactly the kind of questions you want to ask. You may also come across other prospective places to study at such events. Education fairs take place around the world and can easily be found through an online search. The annual QS World Grad School Tour in around 40 countries, enables you to meet more than 150 universities offering masters and PhD programs **www.topgradschool.com**, and the QS World MBA Tour offers you the opportunity to meet many of the world's leading business schools in more than 45 cities every year **www.topmba.com**.

One of the best sources of information is alumni. Having already graduated, they have a unique perspective, an inside view, on their program and the university. This experience can be even more relevant if they have come from a similar background to you, sharing some of your worries and hopes. Most importantly, advice from alumni can cut through the marketing material a university produces and get to the heart of the actual experience you will have and the benefits that a degree from that institution might have for your future career. Alumni tend to have an honest and balanced approach to their university experience and usually provide useful information. Locating an alumnus to speak to generally requires the help of the university, which should be willing to put you in touch with someone nearest to where you live. A number of universities will actually use alumni more directly in the student recruitment process and arrange interviews between former and prospective students as part of the application process.

Premium value of further study

Future salary may not be a major factor in your choice of university, but a sense of potential future earnings helps. To begin with, the UK Association of Graduate Recruiters publishes a salary report, which reveals that graduates, on average, achieve a 50 per cent premium over non-graduates' earnings. The premium for graduate education spans all professional sectors and continues to increase as each further degree is added. QS research on reported salaries across the EU and North America at four stages of higher education: first degree, masters, PhD and MBA shows that first degree salaries vary significantly by industry sector. Consulting/professional services, financial services and energy pay the highest average starting salaries with the manufacturing/automotive, public sector/non-profit and retail sectors reporting the lowest. Starting salaries, however, are not always indicators of long-term earnings potential. Career decisions will always be based on more than just salary, with work-life balance, a stimulating environment and assignments and travel being important factors.

Employers place a high premium on further higher education: masters, PhD and MBA. According to QS research, masters degrees can achieve anything between an eight and a 79 per cent premium on a first degree, with some of the lower paid sectors at first degree level, placing a particularly high premium on masters and PhDs, which are no longer simply a route to a professorship. Many employers actively seek to recruit PhDs and offer salary premiums, which vary between 25 and 105 per cent, over and above graduate starting salaries. The aerospace/defence industries offer the highest premium for PhDs, followed by manufacturing/automotive, and the public sector/non-profit. Employers continue to place the greatest salary premium on the MBA qualification, with salaries of between 160 and 248 per cent of equivalent first degree salaries.

Careers sharpened here

The University of Queensland

When you are competing for careers where graduate qualifications are standard, The University of Queensland will give you the edge you need.

You will get a world-class degree with all the benefits of UQ's international reputation. The independent UK Times Higher Education Supplement places UQ in the top 50 universities in the world – the only university in Queensland to rank so highly. So you will enjoy all the benefits of learning from some of Australia's most awarded lecturers, at the forefront of their fields – and a world-class degree that carries UQ's international reputation for excellence. With credentials like that, employers will be impressed.

Students at UQ choose from a range of high-quality study options. This includes PhD, Master of Philosophy, Research and Coursework Masters, Bachelors, Graduate Diplomas and Graduate Certificates.

Students at UQ study across three superb South-East Queensland campuses at St Lucia, Ipswich and Gatton. UQ St Lucia, The University's largest campus, is situated in Brisbane, a dynamic capital city known for its excellent climate, safe environment and superb quality of life.

Visit the weblink below and fill in our online enquiry form to make contact with your personal advisor and to find out more about furthering your career and advancing your education in one of the world's leading institutions.

Online enquiry form **www.uq.edu.au/international/enquiry**

Web **www.uq.edu.au/international**

Phone **+61 3 8676 7004**

CRICOS Provider Number 00025B

THE UNIVERSITY
OF QUEENSLAND
AUSTRALIA

ST LUCIA   IPSWICH   GATTON

Find your

International Masters or PhD

The QS World Grad School Tour will visit
49 cities in 29 countries
please register at

topgradschool.com

Choosing a masters program

Choosing the right university for a graduate masters program often requires more detailed research than at undergraduate level. In most cases, the decision to read a masters degree tends to have a closer relationship with your career, whether after a period of employment, or directly after your first degree, and so you need different information before you can take an informed decision. All the advice in chapter one, about gathering the right information before selecting a university, should be employed, but more time should be spent on defining your specific career objectives and how your program of study will support you in achieving them. University masters programs recognize the importance of a close relationship between the degree and the labour market and tend to keep very detailed data on the employment opportunities for their graduates, the number receiving offers after graduation, salary levels and industry sectors. Such information should be available to all prospective masters students, in addition to the names of companies that regularly recruit on campus.

A way to gain additional insights into masters programs is to seek the advice of current or former university lecturers and tutors. You will have consulted your teachers at school before applying for your first degree, and the advice of university staff on where to take your masters program and what particular degree might be most appropriate to fulfil your ambitions can be absolutely crucial. Academic members of staff tend to be part of a close-knit international community, where university-to-university links exist, offering you access to 'inside knowledge' on the best masters program for you. They are generally only too willing to offer impartial advice on your study choices and can also help you in weighing up a number of choices before you make your final decision.

Length of program

The length of masters programs is an additional factor that should be considered when choosing which program to apply for. In most of Europe, following the Bologna reforms in higher education, the majority of masters programs last two years of being taught and doing research. Other countries such as Canada, New Zealand and the US have a similar structure. However, some countries, most notably Australia, The Netherlands and the UK offer one-year, largely taught programs, halving the time you spend away from home and your career. Although both models result in very similar academic qualifications, your personal circumstances, particularly financing, may dictate whether the one-year or the longer masters program is preferable.

Funding

Perhaps the most important consideration when choosing a masters program is what opportunity you may have to receive financial aid, either from a university or another funding organization. Your decision may well be guided by who offers the broadest range of funding opportunities and what kind of financial aid is provided. In the most popular countries for international students, universities and other bodies tend to fund masters students more willingly than undergraduates. In 2008, 46.5 per cent of all international graduate students at US universities were funded by the universities themselves through scholarships, teaching assistantships and other forms of financial aid, compared with only 11.4 per cent of undergraduate students. This pattern is repeated in Australia, Canada and the UK with a focus on particular academic subjects and specified outcomes related to the funding program. Masters funding, however, is extremely competitive and tends to attract candidates of exemplary academic record with clear reasons for why they want to study at the graduate level. Chapter four (Fees, finance and funding) includes specific advice on funding your masters degree.

Choosing a PhD program

With governments and other organizations prioritizing the acquisition of knowledge and investing significant sums in research and development, it is no surprise that the popularity of PhD study is growing. However, making the right decision on where to pursue your PhD degree tends to be more complex than at other levels of university education. Because so much of the work undertaken for a PhD is done on a one-on-one basis, or in a small research group, choosing the right program tends to revolve around the research record of individual academic faculty in your field, that you are likely to work with, and the potential ways in which your work will be funded.

One of the benefits of university ranking systems is that they tend to reflect research output, one of the academic qualities most relevant to PhD study. Many rankings pinpoint how good individual academic areas are in terms of research, whether measured by how well used or cited a piece of research is (one of the key criteria in the THE-QS World University Rankings) or the perceived quality through peer review. This is the overriding consideration for any prospective PhD student, for it is in this area that their reputation and future will depend, so the need to gather this information is absolutely vital.

Funding

Funding, too, is critical and can dictate where you apply. University and other scholarship schemes encourage the recruitment of international PhD students and link funding with research support for other academic members of staff or, in the US and increasingly in Australia and the UK, through teaching assistantships. Depending on your field of study, it is likely that there will be funding available to you if your research proposal is of an excellent quality and focused in the appropriate academic area. In a number of European countries, the offer of PhD admission is parcelled with a faculty position where you are expected to contribute to the teaching and administration of your department. The benefit of this approach is that you not only receive funding to cover your tuition fees, but you are a salaried member of staff with a different immigration status from other international students. Chapter four (Fees, finance and funding) includes specific advice on funding your PhD.

PhD applications

The application process is also very different for PhD students (see chapter five How to apply to university) but can help you choose the best program. In the course of defining and writing your research profile, you will need to make contact with prospective academic supervisors to discuss whether they will be willing to accept you as their student. This point of contact is one of the best opportunities you will have to discover whether you feel you will 'fit in' with the department that will potentially be your 'home' for between three and five years. If a potential supervisor is responsive, friendly and interested in you and your research, then you have probably found the right place. If you find this communication difficult, then you should probably continue your search.

Finally, you should consider the structure and style of instruction of your future PhD program. PhD degrees are traditionally research intensive, but many universities now require students to participate in taught classes before the research aspect begins. In most countries, including those in the European Union, the first year of a PhD program is routinely structured around classes to establish your methodology and research practices. When this is successfully completed, the research phase begins. Before you make your final decision, you should ensure that you understand how the program will be structured and how this will impact on your time spent studying; this includes any requirements that you might have to fulfil before progressing to the research element of your degree.

جامعة الملك فهد للبترول و المعادن
King Fahd University of Petroleum & Minerals

WORLD-CLASS EDUCATION DELIVERED IN SAUDI ARABIA

COLLEGES

SCIENCES
chemistry, mathematics, physics, and earth sciences

ENGINEERING SCIENCES
chemical, civil, electrical, mechanical, petroleum, and aerospace

INDUSTRIAL MANAGEMENT
management information systems & accounting, finance & economics, and management & marketing

COMPUTER SCIENCES & ENGINEERING
computer engineering, information & computer science, and systems engineering

ENVIRONMENTAL DESIGN
architectural engineering, architecture, city & regional planning, and construction engineering & management

APPLIED & SUPPORTING STUDIES
prep-year program, English language department, physical education, Islamic & Arabic studies, general studies, and skills development

King Fahd University of Petroleum & Minerals (KFUPM) was established in 1963 in Dhahran, Saudi Arabia. KFUPM quickly blossomed into a world renowned center for education and research. With faculty drawn from the best from all over the world, and students attracted from the top 2% of potential applicants, KFUPM has become culturally diversified and intellectually innovative. KFUPM's graduates have achieved positions of trust in all sectors of the Kingdom and around the globe. Today, with a clear vision and an ambitious mission, KFUPM is a symbol of advancement and a model for university of the future:

EXCELLENCE IN EDUCATION
- ABET Accredited Eng'g Programs
- AACSB Accredited Mgmt Programs
- English as Medium of Instruction
- Skills Development Programs
- Rich Graduate Programs

EXCELLENCE IN RESEARCH
Research Institute
- Communications & IT
- Economics & Management Systems
- Engineering Research
- Environment & Water
- Petroleum & Minerals
- Refining & Petrochemicals
Centers for Research Excellence
- Corrosion
- Nanotechnology
- Refining & Petrochemicals
- Renewable Energy
Ample Research Funds

DHAHRAN TECHNO-VALLEY
- King Abdullah Science Park
- Prince Sultan S&T Center
- Innovation Centers
- Business Incubators
- Industry Liaison Office

INTERNATIONAL COOPERATION
- International Advisory Board
- Alliances with Renowned Institutions
- Distinguished Scholars Program
- Student Exchange Program

STATE-OF-THE-ART CAMPUS
- Full and Integrated IT Facilities
- e-University
- e-Learning
- e-Library
- e-Business

KFUPM

www.kfupm.edu.sa

Dhahran, Saudi Arabia

focusing on quality education and innovative research

www.topuniversities.com

NEW in 2009!

QS TOP UNIVERSITIES TOUR - ASIA

Delhi
Mumbai
Shanghai
Hong Kong
Singapore

OCTOBER 2009

The best degree study worldwide for
top-tier international students, presented
by an international selection of the
world's top 500 universities

**For more information, please log on to
www.topuniversities.com/fairs**

 THE - QS World University Rankings

Profiles of the world's top 100 universities

Knowing that a university is highly ranked is important, but hearing about its history, special expertise, famous alumni, and from students adds a different dimension that will help you decide whether it is the right place for you. The following pages profile the top 100 universities in the THE-QS World University Rankings, starting with Harvard University at number one. On the following page, you will find an alphabetical list, so that you can easily locate the profile you are interested in.

The profiles look at some of the reasons you might wish to consider each university as a study choice. They identify unique features, latest developments and subjects the institution is known for and give the foundation date and web address. Renowned former students are mentioned and, in most, an anecdotal comment by a current or recent student gives a more personal view. A factfile summarizes useful data, including ranking positions in various subjects, student and faculty numbers, and tuition fees. A map locates each university in its country context, so you know where you will be.

An international network of experts and journalists, have collected information from various public sources to compile the profiles. The intention is to give you a real-life flavour of the top 100 universities and a complementary view to university websites. However, a profile, can only provide a snapshot from one writer's perspective, and student comments are highly individual, and may not reflect general opinions. Nevertheless, these profiles are a starting point for your further research and may help form your own questions to staff or students, as you search for your ideal program and study destination. They may also awaken interest in an institution that you had not considered, or make you realize what is important to you, such as whether a university is located in a major world city or on a campus in beautiful scenery.

Notes on the factfiles

The dedicated research team behind the THE-QS World University Rankings 2008 has complied the factfiles. Each gives you a user-friendly overview of the information behind the rankings, (see chapter six, Information and resources, for the full rankings table and data for the top 200). While some of the profile texts refer to costs a student may face in local currencies, the factfiles use US$ throughout (exchange rates as at 01.05.08) to facilitate comparison. Any apparent disparity between factfile data and profile text, or university websites, results from different data collection dates, sources or data definitions. For example, student numbers in the factfiles are for full-time equivalent (FTE) students, counting students, who do not take a full course load, only as the fraction of a full-time student that they represent, rather than as individual students. Additionally, many universities have students that are neither undergraduates nor postgraduates, such as foundation year, diploma and some language students. Universities also all have different ways of counting distance learning and exchange students, among others, and this can lead to numbers published on university websites, being different from the official statistics of registered students provided for a rankings exercise. Student numbers marked with an asterisk in these factfiles indicate an estimate that has been made in the absence of an accurate FTE figure being provided, based on the average ratio between FTE and headcount across other institutions in the country or region.

These complex issues underline the imperative of your own further research, and the need for you to verify important data, directly with the institution, such as tuition fees, for your chosen course, before you take action based upon it. Any factual clarifications received by the publisher will be posted on **www.topuniversities.com** as appropriate, which also has direct electronic links to all the universities profiled.

World's top 100 universities* alphabetically with rank

University of Aarhus **81=**
University of Alberta **74**
University of Amsterdam **53**
University of Auckland **65**
Australian National University **16**
University of Birmingham **75**
University of Bristol **32**
University of British Columbia **34=**
Boston University **46**
Brown University **27**
University of California, Berkeley **36**
University of California, Davis **89**
California Inst of Technology (Caltech) **5**
University of California, Los Angeles (UCLA) **30=**
University of California, San Diego **58**
University of California, Santa Barbara **98**
University of Cambridge **3**
Carnegie Mellon University **21**
Case Western Reserve University **90**
University of Chicago **8**
Chinese University of Hong Kong **42**
Columbia University **10**
University of Copenhagen **48**
Cornell University **15**
Dartmouth College **54**
Delft University of Technology **78=**
Duke University **13=**
École Normale Supérieure, Paris **28**
École Polytechnique **34=**
Ecole Polytechnique Fédérale de Lausanne **50=**
University of Edinburgh **23**
Emory University **62**
ETH Zurich (Swiss Federal Inst of Tech) **24**
University of Geneva **68**
Georgia Institute of Technology **83=**
University of Glasgow **73**
Harvard University **1**
Hebrew University of Jerusalem **93=**
Heidelberg Universität **57**
University of Helsinki **91=**
University of Hong Kong **26**
Hong Kong U of Science & Tech **39**
Johns Hopkins University **13=**
University of Illinois **71**
Imperial College London **6**
Katholieke Universiteit Leuven **72**
King's College London **22**
KAIST (Korea Adv Inst of Sc & Tech) **95**
Kyoto University **25**
Leiden University **64**

London School of Economics & Political Science (LSE) **66**
Ludwig-Maximilians-Universität München (LMU) **93=**
Lund University **88**
University of Manchester **29**
Massachusetts Inst of Technology (MIT) **9**
McGill University **20**
University of Melbourne **38**
University of Michigan **18**
University of Minnesota **87**
Monash University **47**
Université de Montréal **91=**
Nanyang Technological University **77**
University of New South Wales **45**
New York University (NYU) **40**
Northwestern University **33**
University of Nottingham **86**
Osaka University **44**
University of Oxford **4**
Peking University **50=**
University of Pennsylvania **11**
University of Pittsburgh **97**
Princeton University **12**
Purdue University **99=**
University of Queensland **43**
Rice University **78=**
Seoul National University **50=**
University of Sheffield **76**
National University of Singapore **30=**
University of Southampton **99=**
University of St Andrews **83=**
Stanford University **17**
University of Sydney **37**
Technische Universität München **78=**
University of Texas at Austin **70**
University of Tokyo **19**
Tokyo Institute of Technology **61**
University of Toronto **41**
Trinity College Dublin **49**
Tsinghua University **56**
University College London (UCL) **7**
Uppsala University **63**
Utrecht University **67**
University of Virginia **96**
University of Warwick **69**
University of Washington **59**
Washington University in St. Louis **60**
University of Western Australia **83=**
University of Wisconsin-Madison **55**
Yale University **2**
University of York **81=**

* according to the THE-QS World University Rankings 2008

1 (1) Harvard University
Founded 1636   **www.harvard.edu**

USA

Cambridge●

Washington, DC●

Arts & humanities	1
Engineering & IT	19
Life sciences & biomedicine	1
Natural sciences	4
Social sciences	1
Academic survey position	2
Employer survey position	4
Student faculty ratio	5.7:1
International faculty	29.5%
Undergraduates	8,044
Postgraduates	13,528
International students	19.2%
Research strength (Scopus) papers	44,411
Research strength (Scopus) citations	517,932
Impact (citations per paper)	12

Top of the THE-QS World University Rankings since they first appeared in 2004, Harvard is America's oldest and the world's richest university. Now creating an entire new campus, largely to encourage interdisciplinary study, like almost everything that Harvard does, the scheme is ambitious almost without precedent: a small city in Boston's Allston section, just a short footbridge's walk across the Charles River from Harvard's long-time Cambridge home. The vastly expanded science and technology programs will be anchored by two 500,000-square-foot research facilities. It will take a decade for the new campus to take shape. Harvard isn't waiting around. It already conducts groundbreaking medical research, largely in its affiliated hospitals, which are among the best in the world, while the library is the largest at any academic institution, with nearly 16 million volumes. The university is trying to increase the number of women on the faculty after a controversy in which a former president was quoted (largely out of context) theorizing that women did not have the innate ability to succeed in the sciences. Now Harvard has its first woman president and an initiative to support tenure-track women. International activities include the opening of offices in Shanghai and Beijing. Nine applicants vie for every seat in the entering class. Following complaints that teaching is an afterthought for faculty more concerned with research and writing, a university review has recommended improving its quality and rewarding successful teachers by encouraging faculty to share course materials and teaching practices, and linking good teaching to salaries and career advancement.

Harvard's faculty has produced 43 Nobel laureates, its alumni another 32, and alumni have served as leaders in every field, from eight US presidents (including George W Bush and Barack Obama) to Benazir Bhutto and Al Gore. Some of the most famous, however, are the ones who dropped out, including Microsoft's Bill Gates (he reportedly quit when Harvard objected to his use of university computers for private business), Polaroid founder Edwin Land, publishing magnate William Randolph Hearst, and actor Matt Damon.

Generous financial aid made Harvard possible for Wojtek Kaszynski, an undergraduate from Poland who is majoring in applied mathematics. He doesn't dispute that students aren't always delighted with the teaching at Harvard. "The best researchers are not always the best teachers and the faculty will not actively seek you out. It's up to the students to be proactive and meet faculty." But he added: "My experience is that if I wanted to meet a particular professor, I certainly could."

2 (2=) Yale University

Founded 1701   www.yale.edu

USA

New Haven ●
Washington, DC ●

Arts & humanities 5
Engineering & IT 58
Life sciences & biomedicine 7
Natural sciences 17
Social sciences 7

Academic survey position 8
Employer survey position 12

Student faculty ratio 3.9:1
International faculty 31.0%
Undergraduates 5,296
Postgraduates 6,037
International students 15.9%

Research strength (Scopus) papers 23,073
Research strength (Scopus) citations 222,546
Impact (citations per paper) 10

A university that numbers both George H W Bush, George W Bush, Bill Clinton and John Kerry, among its graduates, must be providing a broad education. In fact, Yale does have one of the broadest curricula in American higher education, requiring its undergraduates to take at least three classes in each of four groups: languages, culture, social sciences, and science and maths. All students are required to learn a foreign language and to submit a senior essay or project, unusual at American universities. Named after Elihu Yale, who gave the young school 417 books and a portrait of King George I in 1716, Yale is in New Haven, Connecticut, a small city plagued with problems of urban poverty. Yale also seeks to make itself affordable for the broadest possible range of students. Families with combined incomes below US$45,000 a year are no longer required to pay anything towards their children's education at the school, a groundbreaking shift, followed by other leading universities. International students are eligible for the same financial aid as US citizens. Many of the programs at Yale have small classes; nearly a third of the classes enrol fewer than ten students, and three-quarters have fewer than 20. The law school has 124 full- and part-time faculty for its 664 students. Only one in ten applicants is admitted, the lowest proportion in the country. Undergraduates are divided into 12 residential colleges. More than US$400 million a year in research is conducted at the university. A strong international focus includes the recruitment of Tony Blair to lecture on Faith and Globalization. The 'Center for International Experience' has been running for eight years and enables hundreds of students each year to experience other cultures through study, work or research abroad.

Other alumni include Presidents William Howard Taft and Gerald Ford, and Senator Hillary Rodham Clinton; actors Jodie Foster, Sigourney Weaver, Sam Waterston, and Meryl Streep; former and current CEOs of FedEx and Coca Cola; 12 Nobel laureates; and Samuel F B Morse, the inventor of the telegraph.

"The biggest advantage of Yale is that it represents a sort of bubble of ideas from different perspectives," said Komli-Kofi Atsina, a student from Ghana who just received his undergraduate degree in molecular biophysics and biochemistry and is going on to medical school at the University of Pittsburgh. "It is a place that is so representative of the wide diversity around the world, a melting pot for crazy ideas, genius ideas, different kinds of ideology. In that respect, it's a great place for learning."

3 (2=) University of Cambridge
Founded 1209   www.cam.ac.uk

Arts & humanities	4
Engineering & IT	5
Life sciences & biomedicine	2
Natural sciences	3
Social sciences	5
Academic survey position	3
Employer survey position	1
Student faculty ratio	4.7:1
International faculty	41.4%
Undergraduates	12,300
Postgraduates	6,253
International students	26.7%
Research strength (Scopus) papers	28,037
Research strength (Scopus) citations	222,741
Impact (citations per paper)	8

The University of Cambridge celebrates its 800th anniversary in 2009 with a £1 billion fundraising campaign, regaining its lead over Oxford in the rankings, having been level with its ancient rival last year. Only Harvard and Yale outscore it. Cambridge scores more highly in national assessments of teaching and research in recent years. Traditionally supreme in the sciences, where it was ranked best in the world in successive years, Cambridge has also strengthened the arts and social sciences. There have been plenty of high-profile developments in recent years, but funding has remained a concern. The anniversary campaign hopes to narrow the gap with the US Ivy League. Already, there is to be a new centre on the Cambridge Biomedical Campus to address the growing threat to public health posed by obesity, diabetes and related diseases, and, as part of a unique collaborative agreement, the Japanese government has located a new research satellite at the Nanoscience Centre. A third of places are held by postgraduates, more than half of whom are from overseas and this is where any growth is likely to come. The university dominates the small city of Cambridge, 50 miles northeast of London. All students belong to one of 31 colleges, which, with few exceptions, are dotted around the city centre. Many boast historic buildings, several along the banks of the River Cam, where students and tourists go punting when the weather allows. Three colleges are for women only, while the rest are mixed. International students are guaranteed university-owned accommodation if they want it and are eligible for a limited number of scholarships.

The 81 'affiliates' of the university who have won Nobel prizes cover every category. They include Francis Crick and James Watson, who mastered the structure of DNA, and, more recently, Amartya Sen for his work in development economics, and geneticist John Sulston. Stephen Hawking has become one of the world's best-known scientists, while the student drama company Footlights has produced a stream of stars for the cinema and theatre worldwide.

Denise Law, an engineering student from Hong Kong, applied to Cambridge because she felt it was one of the few UK universities that could compete with US institutions. "It's a lovely city with great heritage and very nice and helpful people," she said. "Plus, the education and facilities are first class." However, the workload took her by surprise: "You're expected to make the most of supervisions by asking questions and taking the initiative, as opposed to the 'spoon feeding' of A levels. The learning curve is steep, although I was told that no one was ever kicked out for finding the material difficult."

4 (2=) University of Oxford
Founded 12th century **www.ox.ac.uk**

Arts & humanities 3
Engineering & IT... 14
Life sciences & biomedicine 5
Natural sciences... 5
Social sciences 6

Academic survey position 6
Employer survey position 2

Student faculty ratio 4.5:1
International faculty 38.1%
Undergraduates 12,173
Postgraduates 6,723
International students 27.8%

Research strength (Scopus) papers.................. 27,327
Research strength (Scopus) citations............. 220,681
Impact (citations per paper)...................................... 8

Oxford is the oldest university in the English-speaking world, and also probably the best known. Having caught Cambridge in the THE-QS World University Rankings last year, it has slipped behind its ancient rival again, but remains in the top five. Oxford comes out on top in some UK league tables, but the two are invariably mentioned in the same breath when leading universities are discussed. The 39 Oxford colleges select their own students and are responsible for much of the teaching, especially in the arts and social sciences. Traditionally, Oxford's strengths have been in these subject areas, which have provided most of the 25 UK prime ministers educated at the university. But the sciences have been growing in quality: a £60 million development houses the world's largest chemistry department, for example, and the controversial Biomedical Sciences Building opened in 2008. The building, which was the subject of intense, and sometimes illegal, protests, will rehouse research animals in one of the most advanced facilities in the UK. The Saïd Business School, established in 1996, has also carved out a strong reputation. Most of the colleges and other university buildings are in, or close to, the centre of the city of Oxford, which is within reach of some of England's most picturesque countryside and only an hour by train from London. Overseas students are guaranteed residential accommodation. Several hundred international students each year benefit from a range of scholarships and bursaries, the biggest of the schemes being the Rhodes and the Clarendon Fund Scholarships. Details appear in the university's International Student Guide. In May 2008 Oxford launched a £1.25 billion fundraising campaign for the university, which started with the news that £575 million had already been donated.

Among scores of famous alumni are Erasmus, philosopher Thomas Hobbes, playwright Oscar Wilde, author JRR Tolkein and chemist Dorothy Hodgkin, the only British woman to win a Nobel prize. More recent alumni include President Bill Clinton and Tim Berners Lee, inventor of the World Wide Web.

Jenny Rigterink, who studied English language and literature, said: "The pros are the unparalleled teaching and resources at your fingertips, but the cons are a stagnant social scene that seems far too old for its audience. Oxford will transform your life. The majority of people seem willing to let Oxford change them, but Oxford is begging for a generation that will turn things upside down." Her advice to potential overseas applicants: "If you're foreign, make contact with potential tutors before you apply."

5 (7=) California Institute of Technology
Founded 1891   www.caltech.edu

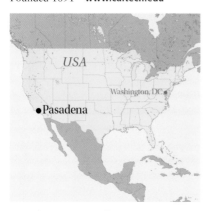

Arts & humanities	213
Engineering & IT	4
Life sciences & biomedicine	16
Natural sciences	7
Social sciences	78
Academic survey position	20
Employer survey position	133
Student faculty ratio	5.4:1
International faculty	85.1%
Undergraduates	913
Postgraduates	1,220
International students	24.5%
Research strength (Scopus) papers	12,037
Research strength (Scopus) citations	137,743
Impact (citations per paper)	11

One of America's smallest major research universities, with little more than 2,000 students, California Institute of Technology (Caltech) is also one of its best. Students boast the highest average scores in the nation on the SAT university entrance examination, and enjoy a high faculty-student ratio. There are more than twice as many men as women. Research is closely integrated with education. Expectations here are high. Every student has to take at least five terms of mathematics, two of chemistry, one of biology and five of physics, including quantum mechanics, special relativity, and statistical mechanics. To deal with the stress of this, collaboration is encouraged. So is a sense of humour. During final examination weeks, Wagner's 'Ride of the Valkyries' is broadcast from loudspeakers across the campus every day at 7am. Despite Caltech's small size, there are still grand construction plans. A new astronomy and astrophysics centre was completed in 2008, a chemistry and chemical engineering laboratory is due in 2009, as is an information science and technology centre.

Fourteen Caltech professors, 17 alumni, and four professors, who were also alumni, have won the Nobel prize for breakthroughs in almost every major scientific field. They made the first astronomical survey of the entire sky visible from the Northern Hemisphere, and virtually invented seismology. It was Caltech physicist Carl Anderson who discovered anti-matter, chemist Linus Pauling who showed how atoms link up to form molecules, psychobiologist Roger Sperry who devised the left brain/right brain theory, and geophysicist Charles Richter, who invented the scale for measuring earthquakes. Among its international alumni are former Israeli foreign and defence minister Moshe Arens and Steingrímur Hermannsson, the former prime minister of Iceland. Alumni also include Chester Carlson, the inventor of photocopying, Intel chairman Gordon Moore, and Frank Capra, director of the film classic 'It's a Wonderful Life'.

Todd Gingrich was drawn to Caltech as an undergraduate because he wanted a challenge; he had already jumped ahead to university courses while he was still in high school and wasn't disappointed. "There's sort of this perception, which now that I'm here I can verify, that it's reasonably hardcore. The school's small size is mostly an advantage — people all know each other, you're living with a group of your good friends, and people are always looking out for you in a way that doesn't happen in a bigger school. I have this amazing network of peers in every field of math and science and I use it all the time." Many of these students live in small residential houses. "It's almost as if a bunch of nerds had taken over all the frats," he said.

6 (5) Imperial College London
Founded 1907   www.imperial.ac.uk

Arts & humanities 208
Engineering & IT... 7
Life sciences & biomedicine 11
Natural sciences.. 14
Social sciences 85

Academic survey position 25
Employer survey position 5

Student faculty ratio 4.2:1
International faculty 41.9%
Undergraduates 8,205
Postgraduates 4,410
International students 39.6%

Research strength (Scopus) papers................. 21,823
Research strength (Scopus) citations............. 151,172
Impact (citations per paper)...................................... 7

Imperial College is an academic powerhouse considered to rival Oxford and Cambridge in its specialisms of science, technology, medicine and engineering. The subjects make it one of the most male-dominated universities in the UK, although the number of female students doubled during the 1990s and is now up to a third. Faculty include Nobel prize winners and 61 Fellows of the Royal Society. It was also one of the most successful institutions in the latest UK research assessment exercise. Imperial College has built one of the largest and most powerful medical schools in Britain and a management school that is making its mark internationally. Language courses are available as joint degrees with management or sciences. The integrated medical school and hospital trust spans five hospitals and describes itself as the UK's first academic health science centre 'delivering breakthroughs in medical research directly to its patients'. Imperial College can claim the invention of penicillin and of magnetically levitated trains among its successes. It is also respected for strong links with government and industry, boasting the largest external research income in the UK. Imperial College left the University of London in time for its centenary in 2007, in order to capitalize on a reputation that puts it just outside the top five universities in our world rankings. Student services have now been replicated by the college itself. Imperial College's headquarters could hardly be in a more glamorous part of London. South Kensington's cosmopolitan vibe and museums show off London at its best. That can increase the cost of living, but overseas students are guaranteed college-owned accommodation.

Famous alumni include the four-minute miler and academic Sir Roger Bannister, politicians Rajiv Gandhi and Trevor Philips, writers Simon Singh and HG Wells and pop star Brian May.

Natsuko, who graduated with an MSc in biochemistry in 2004 and went on to study for a PhD at Imperial College, chose it because of its worldwide reputation and its location. "London was scary at first as I had never lived in such a large city, but I soon got used to it and discovered what an exciting place it is to be as a student," she said. "Imperial does work you hard, so you need to be committed and disciplined to be successful. But it really does pay off in the end. Many employers are interested in Imperial College graduates and you get a great network of people who can help you in your future career."

7 (9) University College London (UCL)

Founded 1826   www.ucl.ac.uk

Arts & humanities	29
Engineering & IT	96
Life sciences & biomedicine	25
Natural sciences	88
Social sciences	31
Academic survey position	34
Employer survey position	13
Student faculty ratio	4.5:1
International faculty	38.2%
Undergraduates	11,354
Postgraduates	6,024
International students	37.7%
Research strength (Scopus) papers	29,899
Research strength (Scopus) citations	221,453
Impact (citations per paper)	7

University College London describes itself as 'London's Global University', hosting many international students from across the world. These numbers are expected to grow still further in the next few years, as UCL develops courses in global citizenship and leadership to be integrated into all undergraduate programs. Parts of UCL, such as the Royal Free Hospital are in the north of the city, but most of campus life is based in busy, central London, Bloomsbury, where students have immediate access to London University's, underused, central students' union facilities. Further afield, UCL will become the first British university with a campus in Australia, establishing a School of Energy and Resources in Adelaide, in agreement with the Government of South Australia. UCL is comfortably the largest of the University of London's colleges and has begun to award its own degrees.

UCL is committed to teaching in small groups, especially in the second and subsequent years of degree courses and prides itself on excellence in biomedicine, Slavonic and East European studies, among many other subjects. It pioneered degrees in architecture and law, and has an excellent reputation in art with the Slade School of Fine Art. During the 1990s it took in a number of specialist schools and institutes, mainly in medicine or dentistry, adding to an already large medical school. In the latest development, five top medical research centres and hospitals are coming together to create what UCL claims will be 'Europe's leading health research powerhouse'. The new academic health science partnership, UCL Partners, will support more than 3,500 scientists, researchers and consultants, with an annual turnover around £2 billion. The college launched the biggest-ever UK university fundraising campaign to support further developments.

Alumni include Indian leader Mahatma Gandhi, Japanese Prime Minister Junichiro Koizumi, the inventor of the telephone Alexander Graham Bell and UK TV presenter Jonathan Dimbleby. Twenty alumni or former staff members have won Nobel prizes.

Erik Moore, from Australia, who is studying part-time for an MSc in Environmental Design and Engineering, said: "By offering the flexibility of working and studying at the same time, I feel I've really got the most I could from my degree at UCL. It's been the right mix of academic work, twinned with practical work and with loads of extra guest lectures for those that want to learn more. The standard of teaching has been exceptional and with a mix of international students from a range of different backgrounds, I've learnt a lot about how design works in different sectors."

8 (7=) University of Chicago
Founded 1890   www.uchicago.edu

Arts & humanities 9
Engineering & IT... 83
Life sciences & biomedicine 35
Natural sciences.. 12
Social sciences 8

Academic survey position 15
Employer survey position 18

Student faculty ratio 5.4:1
International faculty 24.8%
Undergraduates 4,880
Postgraduates 7,868
International students 19.9%

Research strength (Scopus) papers................. 15,402
Research strength (Scopus) citations 144,187
Impact (citations per paper).................................... 9

Student protests persuaded the University of Chicago to preserve the unique essay questions for which its admissions process is famous. It's just one way that Chicago students have been fiercely protective of the intellectual seriousness summed up in its heady credo: "Dedicated to the primacy of research, the intimate relationship of research to teaching, and the amelioration of the condition of humankind." So influential is the economics taught here that it has given rise to an entire field known as the Chicago School. Several members of the vaunted economics faculty are among the more than 80 Nobel laureates that have been associated with the university. Chicago also has the oldest sociology department in the US, and was an early practitioner of interdisciplinary scholarship. This is a place that takes higher education very seriously. Its ten-week quarters accelerate a learning process divided elsewhere into much longer semesters. Students are constantly subjected to examinations that test them on the rigorous core academic requirements, including a foreign language and cross-cultural studies. The university has surpassed a US$2 billion fundraising target and is putting that much into new facilities. It is also setting aside US$400 million — including US$100 million from a single anonymous donor — for student financial aid, entirely eliminating the need for loans for its middle-class students. The flip side of Chicago's notorious seriousness is that it's not an especially fun place. "Our un-fun-ness has been the subject of both mirth and pride," a task force on the matter put it. Some say Chicago is the only school in America where the undergraduates are under more stress than the graduate students.

The Graduate School of Business, second-oldest in the world, is consistently ranked among the best and has recently been renamed the University of Chicago Booth School of Business following the US$300 million donation by alumnus David Booth, the largest donation in the university's history and largest gift to any business school in the world. Other alumni include former US Attorney General John Ashcroft, former World Bank President Paul Wolfowitz, authors Kurt Vonnegut Jr and Philip Roth, composer Philip Glass, astronomer Edwin Hubble, the Reverend Jesse Jackson, director Mike Nichols, and the current or former presidents of other universities on this list, including Northwestern and Caltech. President Barack Obama taught at the university law school from 1992 to 2004.

It was Chicago's competitiveness that attracted Bonginkhosi Mzileni, a student from Swaziland majoring in chemistry. "It is tough. I found it even harder than I expected. We do get a lot of work every week and the quarter system puts you under a lot of pressure." But in the end, he said, succeeding at a school known for being so competitive is likely to serve him well in his career.

9 (10) Massachusetts Institute of Technology (MIT)
Founded 1861   **www.mit.edu**

Arts & humanities	20
Engineering & IT	1
Life sciences & biomedicine	8
Natural sciences	1
Social sciences	10
Academic survey position	5
Employer survey position	6
Student faculty ratio	6.6:1
International faculty	7.9%
Undergraduates	4,130
Postgraduates	5,851
International students	25.4%
Research strength (Scopus) papers	25,181
Research strength (Scopus) citations	223,472
Impact (citations per paper)	9

Every January, MIT, in the small city of Cambridge across the Charles River from Boston, runs an 'Independent Activities Period' during which students can select such non-credit subjects as chocolate sculpture making, palmistry, the symbolism of the Star Wars films, and how to make chain mail. It is a whimsical break from the intensity of the demanding academics at a school whose students are required to take two semesters each of calculus and physics, one each of biology and chemistry, and various courses in the humanities, arts, and social sciences. What makes MIT so tough, beyond the pressure its high-achieving students famously put on themselves, is the concept of the 'teaching laboratory' it pioneered, combining teaching with applied research, also making it one of the leading research institutions in America. Research teams at MIT have developed a single-electron transistor, invented a process similar to photosynthesis to produce hydrogen, and invented a gas with super-high temperature fluidity. Undergraduates, too, work with faculty through the Undergraduate Research Opportunity Program. More than half the undergraduates who have declared a major are enrolled in engineering, the field in which MIT is indisputably pre-eminent. This work is conducted in a collection of radically innovative buildings, many recently completed, including the Frank Gehry-designed Ray and Maria Stata Center for Computer, Information, and Intelligence Sciences and a huge new brain and cognitive sciences complex. MIT's president, Susan Hockfield, a neuroscientist and the first woman to hold the post, has challenged MIT to find solutions to the world's energy crisis. The university was also the first to put all the teaching materials used in its courses on the Internet without charge. In addition to its science disciplines, MIT has a top-flight business school, the Sloan School of Management, which attracts mostly mid-career managers.

More than 70 past and present MIT faculty and alumni have won the Nobel prize, 31 have received the National Medal of Science, and four have been awarded the Kyoto Prize. MIT leads all universities in America in patents granted.

Even chocolate sculpture making fails to completely lighten the mood at a place where the stakes are so high. "In the dorm that I live in, people tend to keep to themselves. They're generally not outgoing. It's a little cold," said Dzikimaki Matara, an undergraduate from Zimbabwe who is majoring in mechanical engineering. He, like two-thirds of his colleagues, alleviates his stress by playing intramural sports. Among the many new facilities is a fitness centre with two swimming pools and international-scale squash courts. "The workload is really much heavier than anywhere else," he said.

10 (11) Columbia University
Founded 1754   www.columbia.edu

Arts & humanities	7
Engineering & IT	63
Life sciences & biomedicine	20
Natural sciences	23
Social sciences	11
Academic survey position	16
Employer survey position	21
Student faculty ratio	5.3:1
International faculty	6.4%
Undergraduates	6,728
Postgraduates	13,828
International students	22.5%
Research strength (Scopus) papers	29,243
Research strength (Scopus) citations	252,414
Impact (citations per paper)	9

One of America's oldest universities, opened under a royal charter from King George II, is now undergoing one of the most ambitious expansions in the history of American higher education: a US$7.4 billion explosion out of its fortress-like Morningside Heights campus in Manhattan into neighbouring Harlem. The expansion will take 30 years and add 6.5 million-square-feet of labs, classrooms, offices, and housing. It's partly New York that puts Columbia in such high demand. The only Ivy League school in the city, Columbia attracts so many applicants that it has become one of the hardest American universities to get into, and can pick from the cream of the student crop. One in five students is from outside the United States — the fourth-largest proportion of international scholars at any American university. Many are Asian, enrolling in engineering, public affairs, business, and social sciences programs. Going the other way, Columbia students join summer language programs in Beijing, business internships in Shanghai and architecture field study in France.

An aggressive licensing program has resulted in the awarding of some 100 patents a year for Columbia discoveries and breakthroughs. The modern science of anthropology was invented here, as was the field of modern genetics, the laser, and system initial protocol, or SIP, the basis for instant messaging. The School of International and Public Affairs founded in the wake of World War II, is among the world's best, and the highly selective Graduate School of Journalism is considered the best in America. Columbia, like the city it calls home, is a comparatively noisy place. Its early graduates included some of the leaders of the American Revolution. Its students were in the forefront of the 1960s antiwar movement and it remains a hotbed of political activism.

Among Columbia's prominent alumni have been many who may have made King George regret his royal charter. They include John Jay, the first chief justice of the United States; Alexander Hamilton, the first secretary of the treasury; Gouverneur Morris, the author of the final draft of the US Constitution; and Robert Livingston, who helped draft the Declaration of Independence. More recent graduates have included Presidents Theodore Roosevelt, Franklin D Roosevelt, Dwight D Eisenhower and now Barack Obama. Former Secretary of State Madeleine Albright, author Isaac Asimov and anthropologist Margaret Mead are others. Martin Chalfie, Professor of Biological Sciences, won a share of the 2008 Nobel prize for chemistry.

Columbia's best asset is New York, said Stephanie Lew, an undergraduate. "The only thing that's a negative here is accommodation. They just don't have the best housing. I guess that's New York City for you." She also appreciates the school's diversity. "It's an environment that's very accepting. Everyone expresses themselves and their cultures."

11 (14) University of Pennsylvania
Founded 1740 **www.upenn.edu**

Arts & humanities 40
Engineering & IT... 78
Life sciences & biomedicine 41
Natural sciences... 47
Social sciences 22

Academic survey position 32
Employer survey position 24

Student faculty ratio 6.9:1
International faculty 27.3%
Undergraduates 10,734
Postgraduates 10,550
International students 18.4%

Research strength (Scopus) papers.................. 30,561
Research strength (Scopus) citations 262,252
Impact (citations per paper).................................... 9

'Penn' was founded by Benjamin Franklin and boasts that it carries on his principles of entrepreneurship, innovation, invention, and the pursuit of practical knowledge. It has 174 research centres and institutes and conducts more than US$700 million a year in research. The 4,800 faculty include 11 Nobel laureates (there is a similar number of alumni with Nobels). An ongoing US$3.5 billion fundraising campaign aims to add a nanoscale research building and new clinical, research, and educational facilities for the school of medicine, America's oldest. It will also help pay for more faculty, student financial aid, new programs and research. Like Franklin, a statue of whom sits at the centre of the campus, Penn is well-rounded. Its Wharton School, the world's first collegiate school of business and largest global business school, is consistently regarded among the top three in America. Its school of nursing ranks in the top two and its school of arts and sciences and graduate schools of education, law, medicine, and veterinary medicine in the top ten.

The university has a global emphasis that is evident in its programs. Penn's Solomon Asch Center for the Study of Ethnopolitical Conflict advises foreign governments; medical school faculty and students treat HIV-infected patients in Botswana. The graduate school of education has teamed up with Beijing and East China Normal universities to offer the first education doctorates in China. Penn suffers somewhat from its West Philadelphia setting, separated from the city centre by an industrial wasteland to the east that even a university task force described as 'unattractive.' Urban blight afflicts the residential neighbourhood to the west. The university hopes to transform both with an ambitious expansion, starting with a new 'East Campus.' Almost half of Penn students and many staff already participate in some 300 volunteer and community service courses.

Nine signers of the American Declaration of Independence and 11 signers of the Constitution are associated with the University of Pennsylvania. Eadweard James Muybridge, who pioneered motion photography, began his experiments under the university's auspices.

"It is not the best feeling in the world to be at the edge of West Philly, but I sincerely believe that the campus has become a lot safer than it was a couple of years ago or when my sister went here," said Schuchi Kothari, an undergraduate business major from India. "There have been a few incidents but everyone has come out safe. I do not feel unsafe walking around campus alone. There are security officers at every corner and street and the campus is well protected. The university does a great job of dealing with an area that most people would perceive as less than ideal."

12 (6) Princeton University
Founded 1746   www.princeton.edu

Arts & humanities 6
Engineering & IT.. 15
Life sciences & biomedicine 22
Natural sciences.. 6
Social sciences 9

Academic survey position 7
Employer survey position 31

Student faculty ratio 8.3:1
International faculty 32.5%
Undergraduates 4,845
Postgraduates 2,416
International students 19.4%

Research strength (Scopus) papers................. 13,243
Research strength (Scopus) citations 117,548
Impact (citations per paper)...................................... 9

The second-smallest of the Ivy League universities, Princeton is planning a new campus in central New Jersey to be built on a 400-acre, university-owned forest area, which the university claims will 'integrate the campus into natural systems of the environment.' But Princeton already has a reach far beyond its size. It accepts fewer than one in ten applicants (some no doubt attracted by the pioneering financial-aid policy, replacing loans with outright grants even for international students). It has see-sawed with Harvard in the American league tables, and even stolen some top faculty from its rival. All full-time faculty members must teach in addition to doing research: another tweak at Harvard, where students have complained that professors are more interested in what they're doing in the lab than in the classroom. Ten Princeton faculty members are Nobel laureates. All undergraduates are required to submit a senior thesis, something most other US universities make optional. All must also successfully complete two courses each in literature and the arts, science and technology, and social analysis, plus one course each in epistemology and cognition, ethical thought and moral values, historical analysis, and quantitative reasoning. Even engineering students have to take at least seven humanities and social sciences courses.

The emphasis on teaching doesn't mean that Princeton doesn't have a robust tradition of research. Some US$220 million a year in research is conducted here, US$77 million of it at the Princeton Plasma Laboratory, which the university administers on behalf of the US Department of Energy. Since the millennium alone, it has established the Lewis-Sigler Institute for Integrative Genomics to encourage interdisciplinary collaboration between biologists and scientists in physics, chemistry, chemical engineering, molecular biology, and other fields; the Princeton Neuroscience Institute, which does the same thing in the area of brain and nervous system studies; and the Princeton Center for Theoretical Physics, which combines various departments to do research on everything from the Big Bang to quantum computing. The university's engineering school specializes in dissecting the connection between technology and economics, politics, the arts, and other fields.

Princeton alumni include US presidents James Madison and Woodrow Wilson, after whom the university named its Woodrow Wilson School of Public and International Affairs.

"It's a small university for the Ivy League, and there's a lot of focus on the undergraduates," said Ritu Kamal, a bioengineering undergraduate from India. "The faculty are willing to take undergraduates into their labs and give them a lot of personal attention. In science departments, students do a lot of hands-on lab work alongside grad students who are doing research that will probably be published. "I worked with stem cells. It doesn't get much more cutting-edge than that," she said.

13= (13) Duke University
Founded 1838 **www.duke.edu**

Arts & humanities 21
Engineering & IT.. 111
Life sciences & biomedicine 21
Natural sciences... 79
Social sciences 26

Academic survey position 30
Employer survey position 23

Student faculty ratio 4.2:1
International faculty 6.6%
Undergraduates 6,372
Postgraduates 6,959
International students 14.6%

Research strength (Scopus) papers.................. 23,423
Research strength (Scopus) citations 208,965
Impact (citations per paper)...................................... 9

Considered one of the pre-eminent universities of the American South, Duke describes itself as a 'global gateway', requiring its students to take foreign language and international courses. Many of the students are pre-med, intending to go on to medical school, while others are engineering majors. All undergraduates enrol in either the Trinity College of Arts & Sciences or the Pratt School of Engineering, and half study abroad at some point — five times the US average. The business school plans to establish a network of campuses around the world to conduct research and deliver programs in key economic and cultural centres, including New Delhi, St Petersburg, Dubai, London and Shanghai. Undergraduates will also be pushed to take part in a US$30 million 'civic engagement program', which was one result of soul-searching at Duke in the wake of, what turned out to be, unfounded allegations that members of one of its sports teams had raped a black woman. The scheme involves community service over a summer or semester, largely in the surrounding city of Durham, North Carolina, with an organization that promotes awareness about sexual health, rape prevention, and alcohol and drug use.

The controversy distracted deserved attention from Duke's decidedly forward-looking work in the sciences. Anchoring the so-called Research Triangle in North Carolina's Piedmont region (its other corners are North Carolina State University and the University of North Carolina), Duke has sprouted cutting-edge facilities on its Gothic revival-style campus that have given the university a lead in fast-growing and emerging fields more closely associated with rivals in the North. They include the new US$97 million Fitzpatrick Center for Interdisciplinary Engineering, US$41 million Institute for Genome Sciences and Policy, and US$115 million French Sciences Building. Duke's Levine Science Research Center is the largest single-site interdisciplinary research facility at any American university.

Prominent alumni have included President Richard Nixon, Senator Elizabeth Done, and the former president of Chile, Ricardo Lagos; Melinda Gates, co-founder of the Bill and Melinda Gates Foundation; and the current or former heads of companies including Bear Stearns, Boston Scientific, Cisco Systems, ExxonMobil, General Motors, Northwest Airlines, PepsiCo, and Pfizer.

Shian Ling Keng, an undergraduate from Malaysia who majored in biology, said: "My experience as an international student is that it was difficult for me to fit into the social environment here, maybe because of the cultural differences. People feel like partying and drinking are the main way of social interaction, and I just don't party or do those things. But after a while I found that there were people who shared my interests and I found my niche."

13= (15) Johns Hopkins University
Founded 1876   www.jhu.edu

Arts & humanities	22
Engineering & IT	67
Life sciences & biomedicine	3
Natural sciences	45
Social sciences	41
Academic survey position	24
Employer survey position	118
Student faculty ratio	3.9:1
International faculty	6.6%
Undergraduates	5,425
Postgraduates	8,915
International students	15.3%
Research strength (Scopus) papers	36,561
Research strength (Scopus) citations	353,929
Impact (citations per paper)	10

Although it can demonstrate quality across the board, Johns Hopkins is famous mainly for its medical school. It was here that neurosurgery, urology, endocrinology, paediatrics and renal dialysis were developed. The school receives by far the most government research funding in America and the Bloomberg School of Public Health alone gets a quarter of all federal research money awarded to the 28 US schools of public health. No wonder a disproportionate number of Johns Hopkins undergraduates are pre-med, planning for careers in medicine. A US$950 million construction project will add two new clinical towers, for cardiovascular and clinical care, by 2010/11. The university's Whiting School of Engineering is also highly selective, and bioengineering is a popular major that spans both of the university's principal strengths. Seventy per cent of engineering students and 50 per cent of other undergraduates work with faculty on primary research for pay or academic credit. This tradition of close student-faculty interaction dates from Johns Hopkins' legacy as America's first university modelled on the European research institution, teaching through seminars instead of solely through lectures. Its renowned School of Advanced International Studies is named after Cold War architect Paul Nitze, who co-founded it in 1943. That division is based in Washington, 45 minutes by train from the university's park-like, Georgian-style main campus in Baltimore. Johns Hopkins has been aggressive about extending its reach globally. Its Bologna campus houses the only full-time, resident American graduate school of international relations in Europe. It has a centre in Florence for its Italian studies program, another in Nanjing, and two in Singapore, one a collaboration between its Peabody Institute of Music and the National University of Singapore to establish a music conservatory.

Alumni include President Woodrow Wilson, Vice President Spiro Agnew, novelist John Barth, New York Mayor Michael Bloomberg, pianist Andre Watts, Nobel economics winner Merton Miller, Nobel peace prize winner Jody Williams, biologist and author Rachel Carson, and IBM Chief Executive Samuel Palmisano.

"If you're interested in doing research, it's right there. You just have to ask," said Kristy Gangaram, an undergraduate from Trinidad and Tobago majoring in public health. "On campus, you can look in windows and see students working in the labs until well into the night." One thing that's less popular with students is the neighbourhood surrounding the main undergraduate campus. "Baltimore is an inner city so you have to be cautious," she said. "But we have a blue light system and when you feel unsafe, you press the button under a blue light and a security officer is there in 30 seconds."

15 (20=) Cornell University
Founded 1865   www.cornell.edu

Arts & humanities	14
Engineering & IT	24
Life sciences & biomedicine	18
Natural sciences	11
Social sciences	17
Academic survey position	12
Employer survey position	14
Student faculty ratio	6.7:1
International faculty	5.8%
Undergraduates	13,500
Postgraduates	6,275
International students	17.4%
Research strength (Scopus) papers	27,000
Research strength (Scopus) citations	205,800
Impact (citations per paper)	8

Ambitious partnerships with universities in India, Singapore, and China, and a medical campus in Qatar, have led Cornell to call itself the world's first transnational university. But its attention is also firmly rooted at home, where it has been working to move back up the pre-eminent American league tables. Cornell's large size makes it the most comprehensive university in the elite Ivy League, with 70 undergraduate specialities. It is also unique in a country whose universities are divided between public and private. Cornell is partly private and also partly run and financially underwritten by the state of New York, in whose rural (and often very cold and snowy) west central reaches it is set. It also has specialties unusual among the Ivies. Its College of Agriculture and Life Sciences is the third largest in the United States, and usually rated the best. So is its School of Hotel Management, which has the largest faculty and curriculum of any program of its kind and attracts a sizeable international enrolment. The College of Veterinary Medicine is the nation's most respected; among other things, where Salmonella was discovered. Despite its location a distant five hours' drive northwest of New York City, Cornell is one of America's most international campuses. It is also aiming to be one of the greenest and is on course to reduce its utilities emissions by 2012, by one third of the 1990 level. An enormous amount of research is conducted at Cornell. Annual research expenditures exceed US$600 million. The university ranks first in National Science Foundation funding for academic science and engineering. Cornell has set out to raise US$4 billion to build on these strengths, a significant amount of it for a new biomedical research centre attached to its satellite Weill Cornell Medical College in New York City.

Forty Nobel laureates have been affiliated with Cornell, and there are three on the current faculty. Alumni include US Supreme Court Justice Ruth Bader Ginsburg, former US Attorney General Janet Reno, the former presidents of Taiwan and Cuba and the former prime minister of Iran; the inventors of the iPod, the pacemaker and the Heimlich Manoeuvre, and the founders or heads of businesses including Citigroup, Grumman Aerospace Corporation, and Burger King.

Undergraduate Arthur Change said he was attracted to come to Cornell from Hong Kong for a business degree with the "...whole Ivy League experience. It has exceeded my expectations. With the connections you gain from Cornell, you can really do anything you want. Definitely the weather is tough, but everybody survives it," he said.

16 (16) Australian National University
Founded 1946   www.anu.edu.au

AUSTRALIA

Canberra ●

Arts & humanities 12
Engineering & IT... 36
Life sciences & biomedicine 37
Natural sciences 21
Social sciences 14

Academic survey position 17
Employer survey position 58

Student faculty ratio 7.6:1
International faculty 46.5%
Undergraduates 7,532
Postgraduates 3,586
International students 23.3%

Research strength (Scopus) papers.................. 11,571
Research strength (Scopus) citations 61,608
Impact (citations per paper)..................................... 5

The Australian National University (ANU) was the first to be created by an act of the federal parliament and the first university founded in the national capital, Canberra. The ANU is the only Australian member of the International Alliance of Research Universities and one of the nation's Group of Eight research-intensive institutions. The university is consistently placed among the best in the world and again finishes above all its Australian peers in this year's rankings. The ANU campus of 10,000 trees spreads over 145 hectares, adjacent to the city centre of Canberra, but there are also smaller sites, including the astronomy observatories at Mt Stromlo west of Canberra and Siding Spring near Coonabarabran in western New South Wales. The university launched a Korean Institute in 2008 and also signed a memorandum of understanding with Yonsei University, in Seoul. Academics at the ANU carry out research and teaching in seven colleges that cover the arts, Asian and Pacific studies, economics and business, engineering and IT, science, medicine and health sciences, and law.

The ANU has four Nobel laureates among many of its distinguished scholars who have achieved international recognition: John Eccles, John C Harsanyi and, joint-winners, Rolf Zinkernagel and Peter Doherty. It also has more Federation Fellows (lucrative fellowships awarded by the Australian Research Council) than any other Australian university and also claims more members of the Royal Society on its staff than any of its Australian counterparts. Kim Beazley, the former leader of the Labour Party and once deputy prime minister, now Professor of Political Science and International Relations at the University of Western Australia, became the ANU Chancellor in January 2009.

Many of Australia's brightest young people enrol at the ANU, but almost a quarter of the students are from other countries. Yew Kuen Tan, who graduated with a bachelor of medical science, was president of the Malaysian Students Association and acted as a mentor for new students through a scheme linking first-years with those in later years to learn from their knowledge and experience of campus life. He was awarded a full scholarship to the ANU but says one of the main reasons he opted for Canberra was that it was quiet and good for study. He praises the university's student support services and says his course consisted of a well-balanced system of assignments and examinations. "I think the lecturers are fantastic. "The ones I know are well aware that many international students have English as a second language so they speak slowly. They know that Asian students, particularly, tend not to question authority and do not speak out but, because they are so approachable, help to overcome that."

17 (19) Stanford University
Founded 1891   www.stanford.edu

USA

•Palo Alto   Washington, DC•

Arts & humanities	8
Engineering & IT	3
Life sciences & biomedicine	6
Natural sciences	8
Social sciences	3
Academic survey position	4
Employer survey position	8
Student faculty ratio	9.2:1
International faculty	4.9%
Undergraduates	6,543
Postgraduates	9,565
International students	21.5%
Research strength (Scopus) papers	34,423
Research strength (Scopus) citations	315,286
Impact (citations per paper)	9

Stanford University's US$1 billion a year in research and its small-scale teaching have made it an incubator for the likes of Google, Yahoo!, Cisco Systems, eBay, Sun Microsystems, and 350 other cutting-edge companies that have, in turn, helped fuel California's high-tech boom. Leland Stanford, who made his fortune selling provisions to miners during the 1850s California gold rush, also gave the school his ranch (students still call the university 'the farm') making it one of the largest campuses in America, whose distinctive red-tile-roofed buildings sit on 8,000 roomy acres in the otherwise densely populated San Francisco Bay area. It may be a big place, but Stanford boasts small classes with individualized instruction: the majority of classes have fewer than 20 students. Classes are small at the graduate level, too. And it's an impressive faculty, including 16 Nobel laureates. The university's Undergraduate Research Program not only encourages students to work with faculty on research; it funds them to design their own research projects to the tune of more than US$4 million a year. A Stanford surgeon performed the first human heart transplant in the US and the world's first heart/lung transplant; a lab at Stanford was the first to isolate stem cells. The Stanford Institute for Stem Cell Biology and Regenerative Medicine is today among the top such research centres in the world. The National Research Council also ranks Stanford's programs the best in America in computer science, electrical engineering, and mechanical engineering, and rates it highly in aeronautics and astronautics, and civil engineering. One quarter of the US$4 billion being collected in an ambitious fundraising campaign is earmarked to encourage multidisciplinary research, in which Stanford has already launched several initiatives. Philip Knight, founder of Nike and Stanford alumnus, pledged US$105 million, of which US$100 million will go towards the large new business school campus.

Other alumni include Hewlett Packard co-founders William Hewlett and David Packard; the four US Supreme Court justices; US President Herbert Hoover; former Israeli Prime Minister Ehud Barak; Dolby Laboratories founder Ray Dolby; golfer Tiger Woods, and Sally Ride, the first American woman in space.

"Stanford has good resources, it has good libraries, it has good research, and the professors are very easy to approach," said Pumsaran Tongliemnak, a doctoral candidate from Thailand who is studying education economics. "They're world-class, but they're unassuming and students can approach them more easily than at other institutions." As for the students: "They have the mentality of work hard, play hard, and they have a lot of creativity," he said. "They're just not the type that go to the library all the time."

18 (38=) University of Michigan
Founded 1817   www.umich.edu

Arts & humanities	19
Engineering & IT	38
Life sciences & biomedicine	31
Natural sciences	35
Social sciences	20
Academic survey position	23
Employer survey position	19
Student faculty ratio	7.2:1
International faculty	17.2%
Undergraduates	25,629
Postgraduates	13,597
International students	11.1%
Research strength (Scopus) papers	37,129
Research strength (Scopus) citations	276,795
Impact (citations per paper)	7

More than 107,000 people can fit inside the football stadium at the University of Michigan, the most at any university. And there's seldom an empty seat. Michigan fields some of the most dominant university sports teams in America and has more alumni (420,000) than any other US school. But while athletics garners much of the attention here, Michigan, which has taken a dramatic leap in the rankings, also conducts an almost unrivalled US$876 million a year in research, a tradition that began with government grants in the Cold War and the space race in the days when nearby Detroit was the world centre of the automotive industry. One in five undergraduates specialize in engineering, which is also the pre-eminent graduate program. Michigan has top-flight laboratories for research into manufacturing engineering, manufacturing systems, and, not surprisingly, transportation. Now, with the auto industry struggling, Michigan has announced the University Research Corridor, with Michigan State and Wayne State universities, to help reinvigorate the local economy by incubating technology and alternative energy companies. The first American university to use the seminar method of teaching, Michigan offers more than 70 seminars for first-year students, each capped at an enrolment of 20. Later, students can find themselves in huge lecture classes taught by graduate students rather than faculty. But 900 undergraduates a year do have a chance to work with faculty on research. A multibillion-dollar fundraising campaign will underwrite nearly 170 more endowed professorships along with student financial aid and buildings including a hospital, drama centre, the new Gerald R Ford School of Public Policy, and a new home for the school of public health. In the middle of the 'credit crunch' retail pioneer Alfred Taubman gave US$20 million to the university taking his total gifts to a massive US$80 million.

President Gerald R Ford played football at Michigan. Other Michigan athletes have gone on to high-profile careers in sports, and so many astronauts have graduated that there is an alumni chapter on the moon, marked by a plaque left on the lunar surface by the all-Michigan crew of Apollo 15. Other alumni include the playwright Arthur Miller, actors James Earl Jones and Lucy Liu, Madonna, Iggy Pop (though he never graduated), and Swedish Holocaust hero Raoul Wallenberg.

"The research facilities are sensational," said Simon Schenk, an Australian who just received his doctorate in kinesiology with articles published about his groundbreaking research into exercise, obesity, and diabetes in high-profile scientific journals. "That's one of the fortunate things at Michigan. Typically people might think of kinesiology as teaching physical education or something. But we were really at the cutting edge of basic science."

19 (17) University of Tokyo
Founded 1877   www.u-tokyo.ac.jp

Arts & humanities 28
Engineering & IT.. 9
Life sciences & biomedicine 15
Natural sciences.. 10
Social sciences 21

Academic survey position 14
Employer survey position 50

Student faculty ratio 5.2:1
International faculty 5.4%
Undergraduates 14,085
Postgraduates 14,242
International students 8.5%

Research strength (Scopus) papers.................. 44,543
Research strength (Scopus) citations 246,610
Impact (citations per paper)...................................... 6

For the second year in a row, Tokyo University is the only Asian institution in the top 20 of the THE-QS World University Rankings. It is the oldest university in Japan and the most prestigious, receiving by far the biggest direct government grant. Like other Japanese universities, it has been struggling with annual cuts in government subsidies and has been trying to raise ¥13 billion in endowment to compensate. The university has five campuses, two in the heart of Tokyo. It started out as a law school, before setting up science and liberal arts departments. The legacy of a training institution in a country of powerful bureaucracy persists to this day. Its law graduates, for example, dominate the top civil service posts. President Hiroshi Komiyama is careful not to specify any particular area of strength, emphasizing instead the university's pursuit of excellence in all aspects of education and research. Tokyo is the only university in Japan that has a system of two years of general education before students choose their specialisms. The Komaba Campus, which houses the college of arts and sciences and two graduate schools, is the cornerstone of general education, attended by all freshmen and sophomores. It has also been designated as a 'centre of excellence' for three new areas of research by the Japanese Ministry of Education and Science. The university is striving to raise its international profile, attracting overseas students and researchers, which is also the educational ministry's objective. The number of international students still remains relatively low, although visiting foreign researchers are more numerous. The university closest to Japan's centre of power is also male dominated: only nine per cent of the faculty are women.

In a country where Nobel prize triumphs make huge newspaper headlines, Tokyo University's record has not been illustrious, with only a single faculty, Professor Emeritus Masatoshi Koshiba, in 2002, for physics. Six alumni have won Nobels, the latest Professor Yoichiro Nambu, a graduate of the Department of Physics, who was awarded a share of the 2008 physics prize. Faculty also includes architect Tadao Ando, winner of the 1995 Pritzker Architecture Prize. Notable alumni include six prime ministers since 1946, mathematician Kunihiko Kodaira (Fields Medal winner), Nobel literature laureates Yasunari Kawabata and Kenzaburo Oe, writer Yukio Mishima, Nobel physics laureate Leo Esaki and industrialist Eiji Toyoda.

"International atmosphere is definitely lacking," said a second-year student of literature. "I have yet to come across any undergraduates with a powerful personality, they all seem to be obedient people who follow the rule without a question."

20 (12) McGill University
Founded 1821   www.mcgill.ca

Arts & humanities 13
Engineering & IT.. 18
Life sciences & biomedicine 10
Natural sciences 22
Social sciences 14
Academic survey position 11
Employer survey position 36

Student faculty ratio 4.8:1
International faculty 18.2%
Undergraduates 17,558*
Postgraduates 5,040*
International students 26.1%

Research strength (Scopus) papers.................. 18,955
Research strength (Scopus) citations............. 122,350
Impact (citations per paper)...................................... 6

McGill University's research pillars have traditionally been medicine and law, giving the university a reputation in the fields of neurosciences, genomics, cancer, human rights and social policy. The engineering faculty has spawned specialties in nanotechnology and biomedical engineering. It also has a dental faculty, a school of environmental sciences, a large music faculty and a full complement of arts and sciences. Determinedly international, McGill attracts more than a third of its non-Canadian students from the US, but nearly half of the international contingent claim a first language other than English. France and China both send large numbers to the Montreal university. McGill is one of Canada's most research-intensive universities, with the country's highest per-faculty research funding in three of the past four years. A new medical research centre, is edging towards completion on the Glen Campus with the aid of CA$100 million in federal funding. Among current researchers, Henry Mintzberg is the most distinguished of contemporary management authors; legal scholar Payam Akhavan is an authority on human rights and genocide; Mark Wainberg is an internationally recognized scientist in the field of HIV/AIDS research; environmental scientist Nigel Roulet is a contributing author to the 2007 Nobel prize winning International Panel on Climate Change; and Michel Tremblay's research has provided breakthroughs in the genetics of breast cancer, diabetes and obesity. They follow some illustrious predecessors. In 1948, John Humphrey, a McGill graduate and law professor, authored the first draft of the Universal Declaration of Human Rights.

Four McGill graduates have won Nobel prizes: Andrew Victor Schally (medicine, 1977), Val Fitch (physics, 1980), David Hubel (medicine, 1981) and Rudolph Marcus (chemistry, 1992). Ernest Rutherford uncovered the alpha particle and Norman Bethune designed the world's first mobile medical unit and became a hero in China during the Second World War for training thousands of Chinese medics and doctors. Other notable alumni include poet and musician Leonard Cohen; and William Shatner, best known as Captain James T Kirk of Star Trek, though the university can also lay claim to real astronauts in Dave Williams, Robert Thirsk and Julie Payette.

Astrophysics student Andrew McCann was attracted from Dublin by McGill's reputation and active and lively department. "Very few universities in the world research my particular area of study, and there are many talks and seminars of interest, as well as highly motivated students and teachers," he said. He was disappointed by what he believed to be insufficient information on financial aid for international students, but he says that did not mar the academic excellence he saw at the university.

21 (20=) Carnegie Mellon University
Founded 1900   www.cmu.edu

Arts & humanities	113
Engineering & IT	6
Life sciences & biomedicine	73
Natural sciences	80
Social sciences	35
Academic survey position	37
Employer survey position	33
Student faculty ratio	7.5:1
International faculty	13.7%
Undergraduates	5,674
Postgraduates	3,917
International students	28.0%
Research strength (Scopus) papers	10,872
Research strength (Scopus) citations	58,966
Impact (citations per paper)	5

Carnegie Mellon is the self proclaimed 'global university' with faculty members working all over the world and with campuses in Qatar and South Australia. Its scale and culture have encouraged the faculties to collaborate across disciplines, with unconventional partnerships among seemingly unrelated fields. Best known for science and technology, Carnegie Mellon has top drama and business programs, and has seen applications double in the last ten years. Carnegie Mellon was founded as a technical school by the Scottish-American industrialist Andrew Carnegie (members of the band, which includes bagpipers, still wear kilts) to train the children of the working-class poor in industrial Pittsburgh. Its School of Computer Science is one of the best in the world and includes the pre-eminent Robotics Institute, the largest at any US university, which developed robots to clean up nuclear waste at Three Mile Island and Chernobyl. It has 16 Nobel laureates on its faculty and maintains a branch campus in California's Silicon Valley.

Carnegie Mellon's highly regarded business school also takes advantage of its presence at a university that specializes in technology, while the Heinz School of Public Policy and Management studies urban and social issues, with an equally interdisciplinary approach. Its Human-Computer Interaction Institute integrates computer science, design, social science, and learning science. Not surprisingly, the campus is among America's most wired, and the home to a 10-teraflop Cray XT3 computer called Big Ben, capable of ten trillion calculations per second, or as much processing capacity as 30,000 personal computers. Scientists have used it to model earthquake soil vibration, forecast severe thunderstorms and Comet Shoemaker-Levy 9's impact with Jupiter. Concerned about public perceptions that universities with robust research programs neglect undergraduate teaching, Carnegie Mellon was also one of the first universities in America to establish a centre aimed at helping faculty improve their classroom teaching.

Alumni include James Gosling, creator of the Java programming language, Sun Microsystems co-founders Andy Bechtolsheim and Vinod Khosla, and astronaut Judith Resnik, who died in the Challenger disaster. Carnegie Mellon's conservatory-style drama program has graduated the likes of George Peppard, Jack Klugman, Holly Hunter, Ted Danson, Blair Underwood, and producer Steven Bochco.

"When I told people I was going to Carnegie Mellon, they thought that I was going to be an engineer," said Jen Johnson, an anthropology undergraduate who describes herself as technologically unskilled. "And when I told them I wasn't, they assumed I must be in the drama school. In fact, you get to know a lot of people outside of your field. We all feed off each other's energies that way. You're surrounded by a wide array of different types of thinking."

22 (24) King's College London
Founded 1829   www.kcl.ac.uk

Arts & humanities 38
Engineering & IT.. 129
Life sciences & biomedicine 34
Natural sciences.. 107
Social sciences 48

Academic survey position 46
Employer survey position 26

Student faculty ratio 6.8:1
International faculty 32.5%
Undergraduates 12,075
Postgraduates 5,114
International students 20.6%

Research strength (Scopus) papers.................. 14,859
Research strength (Scopus) citations 97,876
Impact (citations per paper)...................................... 7

King's College has been rising up the THE-QS World University Rankings and UK league tables. It set itself the goal of reaching the top 25 in the world by 2016, but has already achieved this. A member of the Russell Group of 20 leading research universities, King's is one of the oldest institutions in UK higher education. Having been known primarily for science, it now also excels in Portuguese, Byzantine Greek, law and war studies. Previous achievements include discovering the structure of DNA with a Cambridge team. Its prime location on London's Strand, is another attraction for international students. A £500 million redevelopment on five sites close to the River Thames is nearly complete. It includes the largest university building in London, where 2,800 study health and life sciences. Biomedical sciences, medicine and dentistry have also acquired new buildings. Science students dominate, but there is a wide range of interdisciplinary combinations. Alongside their degree, all students can take lectures on ethics, philosophy, theology, biblical studies and Christian doctrine. Health subjects have been the fastest-growing in recent years: King's is the only UK university to have five Medical Research Council centres and boasts Europe's largest centre for medical and professional healthcare education. Links with China were extended in 2008 with the establishment of the Centre for the Study of Christianity in China. Other activities include collaboration on studies of traditional Chinese medicine and links between the law school and Tsinghua University, in Beijing.

Famous alumni include the Romantic poet John Keats, Archbishop Desmond Tutu, and conductor John Eliot Gardiner. An array of distinguished staff is headed by Rosalind Franklin and Maurice Wilkins, the discoverers of DNA, Lord Lister, pioneer of antiseptic surgery, and Sir Edward Appleton, whose work on atmospheric layers paved the way for modern telecommunications. Florence Nightingale established the first professional school of nurse training at St Thomas's Hospital, now also part of the medical school.

Joanne Ooi, a Malaysian student studying medicine, chose King's on the basis of its international reputation and came with high hopes. "I'm delighted to say the King's experience has far exceeded my expectations," she said. "In a typical day I am fortunate enough to sample the best of all the worlds that college life could possibly offer. I attend lectures by world-class academics with students from diverse backgrounds in history-rich surroundings. I enjoy the excellent social and cultural opportunities of London by taking just a short walk down the Thames. I may have travelled halfway across the globe to get to King's, but I feel right at home here!"

23 (23) University of Edinburgh
Founded 1582   www.ed.ac.uk

Arts & humanities	26
Engineering & IT	60
Life sciences & biomedicine	32
Natural sciences	82
Social sciences	54
Academic survey position	36
Employer survey position	19
Student faculty ratio	7.5:1
International faculty	32.6%
Undergraduates	15,764
Postgraduates	4,936
International students	19.3%
Research strength (Scopus) papers	14,441
Research strength (Scopus) citations	106,473
Impact (citations per paper)	7

Founded as the 'Tounis (Town's) College,' the University of Edinburgh's local roots are matched by an international outlook. It is Scotland's largest and most research-intensive university. Its cutting edge research in medicine has been boosted by the opening of the £49 million Queen's Medical Research Institute, which brings together hundreds of elite researchers in inflammation research, cardiovascular medicine and reproductive biology, who will work together on conditions from diabetes and heart disease to cancer and menstrual disorders. Work has begun on the £60 million Scottish Centre for Regenerative Medicine which is due to be completed by 2010 and will include researchers from a range of disciplines, including stem cell research. Edinburgh is also increasing its existing strength in informatics, a discipline covering computer science, artificial intelligence, cognitive science and linguistics. It is a prominent player in Scotland's pioneering 'research pooling' ventures in physics, chemistry, geosciences, engineering and mathematics, enabling researchers in different universities to work together and share expensive equipment. It is also drawing on American experience to develop an ambitious £350 million fundraising campaign with a top priority on increasing the number of scholarships and bursaries. Edinburgh is often stereotyped as Scotland's 'Oxbridge', attracting wealthy, privately educated English students. But it has been strenuously combating its elitist image with widening access schemes, and is already putting some £15 million into scholarships. Edinburgh offers a blend of innovation and tradition: Old College, designed by alumnus Robert Adam, dates from the late 18th century and is in the centre of a World Heritage Site. The historic city is a magnet for tourists, especially during the Edinburgh Festival, but its leisure facilities are thoroughly up-to-date.

Notable Edinburgh graduates include Charles Darwin, David Hume, James Hutton and writers Sir Walter Scott, Robert Louis Stevenson and Sir Arthur Conan Doyle. Two of today's best known Scottish writers have Edinburgh connections: Ian Rankin, creator of detective John Rebus, is an Edinburgh graduate, while Alexander McCall Smith, author of the 'No. 1 Ladies' Detective Agency', was professor of medical law until he retired to concentrate on writing.

Wen Hao Zou from China, who took a business and accountancy degree, said: "My father runs a small business so I want to learn some new things. I realize here [the course] is more practical and I think it's very useful. The first time I came to Edinburgh, I was carrying my bags and someone stopped in a car and gave me a lift. It's friendly; I could never imagine this happening in London. Edinburgh University has a lot of international students and we have a lot of fun."

24 (42) ETH Zurich (Swiss Federal Institute of Technology)
Founded 1855   www.ethz.ch

Arts & humanities	202
Engineering & IT	13
Life sciences & biomedicine	67
Natural sciences	15
Social sciences	160
Academic survey position	38
Employer survey position	106
Student faculty ratio	10.6:1
International faculty	54.7%
Undergraduates	7,161
Postgraduates	6,838
International students	25.9%
Research strength (Scopus) papers	18,035
Research strength (Scopus) citations	120,474
Impact (citations per paper)	7

The Eidgenössische Technische Hochschule (ETH Zurich), is Switzerland's largest and oldest federal university. It was the country's only federal higher education institution until 1969, when Lausanne's École Polytechnique also acquired federal status. ETH's departments of architecture, civil engineering, mechanical engineering, chemistry, forestry, plus a department including mathematics, natural sciences, literature and social and political sciences, were key players in the modernization of Switzerland and in the brilliant engineering works, especially roads, railways, bridges and tunnels, which marked the late 19th and early 20th centuries.

Entrance to ETH is open to all Swiss citizens who have passed the Matura school-leaving exam, while foreign students have to sit a separate admissions exam. For all, there is a rigorous selection after the first two semesters. ETH was among the first European universities to adopt the three-plus-two degree structure of the Bologna process, and the changeover from four and five year degrees appears not to have been traumatic for the institution. The 34 masters programs available at ETH outnumber the 24 bachelors degrees, most of which are, in any case, merely the basis for a subsequent masters program. ETH claims that its work in chemistry, physics and architecture is among the most advanced in the world, and that the Department of Biology is rapidly reaching the same level. A basic element of research policy is the creation of inter-disciplinary 'platforms' for work on a specific field. A new nanotechnology laboratory has received planning permission and the US$90 million facility should be ready and in use by 2011.

ETH has an impressive list of 21 Nobel prize winners. Albert Einstein, who studied there from 1896 to 1900, returned to teach physics from 1912 to 1916. Others include Wilhelm Conrad Röntgen (physics 1901) and Felix Bloch (physics 1952), while the most recent is ETH professor Kurt Wüthrich (chemistry 2002).

Laila Hossain is a British PhD with a chemistry degree from Bristol University. At the ETH she is working in the department of chemistry and applied biosciences. "The ETH is very multi-cultural and very interdisciplinary. You meet and work with people from many different countries, and one's own research group often works with people from research groups in completely different fields. There are lots of lectures by key speakers from around the world, not just on one's own subject, but on all kinds of themes. The atmosphere here is very focused and very professional. Everyone seems eager to help, but the standards are very high and they expect a great deal of effort and dedication," she said.

25 (25) Kyoto University
Founded 1897   **www.kyoto-u.ac.jp**

Arts & humanities	37
Engineering & IT	22
Life sciences & biomedicine	24
Natural sciences	13
Social sciences	42
Academic survey position	22
Employer survey position	78
Student faculty ratio	7.8:1
International faculty	6.5%
Undergraduates	13,235
Postgraduates	9,162
International students	4.6%
Research strength (Scopus) papers	32,339
Research strength (Scopus) citations	172,694
Impact (citations per paper)	5

Kyoto University, in the ancient capital of Japan, is the oldest in the country outside Tokyo. Initially, the university consisted of science and engineering, medicine and law, but it has expanded to cover nearly all aspects of education and research, including medicine and nuclear energy. The university's commitment to academic freedom has long been a hallmark of the institution, even in pre-war Japan under a military government. But the overseas composition of this prestigious university is limited. Language is a major barrier as nearly all lectures and seminars are in Japanese, although many faculties accept postgraduate theses in English. Competition for undergraduate places is intense, based on national entrance exams and the university's own entrance exam, both of which are set in Japanese. There is a special selection process for foreign students and foreign educated Japanese. Kyoto, like Japan's 81 other former national universities, faces a one per cent subsidy cut for the next three years and has begun actively seeking endowment for the first time in its history, as well as placing greater reliance on the private sector for research grants. So far, the fact that Kyoto is more than 500 kilometres, or two hours' bullet train ride, away from the capital has somewhat shielded the university from political influences, academics say. Only a handful of Kyoto university lecturers and professors are on government advisory panels. However, young ambitious academics seeking media exposure are attracted to positions at Tokyo-based universities, often of less prestige. The university has an even lower ratio of international faculty members than Tokyo, although the number of foreigners has grown substantially in the last three years.

Perhaps it is because of its liberal tradition that the university has produced more Nobel prize and Fields medal winners than any of its Japanese rivals, the latest within the past year. In 1949 physicist Hideki Yukawa, a Kyoto professor, was the first Japanese ever to win a Nobel prize. Since then, it has produced three winners in physics and science, most recently in 2008 when Dr. Toshihide Masukawa won the Nobel prize for physics. Makoto Kobayashi, his fellow laureate for the discovery of the origin of the broken symmetry which predicts the existence of at least three families of quarks in nature, was also a research associate at Kyoto. In 1999, mathematician Shigefumi Mori won the Fields medal.

"It's a liberal school," says a US PhD student, who completed a thesis on British-Japanese relations in the late 19th century. "I think analysis approaches are not as strong as at American universities."

26 (18) University of Hong Kong
Founded 1911   www.hku.hk

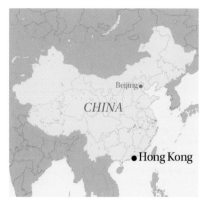

Arts & humanities	46
Engineering & IT	69
Life sciences & biomedicine	39
Natural sciences	103
Social sciences	34
Academic survey position	43
Employer survey position	65
Student faculty ratio	7.1:1
International faculty	57.9%
Undergraduates	9,062
Postgraduates	6,836
International students	24.1%
Research strength (Scopus) papers	12,678
Research strength (Scopus) citations	69,447
Impact (citations per paper)	5

The University of Hong Kong, (HKU), the then colony's first university, has long had an international outlook. The university's coat of arms features two Chinese phrases from Confucius: 'Illustrious Virtue' and 'the investigation of things,' combined with the Latin motto 'Sapientia et virtus' meaning 'wisdom and virtue.' The university's international outreach is reflected in more than 400 formal links with overseas universities and ongoing student exchanges with over 180 partner institutions. There are big expansion plans as it approaches its centenary in the form of a new Centennial Campus. Due to be completed in 2011, the 42,000-square-metre state-of-the-art campus will allow the university to enhance its teaching and research facilities as well as increase its student numbers by over 3,000 in preparation for the territory-wide introduction of a four-year degree structure. Included in the plans are another 1,800 residential places.

As Hong Kong's pre-eminent research institution, the university receives the lion's share of government research grants. It dedicates itself to providing 'outstanding teaching and world-class research'. One half of this commitment was demonstrated in 2003 when the influenza research team at its Faculty of Medicine identified the coronavirus that triggered the 2003 SARS epidemic. While the faculty members and researchers worked to discover the origins of the virus and its mode of transmission, they also met with local and international media to explain its causes and educate the public on keeping the virus at bay. From this experience, the university was subsequently appointed by the Chinese government to establish a State Key Laboratory of Emerging Infectious Diseases and a State Key Laboratory of Brain and Cognitive Sciences, the only such laboratories outside Mainland China. The MBA program offered by the Faculty of Business and Economics also has a highly-regarded reputation, particularly in Asia. Its curriculum was further enhanced by partnerships that will allow students to take classes at London Business School and Columbia Business School.

Famous alumni include Dr Sun Yat-sen, founding president of the Republic of China, who attended Hong Kong College of Medicine for Chinese, HKU's predecessor institution, and whose statue stands at the heart of the modern university. More recent graduates are found throughout the Hong Kong SAR Government and among the senior management of private firms.

Alexander Schindler from Germany, who is in year three of his LLB at the Faculty of Law, was initially surprised by the diversity and competitiveness of his fellow-students. "The program exceeded all my expectations," he says. "Scholars from all major jurisdictions offered a rich learning experience with special priority on business and financial law due to Hong Kong's position as an international trade centre.

27 (32) Brown University
Founded 1764 www.brown.edu

Arts & humanities	27
Engineering & IT	93
Life sciences & biomedicine	50
Natural sciences	106
Social sciences	65
Academic survey position	48
Employer survey position	99
Student faculty ratio	9.6:1
International faculty	15.8%
Undergraduates	5,863
Postgraduates	2,093
International students	12.8%
Research strength (Scopus) papers	9,235
Research strength (Scopus) citations	73,505
Impact (citations per paper)	8

Founded on College Hill, overlooking Providence, Rhode Island, Brown University was the first US school to admit students of all religious persuasions and the first Ivy League university to be headed by a black woman president. Its undergraduate engineering program is the oldest in the Ivy League and it has the only undergraduate Egyptology department in the western hemisphere as well as an undergraduate program in the history of mathematics that was, until recently, the only one of its kind in the world.

Brown has embarked on an ambitious, US$1.4 billion plan to increase the size of its faculty, expand research, and improve facilities. "...our programs are not recognized as leaders as consistently as many in other great research universities," a task force concluded. Brown has also been reviewing its so-called New Curriculum, under which there are no distribution requirements and grades are optional, meaning students get to choose from any of 2,000 courses in 40 departments while forgoing the ruthless competition characteristic of other Ivy League schools. Whatever insecurities might have prompted these self-evaluations, students continue to flock to Brown. Less than 14 per cent of applicants are accepted in each year's entering class. Once enrolled, a survey found, these students are the happiest in America, enjoying the atmosphere of a comparatively small school. Brown conducts a relatively modest US$134 million in sponsored research. The young medical school integrates premedical and medical education into a seamless, eight-year program; Brown also ranks in the top five for students accepted to other medical schools. Its "Boldly Brown" campaign has already resulted in the Sidney E Frank Hall for Life Sciences, the most expensive building in university history, with 30 laboratories designed to encourage scientific collaboration. The university describes its new 'Mind, Brain and Behaviour' building as an attempt to make intellectual meeting places available because 'that's how you create an intellectual powerhouse'.

Alumni include former US Secretary of State and Chief Justice Charles Evans Hughes, Prince Faisal Ben Al Hussein of Jordan, Prince Nikolaos and Princess Theodora of Greece and Denmark, Lady Gabriella Windsor, daughter of Prince Michael of Kent, John D Rockefeller Jr, and Allegra Versace.

The students are competitive with themselves, not with other people, said Guy Bloembergen, an undergraduate from the Netherlands. "I have friends who are very artsy people and aren't particularly good at science, but they can take a science course and not have to worry too much about the grade. They can focus on the class." Guy said he was drawn to Brown by the openness of the curriculum. "That was probably the biggest pull for me."

28 (26) École Normale Supérieure (ENS)
Founded 1794   **www.ens.fr**

Paris●

FRANCE

Arts & humanities	34
Engineering & IT	100
Life sciences & biomedicine	136
Natural sciences	19
Social sciences	113
Academic survey position	44
Employer survey position	139
Student faculty ratio	9:1
International faculty	6.3%
Undergraduates	434
Postgraduates	1,762
International students	15.4%
Research strength (Scopus) papers	3,202
Research strength (Scopus) citations	20,864
Impact (citations per paper)	7

The École Normale Supérieure in Paris is one of the great institutions of revolutionary France, a pioneering 'grande école' created to train university and lycée teachers for the 'agrégation,' the competitive high-level teaching examination. Today ENS is France's elite training-ground not only for academics and researchers, but for those seeking careers in the upper echelons of the civil service, business or politics. Entry is generally by the traditional concours (competitive exams) preceded by two years' post-baccalauréat study in preparatory classes, but there are alternative entry methods for foreign applicants.

ENS is the only grande école catering for students of both humanities and sciences. Its watchwords are 'interdisciplinarity' and 'education through research'. Studies last three or four years, leading to a licence (bachelors equivalent) and masters, awarded jointly with another higher education establishment. Many students, including most on humanities courses, take the agrégation. ENS graduates might otherwise continue at other grandes écoles to train as senior technocrats or follow careers in sought-after fields such as the media or publishing. The school has agreements with about 60 universities worldwide through which it exchanges about 150 students each year. About 60 foreign academics visit annually for a month at a time; and nearly 300 international researchers stay for periods of up to two years. The ENS International Division caters for foreign students. Candidates are rigorously tested by a panel of professors from French and foreign universities, who evaluate their capacity for analysis, conceptualization and synthesis, scientific and literary knowledge, intellectual curiosity and relevance of their chosen projects. About 20 foreigners were accepted for the 2007 session.

Among ENS alumni are numerous eminent scientists, writers, philosophers, social scientists and politicians, including many winners of Nobel prizes, Fields medals and CNRS gold medals. Graduates include Louis Pasteur, Jean-Paul Sartre, Michel Foucault, Jacques Derrida, Simone Weil, Pierre Bourdieu, Romain Rolland, Charles Péguy, Jean Jaurès, Léon Blum and Georges Pompidou. Samuel Beckett taught here.

Klaus Speidel, 27 was admitted to ENS to study for a masters in philosophy after studying philosophy for two years at Munich University (LMU). He says interdisciplinarity and a close relationship with lecturers are the school's strong points. "The ENS has a system of personal tutors, which you choose at the beginning, and they sustain you in your choices, discuss and correct your work, and so on." But he regrets that students are not encouraged more to talk during their studies. "Class participation is nearly impossible in France, and I miss it," he says. "It's clear people who attend the ENS are clever, but the teachers mainly give lectures, even if the classes are called seminars."

29 (30) University of Manchester
Founded 1824   www.manchester.ac.uk

Arts & humanities 66
Engineering & IT... 45
Life sciences & biomedicine 57
Natural sciences.. 111
Social sciences 66

Academic survey position 51
Employer survey position 7

Student faculty ratio 7.6:1
International faculty 32.7%
Undergraduates 23,029
Postgraduates 5,658
International students 20.1%

Research strength (Scopus) papers................. 20,109
Research strength (Scopus) citations............. 108,641
Impact (citations per paper)...................................... 5

England's oldest civic university became Britain's first chartered university of the 21st century and the largest single-site institution in the country when Victoria University of Manchester merged with UMIST in 2004. Since the merger, the University of Manchester has set its sights on becoming a world giant by 2015 in terms of academic achievement and reputation. It is already well on its way to achieving its aims, albeit with work still to do in balancing the books. Voted University of the Year in the Times Higher Education's annual awards of 2005, it was one of the leading universities in the UK 2008 Research Assessment Exercise. Such impressive results have helped make Manchester the UK's most popular university among British and international students applying for places on undergraduate courses, which are being reviewed to ensure that teaching does not take a back seat to research. There are more than 50 specialist research centres and groups at Manchester, focusing on areas ranging from cancer treatments and genetic disorders to artificial intelligence and aeronautics. The university boasts the world-famous Jodrell Bank Observatory, the £35 million Manchester Interdisciplinary Biocentre, the Photon Science Institute, and the £40 million Integrative Centre for Molecular Cell Biology. Other new facilities include the Brooks World Poverty Institute and a new centre for cancer research.

Manchester is funding these developments with a massive £360 million capital investment program. As well as improving academic facilities, the money is being used to enhance the university's city centre campus, a 'mini-metropolis', with shops, accommodation, and social and sporting facilities. Manchester guarantees university accommodation for the duration of a course for all fee-paying overseas students. Its huge student population helps to make the city of Manchester one of the most vibrant in the UK, which sees itself as the capital of the north of England.

Alumni include more than 20 Nobel prize winners such as Ernest Rutherford, who split the atom. WS Jevons formulated the principles of modern economics, while AJP Taylor was the best-known historian of his generation. Tom Kilburn and Sir Freddie Williams were among the pioneers of computers in the 1940s.

Tomomi Kimura, a life sciences PhD student from Japan, said she felt the convenient, compact, and comprehensive facilities on campus and in the city were among the university's greatest assets, along with its strong academic reputation. "It is easy to get everything you need at Manchester, and the facilities are excellent," she said. "The student accommodation is very good and conveniently located, and arranged so that it is easy to make friends."

30= (41) University of California at Los Angeles (UCLA)
Founded 1919   www.ucla.edu

Arts & humanities	10
Engineering & IT	16
Life sciences & biomedicine	11
Natural sciences	18
Social sciences	13
Academic survey position	10
Employer survey position	29
Student faculty ratio	11.8:1
International faculty	3.5%
Undergraduates	25,291
Postgraduates	11,367
International students	7.5%
Research strength (Scopus) papers	36,940
Research strength (Scopus) citations	322,515
Impact (citations per paper)	9

You've already been to UCLA if you've ever watched an American movie. Convenient for the Hollywood film studios, the university has been the backdrop for such classics as Legally Blonde and American Pie 2. But UCLA's real contribution to the entertainment industry has been with its School of Theater, Film, and Television, whose undergraduate division is usually ranked first in the nation. It encompasses the largest university-based film and television archive in the world. Film directors Francis Ford Coppola and Rob Reiner, actors James Dean and Tim Robbins, and agent Mike Ovitz all attended UCLA. The benefits of being at the centre of the entertainment world have worked both ways. Record executive and Dreamworks co-founder David Geffen gave UCLA US$200 million for what is now called the David Geffen School of Medicine. The medical school is now ranked with America's best medical schools; it was UCLA physicians who identified the first AIDS cases. There are nearly 300 research centres, labs, and institutes at UCLA, including a prestigious civil rights research centre it 'stole' from Harvard by offering more money and free space. Five of the 4,000 UCLA faculty (and four of the school's alumni) have won the Nobel prize, a distinction considered important enough that two have campus buildings named in their honour.

Money has been flowing for construction at UCLA: some US$2 billion worth of new facilities are going up, prompting some people to call the school the University of Construction at Los Angeles. The latest project (expected completion 2009) is the Aquatic Center which will house elite sports and also be available for recreational use. UCLA has the largest enrolment of any university in California, nine out of ten students come from the state. UCLA has more than 50,000 applicants every year, more than any other university in the US. The voluntary General Education Cluster Program allows entering students to work on research with faculty on interdisciplinary topics by combining lecture classes with lab work and discussion sessions. Or they can take a Fiat Lux Freshman Seminar in groups of no more than 20, an honours-style course meant to encourage intellectual discourse by investigating a specific question or topic, with no grades or homework.

"Los Angeles is a place where strange encounters occur, something I happen to like without being able to say that you can be prepared for it in advance," said Stanislav 'Stas' Shvabrin, a graduate student from Russia who was drawn to the university's highly regarded Slavic Studies department. "It's an inscrutable, impossible city that grows on you the way very few places do."

30= (33=) National University of Singapore (NUS)
Founded 1905   www.nus.edu.sg

Arts & humanities 30
Engineering & IT.. 11
Life sciences & biomedicine 17
Natural sciences.. 31
Social sciences 18

Academic survey position 18
Employer survey position 26

Student faculty ratio 13.8:1
International faculty 51.8%
Undergraduates 22,776
Postgraduates 5,196
International students 34.9%

Research strength (Scopus) papers................. 21,256
Research strength (Scopus) citations............... 86,701
Impact (citations per paper)..................................... 4

The National University of Singapore has forged a global reputation and now ranks in the top quartile of the world's universities. Privatised in 2006, the university continues to receive a government subsidy as the island-state seeks to maintain the highest all-round standards in education. It is set on a 1.5-square-kilometre campus at Kent Ridge, scene in February 1942 of the heroic last stand by the Malay Regiment, and is a beacon for the huge investment in education at all levels made by the government of the Republic of Singapore. The law school has moved to a new site at Bukit Timah, in the centre of the island. Student intake is from a wide spectrum of countries. More than two-dozen nationalities are represented in the law school, while student exchange programs take Singaporean students to a number of countries including China, Canada, Australia and the US. NUS plays a leading role in the Association of Pacific Rim Universities (APRU), as well as in the International Alliance of Research Universities. The university has five overseas colleges: Bio Valley, Silicon Valley, Shanghai, Stockholm and Bangalore. Facilities in Singapore are of the highest international standard and include six libraries and four museums, including the Raffles Museum of Biodiversity Research, which showcases over 500,000 specimens of flora and fauna. The university has announced a Centre of Excellence in Translational Cancer Research, which it hopes will become a world leader, under the directorship of Professor Daniel Tenen, formerly of Harvard Medical School.

Among its leading graduates NUS can number Goh Chok Tong, former Prime Minister of Singapore, Kishore Mahbubani, Dean of the Lee Kuan Yew School of Public Policy at NUS and Choo San Goh, prominent choreographer of the Washington Ballet. Of the current staff, Wong Lim Soon of the School of Computing has established an international reputation in database theories.

Reben Ng, who graduated in psychology and is reading for a masters at NUS, exemplifies the university's international approach. He was the first to qualify for an International Council of Psychologists award, usually made to academics that have completed a PhD and five years' research, on the basis of his undergraduate research paper as a result of his internship with the Singapore police after only two years at NUS. He said: "When I first stepped into NUS, I never expected that my university life would be so rich. In retrospect I realize I was given the opportunity to learn in three ways: from books, through travels and by interacting with people who were totally different from me."

32 (37) University of Bristol
Founded 1876   www.brist.ac.uk

Arts & humanities	90
Engineering & IT	131
Life sciences & biomedicine	46
Natural sciences	89
Social sciences	150
Academic survey position	83
Employer survey position	16
Student faculty ratio	7.6:1
International faculty	28.2%
Undergraduates	12,451
Postgraduates	3,674
International students	16.9%
Research strength (Scopus) papers	13,824
Research strength (Scopus) citations	88,879
Impact (citations per paper)	6

Bristol has been moving steadily up the THE-QS World University Rankings since they were first published in 2005. Having resisted the dash for growth that many of its competitors have displayed, the university is among the most popular in Britain, with more than ten applicants for every undergraduate place. A prominent member of the Russell Group of research-intensive universities, Bristol has a strong research reputation across a wide variety of traditional disciplines. In the UK Research Assessment Exercise (RAE) in 2001, 36 departments received the top 5 or 5* ratings. Bristol produced another strong set of results in the 2008 RAE. In computer science, drama, economics, education, epidemiology and public health, geography, mathematics and philosophy, at least 30 per cent of the research was considered 'world-leading'. Distinguished faculty members now include Professor Michael Berry, one of the world's top physicists, and Professor Peter Fleming, whose work is credited with saving the lives of 100,000 babies worldwide. Bristol is an old, city-based institution owning 400 hectares of land and 370 buildings. It is in the middle of a £250 million investment program of new buildings, equipment and staff appointments. Major investments are planned in physics, mathematics, biological sciences, library and IT facilities, as well as new premises for the students' union and student support services. The university and the United Bristol Healthcare Trust have joined forces to build a new £6.6 million Clinical Research and Imaging Centre at St Michael's Hospital. The city of Bristol, the largest in the southwest of England, is attractive and prosperous. Although relatively expensive by UK standards, it is also generally popular with students.

Four Nobel laureates have worked at Bristol: Paul Dirac (1933), Cecil Frank Powell (1950), Hans Albrecht Bethe (1967) and Sir Neville Francis Mott (1977). There are 30 fellows of the Royal Society and nine fellows of the British Academy on the active and emeritus staff. Other famous Bristol alumni include: Sir Liam Donaldson, chief medical officer of England; Will Hutton, chief executive of The Work Foundation; Josh Lewsey, the rugby union international; and Lembit Opik, the UK Member of Parliament (MP).

Matthew Seow, a fourth year electrical and electronic engineering student said: "The university's biggest strength is that it has managed to get that tricky balance between academic achievement, activities outside academia and social life, close to perfection. It's quite hard to think of weaknesses but I guess it could do a bit more to integrate international students into the general student body and vice-versa. Studying at Bristol University was the best thing that's ever happened to me, and the whole experience has definitely exceeded my expectations."

33 (29) Northwestern University
Founded 1851   www.northwestern.edu

Arts & humanities	108
Engineering & IT	81
Life sciences & biomedicine	72
Natural sciences	114
Social sciences	29
Academic survey position	62
Employer survey position	37
Student faculty ratio	8:1
International faculty	6.7%
Undergraduates	8,574
Postgraduates	8,282
International students	13.4%
Research strength (Scopus) papers	15,559
Research strength (Scopus) citations	104,021
Impact (citations per paper)	7

Although a major private research university of some 17,000 students, the Northwestern campus at Evanston has the feel of a small college. At exactly 9pm on the Sunday before finals week each term, students traditionally lean out their windows and collectively unleash a primal scream. Nearly three-quarters of classes have fewer than 20 students, and the 1,000 undergraduate faculty (not graduate assistants) teach more than 95 per cent of the courses. The research agenda at Northwestern is ambitious. Founded in an office over a hardware store, by Chicago civic leaders anxious to win respect for their gritty frontier town, it now has five doctoral programs ranked in the top ten per cent in America by the National Research Council and ten others in the top 25 per cent.

Many international students come to Northwestern to attend its top-rated Kellogg School of Business, where a third of the students are from outside the US. Its Global Initiatives in Management includes two weeks of field study in such places as Central Europe, China, Russia, and Vietnam. Northwestern's small Chicago-based School of Law includes a nine-month masters program for graduates of foreign law schools to learn American law and legal processes. The Center for Wrongful Conviction, staffed largely by students from the law school and the university's Medill School of Journalism, famously proved innocent nine inmates on Illinois's death row, causing the state's governor to declare a moratorium on executions. The university's McCormick School of Engineering is among the top-rated in America, with a program that gives first year students the chance to work with real engineers on projects with major companies. "Engineering First" stemmed from concern that engineering education previously emphasised scientific analysis at the expense of practical design. A 50-year development plan for the Northwestern campus, now alongside Lake Michigan, includes new facilities for molecular therapeutics and diagnostics, even encroaching into the lake to make more space for residential accommodation.

The theater program has graduated the likes of Charlton Heston, Warren Beatty, Ann-Margret, Patricia Neal, Clancy Brown, Shelley Long and Tony Roberts. Other prominent alumni include the chairman and CEO of General Dynamics, the president and CEO of the Campbell Soup Company, and the president of Cornell University.

"You find people from all over the world, and they're definitely some of the smartest people to get in here," said Ruchit Duggal, an undergraduate from India who is majoring in both economics and computer engineering. "There's a good mix of cultures. It's not inside the city, but if you need to go into the city, it takes maybe 30 minutes," he said. "The only negative I've found is the weather in the winter, which gets you down a bit."

34= (33=) University of British Columbia
Founded 1908   www.ubc.ca

Arts & humanities 18
Engineering & IT... 22
Life sciences & biomedicine 14
Natural sciences 20
Social sciences 12

Academic survey position 13
Employer survey position 59

Student faculty ratio 9:1
International faculty 7.8%
Undergraduates 30,851
Postgraduates 7,113
International students 13.5%

Research strength (Scopus) papers................. 23,748
Research strength (Scopus) citations 154,465
Impact (citations per paper)....................................... 7

Out on Canada's West Coast, the University of British Columbia (UBC) offers a full range of programs in the arts, sciences, medicine, law, commerce and other faculties. Its main campus is in Vancouver and there is a small campus in the province's Okanagan valley. There are international students from over 140 countries. Those who teach and research are similarly cosmopolitan: 43 per cent earned their first degrees from institutions outside Canada. Neurosciences has become a leading discipline, with UBC's Brain Research Centre bringing together 175 interdisciplinary investigators. Physics and astronomy researchers are among the most cited in Canada. In 2005, New Scientist ranked UBC ninth in North America for life-science patents, the only Canadian university on the list. Technologies invented by UBC researchers have broken the US$100 million mark in cumulative licensing revenue. Burgeoning sales revenues have helped UBC develop what it terms its 'world renowned biotech industry'. The university also boasts a strong creative writing program, and is particularly proud of the fact that its runs Canada's largest program in Asian Studies and the largest Asian library collection. Its Museum of Anthropology is known internationally for a strong Pacific Northwest Collection.

UBC's mission is to "prepare students to become exceptional global citizens, promote the values of a civil and sustainable society, and conduct outstanding research to serve the people of British Columbia, Canada, and the world". It says its values are of excellence in research and teaching, global citizenship, sustainability and civil society. The late Michael Smith, a Nobel laureate in chemistry taught for decades at UBC, while physics researcher Carl Wieman, recently hired to spearhead reforms in the teaching of science, is the newest Nobel laureate. Opera singer Ben Heppner is a graduate of its School of Music, while former Canadian prime ministers Kim Campbell and John Turner also call UBC their alma mater.

Deniz Kuran, of Istanbul, Turkey, chose to study at UBC "because I knew it was one of the top universities in Canada. "Its location was one of the school's strong points. "I had heard Vancouver was one of the best cities to live in the world and also has some of the mildest weather in the country." Studying for her Bachelor of Commerce in Human Resources Management and International Business she enjoys "strong company connections and good professors". While UBC met her academic and social expectations, she says the large student population can pose problems and "can be too much for some students who might feel lost sometimes."

34= (28) École Polytechnique
Founded 1794 **www.polytechnique.edu**

Engineering & IT	31
Life sciences & biomedicine	278
Natural sciences	26
Social sciences	204
Academic survey position	89
Employer survey position	44
Student faculty ratio	3.7:1
International faculty	18.2%
Undergraduates	1,000
Postgraduates	1,496
International students	24.9%
Research strength (Scopus) papers	4,357
Research strength (Scopus) citations	20,288
Impact (citations per paper)	5

For over two centuries, France's most prestigious engineering grande école, École Polytechnique, has trained distinguished scientists, captains of industry, military chiefs and political leaders, as well as engineers. It is now to be a founding member of the Paris Institute of Technology, one of the new collegiate universities in France with 11 engineering schools and one business school sharing an ambitious global aim. Founded as the École centrale des travaux publics by Lazare Carnot and Gaspard Monge, it was re-established as a military academy by Napoleon in 1804, with the motto 'Pour la patrie, les sciences et la gloire' ('For the nation, science and glory'). The Defence Ministry remains its supervisory authority. Students have military status and wear a distinctive uniform on special occasions. Women were first admitted in 1972. Entrance is through a competitive exam after two years of study in post-baccalauréat preparatory classes, though nowadays there is an alternative selection procedure for foreign students. The school, nicknamed 'X', has an undergraduate program, graduate school and many research laboratories mostly run in association with other institutions such as CNRS, the national centre for scientific research. École Polytechnique specializes in biology, chemistry, computer science, economics, pure and applied mathematics, mechanical engineering, physics and social sciences. But all students must study a broad range of subjects including two languages and general cultural courses, and follow several work placements. Reforms in 2000 extended by a year the traditional three-year undergraduate engineering program: one year each military service, common studies and specialization, and introduced a civilian service option. A year is spent at another university, possibly abroad. Annual intake is 500, with foreigners of 40 nationalities represented among the undergraduates. Half the masters students are from abroad and a third of the doctoral candidates. In 1976 the school moved from its historic site in the Paris Latin Quarter to its present campus at Palaiseau, south of the capital, where all students are housed.

Alumni include presidents Sadi Carnot and Valéry Giscard d'Estaing, astronauts Jean-François Clervoy and Philippe Perrin, scientists André-Marie Ampère, Paul Lévy, Henri Poincaré and Nobel prize winner for economics, Maurice Allais. Alfred Dreyfus and Generals Foch and Joffre are among military Polytechniciens.

British undergraduate Harry Robertson had high expectations of both the quality of the education and the student lifestyle, and was not disappointed. He identifies the school's strengths as "the diversity and quality of its education, its budget per student (École Polytechnique is very highly subsidised), and the student lifestyle: there are an incredible number of clubs, activities and sport. Its weaknesses are that it is little known abroad, especially compared to the top British and US universities, and its relatively small size."

36 (22) University of California at Berkeley
Founded 1868   www.berkeley.edu

Arts & humanities 2
Engineering & IT... 2
Life sciences & biomedicine 4
Natural sciences.. 2
Social sciences 2

Academic survey position 1
Employer survey position 10

Student faculty ratio 19.5:1
International faculty 30.4%
Undergraduates 24,121
Postgraduates 9,652
International students 7.4%

Research strength (Scopus) papers.................. 28,257
Research strength (Scopus) citations 237,744
Impact (citations per paper)...................................... 8

The first and flagship campus of the University of California, Berkeley, can trace its origins to the gold rush era, when the nascent state was seeking cultural legitimacy. With a generous amount of space set aside for its campus in the hills above San Francisco Bay, and a curriculum modelled after Harvard's and Yale's, Berkeley was an ambitious place. It still is. Thirty-five of its 36 graduate programs are ranked in the top ten by the National Research Council, including the best overall in chemistry, English, German, mathematics, and statistics; the highest score in America. It produces more PhDs than any other US university, its library holdings are the nation's fourth largest, and it also ranks first in the number of its research programs the NRC considers 'distinguished.' Research has always been Berkeley's great strength, particularly in the sciences. It was here that the first cyclotron, or circular particle accelerator, was developed by physicist Ernest O Lawrence, who, along with other Berkeley scientists, went on to help produce the atomic and hydrogen bombs at a secret base in Los Alamos, New Mexico. Berkeley researchers also discovered the anti-proton and elements including plutonium, isolated the polio virus, and contributed to the invention of the laser. Twenty members of the faculty have won the Nobel prize and seven laureates still work there.

Research opportunities aren't limited to the university's graduate students. Undergraduates can apply to take part in the Undergraduate Research Apprentice Program and work side-by-side with faculty in any discipline. Just over three per cent of Berkeley students come from countries other than the US. In addition to groundbreaking science, Berkeley is famous as a centre of the Free Speech Movement, which began there in the 1960s, and for student and faculty activism. Its latest venture is a US$593 million Student Athlete High Performance Center to add to the impressive sports facilities, which had to overcome concerns that it would be built on an active earthquake fault.

Alumni include former Pakistan President Zulfikar Ali Bhutto, Vietnam-era Defense Secretary Robert McNamara, California governor and onetime US presidential candidate Jerry Brown, Apple Computer co-founder Steve Wozniak, Intel CEO Paul Otellini, MySpace creator Tom Anderson, Vodafone CEO Arun Sarin, Korean Airlines president Choon Kun Chom, The Gap CEO Don Fisher, and Stephen Bechtel, founder of the controversial worldwide engineering firm that bears his name.

"What I find most remarkable about Berkeley is that it is a public university and yet it is doing so well academically, especially in a society like America," said Arpita Roy, a doctoral student in cultural anthropology from India. "It tells me that money is not everything, and that good research can be accomplished even under financial constraints."

37 (31) University of Sydney
Founded 1850   www.usyd.edu.au

Arts & humanities 17
Engineering & IT.. 41
Life sciences & biomedicine 27
Natural sciences.. 44
Social sciences 27

Academic survey position 26
Employer survey position 34

Student faculty ratio 10.8:1
International faculty 40.2%
Undergraduates 27,253
Postgraduates 9,142
International students 24.7%

Research strength (Scopus) papers.................. 18,785
Research strength (Scopus) citations 93,773
Impact (citations per paper)...................................... 5

Australia's oldest university celebrated its 150th anniversary with the Sydney Olympics in 2000 and enjoys a big reputation for research. Sweeping lawns and Gothic Revival sandstone architecture give the main campus, on the edge of the Sydney Central Business District, a sense of old world higher learning that continues within the grand quadrangle and the Great Tower, which is its focal point. Sydney is a member of Australia's Group of Eight research-intensive universities and has links with many of the world's leading research institutions. This global network covers research collaboration, joint teaching projects as well as staff and student exchanges across Europe, North America and Asia. The university is one of only three Australian institutions in the Association of the Pacific Rim Universities. A seven-floor medical research and teaching facility was opened in November 2008, as part of a AU$950 million redevelopment of the North Shore Hospital, which will be completed in 2013.

The university offers full fee scholarships with stipends to cover living expenses to outstanding international candidates for the Doctor of Philosophy program. Merit scholarships are also offered to international students completing Australian final-year high school examinations, as well as to continuing undergraduate students. All Sydney undergraduates are eligible for scholarships awarded for outstanding academic achievement. The university does not guarantee residential accommodation for international students, although many find places in campus colleges or residences. It advises arriving 14-days early to attend orientation sessions and find a place to live.

Renowned graduates include Nobel laureates Professor Russell Robinson, Sir John Cornforth and Dr John Harsanyi, former president of the World Bank James Wolfensohn, academic and businesswoman Jill Ker Conway, film makers Phil Noyce, Jane Campion and Bruce Beresford, writers Germaine Greer and Clive James, and three Prime Ministers, including Australia's first, Andrew Barton, and the Governor of New South Wales and Chancellor of the University, Her Excellency Professor Marie Bashir.

Diego Poveda, from Bogota, in Colombia, initially hoped to study in America or Britain, but the cost was more than his parents could afford, so he opted for Australia. A chemical engineering graduate, he has no complaints about his lecturers, his studies or the university. "In large part it has met my expectations. When I saw the curriculum, I realized that it balanced theoretical classes and problem-based learning, which really put a smile on my face as I could see how learning about systems could be applied in a chemical plant," he said.

38 (27) University of Melbourne
Founded 1853   www.unimelb.edu.au

Arts & humanities	16
Engineering & IT	28
Life sciences & biomedicine	26
Natural sciences	27
Social sciences	19
Academic survey position	21
Employer survey position	9
Student faculty ratio	10.2:1
International faculty	15.3%
Undergraduates	25,589
Postgraduates	9,088
International students	27.1%
Research strength (Scopus) papers	17,796
Research strength (Scopus) citations	99,197
Impact (citations per paper)	6

Melbourne is Australia's second oldest university and it attracts a large number of students from socially advantaged homes and top private schools. But it claims to offer the nation's largest scholarship scheme, 8,000 scholarships worth AU$100 million over three years for highly able students. Being large, venerable and of high prestige, the university has huge financial, intellectual and locational assets. Its centralized campus, a few minutes' tram ride from the central business district, is in the heart of cosmopolitan Carlton. There are other small campuses dotted around Victoria that focus on agriculture, forestry and rural medicine. Melbourne has begun to transform itself along the lines of the Bologna model for European universities, becoming the first university in Australia to introduce a comprehensive graduate school system. Students will enrol in a new set of six broad undergraduate degrees leading to professional graduate programs such as architecture, law and teaching, or to the workplace, or higher research degrees such as PhDs. From 2008, law, architecture, building and planning, as well as nursing and some education courses will be offered only as graduate programs. Other professional degrees, such as medicine, dentistry and engineering, will also become graduate-entry only. Melbourne expects to peak at around 50,000 but towards 2015 it will drop to current levels or below. Some 20 per cent of these students will be in new graduate schools and a further 10-15 per cent engaged in post-graduate research.

Many of Melbourne's academics are among Australia's most accomplished and sought-after scholars accounting for 250 memberships of the four Australian learned academies. Melbourne has three Nobel laureates on its staff, Peter Doherty, Sir Clive Granger and Sir James Mirrlees. The university received AUS$90 million in 2008 for the Peter Doherty Institute of Infection and Immunity. Melbourne has led the recent Thomson Scientific Australian citation survey making 'Top Three' appearances in 21 fields (11 by total citations and ten by impact) and in both citations and impact in five fields: neurosciences, physics, microbiology, pharmacology and psychology/psychiatry.

Nicklas Sandstrom, a Swedish medical student who came to Melbourne after completing a year's military service, was attracted by the university's problem-solving approach. He will have to repay a Swedish government loan covering the AU$200,000 cost of his six-year medical degree after he graduates. "I've learnt a lot more than I expected and have no complaints about the teaching so far," he said. "The problem-based approach and tutorials are different to the teaching back home where they don't have the small discussion groups. You remember more and learn more while interacting, rather than just looking at slides in a lecture."

39 (53=) Hong Kong University of Science and Technology
Founded 1991   www.ust.hk

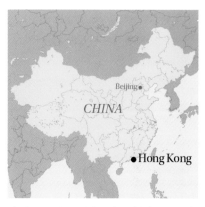

Engineering & IT	24
Life sciences & biomedicine	67
Natural sciences	59
Social sciences	69
Academic survey position	71
Employer survey position	67
Student faculty ratio	10.1:1
International faculty	68.1%
Undergraduates	5,868
Postgraduates	2,546
International students	28.4%
Research strength (Scopus) papers	8,493
Research strength (Scopus) citations	33,571
Impact (citations per paper)	4

The Hong Kong University of Science and Technology (HKUST) is the youngest institution in this year's top 100, conceived with the goal of propelling Hong Kong towards a knowledge-based economy. The teaching faculty is organized around four schools: science, engineering, business and management, and humanities and social science. A fifth school, the HKUST Fok Ying Tung Graduate School in Nansha, Guangzhou, is now open and is expected to be fully operational in 2009, capitalizing on the region's dynamic growth. The main campus is also being expanded to accommodate a projected rise in students with the introduction of the government-initiated four-year degree program. The campus will dramatically increase in size by 2012, with the addition of new student residences and more teaching and research facilities.

More than half of the faculty members are from outside Hong Kong and Mainland China, almost a quarter coming from North America. The EMBA program, run jointly with the Kellogg School of Management, is consistently ranked among the best in the world, attracting over 50 per cent of its students from outside Hong Kong. The MSc in Global Finance, offered jointly with the Leonard N Stern School of Business of New York University, is the first executive format finance program in the Asia-Pacific Region.

HKUST laboratories have already made many groundbreaking discoveries, including the fabrication and characterization of the world's smallest carbon nanotubes, genetic associations in schizophrenia and the development of anti-ageing drugs. Two departments in the engineering school are ranked among the world's top leaders in the number of papers published in key international journals. In 2006 the Institute for Advanced Study was inaugurated at HKUST, with a mission to further scientific advancement by inviting the world's foremost scientists to work in partnership with local academics in the fields of nanotechnology and nanoscience, biotechnology and bioscience, information technology, the environment and sustainable development. The 13-member international advisory board consists of nine Nobel laureates.

Gesche Haas, from Bonn, chose to join a Global Business program over other offers in Germany and the UK, but even she was surprised by the quality of the university and the study and living environment. "Professors at HKUST received their PhDs and other qualifications from prestigious universities all over the world," she says. "They also have a lot of work experience and are well connected to many companies." She added that the university still has a lot to do to make itself better known to an international audience, saying that "HKUST's real potential does not seem to be fully understood by the entire world yet."

40 (49) New York University (NYU)
Founded 1831   **www.nyu.edu**

Arts & humanities	15
Engineering & IT	243
Life sciences & biomedicine	53
Natural sciences	53
Social sciences	23
Academic survey position	35
Employer survey position	45
Student faculty ratio	7.5:1
International faculty	5.6%
Undergraduates	20,385
Postgraduates	14,775
International students	12.3%
Research strength (Scopus) papers	16,293
Research strength (Scopus) citations	129,999
Impact (citations per paper)	8

The largest private, non-profit university in the US, NYU is growing even bigger by merging with the Polytechnic University, giving it an instant engineering school. It is also opening a branch in Abu Dhabi, in the United Arab Emirates in 2010, the first complete liberal arts campus developed abroad by a US research university, which will infuse money into the main campus, in exchange for borrowing members of the faculty on a rotating basis. On top of this, NYU is raising US$2.5 billion to make more financial aid available to students, expand its campus, and add programs and faculty. Eleven NYU faculty members and an equal number of alumni have won the Nobel prize.

Despite NYU's huge enrolment, most classes are of a reasonable size; about 80 per cent have fewer than 30 students. The university is highly regarded in business, law, the sciences, and the performing arts. Its law school, housed in a newly refurbished building, and the Stern School of Business are among the nation's most distinguished. Its Institute of Fine Arts specializes in not only the history of art and archaeology, but also the conservation and technology of works of art, collaborating with New York's superlative museums. And its Gallatin School of Individualized Study lets students create their own curriculum. NYU's interest in international affairs goes beyond its significant proportion (the fifth highest in America) of students from abroad. The undergraduate division of its business school requires, and pays for, all its students to go on an international business trip. The law school's 'global faculty' includes leading legal thinkers from all over the world who come there for at least a term. The university's main campus wraps around Washington Square in bohemian Greenwich Village, the very centre of Manhattan. NYU also has 11 campuses overseas.

Some of NYU's best-known alumni attended the Tisch School of the Arts. They include Spike Lee, Oliver Stone, Alec Baldwin, Amy Heckerling, Ang Lee and Tony Kushner. Among the university's other graduates have been Woody Allen, Angelina Jolie, Burt Lancaster, Martin Scorcese, Billy Crystal, John Cusack, Lou Gossett, Ethan Hawke, Meg Ryan, former New York City Mayor Rudy Giuliani and John F. Kennedy Jr.

"It is all very well to read about globalization, but NYU is about living it," said Devyani Prabhat, a doctoral candidate in sociology from India. "A tremendous diversity of ideas and forward thinkers from all over the planet converge here." "NYU," he said, "is always thinking ahead and not resting on its past glories. Like New York City, it is always two steps ahead of the rest. It is not scared to try new things and does not hide behind tradition."

41 (45) University of Toronto
Founded 1827   www.toronto.edu

Arts & humanities	11
Engineering & IT	10
Life sciences & biomedicine	13
Natural sciences	9
Social sciences	16
Academic survey position	9
Employer survey position	52
Student faculty ratio	24.2:1
International faculty	25.7%
Undergraduates	46,778
Postgraduates	12,029
International students	9.8%
Research strength (Scopus) papers	38,828
Research strength (Scopus) citations	267,076
Impact (citations per paper)	7

The University of Toronto aims high with its stated mission and purpose: 'It is this human right to radical, critical teaching and research with which the University has a duty above all to be concerned; for there is no one else, no other institution and no other office, in our modern liberal democracy, which is the custodian of this most precious and vulnerable right of the liberated human spirit.' That bold statement is an indication of the role assumed by Canada's biggest university. There are three campuses, with the majority of students based at its 180-year-old downtown location. A new Science Research building was opened in 2008 on the Scarborough campus, accommodating principal investigators and post doctoral fellows as well as student researchers. In its latest figures, it accumulated C$854 million in research grants and contract support and has spun off 103 companies. Its research library is one of the top four in North America and has more than 15 million holdings. Research achievements have also been mammoth. It developed the first electronic heart pacemaker, artificial larynx, single-lung transplant, nerve transplant and artificial pancreas. Scientists have joined forces with colleagues at Kyoto University in the area of stem cell research to bring therapies to the market more quickly.

Alumni include authors Margaret Atwood and Michael Ondaatje, film directors David Cronenberg and Norman Jewison, eBay's Jeff Skoll and former Canadian prime ministers Paul Martin and Lester B Pearson. Sir Frederick Banting and J J R Macleod won the Nobel prize in 1923. Communications guru Marshall McLuhan was a faculty member. John C Polanyi won the 1986 Nobel prize in chemistry for pioneering work that led to the development of the laser. Geneticist Tak Mak was the first to clone a T-cell gene, a key part of the immune system.

Audre Kapacinskas from Chicago, who took peace and conflict studies, psychology and economics, appreciated the size and flexibility that she found at the institution. She says requirements to complete credits in diverse academic areas like humanities and science meant she could try something different while focusing on what interested her. "It's a nice cross between European and US systems." Weaker points have been a frustrating student web service and a lack of student involvement to bolster school spirit. But the university far exceeded her expectations: "I came for a fantastic city, nice campus, and variety of courses. The people I've met and the professors I've had have made it an exceptionally positive experience. You develop a friendly, caring community around you, but you still have the resources of a large research institution at your disposal."

42 (38=) The Chinese University of Hong Kong
Founded 1963   www.cuhk.edu.hk

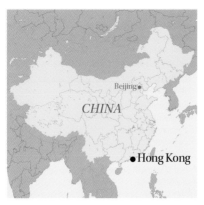

Arts & humanities	111
Engineering & IT	74
Life sciences & biomedicine	64
Natural sciences	105
Social sciences	66
Academic survey position	74
Employer survey position	95
Student faculty ratio	7.8:1
International faculty	42.0%
Undergraduates	10,515
Postgraduates	3,175
International students	20.8%
Research strength (Scopus) papers	12,172
Research strength (Scopus) citations	51,997
Impact (citations per paper)	4

The Chinese University of Hong Kong (CUHK) is a comprehensive research university with philosophical foundations built on the traditions of bilingualism and multiculturalism. As such, it is in a unique position to attract more overseas students and faculty, and to position itself as a university of choice in Asia. Five new colleges will be built in the next few years as the university prepares to increase its undergraduate intake in preparation for Hong Kong's move towards a four-year degree structure in 2012. A 'Campus Masterplan' for 2021 promises a 'pedestrian-friendly' and sustainable campus, conserving places of cultural significance while providing academic and recreational venues that will enhance college life. Established through the amalgamation of three colleges, with the addition of a fourth college in 1986, the university is the only one in Hong Kong that follows a collegiate structure and a bilingual policy that places equal emphasis on English and Chinese. Three-quarters of the full-time students are undergraduates, but there are also several thousand students in professional and continuing education leading to higher degrees. With the largest campus in Hong Kong (134 hectares) the university provides over 6,000 hostel places and its member colleges play important roles in fostering an intellectual community and providing pastoral care and support. Of the ten previous Rhodes Scholars from Hong Kong, seven are from the university.

CUHK has an international faculty, nearly half coming from outside China and 93 per cent holding overseas qualifications. Many of the academics have distinguished themselves with research in the medical and scientific fields, including the first successful cloning of the plant gene, the development of the world's smallest Bluetooth communications module, the formulation of network coding theory, and breakthroughs in minimally invasive surgery and detection of foetal DNA in maternal plasma. The university's MBA programs are also highly-regarded. The Faculty of Business Administration was among the first in Asia to be accredited internationally.

The university is the only one in Hong Kong to have had Nobel laureates on its staff, such as C N Yang, (physics 1957) and Sir James Mirrlees, (economics 1996).

Sarah Moore worked in London for seven years before her decision to take a full-time MBA at CUHK. Motivated by China's integration into the world economy and a truly multicultural learning environment at the university, she has no regrets about relocating to Hong Kong: "Given China's increasing importance as a global economic power Hong Kong is an ideal place to develop myself and gain invaluable experience that will benefit my career."

43 (33=) University of Queensland
Founded 1909   www.uq.edu.au/international

Arts & humanities	67
Engineering & IT	61
Life sciences & biomedicine	32
Natural sciences	58
Social sciences	39
Academic survey position	41
Employer survey position	38
Student faculty ratio	11.7:1
International faculty	49.6%
Undergraduates	22,573
Postgraduates	5,623
International students	18.1%
Research strength (Scopus) papers	15,993
Research strength (Scopus) citations	81,575
Impact (citations per paper)	5

The University of Queensland (UQ) is the oldest and most highly respected of the state's seven universities. It is large by Australian standards and is the biggest in Queensland. UQ was founded in 1909 and its first lectures held two years later when 83 students, including 23 women, turned up for classes at Government House in the centre of the city. Today, the main campus is located on a tranquil site on the bend of the Brisbane River, about six kilometres from the central business district. But UQ also operates on 50 locations across the state in hospitals, on tropical islands and even has its own experimental mine. It is probably best known for a series of world-class research institutes and centres which specialize in molecular bioscience, bioengineering and nanotechnology, social science, sustainable minerals, magnetic resonance capabilities and neuroscience.

The university is a founding member of Australia's Group of Eight research-intensive universities. UQ accounts for about 70 per cent of Queensland's research, as well as being one of the top three universities in Australia in this regard. The university will be at the forefront of renewed global efforts to eliminate malaria, thanks to a new AusAID-funded support centre at its School of Population Health. UQ will also lead a large-scale partnership with the Chinese Academy of Sciences on clean energy technologies, targeting clean coal, hybrid and fuel cell vehicles, hydrogen production and energy storage. It is helping to increase medical support in rural communities through its new AU$4.2 million advanced clinical training facility. The university also continues to pay tribute to Steve Irwin, the 'crocodile hunter' who died in 2006, by working with his former team on the wildlife reserve on Queensland's Cape York Peninsula that bears his name. The university praised Irwin for making a 'significant contribution' to crocodile research in Australia by 'developing new methods to track these often wary animals'.

UQ's alumni include Nobel prizewinner Professor Peter Doherty as well as former state premiers, a governor-general and chief justices as well as Oscar-winning actor Geoffrey Rush and a list of famous business people, writers, artists, doctors and engineers.

Camryn Allen was drawn to UQ in 2002 as a study abroad student from California's San Diego. She felt so at home that she stayed on to complete her PhD in a study of koalas, and plans to continue her research there. Ms Allen says because the university was flexible about her studies and offered unique research opportunities in her particular area of interest, it was her "number one choice". At the school of animal studies, she spent her time with a koala research group that created a ground-breaking artificial insemination technique for the animals.

44 (46) Osaka University
Founded 1931   www.osaka-u.ac.jp

Arts & humanities	154
Engineering & IT	49
Life sciences & biomedicine	36
Natural sciences	40
Social sciences	146
Academic survey position	53
Employer survey position	153
Student faculty ratio	6.2:1
International faculty	4.4%
Undergraduates	16,204
Postgraduates	8,037
International students	5.4%
Research strength (Scopus) papers	28,130
Research strength (Scopus) citations	151,370
Impact (citations per paper)	5

The sixth-oldest national university in Japan, Osaka University was established in 1931 in the heart of one of the commercial centres of Japan, 500 kilometres south west of Tokyo. Its roots lie in a local medical college founded in 1869. At the outset, the university consisted only of medical and science faculties. Today, those subjects are considered the backbone of the university, which operates its own hospital. However, all undergraduates take liberal arts programs for the first three semesters.

The latest stage in its development came in October 2007, when the university merged with Osaka University of Foreign Studies, which specialized in studies of more than 20 modern languages, including Urdu and Swahili, making it the largest national university in Japan. After the integration, Osaka University has 11 schools, 15 graduate schools, five research institutes and two hospitals. There are three campuses in Suita, Toyonaka and Minoh cities and Nakanoshima. The university has the motto 'Live locally, grow globally', underlining the international ambitions which have been at the heart of its activities since the 'semi-privatization' of Japanese universities two years ago. About half of all foreign students receive grants through the university, including some from the Japanese government. Plans are afoot to send more Japanese students abroad with the aim of giving a third of the university's undergraduates overseas exposure. Osaka already has exchange programs with numerous European and American institutions, including Nottingham University and University College London. Yale University may soon be added to the list, following discussions in 2008 about future collaborations between the two institutions, as well as to encourage Osaka students to pursue further study at Yale.

Among the university's most cited scientists is Shizuo Akira, 54, winner of the 2004 Robert Koch prize for his discovery of the 'toll-like receptor' that activates immune system cells upon recognition of pathogenic organisms. He was also recently named 'the hottest researcher' by Thomson Scientific for outnumbering his peers in citation. Professor Akira currently leads a government-funded project that seeks to combine microbiology with immunology at the university's Research Institute of Microbial Disease. "We have great facilities for medical research, backed by our long tradition. We also get a lot of bright students in our department," says Professor Akira, who also cites robotic engineering as an area of strength for the university. Alumni include Manga author Osamu Tezuka, Sony founder Akio Morita, and Nobel physics laureate Hideki Yukawa.

"The university provides an excellent atmosphere for research," says Ngan Chew Yee, a Malaysian student currently researching into anticancer drug mechanisms. "The graduate school of medicine provides an almost unlimited source of information and excellent student guidance by the 'sensei' (professors)."

45 (44) University of New South Wales
Founded 1949   **www.unsw.edu.au**

Arts & humanities 51
Engineering & IT.. 27
Life sciences & biomedicine 50
Natural sciences... 39
Social sciences 28

Academic survey position 29
Employer survey position 17

Student faculty ratio 14.8:1
International faculty 27.2%
Undergraduates 23,083
Postgraduates 7,326
International students 23.2%

Research strength (Scopus) papers.................. 15,999
Research strength (Scopus) citations 76,481
Impact (citations per paper)...................................... 5

The University of New South Wales (UNSW) is one of the heavyweights of Australian higher education, offering more than 665 programs in 75 schools to undergraduates and postgraduates. The university's main campus is in Kensington, an inner suburb of Sydney, but six others are scattered around the city. One of its most famous colleges, the Australian Defence Force Academy, is the nation's principal military training institute, based in Canberra. Construction has begun on the Lowy Centre for Cancer Research to bring together Australia's leading childhood and adult cancer researchers, making it the largest integrated cancer research institute in the Southern Hemisphere. Another strategic priority is environmental sustainability; the UNSW Climate Change Research Centre, bringing together more than 60 researchers from various disciplines across the university and making it one of the largest centres of its kind. The university is also 'walking the talk' with sustainability initiatives aimed at making the UNSW campus the greenest in Australia. The latest research development is the AU$20 million National Institute of Virology, which will be part of the university's growing effort to combat HIV Aids.

Although the origins of the University of New South Wales can be traced back to the founding of the Sydney Mechanics Institute in 1843, it was not until 1949 that it became a university. Initially, the university's core focus was on teaching and research in science and technology but the courses also included humanities and commerce subjects and they are still a crucial component today, along with engineering, law and medicine. Now a member of Australia's Group of Eight research-intensive universities, UNSW is also a founding member of Universitas 21, the international alliance of 20 leading universities in 11 countries. Its researchers maintain more than 2,000 separate international and academic links with 500 universities and research organizations across 90 countries.

Catherine Nawangpalupi came with her four-year-old daughter and husband from the Indonesian island of Java to undertake a PhD in the Faculty of Built Environment after completing a masters degree in engineering at the university in 2001. "I initially decided on UNSW after comparing the ranking of its engineering course with others and it was one of the best," she says. "My supervisors and other staff give me a great deal of support and I find that excellent although the library resources are not as good as when I did my masters." Ms Nawangpalupi says, as well as receiving help with her studies, she also has the opportunity to tutor undergraduate students. She believes the experience in conducting her research and tutoring will be of great use when she returns to teach at a private university in Java.

46 (47) Boston University
Founded 1839   **www.bu.edu**

Arts & humanities	49
Engineering & IT	106
Life sciences & biomedicine	43
Natural sciences	98
Social sciences	46
Academic survey position	49
Employer survey position	89
Student faculty ratio	9.3:1
International faculty	5.1%
Undergraduates	17,715
Postgraduates	10,162
International students	13.0%
Research strength (Scopus) papers	14,764
Research strength (Scopus) citations	123,658
Impact (citations per paper)	8

Long in the shadow of MIT and Harvard just across the Charles River, Boston University (BU) has taken the head-down approach of the also-ran that has to work harder. It lobbies aggressively for the government money that has paid for such things as a new building dedicated to the study of photonics, largely for military applications. Its new high-rise residence halls and state-of-the-art fitness centre and arena were partly underwritten by, and are named after, an insurance company rather than an academic or alumnus. But BU also has a tradition of social activism. Alexander Graham Bell was a professor at BU when he invented the telephone. Alumni include the civil rights leader Martin Luther King Jr The School of Education took over the management of a nearby failed public school system in an attempt to turn it around, and its medical school merged with a city hospital that largely serves urban, low-income patients. A new ambulatory care building, partly funded by tax credits, is designed to provide care to many more patients 'regardless of their ability to pay'.

BU was the first university to award a PhD to a woman, and the first to open all of its divisions to women. Today, more than half of the degree students are women. About one student in eight comes from outside the US. Many are drawn by the business school, which offers an unusual combined MS-MBA degree rooted in the connection between information technology and business management. BU is also pre-eminent in engineering, where much of BU's US$312 million a year research takes place. And yet, bucking the trend of other universities to focus on the sciences, BU has now turned to the arts. One of the few major research universities to also house a conservatory for the performing and visual arts, the university is renovating its College of Fine Arts.

Alumni of the College of Fine Arts include actors and actresses Faye Dunaway, Geena Davis, and Olympia Dukakis. The business school has graduated Benetton Group chairman Alessandro Benetton and Shin Yong-Il, CEO of Deutsche Asset Management. Others include Ishrat Husain, governor of the State Bank of Pakistan, and Faisal al-Fayez, former prime minister of Jordan. Among six Nobel prize-winners are Derek Walcott and Elie Wiesel.

Despite its size, students say, BU offers personal attention. "It has a community feeling," says Masayo Nishida, a student from Japan who is working toward her doctorate in sociology. "In general, the professors are very approachable." Like many students, she was also drawn by the university's location. "Boston is attractive because it is not a huge city but also not a typical college town in the middle of nowhere so I can concentrate on my studies and also enjoy cultural life."

47 (43) Monash University
Founded 1958   www.monash.edu.au

AUSTRALIA

Canberra●
Melbourne ●

Arts & humanities	33
Engineering & IT	47
Life sciences & biomedicine	30
Natural sciences	53
Social sciences	25
Academic survey position	28
Employer survey position	15
Student faculty ratio	11.1:1
International faculty	46.1%
Undergraduates	32,865
Postgraduates	8,801
International students	34.5%
Research strength (Scopus) papers	13,203
Research strength (Scopus) citations	59,943
Impact (citations per paper)	5

Monash University has more students, more staff and more campuses around the world than any other in Australia. It was the first university created in Victoria since the University of Melbourne, 105 years earlier. From an initial intake of 347 students, Monash grew rapidly. The university also developed a wide range of courses in arts, commerce, engineering, education, law, medicine and science, and in 1990 began expanding, first around Melbourne, then outside the city and, finally, beyond Australia. In 1998, the Malaysian Ministry of Education invited Monash to set up a campus near Kuala Lumpur together with the Sunway Group. A second offshore campus followed in South Africa in 2001. More than 3,000 students are now based on the Malaysian and 1,100 on the Johannesburg campus. Study centres have been established in London, UK and in Prato, Italy. Monash is now a network of eight campuses and has partnerships with 110 institutions around the world. International students are encouraged to apply for scholarships including International Scholarships for Excellence, which provide up to AU$6,000 a year and Monash Global Scholarships, which provide a AU$6,000 one-off grant.

Monash is one of the Australian Group of Eight research-intensive universities and is home to 75 research centres. The university is best known for three large science and technology projects: the AU$300 million Science, Technology, Research and Innovation Precinct, the Australian Stem Cell Centre which is one of the major tenants of the precinct, and a AU$207 million synchrotron, the first to be built in Australia. Work has begun on the Melbourne Centre for Nanofabrication, which will be built next to the Clayton campus. A new regenerative medicine research facility opened in 2008 and houses a multi-million-dollar aquarium with thousands of tropical fish. Researchers are seeking breakthroughs in fields such as heart disease.

Famous alumni include federal government ministers Simon Cean and Tony Robinson, novelist Peter Carey, and America's Cup skipper John Bertrand.

Shyamala Nataraj came from India to complete a masters in bioethics at Monash's main campus in Melbourne and went on to a PhD in public health: "Melbourne is such a lovely city to live in," she said. "I spent some time in the US and considered studying, but didn't want my son growing up there, so I brought him with me while my daughter is studying in America. Most of the teaching at Monash is good while some is excellent. The only limitation is that the content and context of the curriculum is "very Western," she said.

48 (93=) University of Copenhagen
Founded 1479   www.ku.dk

Arts & humanities	58
Engineering & IT	281
Life sciences & biomedicine	59
Natural sciences	75
Social sciences	31
Academic survey position	65
Employer survey position	196
Student faculty ratio	3.9:1
International faculty	20.1%
Undergraduates	11,341
Postgraduates	8,911
International students	15.4%
Research strength (Scopus) papers	15,805
Research strength (Scopus) citations	111,952
Impact (citations per paper)	7

Situated in a number of impressive buildings scattered around 'wonderful, wonderful Copenhagen', Denmark's top university has over 100 institutes, departments, laboratories, and research centres. The university, which enjoyed a spectacular rise up the world ranking this year, is one of the ten members of the International Alliance of Research Universities, which includes Oxford, Cambridge and Yale. It is also a leading member of the Øresund University Partnership, which brings together 14 universities from eastern Denmark and southern Sweden; the largest concentration of higher research and educational programs in Scandinavia. To appeal to an international audience, the university offers a significant number of courses in English each semester, across all faculties and disciplines. However, all degree courses require proficiency in Danish. A new centre for internationalization and parallel language competencies opened in August 2008. Students from Denmark and other EU countries do not pay tuition fees, but those from other countries have done so at all Danish universities since 2006/07. At Copenhagen, undergraduates will pay €10,000 in 2009-10. Charges for masters courses vary according to faculty. The six faculties offer approximately 200 study programs in the humanities, health sciences, social sciences, law, science and theology.

The university's research profile is focused on what it calls four major interdisciplinary research priority areas: Religion in the 21st Century, Body and Mind, BioCampus (biotechnology), and Europe in Transition. The spirit of this research is perhaps best illustrated by ground-breaking research into breast cancer. A project run by the university's Institute of Molecular Biology and the Finsen Laboratory at Copenhagen University Hospital has shown that one particular enzyme, uPA, (urokinase-type plasminogen activator), causes breast cancer to spread throughout the body.

Alumni include several prime ministers of Denmark, including Poul Nyrup Rasmussen, Nobel laureates Aage Niels Bohr and Ben Roy Mottelson, who won the physics prize in 1975, and Niels Kaj Jerne, a winner in medicine and physiology in 1984; the existentialist Søren Aabye Kierkegaard; and Sir Ove Arup, the structural engineer.

Fabrizio Loce-Mandes from Perugia in Italy studied anthropology at the University of Copenhagen as a student on the Socrates/Erasmus exchange program last year. "Conditions for international students in Copenhagen are very unique. We are very close, and there are great opportunities for experiencing things and meeting new people, because everything is close by. I have become enchanted because I, like the Danes, enjoy being able to walk safely down the street at night."

49 (53=) Trinity College Dublin
Founded 1592   www.tcd.ie

Arts & humanities	32
Engineering & IT	135
Life sciences & biomedicine	97
Natural sciences	66
Social sciences	59
Academic survey position	54
Employer survey position	43
Student faculty ratio	9:1
International faculty	46.5%
Undergraduates	9,852
Postgraduates	2,831
International students	17.5%
Research strength (Scopus) papers	4,755
Research strength (Scopus) citations	27,347
Impact (citations per paper)	6

Trinity College Dublin is Ireland's oldest university and is the sole constituent college of the University of Dublin. Most of the college's activities are based on the 47-acre city centre campus, which contains much of Dublin's finest architecture. The west end of the campus is laid out in five quadrangles with buildings from the 18th century including the Old Library which houses the priceless Book of Kells, written in the ninth century. The magnificent legal deposit library is also an invaluable resource to scholars.

At the heart of Trinity's strategy to meet the goal of a world reference point in key themes is a focus on interdisciplinarity. Its flagship interdisipinary institutes are in areas such as nanostructures/nanodevices, molecular medicine, neuroscience, and international integration studies. The Irish government is pouring money into science and research and wants to double the number of PhD students within the next few years. The college was well poised to tap some of the additional funds and now almost one in three students are postgraduates. The €100 million nanoscience facility, the Naughton Institute opened at the beginning of 2008. However, funding at undergraduate level is a problem and the average student/staff ratio is high by international standards. Trinity plans to limit its undergraduate student population. It is fortunate that more than half of its Irish students have at least 500 out of a maximum of 600 points in the Irish schools' leaving certificate. However, it has also met its target of 15 per cent intake of non-traditional learners.

One of its first students, James Ussher, was a notable religious scholar and since then many of its alumni have helped shape the history of Ireland and of the English-speaking world. They include George Berkeley, Jonathan Swift, Edmund Burke, Theobald Wolfe Tone, Edward Carson, Oscar Wilde, Oliver Goldsmith, and William Rowan Hamilton. Two alumni have won Nobel prizes: Ernest Walton for physics in 1951 and Samuel Beckett for literature in 1968. Both Mary Robinson, the former President of Ireland, and Mary McAleese, the current President, were on the staff of its law school.

The grandparents of Meghan Brown from Buffalo, New York, came from Schull, Co Cork in Ireland. But it was not just sentimental attachment that prompted her to study sociology and Spanish in Dublin. "The only way to be successful in a globalized world is to have a world-recognized degree. Trinity offers that," she said.

50= (117=) Ecole Polytechnique Fédérale de Lausanne
Founded 1853 **www.epfl.ch**

Engineering & IT	44
Natural sciences	76
Academic survey position	163
Employer survey position	145
Student faculty ratio	6.2:1
International faculty	63.2%
Undergraduates	3,238
Postgraduates	2,925
International students	41.5%
Research strength (Scopus) papers	9,426
Research strength (Scopus) citations	44,200
Impact (citations per paper)	5

By far the highest new (re)entrant in this year's top 100, the École Polytechnique Fédérale de Lausanne (EPFL) is, with ETH Zurich, one of the twin pinnacles of Switzerland's higher education and research. They are the only two federal (rather than cantonal) institutions and have a common national supervisory system. EPFL has a strongly international vision, since four out of ten students and more than half of the academics are foreign. Many students are from neighbouring Germany and France, but others come from all over the world. In addition to the professors, there are about 2,000 'scientific collaborators', a many of whom also teach. EPFL began life as the Schola Lausannensis, a religious institution for educating the young, and training adults as ministers of the church. It was only in the 19th century that it developed into a modern university, or, rather, as the engineering and technology 'wing' of the University of Lausanne, under cantonal control. Emancipation came in 1969, with the establishment of EPFL as an autonomous federal institution. Today EPFL has an agreement with the cantonal universities of both Lausanne and Geneva to distribute sectors of research among the three institutions, striving for a 'critical mass' on any given project, and to encourage networked, interdisciplinary programs. EPFL has seven departments: architecture, civil and environmental engineering; computer and communication sciences; basic sciences; engineering sciences and techniques; life sciences; humanities; management and technology. The accent is on applied, inter-disciplinary science and technology. One of EPFL's flagship projects is the research and development related to the Alinghi yacht that took the America's Cup for Switzerland in 2003 and 2007. Another is 'Solar Impulse', the development and construction of a solar-powered aircraft to fly round the world.

Alumni include Daniel Borel, one of the founders of Logitech, Aart de Geus, the founder of Synopsis Inc, and André Gorz, the philosopher and economist.

Abhijit Patil, an Indian graduate student in electrical engineering, says: "EPFL is a truly global university. It has state-of-the-art facilities and eminent professors, and in fields like material science is working on cutting-edge technology. Students have excellent living standards and PhD students are paid very well. The negative side is that there is still reluctance in many departments to speak English, which can force foreigners to learn French. Also, in some labs where the Swiss are paid high salaries, the foreigners are paid less. But leaving aside these negative aspects, I believe EPFL is a very good place to pursue advanced studies, and EPFL graduates are recognized even in the best American universities."

50= (36) Peking University
Founded 1898   **www.pku.edu.cn**

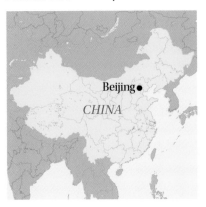

Arts & humanities	23
Engineering & IT	38
Life sciences & biomedicine	19
Natural sciences	16
Social sciences	24
Academic survey position	19
Employer survey position	35
Student faculty ratio	7.4:1
International faculty	5.3%
Undergraduates	14,786
Postgraduates	15,894
International students	7.5%
Research strength (Scopus) papers	20,227
Research strength (Scopus) citations	58,802
Impact (citations per paper)	3

Peking University (Beijing Daxue, or Bei Da) is one of the oldest universities in China. Originally known as the Imperial Capital University, it was renamed the National Peking University in 1912, following the Xinhai Revolution. In 1919, students from the university formed the bulk of the protesters in the May Fourth Movement. In 1920, it became the second Chinese university to accept female students, after Nanjing University. During the Second World War, the university moved to Kunming, where it formed the National Southwestern United University along with Tsinghua and Nankai. It returned to Beijing in 1946. After the founding of the People's Republic of China in 1949, it merged with Yenching University and dropped the 'National' from its name, moving from central Beijing to the Yenching campus on the city's north-west outskirts. It remains there today, literally across the road from its rival Tsinghua.

Peking is one of China's designated 'national key universities', competing with Tsinghua to be regarded as the best university in China. It has one of the largest intakes in China of international students, about 40 per cent of whom are from South Korea. While offering a comprehensive range of courses, Peking University is known mostly for arts and science, and is heavily geared towards scientific research. It has 216 research institutions, including two national engineering research centres. Among the new developments is a 17-floor Stomatology building opened in 2008 for medical care, teaching and research. In recent years, the university has committed to improving its teaching standards. The ultimate goal is to combine continued research with the training of the specialized personnel needed for China's skill-hungry workforce.

Among many famous alumni, perhaps its most notable was Lu Xun, the godfather of modern Chinese literature, though early chancellor and May Fourth Movement leader Cai Yuanpei is a strong contender. Chinese Communist Party co-founders Chen Duxiu and Li Dazhao both worked there; the former as Dean of Letters, the latter head librarian. A young Mao Zedong was a part-time student there, while working as an assistant in the university library.

He Qinzhou from Tianjin, China, who is studying computing, said: "The special thing about here is that it is a very comprehensive university. Almost anything you want to study, Peking University can provide it at a good level. For me, it was a great honour to be able to study here. However, like all Chinese universities at the moment, we are very undeveloped; there is a big disparity between China and the West. China definitely needs to keep improving. I believe that it will not be long before we can get to the same level as the best universities in the world."

50= (51=) Seoul National University
Founded 1946 **www.useoul.edu**

Arts & humanities	76
Engineering & IT	43
Life sciences & biomedicine	40
Natural sciences	31
Social sciences	33
Academic survey position	33
Employer survey position	173
Student faculty ratio	7:1
International faculty	3.6%
Undergraduates	14,476
Postgraduates	9,388
International students	7.6%
Research strength (Scopus) papers	23,571
Research strength (Scopus) citations	93,291
Impact (citations per paper)	4

Pre-eminent in Korea, Seoul National University (SNU) has been building up its international profile. Students come from 33 different countries, more than half of them from China, and there are plans for an international campus where all courses will be delivered in English. Only a small proportion of courses have been offered in English up to now. The university has announced a new scholarship program, to be known as the Silk Road scholarship for foreign students wishing to study social sciences and humanities. The number of foreign universities with which SNU has developed academic exchanges doubled in four years to almost 100, including with Yale, Princeton, Vienna, Tokyo and Toronto. SNU claims to have contributed significantly to South Korea's spectacular economic progress, while spearheading democratization efforts on the peninsula. The proportion of high-ranking government officials with SNU degrees has declined from 81.7 per cent to a still-remarkable 68.8 per cent. A new College of Engineering building was completed in 2008 and a seven-storey research building, a College of Natural Sciences and an Agriculture and Life Sciences Research Institute are on the way. The Gwanak residential campus is still being completed and there are plans to establish a College of Liberal Arts. SNU now has 28 dormitory buildings with 2,600 rooms accommodating 4,500 students.

The best-known alumnus is Ban Ki-moon, the UN secretary-general and former international relations student. SNU's philosophy department also produced Kim Young-sam, president of South Korea from 1993 to 1998. The university was required to weather an international storm when one of its top research scientists, Hwang Woo-suk, was dismissed after claims that his team had produced the first stem cells from human cloned embryos were shown to have been fabricated.

Wei-yi Sun, from Qingdao, China, took a masters in Korean language education after majoring in Korean language education with Chinese literature. "SNU is one of the most prestigious universities in Korea, especially when it comes to Korean language education. Plus, the campus is really beautiful. "But," he said, "the process of being accepted was long and painful, when I applied. I even had to take my English and Korean test the school had requested on the phone, due to visa problems. Even though these experiences were really strenuous, I got to appreciate my life in Korea and at SNU even more thanks to them. A major problem was that SNU had only one Korean class for foreign students to improve their Korean skills."

53 (48) University of Amsterdam
Founded 1632   **www.uva.nl**

Arts & humanities	36
Engineering & IT	171
Life sciences & biomedicine	80
Natural sciences	119
Social sciences	43
Academic survey position	63
Employer survey position	121
Student faculty ratio	7.8:1
International faculty	22.4%
Undergraduates	15,883
Postgraduates	9,280
International students	6.4%
Research strength (Scopus) papers	15,573
Research strength (Scopus) citations	104,601
Impact (citations per paper)	7

The Universiteit van Amsterdam prides itself on ancient roots stretching back to the Athenaeum Illustre, founded to educate students in trade and philosophy. The university has since spread through the city, taking over old buildings and putting up modern structures along Amsterdam's famous canals and courtyards. The university emphasizes its comprehensive approach, taking in every discipline except technology, and offering a classical education that, it boasts, does not just cram students for the job market. It has seven faculties, from the humanities, social and behavioural sciences, to economics and business, medicine and dentistry, and science, offering over 100 international study programs taught in English as well as bachelors degrees taught in Dutch. In the arts and humanities, Amsterdam is particularly strong in European studies, philosophy, film and television studies, linguistics and several areas of language and literature. Among the noted faculty are John Neubauer, specialist in comparative literature, Latin scholar Harm Pinkster, and Mieke Bal, professor of theory of literature and a founding director of the Amsterdam School for Cultural Analysis. Unlike the rest of the university, the laboratories and research institutes of the medical faculty have been extracted from the city and united with three hospitals under the single roof of the academic medical centre. In 2005, a graduate school was created to raise the profile of this part of the medical centre's work. It has over 100 PhD graduations per year, divided over seven research institutes and 80 individual science programs, ranging from genetic factors in cancer biology, to public health screening projects.

The golden age of science at the university was between 1901 and 1910, when three of its professors won Nobel prizes. Now the university's strengths are very much on the mathematical side and where maths touches on physics and astronomy. In recent years it has picked up several Spinoza awards, the 'Dutch Nobels', for work in these disciplines. Particularly distinguished is Edward van den Heuvel, of the university's Anton Pannekoek Astrophysical Institute, who also led an international team researching the origins of gamma-ray bursts, which won an EU Descartes award in 2002. The university can also claim Spinoza awards for Daan Frenkel, in macromolecular simulations, and Ronald Plasterk in molecular biology.

Joan Miller, a British postgraduate quoted on the Reviewcentre website, said: "Academically this university was very good. I participated in some of the best seminars while doing my masters here and some of the research projects are very interesting, if not extremely informative and contributing to a wide range of academic and social areas of interest."

54 (71=) Dartmouth College
Founded 1769   **www.dartmouth.edu**

Arts & humanities	114
Engineering & IT	294
Life sciences & biomedicine	106
Natural sciences	275
Social sciences	108
Academic survey position	151
Employer survey position	56
Student faculty ratio	6.9:1
International faculty	5.8%
Undergraduates	4,127
Postgraduates	1,653
International students	12.6%
Research strength (Scopus) papers	7,335
Research strength (Scopus) citations	58,199
Impact (citations per paper)	8

Dartmouth looks like a Hollywood vision of the quintessential New England university. But its size, the smallest in the Ivy League, and picture-postcard campus shouldn't be mistaken for merely quaint. Admission is among America's most competitive, with barely 15 per cent of applicants accepted. They can choose from some 1,600 courses in 29 departments and ten inter-disciplinary programs. Students study under an unusual academic calendar divided into quarters with three vacation, or leave, terms and up to three terms of off-campus study during the typical run-up to an undergraduate degree. Nearly 60 per cent have a period of study abroad and more than 40 per cent are involved in research conducted in world-class laboratories that are benefiting from a fundraising campaign that has already passed the US$1 billion mark. Among other beneficiaries will be the three professional schools of business, engineering and medicine, and there are plans for a new undergraduate college. The medical school is the fourth oldest and the engineering school the oldest in America, while the graduate school of management was the first in the world.

To unwind, students at scenic Dartmouth famously party, in spite of the university's best efforts to curb social excess. Its Alpha Delta Phi fraternity was a model for the movie 'Animal House', and in a prank that has become a cult favourite on YouTube, prospective students and their parents on a campus tour are interrupted by a bell that triggers 'drinking time.' Students come running from all corners shouting, "Drinking time!" as the marching band appears behind a mascot modelled after a giant beer keg, all as the hapless tour guide tries to be heard above the din explaining that there is, in fact, no more drinking at Dartmouth than at any other school.

Notable alumni include senator and statesman Daniel Webster, poet Robert Frost, and former Surgeon General C Everett Koop. In all, more than 160 Dartmouth graduates have served in the US Congress, and two on the Supreme Court. Alumni also serve, or have served, as the founders or heads of IBM, eBay, General Electric, NBC Television, Goldman Sachs, and the San Diego Padres baseball team.

The academic work is demanding, says Mitalee Patil, an undergraduate from India double-majoring in business and chemistry. "This is the hardest I've ever worked to get good grades. It is good preparation for dealing with the pressures of a job later on when you have deadlines and you're expected to meet them. But she said, "Anytime I looked lost and confused, someone would come over without my having to say anything and ask me if I needed help."

55 (55=) University of Wisconsin-Madison
Founded 1848   **www.wisc.edu**

Arts & humanities	56
Engineering & IT	73
Life sciences & biomedicine	47
Natural sciences	56
Social sciences	40
Academic survey position	45
Employer survey position	113
Student faculty ratio	11.9:1
International faculty	6.8%
Undergraduates	28,341
Postgraduates	10,043
International students	7.3%
Research strength (Scopus) papers	28,079
Research strength (Scopus) citations	186,453
Impact (citations per paper)	7

While some large US research universities have begun dividing themselves up into smaller units to give students the feeling that they are at small colleges, Wisconsin revels in its bigness, touting the size of its library holdings (7.2 million volumes), the number of areas of study it offers (136 undergraduate majors, 155 masters and 110 doctoral programs), the variety of living arrangements, and the hundreds of student organizations. Wisconsin faculty have won 17 Nobel prizes since the 1940s. Students and faculty alike take a break from their studies on autumn Saturdays, when the entire surrounding community turns red to support the school's American football team. The university does just under US$700 million a year in research. It's eighth among all universities in research paid for by the national government, second in non-federally funded research, fourth in total research expenditures, and second in doctorates granted. Wisconsin is particularly highly ranked in the sciences, with an emphasis on agricultural and life sciences. It is also extremely well-regarded for its sociology and education programs. It is a centre for embryonic-stem-cell research and the home of the National Stem Cell Bank, as well as being a principal partner of the US Department of Energy in seeking out new ways to produce energy and biofuels. Supported by financial contributions from its loyal alumni, the university has recently completed a new building for health sciences, genetics and biotechnology, engineering and pharmaceutical studies, as well as a chemistry research tower and a massive addition to its biochemistry building, also renovating its physics building. A new Urban Research Park will target high technology entrepreneurs, particularly in information technology, engineering, medical devices and computer sciences start-up companies.

Prominent alumni have included the aviator Charles Lindbergh, architect Frank Lloyd Wright, former Vice President Dick Cheney, astronaut Jim Lovell, movie producers Walter Mirisch and Jerry and David Zucker, authors Joyce Carol Oates and Eudora Welty, and Major League Baseball Commissioner Allan 'Bud' Selig.

Fan Yang, an undergraduate from China majoring in actuarial science in the business school, has found classes large. "If you're in a general course, there could be more than 100 students in a class, though I have been in more specialized courses with as few as ten," she said. But even in large classes, she said, the faculty "are very patient and very quick to answer questions." She found one other disadvantage: "I think this campus is very friendly, but I do talk with other international students about the distance between us and the American students. Sometimes there is trouble communicating."

56 (40) Tsinghua University
Founded 1911   www.tsinghua.edu.cn

Arts & humanities	85
Engineering & IT	12
Life sciences & biomedicine	56
Natural sciences	28
Social sciences	44
Academic survey position	31
Employer survey position	68
Student faculty ratio	6.1:1
International faculty	3.4%
Undergraduates	11,534*
Postgraduates	15,913*
International students	4.0%
Research strength (Scopus) papers	32,618
Research strength (Scopus) citations	54,433
Impact (citations per paper)	2

Established after the Boxer Uprising, with reparation money paid to the US, as a preparatory school for Chinese graduates pursuing further studies at American universities, Tsinghua became a university in 1925, offering four-year undergraduate and postgraduate programs. Tsinghua's faculty has 34 members of the Chinese Academy of Sciences and 28 members of the Chinese Academy of Engineering, more than any other college or university in China. Half of the international students are Korean; the rest are from more than 50 different countries. Within China, Tsinghua is usually rated as one of the top two universities in the country. Located on the site of Qing dynasty royal gardens in the northwest of Beijing, it is usually considered best in China for engineering and business. Tsinghua has extensive ties with companies in China's burgeoning high-tech sector. Arts and languages are comparatively weak, being mostly a support system for science and engineering students to get through government-mandated tests in various subjects outside their major, necessary to obtain their degrees. Tsinghua is keen to remedy this, and acquired an independent art college in Beijing in 2005. Tsinghua also recently became the first Chinese university to offer a master of laws program in US law, and its law school now ranks as one of the best in China. While the university's appeal to overseas students and researchers has been limited, it has begun to turn national prestige into global recognition. Tsinghua researchers won 23 awards at the 2008 State Science and Technology Awards, the largest haul for any university, making a total of 377 such awards. Many staff and students got involved in the 2008 Beijing Olympics, with academics from engineering, architecture, design, construction and environmental design participating in setting up the Games and 3,000 students volunteering.

Many of China's top scientists, engineers and politicians are Tsinghua alumni. Among them are former premier Zhu Rongji, present Chinese president Hu Jintao, and the Nobel prize for physics laureate Chen Ning Yang. The present faculty includes such luminaries as former Goldman Sachs president John L Thornton and computer scientist Andrew Yao, who received the Turing Prize in 2000.

Salome Woo left her job as a personnel manager in Hong Kong to take Chinese at Tsinghua. "The campus is so beautiful and so amazingly big," she said. "The bicycle is irreplaceable for getting around." She makes the most of the Tsinghua Olympic Pool and is joining extracurricular classes. Her only complaint is an occasional feeling of isolation. Since she spends most of her time in classes with other international students, she has fewer opportunities to learn what the Chinese students are doing and thinking.

57 (60) Heidelberg Universität
Founded 1386   **www.uni-heidelberg.de**

Arts & humanities	48
Engineering & IT	267
Life sciences & biomedicine	48
Natural sciences	43
Social sciences	108
Academic survey position	69
Employer survey position	198
Student faculty ratio	7.7:1
International faculty	15.3%
Undergraduates	23,636
Postgraduates	3,105
International students	19.1%
Research strength (Scopus) papers	14,942
Research strength (Scopus) citations	105,641
Impact (citations per paper)	7

Heidelberg is Germany's best-known university and a member of the League of European Research Universities that includes just 19 others. The university initially acted as an ecclesiastical centre for the Holy Roman Empire but quickly established itself as a hub for philosophers and independent thinkers, developing into a stronghold of humanism in the 15th century. Grand Duke Karl-Friedrich of Baden turned it into a state-owned institution in 1803, when the city was discovered by poets, artists and intellectuals like Friedrich Hölderlin, Johann Wolfgang von Goethe, Joseph von Eichendorff and Robert Schumann. From the early 20th century, one of its outstanding features has been a tradition of interdisciplinary dialogue cultivated originally by Max Weber, the founder of the modern social sciences. Today its roots are firmly planted in the sciences, but it has still managed to keep its metaphysical traditions with large theology and philosophy faculties all of which help attract students and professors from around the globe. No other university in the world played as significant a part in the Large Hydron Experiment in Geneva, dubbed the 'Big Bang Experiment'. The university played a leading role in three of the four experiments in the 'largest science experiment in the world'. Some of Europe's top research institutes are nearby, among them the European Laboratory for Molecular Biology, the German Cancer Research Centre and a number of Max Planck institutes who collaborate with the university's 12 faculties and its own research institutes.

Weber is just one of many illustrious names who studied or taught at the university. They include nine Nobel laureates. Among them are Philipp Lenard, who won the prize for physics for his groundbreaking work on cathode rays, Hans Jensen, also physics for helping to develop the shell nuclear model, and Georg Wittig, for chemistry in 1979. Other notables include the founder of the German Bank, Georg von Siemens, chemist Robert Bunsen, after whom the Bunsen burner was named, and former German chancellor Helmut Kohl.

Oksana Jurevic, a 29-year-old economics student from Lithuania said: "I was attracted to Heidelberg University because of its history and reputation and so far haven't been disappointed. International students must have some degree of German in order to study here, and even though I am not completely fluent, I get a lot of support from the university and its staff. We are also given plenty of opportunity for one-to-one tutorials that you just do not get at other universities, and the standard of teaching is excellent. The city itself also provides a safe and positive environment for international students."

58 (58) University of California, San Diego
Founded 1960   www.ucsd.edu

Arts & humanities	93
Engineering & IT	35
Life sciences & biomedicine	9
Natural sciences	30
Social sciences	38
Academic survey position	27
Employer survey position	206
Student faculty ratio	14.9:1
International faculty	2.1%
Undergraduates	21,567
Postgraduates	4,843
International students	5.6%
Research strength (Scopus) papers	22,325
Research strength (Scopus) citations	200,341
Impact (citations per paper)	9

At barely 50, the University of California, San Diego (UCSD) is modelled on old ones, Oxford and Cambridge, providing the inspiration for its residential colleges for undergraduates. Research, however, is cutting edge, and the school also prides itself on its local impact. Its middle and high Preuss School, dedicated to providing intensive education for motivated low-income students, was ranked among the top ten US high schools in 2007. The university was built alongside the Pacific Ocean in the southern California city of San Diego, joining the highly regarded Salk Institute and Scripps Research Institute in this onetime Navy port. Specializing in science and engineering, it has spun off more than 250 start-up companies, including 63 biomedical start-ups, almost single-handedly transforming San Diego into a centre of biotechnology and telecommunications. UCSD unapologetically looks towards the Pacific Rim, teaming up on science programs with institutions in China, India, and Singapore. The university ranks third among major US research schools in the number of students who go abroad for at least a full academic year, and eighth in the number of international scholars. Student numbers are up 50 per cent in the last ten years. They study on a quarter system similar to the University of Chicago's, instead of the more typical semesters.

UCSD conducts more than US$730 million a year in research, the seventh-highest US total. It's home to one of the government's two supercomputing centres and was the ninth-most-cited institution in the world based on its published research in science and the social sciences from 1995 to 2005. The medical school alternates between first and second in the nation in research funding per faculty member. UCSD's biomedical engineering program, which launched many of those spin-off companies, is considered among the nation's best. Its California Institute for Telecommunications and Information Technology has also made San Diego a centre for wireless technology. The Rady business school, founded in 2001, specializes in the business of technology and will ultimately have about 65 full-time faculty members and 1,200 MBA candidates.

Eight members of the faculty have won Nobel prizes, one a Fields medal, and one the Kyoto prize. Alumni include the designer of the MacIntosh computer, Nobel laureate in medicine Susumu Tonegawa, and biologist Craig Venter.

"It's in a beautiful location, ten minutes from the sea," said Elizabeth Blackburn, a postdoctoral research fellow in physics from Yorkshire, England. "It's a very pleasant place to be most of the time." Within the University of California system, she said, "San Diego has a reputation as one of the harder schools."

59 (55=) University of Washington
Founded 1861   www.washington.edu

Seattle *USA*

Washington, DC

Arts & humanities	182
Engineering & IT	85
Life sciences & biomedicine	44
Natural sciences	85
Social sciences	113
Academic survey position	82
Employer survey position	231
Student faculty ratio	9.8:1
International faculty	4.4%
Undergraduates	26,622
Postgraduates	10,065
International students	7.5%
Research strength (Scopus) papers	35,387
Research strength (Scopus) citations	315,760
Impact (citations per paper)	9

Some US$800 million a year in research is conducted at the University of Washington (UW, locally pronounced U-Dub); more than at any other US public university, or private, except Johns Hopkins. Much of it is linked to the entrepreneurship that has given rise to Pacific Northwest powerhouse conglomerates such as Microsoft and Boeing. Microsoft co-founder Bill Gates, whose parents were alumni, has made substantial financial contributions to a new law school, provided a bioengineering and genome sciences building and a medical school surgery pavilion, funded scholarships to recruit outstanding students and to pay for student research. Microsoft co-founder, Paul Allen, whose father was a U-Dub librarian, has underwritten a new library and Center for Computer Science and Engineering. Home to the Cesar Pelli-designed physics and astronomy building, which includes 20 physics labs built underground to provide the most stable possible environment, the university is now planning a college to be the leader in environmental research and education. Boeing, which designs and manufactures its planes nearby, uses the wind tunnels at the university's top-rated Department of Aeronautics and Astronautics to test new models. U-Dub also has one of America's top-rated medical schools for training primary-care physicians, which opened new inpatient facilities in 2008. The departments of bioengineering and computer science and the school of social work are at the top of their fields, and the law and business schools are highly regarded, nationally. The sprawling campus in Seattle was originally laid out for the 1909 world fair and incorporates some of the original buildings. Families that earn 65 per cent of the state's median income or less can send their children to the university tuition-free, the most generous such allowance in America. Graduate students are eligible for stipends and health insurance, an unusual benefit.

Six current faculty members are winners of the Nobel prize. Prominent alumni include the first man to fly faster than Mach 2, the men who directed the lunar orbiter program and Rockwell International's Apollo work, the head of the space shuttle program, many astronauts, actors Patrick Duffy, Dyan Cannon, and Bruce Lee, musician Kenny G and someone whose contribution may have been even greater: the inventor of the disposable diaper.

Famously rainy Seattle is overcast 60 per cent of the time, but Mathieu Fregeau, a Canadian doctoral student working on plasma generation and propulsion for space flight, doesn't mind the weather. "For me it's like paradise," he said, comparing the city with his native Montreal. "People are very laid back. I enjoy just walking on the campus and meeting everyone."

60 (161=) Washington University in St Louis
Founded 1853   www.wustli.edu

Arts & humanities	236
Life sciences & biomedicine	28
Natural sciences	283
Social sciences	226
Academic survey position	152
Employer survey position	223
Student faculty ratio	4.5:1
International faculty	4.0%
Undergraduates	6,512
Postgraduates	5,285
International students	11.8%
Research strength (Scopus) papers	18,558
Research strength (Scopus) citations	175,872
Impact (citations per paper)	9

Storming into the top 60 after a prodigious, 100-place, leap up the THE-QS World University Rankings, Washington University may not have the name recognition of the best schools in America. It has to add the words 'in St. Louis' to avoid being confused with George Washington University in Washington, DC, the University of Washington, and the nearly 20 other US higher education institutions with 'Washington' in their titles. But, 'Wash U', as students call it, is sixth in the nation in doctoral degrees awarded and fifth in federal research support. Its George Warren Brown School of social work is at the top of its field, as is its school of law's clinical training program. Its medical school is considered among the nation's best; so many of the university's undergraduates are pre-med that they are given their own orientation when they arrive. A new Masters of Public Health program is being introduced in 2009 for people committed to improving the health of vulnerable communities. While those pre-med students find themselves crowded into huge lectures for their introductory science classes, the university's comparatively small size means that the faculty are, otherwise, usually accessible. Almost all are involved in research, and undergraduate and graduate students have the chance to work alongside them. Wash U also disburses significant financial aid, about US$53 million a year, including to international students. Its quiet, Gothic-style campus borders a large public park and quiet suburbs of St. Louis, a city better known for barbecues than academics. The nearest big city, Chicago, is about five hours away by car.

The poet T S Eliot was the grandson of Washington's founder and took a diploma at the university, while American playwright Tennessee Williams was also a student in the 1930s. Steve Fossett, the adventurer, was a more recent alumnus, as was Sam Fox, the US ambassador to Belgium and owner of Harbour Group Industries. The most recent of 22 Nobel laureates was Aaron Ciechanover, who took the chemistry prize in 2004.

Students find the workload tough but the university generally welcoming. Aycan Sagir, a student from Istanbul taking arts and sciences, graduating in 2011, said, "The whole Washington University community is involved in campus life. The students on my freshman floor were very encouraging and helpful and my professors always have time to talk. The advisors really help students with their schedules and course preferences. Our chancellor's wife even has a project called Home Plate, which matches out-of-town students with families in St. Louis for home dinners and to be contacts if we have questions. All this means a lot to me."

61 (90=) Tokyo Institute of Technology
Founded 1881   www.titech.ac.jp

Arts & humanities	252
Engineering & IT	21
Life sciences & biomedicine	229
Natural sciences	57
Academic survey position	99
Employer survey position	123
Student faculty ratio	8.8:1
International faculty	4.6%
Undergraduates	4,911
Postgraduates	5,014
International students	9.6%
Research strength (Scopus) papers	16,815
Research strength (Scopus) citations	61,771
Impact (citations per paper)	4

Founded as Tokyo Vocational School, the Institute has been a national university since 1929. It is the largest higher education institution in Japan devoted to science and technology. The extensive School of Engineering has no fewer than 16 departments and there are graduate schools of decision science and innovation management, as well as the more traditional mathematical and computing sciences, bioscience and biotechnology. There are three campuses: two in the heart of the Tokyo metropolis and one in Yokahama with a view of Mount Fuji. There are courses for undergraduates in the liberal arts and in health and physical education, while a special project encourages programs that will enhance students' creativity. The two libraries, in Tokyo and Yokahama, boast Japan's foremost collection of scientific and technological journals. An Arts and Crafts Education and Research Center opened in September 2008, two months after the opening of a nine-storey, 3,750 square metre Quantum NanoElectronics Research Center. Sometimes referred to as the 'MIT of Japan', Tokyo Tech has one of the ten largest supercomputers in the world, used by more than 10,000 scientists, researchers and students. It is particularly proud of its Integrated Research Institute, established in 2005, restructuring the university's research functions to anticipate future trends and problems in collaboration with industry. The latest big initiative is the Global Edge Institute, which is designed to attract young researchers from all over the world. Successful researchers will be offered tenured posts after five years.

Tokyo Tech, or Tokodai, has stressed its international ambitions in its slogan 'Leading the world in science and technology'. Foreign students come from more than 70 different countries. The overseas enrolment has been increasing by an average of more than six per cent a year for the last five years. Most live in private apartments, but there are two dormitories for foreign students and a separate residence for women, where students in their first year are given priority. The International Student Centre runs Japanese language courses, as well as helping students deal with problems. There are cooperation agreements with 40 universities across Asia. The institute welcomed more than 200 visiting researchers in 2005, when 60 students enrolled in the international graduate course.

Famous alumni include Professor Hideki Shirakawa, who won the Nobel prize for chemistry in 2000 for his work on conductive polymers. Shigeo Hirose, who was awarded a PhD at the Institute and is now a professor there, is a pioneer of robotics. Naoto Kan is a former leader of the Democratic Party of Japan, while Satoru Iwata has been chief executive of Nintendo since 2002.

62 (74=) Emory University
Founded 1836   www.emory.edu

Arts & humanities	130
Life sciences & biomedicine	53
Natural sciences	262
Social sciences	253
Academic survey position	176
Employer survey position	166
Student faculty ratio	5.8:1
International faculty	11.3%
Undergraduates	6,667
Postgraduates	5,310
International students	10.2%
Research strength (Scopus) papers	13,804
Research strength (Scopus) citations	125,061
Impact (citations per paper)	9

Emory claims to be the most ethnically and religiously diverse of America's leading research universities. A comparatively obscure regional school that didn't accept women until 1953 or blacks until 1962, Emory has rocketed to the top ranks of American universities. Rather than a liability, its location in the southern city of Atlanta (it was state segregation law that prohibited the school from admitting blacks until it successfully sued to reverse that policy) has become an asset as the city itself evolved into an economic powerhouse. Atlanta is home to Coca-Cola, CNN and Delta Airlines, among others.

Of the US$411 million a year in research conducted at the university, three-quarters is in the health sciences, focusing on research areas including cancer, the neurosciences, immunity, cardiovascular and epithelial biology, and global health. Emory has added more than 300,000 square metres of space since the millennium for teaching, research, and healthcare, including medical science and neuroscience research buildings, a paediatrics building, a cancer institute, a vaccine research building, and a mathematics and science centre. A new medical education building is also under construction. The university plans to beef up its faculty and significantly increase financial aid to lure top students, and plans to raise another US$3 billion to continue its expansion in Atlanta's tree-lined Druid Hills section. Emory has embarked on a program of 'green' residences, opening two for freshmen in 2008 and planning another for graduate students in 2009.

Emory's research-intensive medical school received more than 60 applicants for every seat in one recent entering class. Its highly ranked school of law is known for its work in child advocacy, human rights law, and environmental law, and encourages its graduates to go into lower-paying public service jobs through a tuition loan forgiveness program. Its Goizueta Business School is also top-rated, particularly for its undergraduate and Executive MBA programs. One thing the university does not have is an American football team, thanks to an early president who thought intercollegiate sports were evil (and, more to the point, too expensive). Alumni include Alben Barkley, an American vice president; Lucius Quintus Cincinnatus Lamar, a US Supreme Court justice, and astronaut Sonny Carter.

Yong Lee, an undergraduate from Indonesia, picked Emory over a smaller liberal arts school. Specializing in economics and international studies, he decided to go into public health. "There's a lot of versatility in terms of the vast range of courses you can take," he said. "I had no idea what I wanted to study. I knew it was going to be business or the social sciences, but I was still up in the air, and Emory has both the liberal arts and the business programs."

63 (71=) Uppsala University
Founded 1477 **www.uu.se**

Arts & humanities	47
Engineering & IT	149
Life sciences & biomedicine	38
Natural sciences	64
Social sciences	80
Academic survey position	52
Employer survey position	193
Student faculty ratio	12.9:1
International faculty	21.1%
Undergraduates	16,797
Postgraduates	6,789
International students	8.6%
Research strength (Scopus) papers	13,977
Research strength (Scopus) citations	95,450
Impact (citations per paper)	7

Uppsala University, situated 40 miles north of Stockholm, is the oldest university in Scandinavia. Most Swedes associate the university with quaint traditions as much as with teaching and research. For example, all Swedes don a peaked white cap when they graduate from senior high school, a tradition that originated at Uppsala. But a prodigious, 40-place leap saw Uppsala join the world's top 100 universities last year and it has retained its place among the elite. The university has nine faculties distributed over three 'disciplinary domains': humanities and social sciences, medicine and pharmacy and science and technology. Of its annual turnover of around SEK4 billion, approximately 60 per cent goes to graduate studies and research. Recent research evaluation by 76 experts from 20 countries judged over 50 research projects at more than 20 of the university's departments to be 'world leading'. Theoretical physics, surgery, and linguistics were among those areas singled out for special praise. The university's '2009 Operational Plan' promises increased funding for research in areas including energy, peace and medicine, following supplementary funding of SEK101.2 million from the state. The picturesque university buildings are located around the historic centre of the city, close to the impressive cathedral. Recent expansion has also seen the university occupy buildings in the southwest of the region. Arguably the pearl in the university's crown is the library with its extensive art and science collections. Known locally as "Carolina", the library's foremost treasure is the Silver Gothic Bible Codex Argenteus, which was seized when the Swedes stormed Prague in 1648.

Students typically belong to one of 13 'nations', named after the provinces of Sweden. Originally a way of showing a student's origins, students are now free to join any nation including Skånelandens, which was established in the 1960s as a legal fiction to get around the compulsory membership for students who prefer not to become affiliated with the traditional nations. In a bid to attract more international students the university has recently started offering masters courses in English. Prominent alumni include eight Nobel laureates and notable scientists like botanist Carl Linnaeus, astronomer Anders Celsius and the founding father of physical chemistry, Svante August Arrhenius. The French philosopher Michel Foucault also studied at Uppsala.

"Uppsala is a brilliant place to study," says Matthew Greig, an Australian studying macro economics. "The best thing about the university is the variety of nationalities. It's a way to really meet Swedish students as well as exchange students. The university provides a lot of information to help foreign students settle and the special student website is full of tips and advice: **www.uppsalastudentkar.nu**"

64 (84) University of Leiden
Founded 1575   www.leiden.edu

Arts & humanities	35
Engineering & IT	288
Life sciences & biomedicine	74
Natural sciences	68
Social sciences	58
Academic survey position	67
Employer survey position	186
Student faculty ratio	14.8:1
International faculty	22.8%
Undergraduates	11,370
Postgraduates	5,260
International students	8.7%
Research strength (Scopus) papers	11,646
Research strength (Scopus) citations	84,368
Impact (citations per paper)	7

Legend has it that William of Orange offered the people of Leiden a choice of rewards for withstanding a Spanish siege: they could be excused from paying certain taxes, or he would establish a university. They chose the university, thinking it would last longer than a tax cut. Whether or not the story is true, the university has endured and continues to rise up the global rankings. It is the oldest in the Netherlands, and gives a venerable academic air to a modestly sized city between Amsterdam and The Hague.

Leiden has a broad academic range, from archaeology and the arts to mathematics and natural sciences. It added a new humanities department for the 2008/09 academic year, bringing seven subjects such as history and philosophy under one roof. There is a strong international focus, with all research masters and PhD students obliged to take a placement abroad. The nine faculties offer some 50 bachelor and 70 (mostly English) masters degree programs while post-academic training is provided in education and environmental science. A separate campus in The Hague specializes in post-academic training in law and political science.

Leiden has an impressive record in the Spinoza awards, the highest Dutch academic award, with ten winners from fields as different as clinical epidemiology and educational psychology, two in languages and linguistics, and four in mathematics and physics. This builds on a tradition that includes two Nobel prizes in physics, for Heike Kamerlingh Onnes and Hendrik Antoon Lorentz, and associations with figures such as Einstein, John Quincey Adams, ethologist Nikolaas Tinbergen and Paul Ehrenfest.

More recently, Leiden has been the place of study for members of the Dutch royal family, as well as former European commissioner Frits Bolkestein and film director Paul Verhoeven.

Roosje Pertz came to Leiden from the Dutch speaking part of Belgium to take the 'book and byte' masters, a course on book publishing and digital media taught in English. "It's very specialized, and not the sort of thing offered in Belgium," says Roosje. It lived up to expectations, particularly with the small size of the class and the flexibility of tutors. "They treat you as an adult, and you can organize your own work. At other universities, or where you are on bigger programs, you are just a number." This freedom was sometimes hard to deal with. "There is structure, but not a firm hand that says you have to do this or that. That is good, but it can also be a bit weird when you come from a more authoritarian university."

65 (50) University of Auckland
Founded 1883   **www.auckland.ac.nz**

Arts & humanities	39
Engineering & IT	56
Life sciences & biomedicine	42
Natural sciences	102
Social sciences	30
Academic survey position	39
Employer survey position	48
Student faculty ratio	14.6:1
International faculty	35.5%
Undergraduates	23,052
Postgraduates	4,160
International students	33.2%
Research strength (Scopus) papers	8,107
Research strength (Scopus) citations	37,028
Impact (citations per paper)	5

The gothic ogee pinnacles and crockets that cap New Zealand's largest university's distinctive clock tower are now surrounded by functional multi-storey structures, an apt symbol of the university's concerted effort in recent years to assert a reputation based on the quality of its research rather than tradition. With six campuses situated throughout the greater Auckland region, Auckland describes itself as New Zealand's 'pre-eminent research-led university'. This bold statement is given credence by the university's lion's share of money awarded through New Zealand's Performance-Based Research Fund, which ranks Auckland first or second in 26 of the 41 subject areas in which it has been assessed. Engineering and medical research were particular areas of excellence, but anthropology, philosophy, music, geology, sociology and theology also scored well. New Zealand's first Science and Technology Park is planned at the University of Auckland's Tamaki Campus, with the support of the government and city council. Business and economics, arts, and science are the largest of the eight faculties with more than 7,000 students apiece. Education has about 6,000, while there are 3,500 students enrolled in medical and health sciences and 2,000 each in engineering, and creative arts and industries. Law is the smallest of the faculties with 1,500 students, and there is a small school of theology. There has been a five-fold increase in international students since 2002, about half of them Chinese.

Notable Auckland alumni include New Zealand's former prime minister Helen Clark and Chief Justice Sian Elias, as well as the novelist Maurice Gee and Tom Schnackenberg, design coordinator for New Zealand's America's Cup wins in 1995 and 2000. Sir Graham Liggins, who pioneered the treatment of babies in the womb, is remembered by the university's Liggins Institute, which carries out research on foetal and child health, and brain development and function.

Heikki Hansen, a PhD candidate at the Yacht Research Unit in the Mechanical Engineering Department, says Auckland has taken great strides in its support for international students in the four years he has been there. "Initially, the postgraduate experience wasn't perfect," he says. "But a lot has changed; the university is much more popular with international students now and has greatly improved its facilities and support." Heikki says locating external funding for research can be difficult compared with European universities, something he puts down to New Zealand's comparatively small size and lack of large businesses. But the quality of research does not suffer. "I have been really impressed with the research produced here, given the relative limitations of money and equipment," he says.

66 (59) London School of Economics & Political Science (LSE)
Founded 1895 www.lse.ac.uk

Arts & humanities	31
Life sciences & biomedicine	264
Natural sciences	265
Social sciences	4
Academic survey position	60
Employer survey position	3
Student faculty ratio	10.2:1
International faculty	54.5%
Undergraduates	3,786
Postgraduates	4,446
International students	66.8%
Research strength (Scopus) papers	2,445
Research strength (Scopus) citations	6,529
Impact (citations per paper)	3

The London School of Economics and Political Science (LSE) describes itself as 'the world's leading social science institution for teaching and research'. An immodest claim perhaps, but when half its departments have been rated 'internationally outstanding', who can blame them? LSE is a top destination for future heads of state and Nobel prize winners. An international feel on campus, therefore, comes as no surprise. The student population spans 24 European Union countries and 113 non-EU countries. The school is planning 20 per cent more places, having acquired former government buildings near its central London headquarters. Despite its name, LSE is multidisciplinary. Law, management and history received the top rating for teaching quality. Business, economics, psychology and mathematics also produced good results. Research specialisms include maths, media, anthropology, communications, economic history, accounting, international relations, and social policy. A pan-European survey showed LSE students to be more active in student associations, more entrepreneurial and more open to working abroad than those at other leading universities. The school's academics have been in the headlines even more than usual during the onset of global recession. The International Growth Centre (IGC) was launched in December 2008 as a partnership between LSE and Oxford University to provide practical help to the governments of developing countries to support growth and improve their ability to cope with effects of the economic downturn.

Some 29 country leaders and 13 Nobel prize winners have studied at LSE. Among them are Italian prime minister Romano Prodi, former Canadian prime minister Pierre Trudeau and Indian former president Shri K R Narayanan. Socialist luminaries Sidney and Beatrice Webb and George Bernard Shaw founded the school. Former UK Labour prime minister Clement Atlee was a lecturer there. LSE is also the alma mater of Rolling Stone Mick Jagger.

Ali Dewji, from Toronto, who took a BSc in international relations and history, describes the institution as an "urban and international academic powerhouse". He said: "On any given day at LSE, I might find myself attending a public lecture given by a minister from Norway, meeting a friend for sushi and a chat about economic growth in Nigeria, practising my Spanish with some Peruvian postgraduates in an elevator on my way to a Debate Society meeting then heading back to my hall of residence to watch the latest episode of a US soap on TV. When I leave LSE, I will have spent three years studying alongside some of the brightest students in the world, whose lives and experiences are themselves part of an LSE education and part of what makes LSE such a unique place to study."

67 (89) University of Utrecht
Founded 1636   www.uu.nl

Arts & humanities	65
Engineering & IT	169
Life sciences & biomedicine	62
Natural sciences	37
Social sciences	91
Academic survey position	59
Employer survey position	169
Student faculty ratio	9.8:1
International faculty	12.2%
Undergraduates	18,311
Postgraduates	9,802
International students	4.3%
Research strength (Scopus) papers	17,256
Research strength (Scopus) citations	115,507
Impact (citations per paper)	7

Utrecht University mixes ancient and modern, boasting a century long heritage plus an ultra-modern campus with buildings by Rem Koolhaas. It can also claim to be the largest Dutch university in terms of student numbers. The university has recently taken steps to further improve the quality of its intake of bachelor students, including quotas and selection processes. Once admitted, students can choose a minor subject from any of the programs offered by the university, while honours programs cater to the needs of outstanding students. International degrees are offered through University College Utrecht, an international bachelor program in economics, and almost 90 international masters programs. Graduate research programs are clustered in six schools, each covering related research masters and PhDs, the aim being to stimulate interactions between the various research areas. There are also 'prestige' masters programs linked to research areas in which Utrecht holds a leading position worldwide. Students are closely involved in the international activities of these research groups and spend part of their program abroad. Utrecht has signed an agreement with the University of California to allow students to study in the US for a period of six months. Research collaboration will also be enhanced.

Utrecht is one of the few Dutch universities that can claim a living Nobel laureate, in the form of Gerard 't Hooft. He shared the 1999 physics prize with Martinus Veltman (his former supervisor at Utrecht, who later went to the University of Michigan) for their work on the weak force, and he still works at Utrecht. Other Nobel laureates are physicists Nicolaas Bloembergen, Peter Debye, Christiaan Eijkman, Willem Einthoven, Wilhelm Röntgen, and Martinus J G Veltman, Tjalling Charles Koopmans (mathematician, physicist, economist) and Lavoslav Ruzicka (chemistry).

One of the 'prestige students' is Leila Kushan, from Los Angeles, who was attracted to a masters in neuroscience and cognition by the length of the program and the prospect of an internship abroad. A further factor was that the university accepts US federal student loans. "I've been very satisfied with the program," she said. "It's research based, rather than theoretical, so I've learned many new skills and techniques. The coordinators are very helpful and there is a sense of community on the program. Since the program is relatively small (only about 40 new students a year) the coordinators encourage student involvement both for arranging social gatherings and organizing academic events like symposia and special courses." Bureaucracy has been a negative aspect of her experience, both in terms of coming to study abroad and the administrative problems of joining a newly established masters program.

68 (105) University of Geneva
Founded 1559 www.unige.ch

Arts & humanities	97
Engineering & IT	288
Life sciences & biomedicine	120
Natural sciences	130
Social sciences	146
Academic survey position	129
Employer survey position	355
Student faculty ratio	10.4:1
International faculty	40.2%
Undergraduates	6,138
Postgraduates	4,378
International students	35.5%
Research strength (Scopus) papers	11,082
Research strength (Scopus) citations	79,592
Impact (citations per paper)	7

Back in the top 100 after a year's absence, the University of Geneva, (Université de Genève) is Switzerland's second largest university after ETH Zurich. It was founded as the Académie de Genève, a seminary specializing in theology and the humanities. Although law was taught as well, theology remained its principal field of study until the late 17th century. During the Age of Enlightenment, interest broadened out to many aspects of 'natural philosophy' and developed further in legal studies. This led, by the mid-19th century, to its complete emancipation from the church and in 1873, with the opening of a medical school, to its re-definition as a university belonging to the canton of Geneva. The university, which goes by the acronym UNIGE, reflects Geneva's character as an international capital and as Switzerland's second-largest city. Geneva hosts scores of international organizations such as the World Health Organization and the Red Cross, and a number of international schools including the École Internationale de Genève. The large number of foreign residents is one reason that more than a third of the students are non-Swiss. Student numbers have been growing steadily, in particular in the faculties of law and of economic and social sciences. International exchanges for faculty and students are strongly encouraged and, since 1996, the number of students taking part in the European Union's Erasmus program has increased five times. The university works on a number of networked projects with the University of Lausanne, Lausanne's EPFL and the University of Neuchatel. UNIGE was a founding member of the League of European Research-Intensive Universities. The Swiss National Science Foundation chose it to head three of its first ten National Centres of Competence in Research, in genetics, materials and 'affective sciences'.

Theologian Jean Calvin was the religious and ideological driving force for its establishment, and Theodore de Beze, one of Calvin's closest disciples, was its first rector. Throughout the centuries, the university has been a refuge for religious and political exiles, who have both drawn from, and contributed to, the institution. Among the nine Nobel prize winners is Werner Arber, laureate in physiology and medicine in 1978.

Andrea Puglisi, from Parma, Italy, a doctoral student in the department of molecular biology, said: "The level of research is very high, and financial resources are excellent, both for salaries and for the labs. In my field the environment is very international: only about ten per cent are Swiss. Academically, the structure and schedule are such that there is a constant exchange of ideas. Also, Geneva is a very pleasant city that combines the efficiency and reliability of Swiss services with the enjoyment of a cosmopolitan capital."

69 (57) University of Warwick
Founded 1965   www2.warwick.ac.uk

Arts & humanities	75
Engineering & IT	164
Life sciences & biomedicine	201
Natural sciences	85
Social sciences	35
Academic survey position	84
Employer survey position	11
Student faculty ratio	10.1:1
International faculty	33.2%
Undergraduates	11,925
Postgraduates	4,607
International students	28.0%
Research strength (Scopus) papers	6,848
Research strength (Scopus) citations	27,543
Impact (citations per paper)	4

Warwick is aiming for a place in the top 50 universities in the world by the time it celebrates its 50th anniversary in 2015. It is already close, despite falling back 12 places in this year's THE-QS World University Rankings. The university has carved out a place among the elite of British higher education, with excellent ratings in both teaching and research. Two-thirds of the work entered for the UK's 2008 Research Assessment Exercise was considered world-leading or internationally excellent. The university did particularly well in film studies, horticulture, history, mathematics and French. The university is divided into four faculties. The faculty of arts teaches everything from classics to film and television studies, whilst the science faculty teaches the key disciplines in their core forms, avoiding the trend for academic dilution. The university also has faculties of social studies and medicine, the latter only founded in 2000 after many years when Warwick concentrated on its well-established links with industry and commerce. The location, near unglamorous Coventry, does not prevent the university from attracting many top students.

Warwick is a member of the Russell Group of elite research universities. It is planning to extend its international activities by allocating a section of its campus to leading overseas institutions. It has also launched an international arm of the National Academy for Gifted and Talented Youth, which the campus hosts. The university's freestanding international research and education group, WMG, has struck a £22 million deal with Siemens to provide access to software for researchers, students and businesses using the new Warwick Digital Laboratory, investigating areas such as digital manufacturing, e-security and mass customization. The student union is well organized and active. Union facilities have been refurbished, one of many improvements to the estate enabled by £335 million of investment. The Arts Centre, the second largest in the UK, was refurbished with a £33 million UK-lottery grant.

Leading academics at Warwick include Lord Bhattacharyya, Director of WMG, economics professor Andrew Oswald, and Lord Skidelsky, who recently retired as Professor of Political Economy. Famous alumni include leading UK politicians Baroness Amos and David Davis, and Tony Wheeler, co-founder of the Lonely Planet travel guides.

Damian King, a physics PhD student at Warwick, said: "Academically Warwick is a very strong university and in physics I have always found that staff contact time is readily available, particularly from my PhD supervisor, although other departments can differ greatly. Being a campus university Warwick won't suit all people, as many will find it isolated. However, with a strong campus life, living in Coventry in your second year and easy links to Birmingham, it's far from boring."

70 (51=) University of Texas at Austin
Founded 1827 www.utexas.edu

Arts & humanities	45
Engineering & IT	32
Life sciences & biomedicine	101
Natural sciences	34
Social sciences	86
Academic survey position	40
Employer survey position	46
Student faculty ratio	18.2:1
International faculty	17.5%
Undergraduates	35,560
Postgraduates	11,562
International students	9.2%
Research strength (Scopus) papers	18,244
Research strength (Scopus) citations	98,728
Impact (citations per paper)	5

Everything is bigger in Texas, or so the saying goes, and that includes its flagship University of Texas at Austin (UT). One of the largest graduate schools in America, it also has more than 35,000 undergraduates and 2,500 faculty on a vast campus centred around the 27-storey UT Tower, six feet higher than the nearby Texas capitol building. Introductory classes for undergraduates are large, too, with as many as 400 students and discussion sessions taught by graduate teaching assistants. The university's slogan is nothing less than: 'We Change People, They Change the World.' Thanks in part to the pull of Texas politicians such as President Lyndon Johnson, whose papers are kept in a campus archive with a robot version of him that leans on a fence and tells jokes, UT has enjoyed federal grants for work in space flight, defence, nuclear physics, and other fields. The university is also a centre of nanotechnology research, spurred on by the demands of the semiconductor industry, which has a strong presence in Texas. Moncrief Oil International pledged a gift that could total US$500 million for the university from the potential proceeds from litigation over the Yuzhno Russkoye gas field in Russia. The money will go towards a program to speed up the development of an alternative energy. Appropriately for a university that was partly funded by oil discovered on its campus, UT's College of Engineering's graduate program in petroleum engineering is considered the best in America. But it also has top-rated divisions of aerospace, chemical, civil, computer, electrical, environmental, and mechanical engineering. UT has one of the biggest cultural archives in the world, including a Gutenberg Bible and the world's earliest known photograph, while its new museum of art is the largest at any US university and its academic library is the nation's fifth largest. The surrounding city of Austin, known for its innovative music scene, is a lively setting.

Alumni include former First Lady Laura Bush, her daughter Jenna, Nobel laureate for literature J M Coetzee, actors Farrah Fawcett, Jayne Mansfield, Tex Ritter, Matthew McConaughey, and Renée Zellweger, singer Janis Joplin, filmmaker Wes Anderson, Dell Computer founder Michael Dell, and Rex Tillerson, chairman and chief executive officer of ExxonMobil.

"It's a huge university," said Assem Nasr, a doctoral student in international communications from Beirut. "I've never seen that many students at one time. I wondered; was I going to be lost in this place? I'm lucky to be in the department of radio, TV, and film, where the professors at least get to know the graduate students, and what you're doing in terms of research."

71 (73) University of Illinois
Founded 1867   **www.uillinois.edu**

Arts & humanities	103
Engineering & IT	20
Life sciences & biomedicine	115
Natural sciences	36
Social sciences	59
Academic survey position	42
Employer survey position	163
Student faculty ratio	12.9:1
International faculty	9.3%
Undergraduates	45,284
Postgraduates	17,658
International students	11.1%
Research strength (Scopus) papers	36,924
Research strength (Scopus) citations	196,285
Impact (citations per paper)	5

More Microsoft employees have come from the University of Illinois (UI) than from any other school, according to founder Bill Gates. The computer has a long association with this university, dating back to the development of ILLIAC, the first computer created and owned by an educational institution. UI's National Center for Supercomputing Applications created the browser on which Microsoft Internet Explorer is based, and is at work today to build the world's fastest supercomputer, capable of performing one quadrillion calculations per second. The university is also home to the world's largest virtual reality chamber at its Integrated Systems Laboratory. The Illinois Center for Cryptography and Information Protection is one of only four university-based cryptography centres in the world. The university also has one of the most highly regarded semiconductor and nanotechnology research facilities in the United States. Student enrolment is expected to grow by another 70,000 by 2018 through an ambitious online education arm called Global Campus. But this school, on the plains of the agricultural Midwest, isn't focused only on information technology. It's a principal partner in a US$500 million research institute backed by BP to study biofuels. Its academic library ranks third in size in the US behind only Harvard and Yale. The engineering library is the biggest in the country. Its Food and Brand Lab studies why consumers buy what they buy, and eat what they eat. And its Soybean Free Air Gas Concentration Enrichment program is studying the effects of atmospheric change on agriculture. The University opened a new Business Instructional Facility, the first 'green' building on campus, in 2008. Illinois is also highly ranked in accounting; civil, environmental, mechanical, electrical, and computer engineering; materials science; analytical science; kinesiology; and library and information sciences, including the new field of digital librarianship.

UI's 3,000 tenured professors include 11 Nobel laureates, while alumni have won another ten Nobel prizes. Alumni include Playboy magazine founder Hugh Hefner, actor Gene Hackman, director Ang Lee, architect Cesar Pelli, and the co-founders of YouTube, co-creators of Netscape, co-founders of Oracle, and inventors of the plasma display.

Hlaing Hlaing Win, a Malaysian undergraduate reading actuarial science, was drawn to the school after her older brother went there to study in the university's top-ranked accounting program. The location is the only downside, she said. She often leaves on the three-hour bus trip to Chicago (there is also a train service, and a university owned airport, served by three commercial airlines), where her brother now lives and works. She also said, "the weather is too cold!"

72 (61) Katholieke Universiteit Leuven
Founded 1425   www.kuleuven.ac.be

Arts & humanities	42
Engineering & IT	56
Life sciences & biomedicine	84
Natural sciences	93
Social sciences	45
Academic survey position	47
Employer survey position	100
Student faculty ratio	15.1:1
International faculty	14.4%
Undergraduates	15,775
Postgraduates	13,827
International students	11.1%
Research strength (Scopus) papers	15,173
Research strength (Scopus) citations	79,475
Impact (citations per paper)	5

The Katholieke Universiteit Leuven (KULeuven) is the largest of Belgium's Flemish universities, with 14 faculties, five hospitals, three affiliated hospitals, and a campus at Kortrijk in West Flanders. For much of its history the academic discourse in French was at odds with the Dutch spoken in the town, but the university has been bilingual since 1911. However, the language divide continued to produce tensions, and following student unrest in 1968 it was decided to split the university. The French speakers set up a new campus, and a new town, at Louvain-la-Neuve, while the Dutch speakers remained in Leuven. The university has now set up a number of international academic programs, taught in English, aimed both at Belgian and international students. Most are masters, although full bachelor degrees are also offered in English in theology and philosophy. The international masters are closely linked to the leading research areas at KULeuven, but span the whole range of disciplines, from theology and philosophy, to law and economics, pharmaceutical science and bio-engineering. KULeuven recently tempted back Catherine Verfaillie, a pioneer of work with adult stem cells, from Minnesota to lead a new stem cell institute. The university also has an international reputation in cryptography, and was home to Vincent Rijmen and Joan Daemen, the two researchers who developed the Rijndael advanced encryption standard adopted by the US government. It is a world leader in Alzheimer's research.

In the 2005 round of 'Flemish Nobels', awarded every five years, KULeuven faculty won three of the five awards. They went to Bart De Strooper (human genetics), Victor Moshchalkov (solid state physics and magnetism) and Frans Van de Werf (cardiology).

Alumni include Frank Vandenbroucke, the present education minister in Belgium's Flemish government, humanist and theologian Desiderius Erasmus, Dr A Q Khan, the founder of Pakistan's nuclear program, and cartographer Gerard Mercator.

British post-doc Simon Reeve was attracted to KULeuven by the prospect of joining a new research group in neurobiology being set up by an American investigator. "With him establishing a lab here, and the lab being a new place, I figured that the support, the funding, the interest would all be at a maximum." The experience has lived up to his expectations, and he has no regrets at choosing KULeuven over a position in the US. "It's a very dynamic environment," he said. "People suggest things and they go ahead." His only regret is that, in the university's English-speaking environment, there is no incentive to learn Dutch and so engage more with the local community. "From one perspective it's an advantage, but from another it's not."

73 (83) University of Glasgow
Founded 1451   www.gla.ac.uk

Arts & humanities	153
Engineering & IT	152
Life sciences & biomedicine	74
Natural sciences	145
Social sciences	180
Academic survey position	124
Employer survey position	115
Student faculty ratio	9.2:1
International faculty	36.4%
Undergraduates	15,346
Postgraduates	3,947
International students	13.1%
Research strength (Scopus) papers	11,468
Research strength (Scopus) citations	79,388
Impact (citations per paper)	7

Glasgow has always attracted a high proportion of undergraduates from the surrounding area, and was the first of Scotland's four ancient universities to start widening access. By 2010, it aims to have a 'truly diverse student community,' with increasing proportions of both international and postgraduate students. The university is also focused on research, having passed the £100 million a year mark for research grants and contracts. It is a leading player in Scotland's research pooling initiatives to bring together researchers from different universities and has a 'Synergy' partnership with neighbouring Strathclyde University. This has created some 200 active collaborations, including a full merger of Strathclyde's department of ship and marine technology with Glasgow's department of naval architecture and ocean engineering. Glasgow's medical faculty has been a pioneer of new teaching methods, establishing an undergraduate curriculum around problem-based learning. The university's faculty of veterinary medicine was only the third European school to win approved status from the American Veterinary Medical Association. The university's neo-Gothic main building dominates Glasgow's skyline. It has been spending around £30 million annually on building projects, and is committed to cutting energy costs and environmental pollution. Its newest buildings are at the forefront of sustainable construction. Sport plays a big part in university life, with two students representing Scotland in 2008: Johnnie Beattie played for the national rugby union team and June McNeill was part of the Scottish netball team at the European Championships.

Glasgow has a distinguished roll of scholars, including physicist Lord Kelvin and economist Adam Smith, who were both students and professors. James Watt conducted some of his early experiments with steam power while working at the university, and John Logie Baird, a pioneer of television, was a student when the First World War intervened.

Zhaofeng Zhou, from China, is doing a PhD in competition law. He said: "There are several reasons why I chose Glasgow: it is the fourth oldest university in the English speaking world and has many famous people associated with it. It has a great reputation for helping international students, running subsidized trips for them, and provides excellent social events for all students. It gives me an excellent chance to improve my English because I work as a senior resident at Murrano Street student village where most of the residents are first-year British students. Some of the best staff are in my research areas of the law school and the campus is very impressive. The thing I like least about the university is the summer holiday because most students go home and the university is too quiet."

74 (97=) University of Alberta
Founded 1908   www.ualberta.ca

Arts & humanities	88
Engineering & IT	46
Life sciences & biomedicine	45
Natural sciences	51
Social sciences	113
Academic survey position	50
Employer survey position	269
Student faculty ratio	10.6:1
International faculty	33.7%
Undergraduates	29,178
Postgraduates	5,419
International students	14.1%
Research strength (Scopus) papers	18,251
Research strength (Scopus) citations	92,738
Impact (citations per paper)	5

Located atop a river valley in Edmonton, the University of Alberta celebrated its centenary in 2008. Undergraduate and graduate students choose from 400 programs, including 60 doctoral in 300 research areas. Of note is native studies, the only such program in Canada that boasts a faculty and not just a department. It also has the country's only faculty of rehabilitation medicine. The University of Alberta developed the first vaccine for hepatitis B; has made numerous discoveries in medicine and swine research, which led to the development of the Edmonton Protocol islet transplant method to treat Type 1 diabetes; and combined the fields of oncology and nanotech engineering to develop devices for faster and less expensive cancer screening. The university is home to the Canadian Circumpolar Institute, of more than 200 researchers focused on the North. In 2007, its industrial design students were the first from Canada ever invited to participate in the International Contemporary Furniture Fair in New York. It's also home to Orlando, the world's largest text base on British women authors, available to scholars and readers worldwide. Last year saw the opening of the Enterprise Square Downtown Campus as a centre of teaching, learning, research and innovation, and the university has received the largest gift of land ever to a Canadian university for research. The St Albert Research Station will be used for agricultural and environmental research.

Distinguished alumni include the Chief Justice of the Supreme Court of Canada, Beverley McLachlin, the physicist and Nobel laureate Richard Taylor and former Canadian prime minister Joe Clark. Distinguished faculty include ecologist David Schindler, recipient of the Stockholm Water prize; computer scientist Jonathan Schaeffer, whose artificial intelligence program solved the game of checkers; paleontologist Phil Currie who digs in the dinosaur badlands of Alberta; and physicians Ray Rajotte and James Shapiro, collaborators on the Edmonton Protocol.

Mohit Dang, from India, who took a commerce degree, chose Alberta because of the province's oil boom and the business school's reputation. "The school has ranked high internationally, and it offers a family business and entrepreneurship major in their Bachelor of Commerce program, which was just what I was looking for." The university's size can be a drawback: "There can be a shortage of individual study space to accommodate so many students," he says. The university, spread out over 35 city blocks, is undergoing further expansion to address the issue of study-space shortage. Mohit loved the university's increasing international presence. "The staff and students come from all walks of life, and the university has a dynamic feel with a truly international environment."

75 (65=) Birmingham University
Founded 1900   www.bham.ac.uk

Arts & humanities	134
Engineering & IT	98
Life sciences & biomedicine	99
Natural sciences	192
Social sciences	126
Academic survey position	115
Employer survey position	53
Student faculty ratio	10.5:1
International faculty	26.4%
Undergraduates	17,373
Postgraduates	6,338
International students	16.2%
Research strength (Scopus) papers	13,238
Research strength (Scopus) citations	79,616
Impact (citations per paper)	6

Birmingham takes immense pride in its self-proclaimed standing as 'Oxbridge of the Midlands', and with good reason. The university can boast two thirds of its departments as nationally or internationally outstanding with research, especially in languages, winning the university 12 5* ratings in the Research Assessment Exercise. Teaching also scores well, with top marks in assessments going to mathematics, biological sciences, physiotherapy and electrical and electronic engineering. It therefore comes as little surprise that eight applicants contest every student place. The university's prestigious medical school has seen the largest expansion in the country with a new £11.8 million student facilities building. The engineering department has also been bolstered, now offering interdisciplinary courses combining technology with subjects as diverse as modern languages and flood management. A total of £225 million has been invested in new equipment, buildings and staff over the last five years.

The university and its partners have won £15 million of funding for three new centres to train scientists and engineers. The Birmingham Business School, the oldest in England, has also won a high level of respect, being one of only a dozen UK business schools in the Financial Times global top 80 for MBA rankings. Like the city itself, the university is a melting pot of cultures and nationalities. Echoing the 26.4 per cent of Birmingham residents who self-defined as 'non-white' in the 2001 census, the university has students from 150 countries. The city, about three miles from campus, has a growing reputation among students, but many opt to use the plethora of bars, shops and restaurants around the university itself.

With a list of alumni featuring four Nobel prize winners as well as the mayor of Shanghai and the prime minister of the Bahamas, Birmingham has had its share of prestigious students. Actor Tim Curry, UK politician Ann Widdecombe, and zoologist and TV presenter Desmond Morris also hail from the university.

Irene Michael, a student who came from Cyprus to study physiotherapy, praised the level of support given by the university to international students. "I think it's great. The university provides a very good induction, with a student union really enabling students to develop." Irene chose Birmingham largely due to the help given to her to get on the course, in the first place. While other institutions at the time gave little or no financial support to international students for her course, Birmingham gave her funding to match the NHS bursary available for home students. "The university also gives free English courses as well as advice on visas and jobs for both students and employers," she said.

76 (68) University of Sheffield
Founded 1897   www.shef.ac.uk

Arts & humanities	140
Engineering & IT	122
Life sciences & biomedicine	110
Natural sciences	211
Social sciences	155
Academic survey position	130
Employer survey position	38
Student faculty ratio	9.1:1
International faculty	26.1%
Undergraduates	17,172
Postgraduates	4,517
International students	16.3%
Research strength (Scopus) papers	13,410
Research strength (Scopus) citations	74,887
Impact (citations per paper)	6

In recent years, student numbers and facilities at the University of Sheffield have been growing. The university has opened a new research campus and the impressive new £23 million Information Commons, which operates 24 hours a day, provides 1,300 study spaces and 500 computers. Further building and the conversion of a former women's hospital added extra facilities for the arts and humanities in 2008, including a state-of-the-art rubber box development for the music department. The university is within walking distance of the city centre, forming a mile-long corridor of academic and residential buildings stretching into the affluent west side of Sheffield. Derbyshire's scenic Peak District is a bus ride away. The university has always had an international outlook, offering dedicated services for overseas students before many of its rivals. Sheffield International College, offers English language and other preparatory courses. The university also houses national teaching centres for the arts and social sciences and for enterprise learning, although research takes top priority in its mission statement. Boeing is the senior partner of an advanced manufacturing research centre, which forms the hub of the new technology park. The university is the lead institution for systems engineering, smart materials and stem-cell technology in a network of European, American and Chinese universities. A lively social scene is based on the student union, which is considered among the best in Britain, town/gown relations are much better and the crime rate lower than in most big UK cities. International students are guaranteed university accommodation, most of which is within walking distance of lectures. By 2009, a £160 million student village program will have replaced the old halls of residence.

Famous alumni range from pioneering aviator, Amy Johnson, to Britain's first astronaut, Helen Sharman. Nobel prize winners include chemist Sir Harry Kroto and Richard Roberts, who took the 1993 prize for medicine. The arts are represented by the playwright Jack Rosenthal and comedian Eddie Izzard; politics and business by former UK Home Secretary David Blunkett, and Penny Hughes, past president of Coca Cola.

Sajeev Jeganathan, from Sri Lanka, likes Sheffield so much that he hopes to find a job in the area when he completes his B Eng in Aerospace Engineering. He chose the university because the breadth of his course offered a variety of employment opportunities, but he would also like to take a masters degree. "I didn't want a big metropolitan city like London or Manchester," he said. "Sheffield is perfect for me. There is a good social life and the Peak District is really close if I want to get away."

77 (69) Nanyang Technological University, Singapore
Founded 1955   **www.ntu.edu.sg**

Arts & humanities 193
Engineering & IT... 26
Life sciences & biomedicine 78
Natural sciences 110
Social sciences 89

Academic survey position 68
Employer survey position 79

Student faculty ratio 12.1:1
International faculty 54.2%
Undergraduates 20,493
Postgraduates 5,270
International students 34.2%

Research strength (Scopus) papers................. 14,168
Research strength (Scopus) citations 35,669
Impact (citations per paper).................................... 3

Nanyang Technological University (NTU) was founded in the final phase of colonial times as Nanyang University. Like the National Union of Singapore, it became private in 2006 but continues to receive government funding. Setting its goals very high, NTU aims, according to The Straits Times, to become 'the MIT of the East'. The university occupies the Yunnan Garden campus designed by renowned Japanese architect Kenzo Tage, close to the world-famous Jurong Bird Park in the west of the island, well served by the republic's reliable and extensive public transport. With 13 schools and departments, including the incorporated National Institute of Education (NIE) and the Nanyang Business School, NTU has high quality facilities throughout, including excellent libraries and laboratories.

NTU has a high reputation for leadership in technological innovation. It was the first higher education institution in Southeast Asia to open a virtual reality theatre that highlights, among other things, research in biological and medical science. The university's Centre for Advanced Media Technology pursues leading-edge work in computer graphics, scientific visualization, simulation and animation. The Reality Theatre is available to all NTU departments for teaching and research. The Centre has been involved in a number of highly innovative projects that include the Augmented Reality Chinese Character Learning system, an example of next-generation technology. The university has also opened a School of International Relations named after a prominent Singaporean Indian, S. Rajaratnam, and, in 2008, an Art and Heritage Museum.

Among the outstanding graduates of NTU is Adrian Yeo, who graduated in 2002 with first class honours from the School of Civil and Environmental Engineering. On his own initiative, he has been delivering potable water to villagers of the tsunami-stricken Indonesian province of Aceh through Water Initiative for Securing Health (WISH). Indonesian Ardian Kristanto Poernomo, another alumnus, was the 2006 winner of the Google India Code Jam in Bangalore, India, an annual competition attracting over 14,000 contestants.

Nguyen Minh An, son of Vietnamese president Nguyen Minh Triet, joined the business school's Nanyang Fellows program, run in collaboration with MIT's Sloan School. "It was great making friends with people from different cultures. That was a very meaningful experience for me. I attended classes and did research with experienced and devoted professors...and I was able to learn more about effective management skills."

78= (63) Delft University of Technology

Founded 1842   www.tudelft.nl

Arts & humanities	203
Engineering & IT	17
Natural sciences	72
Social sciences	267
Academic survey position	98
Employer survey position	79
Student faculty ratio	9.3:1
International faculty	25.8%
Undergraduates	9,453
Postgraduates	5,035
International students	14.6%
Research strength (Scopus) papers	10,950
Research strength (Scopus) citations	37,809
Impact (citations per paper)	3

Delft University of Technology (TUDelft) has chosen Prometheus' flame as its symbol, and also sees itself as bringing technical knowledge to the aid of humanity. Gaining university status only in 1986, TUDelft is inheritor of a tradition of engineering education in the town that dates back to 1842. Delft is a small city between Den Haag and Rotterdam, greatly influenced by the university's presence. More than ten per cent of its 100,000 inhabitants are students and the university has attracted a large number of technology-oriented companies. The university set up an autonomous renewable energy laboratory in November 2008, on a scale equivalent to ten households. TUDelft is already a leading research unit in the solar power field and won the first Frisian Solar Challenge for solar powered boats. Four of the university's eight faculties cover engineering disciplines, the remainder taking on related subjects such as architecture, information technology, applied sciences and technology policy and management. It offers 16 bachelor courses, almost all taught in Dutch, and 29 masters, all taught in English.

The university is particularly strong in nanoscience, and in 2004 attracted substantial funding from the US Kavli Foundation to establish a research institute that now has 16 professors and more than 90 PhD students and postdocs. This is home to two of the university's most noted faculty: Hans Mooij, who works on quantum computing, and Cees Dekker, who received a Spinoza award (the highest Dutch honour for science) in 2003 for his work on carbon nanotubes. The university's other Spinoza winner is René de Borst, who works in the equally strong aerospace engineering faculty. This is also home to Adriaan Beukers, who in 2006, was named the Netherlands' most entrepreneurial scientist.

The commercial relevance of TUDelft's courses was one of the things that attracted Nitesh Bharosa to a bachelors degree and then masters in systems engineering and policy analysis from his home in Surinam. TUDelft has lived up to its promise, and even compared well to UCLA, where Nitesh followed a summer course in 2005. "The teaching methods here are more advanced, they use a lot more technology, including internet resources to provide information. Class material and so on is all online, and that is much appreciated." The one downside is that the town of Delft does not provide much. His one criticism is support for international students. "The university only has one small office that offers you aid in a lot of bureaucratic issues, such as housing and banking. Other universities have a much better focus on international students."

78= (67) Technische Universität München
Founded 1868   www.tu-muenchen.de

Engineering & IT	40
Life sciences & biomedicine	171
Natural sciences	40
Academic survey position	117
Employer survey position	195
Student faculty ratio	7.1:1
International faculty	15.3%
Undergraduates	12,311
Postgraduates	3,381*
International students	17.9%
Research strength (Scopus) papers	14,861
Research strength (Scopus) citations	89,315
Impact (citations per paper)	6

The Technische Universität in Munich (TUM) began life as a 'polytechnic school' and it was more than 100 years before it was allowed to call itself a technical university. The institute has grasped its new title with both hands and has built upon its prestige to such an extent that it was made one of Germany's first three 'elite' universities in 2006. The success of its international graduate school of science and engineering and the two clusters of excellence hosted by TUM, Cognition of Technical Systems and Origin and Structure of the Universe, paved the way to substantial extra funding. There are campuses in Weihenstephan and Garching, where further expansion is planned, as well as in Munich itself. There is also an institute of science and technology in Singapore. The TUM prides itself on its international standing. Continuity in leadership has contributed to its success. Chemistry professor Wolfgang A Herrmann, renowned in Germany for reforming higher education, has been president of the university since 1995, and has been re-elected twice. He was responsible for fundamental structural reforms at the TUM, which were followed by universities elsewhere in Germany and Austria. Unlike most technical universities across Europe, the TUM is strong in the life sciences, offering degrees in a variety of areas including nutrition and food, biotechnology, bioinformatics and medicine. Much of its innovative research and teaching has emerged from interdisciplinary collaboration between its 12 faculties and a number of research centres. The TUM prides itself on allowing scientists freedom to experiment and in 2005 set up the TUM Institute for Advanced Study that claims to add 'entrepreneurial spirit' to the academic world. Female students and academics are actively encouraged at the TUM, where nearly a third of students are women. The TUM aims to become the most attractive technical university for women in Germany and has adopted a number of unconventional measures to meet the needs of women, particularly those with young families.

Alumni include Rudolf Diesel, who invented the engine that bears his name, and the aeroplane designer Willy Messerschmitt. TUM can count six Nobel laureates: four in chemistry, including Robert Huber, 1988, and Heinrich Otto Wieland, 1927. Rudolf L Moessbauer, 1961 and Klaus von Klitzing, 1985 won the prize for physics.

Zouhair Mahboubi, an engineering student, now at Stanford University, said language barriers are reduced by the availability of classes and textbooks in English. "Personally, in my first semester I took most of my classes in English and by the second one I became comfortable enough with the language that I took all of them in German."

78= (92) Rice University
Founded 1891   **www.rice.edu**

Arts & humanities	272
Engineering & IT	110
Life sciences & biomedicine	201
Natural sciences	125
Social sciences	226
Academic survey position	169
Employer survey position	227
Student faculty ratio	8.2:1
International faculty	11.2%
Undergraduates	2,996
Postgraduates	2,082
International students	16.6%
Research strength (Scopus) papers	5,532
Research strength (Scopus) citations	41,675
Impact (citations per paper)	8

Comparatively small for a research university, Houston-based Rice is very rich. Its endowment makes it the fifth wealthiest university in America, per student, it once even owned Yankee Stadium in faraway New York where the fabled New York Yankees play. Those lucky enough to be accepted here (about one in every five who apply) pay considerably less than the tuition charged at other private US universities. Yet they enjoy an enviable student-faculty ratio, a median class size of 13 and a heavily wooded, stately campus in the elegant neo-Byzantine style. The graceful campus is in the midst of an expansion, with great trouble being taken to protect the trees, as the university begins a thorough reinvention of itself. Rice plans to increase its undergraduate enrolment by about 30 per cent and intends especially to attract more international students. In November 2008 the university attempted to defy the downturn in the global economy by launching a US$1 billion fundraising campaign for its 'second century'.

Already renowned for programs in architecture and engineering (more than a quarter of students are engineering majors), Rice also excels in space science, having taken the forward-looking step of ceding part of its enormous campus to build, in 1962, the NASA Manned Space Flight Center: the Johnson Space Center. President John F. Kennedy famously called for a man to be put on the moon by the end of the 1960s in a speech at Rice. The Rice Space Institute is today a world leader in space weather research, plasma environments of distant planets, and solar research.

Prominent alumni include former Newsweek editor and author William Broyles Jr, Pulitzer Prize-winning author Larry McMurtry, Sex and the City author Candace Bushnel, Howard Hughes, NASA astronauts, and former US Attorney General Alberto Gonzalez.

Students are randomly assigned to live in residential colleges on the Oxbridge model. Friendly though it is, Rice is academically demanding. Students unwind by carrying forward a long tradition of pranks, including a monthly jaunt around the campus for some, wearing nothing but shaving cream. Rosa Dominguez, a doctoral student in environmental engineering, took her first degree at a public university in her native Spain. "I wanted to have the experience of a small private school. When I met the Rice faculty, they were all really friendly, helpful and encouraging. And being near the fourth-largest city in the United States, you have a lot of things to do. You're not in the middle of nowhere."

81= (114=) University of Aarhus
Founded 1928   www.au.dk

Arts & humanities	100
Engineering & IT	230
Life sciences & biomedicine	127
Natural sciences	92
Social sciences	94
Academic survey position	105
Employer survey position	340
Student faculty ratio	8.6:1
International faculty	19.9%
Undergraduates	9,835
Postgraduates	7,676
International students	12.8%
Research strength (Scopus) papers	11,870
Research strength (Scopus) citations	85,494
Impact (citations per paper)	7

Aarhus is among the youngest universities in the THE-QS World University Rankings Top 100 and the second largest in Denmark. Until 1970, it was an independent institution and subsequently government-owned, but, the 2003 University Act again accorded Aarhus the status of an independent institution and it has since merged with the Herning Institute of Business Administration and Technology, the National Environmental Research Institute, the Danish Institute of Agricultural Sciences, the Aarhus School of Business and the Danish University of Education. This has added diversity to the university, new subjects, tasks, staff, students, structure and geographical locations. The main campus is located in the University Park in the centre of Aarhus, where the buildings are listed among the ten most important architectural icons in Denmark. The campus, a wide variety of buildings, all composed of the same yellow bricks and roofing tiles, was designed by the late C F Møller, whose firm has been responsible for all subsequent developments including the five new auditoria completed in 2001. More than 50,000 people, or every sixth resident of Aarhus, is either a student or an employee at the university or another higher education institution. As a result, Aarhus has the largest proportion of residents aged 17–34 years in Denmark. Most departments and institutes, and a large number of other educational institutions, are within walking distance of each other. The university collaborates closely with other educational institutions in Aarhus.

The university is a founding member of the Coimbra Group of elite European universities. Its research covers the broadest range of fields of any Danish university. Three-quarters of its resources are allocated, directly or indirectly, to research. Aarhus accounts for almost a quarter of the total number of researchers employed at Danish universities and close to a quarter of the total number of the country's research contributions. The university added new degrees in agriculture, food and environment, an MSc in Agrobiology and an MSc in Sport Sciences in 2008. More subjects will be added over the next few years. Aarhus also offers a growing number of full-time and part-time programs in English, and the summer university, also taught in English, is growing rapidly.

Professor Jens Christian Skou, was awarded the Nobel Prize in chemistry in 1997. Among the well-known alumni are Queen Margrethe II of Denmark, Crown Prince Frederik, Lene Espersen, Denmark's deputy prime minister, and Bjørn Lomborg, the environmentalist.

81= (74=) University of York
Founded 1963 **www.york.ac.uk**

Arts & humanities	111
Engineering & IT	253
Life sciences & biomedicine	150
Natural sciences	216
Social sciences	187
Academic survey position	172
Employer survey position	55
Student faculty ratio	8.1:1
International faculty	37.4%
Undergraduates	7,762
Postgraduates	2,385
International students	20.1%
Research strength (Scopus) papers	6,714
Research strength (Scopus) citations	36,951
Impact (citations per paper)	6

Having established a worldwide reputation as a relatively small university, focused on a limited range of subjects, York is now planning to grow by almost 50 per cent, adding a second campus and moving into new academic areas. The new site is adjacent to the original campus, on the outskirts of the ancient city of York and will take its first students in 2009, when a new college will provide accommodation for 617 students and five staff. Law, theatre, television and film studies will be the first subjects to be added, and the additional space will be used for research, teaching, student colleges, sport, cultural facilities and spin-out companies. Nursing and midwifery courses arrived with the takeover of a nearby college of health studies, and medicine has been offered since 2003, in a joint initiative with Hull University. Although less than 50 years old, the university is a regular fixture near the top of domestic league tables. It appeared in the top 100 of the THE-QS World University Rankings for the first time last year, thanks partly to strong support from employers. York also did well in the 2008 UK Research Assessment Exercise, with English, sociology and health services research all producing the best results in the country, and the university has been among the top performers in the UK's annual National Student Survey. Every student has a supervisor responsible for his or her academic and personal welfare.

Students join one of eight colleges, which mix academic and social roles. Most departments have their headquarters in one of the colleges, but the student community is a deliberate mixture of disciplines, years and sexes. Nursing apart, only archaeology and medieval studies are located off campus, sharing a medieval building in the city centre. International students are guaranteed residential accommodation and most choose to live on campus.

Alumni include Anibal Cavaco Silva, the president and former prime minister of Portugal, Greg Dyke, former director general of the BBC, and now the university's chancellor and MP Harriet Harman, deputy leader of the UK Labour Party. The writer and critic Hermione Lee taught English for more than 20 years and the Marxist intellectual Alex Callinicos was professor of politics.

Gong Lei, a Chinese postgraduate from Beijing, signed up for a second masters course at York, in computer science, having completed one in English for speakers of other languages. She has been impressed by the level of supervision and finds the city welcoming. "I love York, which is like a small town compared with the big cities I am used to. That was one reason for staying on at the university."

83= (97=) Georgia Institute of Technology
Founded 1885   www.gatech.edu

Engineering & IT	8
Life sciences & biomedicine	264
Natural sciences	61
Social sciences	282
Academic survey position	96
Employer survey position	102
Student faculty ratio	20.6:1
International faculty	9.9%
Undergraduates	12,008
Postgraduates	5,461
International students	18.2%
Research strength (Scopus) papers	16,276
Research strength (Scopus) citations	70,914
Impact (citations per paper)	4

'I'm a ramblin' wreck from Georgia Tech, and a hell of an engineer' goes what might be the world's most famous university fight song. But Georgia Tech these days is trying to move away from its perceived narrow focus on engineering, adding interdisciplinary initiatives and collaborations with its fellow Atlanta research institutions and universities and governments worldwide. It is merging its traditional engineering strength with biology, chemistry, medicine and other fields and has already rocketed into the top tier of research centres in nanomedicine, biotechnology, photonics, high-performance computing, and cancer. It added a new Centre for Music Technology in 2008 with 20 researchers from arts, science and engineering. Founded after the American Civil War to help train the leaders of a new manufacturing sector in the largely agricultural South, Georgia Tech is now also looking to extend its reach abroad with research deals in Ireland and France, where it has its own satellite campus in Metz. This new international emphasis extends to Georgia Tech's own Atlanta-based students. Under its international plan, students can take courses in modern languages, global economics, and international affairs, and spend two terms abroad studying or working. The university wants a third of its students to work or study abroad. Georgia Tech plans to increase by 50 per cent the number of undergraduates who do research, and raise the percentage of women students, as two-thirds of the students are men. The school already graduates ten per cent of all black PhDs in engineering in America. Many students live, work, and play in buildings that were added for the 1996 Olympics, during which time Georgia Tech provided the athletes' village and acquired a huge athletics centre that served as the Olympics' aquatics venue. There is also a new, four-building biotech complex and a planned nanotechnology building that will be the largest of its kind in the Southeast.

Prominent alumni include Nobel laureate and former US President Jimmy Carter, who attended Georgia Tech, although he graduated from the U.S. Naval Academy, and the CEOs of American Express, Wal-Mart, Earthlink, AT&T, and Atlanta-based Coca-Cola, along with several NASA astronauts and administrators.

When she was looking to study her specialty of environmental architecture, Maria Gabriela Zapata, said, "the US had the best programs," and Georgia Tech was at the top of her list. She came there from her native Ecuador to pursue a masters degree in building ecology and emerging technologies. "I like the opportunity here to be very closely involved in research," said Ms. Zapata. "There are so many projects and they are open for anybody to take part in."

83= (76) University of St Andrews
Founded 1413   www.st-andrews.ac.uk

Arts & humanities	71
Life sciences & biomedicine	201
Natural sciences	246
Social sciences	243
Academic survey position	192
Employer survey position	47
Student faculty ratio	8.5:1
International faculty	33.1%
Undergraduates	6,040
Postgraduates	1,257
International students	31.4%
Research strength (Scopus) papers	4,690
Research strength (Scopus) citations	28,529
Impact (citations per paper)	6

St Andrews is the oldest university in Scotland and the third oldest in Britain. Its ancient customs and enduring academic reputation have made it a favourite not just for Scottish students, but for English and those from much farther afield, notably the US. The large international intake gives a cosmopolitan feel to this small, coastal community. The windswept scenery is stunning and academic standards high. The town of St Andrews, with 18,000 inhabitants, is steeped in history, and the centre of the golfing world. Many of the main university buildings date from the 15th and 16th centuries, but sciences are taught nearby at the modern North Haugh site. Everything is within walking distance. Although apparently isolated, St Andrews is within easy reach of Dundee, with airport and rail links. The university's popularity soared while Prince William studied there, but its attractiveness has outlived the royal connection and the university is trading instead on good ratings, particularly from its own students. St Andrews has been among the UK's best-liked universities in the National Student Survey. New students (known as 'bejants' and 'bejantines') are given third and fourth-year 'parents' to ease them into university life, and on 'Raisin Monday' give their academic guardians a bottle of wine in return for a receipt in Latin, which can be written on anything. Students from the European Union (apart from the English, Welsh and Northern Irish) will pay no fees, under the Scottish Parliament's latest plans. All international students are guaranteed a place in university-owned residences, which accommodate more than half of all students. Although small, St Andrews offers a wide range of courses. The university's reputation has always rested primarily on the humanities, but a full range of physical sciences is taught, with sophisticated lasers and the largest optical telescope in Britain. A new £8 million building opened in 2008 to house the university's school of international relations and five other prestigious research units in areas such as international security, terrorism and peace studies.

As well as Prince William, the university's royal alumni included King James II of Scotland. More academic connections include Nobel prize winners James Black and Alan McDiarmid, as well as John Napier, the inventor of logarithms. Political luminaries include Alex Salmond, First Minister of Scotland and leader of the Scottish National Party.

Citizen Sigmund, an international relations student from New York, said: "The town itself is extremely charming and majestic. I feel the St Andrews student has perfectly mastered the art of 'work hard, play hard.' St. Andrews is now, and will always be, a home away from home."

83= (64) University of Western Australia
Founded 1911   **www.uwa.edu.au**

Arts & humanities	128
Engineering & IT	147
Life sciences & biomedicine	81
Natural sciences	166
Social sciences	176
Academic survey position	121
Employer survey position	76
Student faculty ratio	11.2:1
International faculty	33.2%
Undergraduates	12,554
Postgraduates	2,923
International students	19.8%
Research strength (Scopus) papers	9,500
Research strength (Scopus) citations	48,736
Impact (citations per paper)	5

The University of Western Australia (UWA) is the oldest and richest university in the giant state where it is based. It has a beautiful campus, adjacent to Perth's most affluent suburbs, and is a mere five kilometres from the city centre. Because of its age, status and reputation, it attracts an even higher proportion of students from the top private schools than any other university in the country and enrols more than eight in ten of the state's top school-leavers. A member of Australia's Group of Eight research-intensive universities, UWA focuses on research into the exploration, production and development of minerals, oil and gas; the management of agricultural and natural ecosystems; the humanities and social sciences; health and bio-medicine, as well as international management and business studies. In 2008 the university opened a new Centre for Integrated Human Studies, set up to tackle issues as diverse as obesity, the well-being of migrants, the health benefits of romance and the health of mining communities. There are strategic partnerships with Australian industry, the professions and government, and numerous links with international universities and research organizations. Because Perth is close to many southeast Asian cities, and has close links with Malaysia and Singapore, many Asian students find it nearer and cheaper to go to UWA than to travel another 3,000 kilometres to the other side of Australia. Most international undergraduates are from Singapore, Malaysia or Indonesia, and the business school delivers programs in Singapore, Manila and Shanghai. The university has colleges adjacent to the campus which provide accommodation for approximately 700 students.

Apart from Nobel laureates Professor Barry Marshall and Dr Robyn Warren who won the 2005 prize for medicine, other notable UWA graduates include a former Australian prime minister and an opposition leader, former WA premiers, five of the last six Australian ambassadors to China and international political leaders, including senior ministers in the Indonesian and Singaporean governments.

Charmaine Kalidas, a Singaporean Indian who took a BSc in zoology, chose UWA because it was in the Group of Eight, and because it was recommended as a place to study and work with animals. The workload is heavy, (she jokingly refers to her lecturers as 'slave-drivers' because of the amount of work they demanded), but she feels that students reap the benefit of the pressure in the annual exams, even if it cuts down on the opportunity to enjoy campus life. "I would give UWA a mark of 85 out of 100 overall," she said, "and I will urge my younger sister to also come here if she wants to go abroad to study."

86 (70) University of Nottingham
Founded 1798   www.nottingham.ac.uk

Arts & humanities 128
Engineering & IT... 140
Life sciences & biomedicine 92
Natural sciences... 192
Social sciences 137

Academic survey position 122
Employer survey position 24

Student faculty ratio 9.6:1
International faculty 31.8%
Undergraduates 20,725
Postgraduates 5,055
International students 22.4%

Research strength (Scopus) papers................. 12,187
Research strength (Scopus) citations.............. 59,621
Impact (citations per paper)..................................... 5

Nottingham University is a campus-based, research-led institution with a strong international presence and reputation. Traditionally one of the most popular universities among prospective British undergraduates, the university also attracts a high volume of applications from overseas. Three attractive campuses with award-winning buildings are all within easy reach of Nottingham city centre. The main University Park campus is set around a lake with extensive greenery, and is regarded as one of the most attractive in the UK. This campus is the focus of university life for most students, and includes 12 halls of residence, a conference and exhibition centre, sports facilities and an arts centre. Adjacent to University Park is Nottingham's medical school. Jubilee campus houses the schools of education, computer science and information technology, and Nottingham's business school. A new research and innovation park is being developed here. Most biosciences students are based at the Sutton Bonington campus, outside the city, which is also home to the university's new school of veterinary medicine and science. Nottingham guarantees international students university accommodation for the first two years of study. Support for them includes a foundation program, offered both in Nottingham and at the university's two overseas campuses, in China and Malaysia. Both have echoes of University Park and its famous clock tower, offering a limited version of the Nottingham curriculum. English language tuition is provided on campus and online by a centre for English language education. Nottingham did well in the 2008 Research Assessment Exercise, with almost 60 per cent of all research defined as 'world-leading' or 'internationally excellent'. In both teaching and research, the university has a strong record in healthcare, nanotechnology, biosciences, the built environment, international relations and cultural studies. Nottingham was named 'entrepreneurial university of the year' at the Times Higher Education Awards in 2008. A new research centre for international finance opened at the university's China campus, during the year.

Distinguished faculty include Nobel prize winners Sir Peter Mansfield in the field of cognitive behaviour and scanning, and economist Sir Clive Granger. The novelist D H Lawrence is the most famous alumnus, but table-tennis champion Deng Yaping enjoys superstar status in her native China, while Dato Seri Najib Razak became deputy prime minister of Malaysia in 2004.

It was Nottingham's "tranquil" environment that first attracted and has impressed Julie Walabyeki, from Uganda, who is taking a Masters in Public Health. She said: "The university and its environment have lived up to my hopes and expectations. My course has been very intensive, but so good that I now want to do a PhD here. As a mature student, I have found the social scene at Nottingham very inclusive."

87 (142=) University of Minnesota
Founded 1851   **www.umn.edu**

Arts & humanities	122
Engineering & IT	140
Life sciences & biomedicine	84
Natural sciences	137
Social sciences	71
Academic survey position	95
Employer survey position	231
Student faculty ratio	13.9:1
International faculty	21.8%
Undergraduates	28,825
Postgraduates	12,461
International students	6.7%
Research strength (Scopus) papers	28,894
Research strength (Scopus) citations	197,657
Impact (citations per paper)	7

The University of Minnesota aspires to be nothing short of one of the three best public research universities in the world. It has seen nearly double-digit percentage growth annually, rising to ninth among US public universities with US$619 million a year in sponsored research. Minnesota anticipated erosion in funding as early as 2005 and embarked on an ambitious, if controversial, restructuring. The university merged several colleges, streamlining departments, but also added a writing requirement and an honours program for undergraduates, expanded undergraduate research, began a training program for new faculty, and channelled funding towards biomedical sciences, clinical research, science and engineering. These are areas in which the university is already strong. The US National Research Council rates many of its programs in the top 20, nationally. With its own nine square mile conservation reserve, the University of Minnesota has also positioned itself as a top school for the study of ecology and evolution. Its Cedar Creek Ecosystem Science Reserve, a half-hour drive from the main campus, is the meeting point of North America's western prairies, northern evergreen forests, and eastern leafy forests, and where the modern science of ecosystem ecology was conceived. Its Saint Anthony Falls Laboratory on the Mississippi is the world's only fluid-mechanics laboratory that uses a natural waterfall as its prime water source. The university's main campus is decidedly urban, making it one of only a handful of US public universities located in a major city (or, in this case, two cities): friendly, and, in the winter, freezing Minneapolis and St. Paul. With architecture that ranges from Norman and Romanesque to contemporary (the art museum was designed by Frank Gehry), the campus flanks the Mississippi, its two halves connected by a bridge, an enclosed walkway, and shuttle buses, and its buildings linked by skywalks and tunnels so its students (it boasts the fourth-largest enrolment in America) can stay out of the cold. Minnesota is also prominent in university athletics, particularly dominant in men and women's ice hockey. It is building a new US$300 million, 50,300-seat American football stadium.

Nineteen past and present faculty or alumni have won Nobel prizes, including the economist Milton Friedman and Ernest O Lawrence, creator of the cyclotron. Other prominent alumni include supercomputer architect Seymour Cray.

Tryggvi Thayer, a doctoral student from Iceland in the College of Education and Human Development, considers the university's large size an asset. "It's very interdisciplinary," he says. "We have access to, and are expected to take, courses from other departments. The breadth of expertise and types of courses that are offered here has a really positive impact on the quality of the education."

88 (106) Lund University
Founded 1666   www.lu.se

Arts & humanities	96
Engineering & IT	126
Life sciences & biomedicine	119
Natural sciences	74
Social sciences	77
Academic survey position	85
Employer survey position	160
Student faculty ratio	12.5:1
International faculty	20.5%
Undergraduates	21,044
Postgraduates	5,703
International students	11.4%
Research strength (Scopus) papers	13,133
Research strength (Scopus) citations	80,392
Impact (citations per paper)	6

Lund is the second-oldest university in Sweden, located in a medieval city of 100,000 people in the south of the country, close to Denmark and northern Germany. Lund has been rated the best place to live in Sweden. It is one of the safest and wealthiest municipalities, the population is the youngest in Sweden and it is home to some world-leading companies. The university has eight faculties and additional campuses in the cities of Malmö and Helsingborg, with a total of over 25,100 students in more than 50 different programs and 800 separate courses. It belongs to the League of European Research Universities and the global Universitas 21 network. The university traditionally centres on the Lundagard park adjacent to Lund Cathedral, with various departments spread in different locations in town, but mostly concentrated in a belt stretching north from the park to the university hospital area and continuing out to the large campus of the Lund Institute of Technology, the university's engineering faculty, on the northeastern periphery of the town. An evaluation of the university's research by 17 external panels in 2008 found the humanities and life sciences to be particularly strong. Leading areas included philosophy, nanotechnology, synchrotron radiation, stem cell and endocrinology research. The centrepiece of the university's research is the climate initiative, which has identified 11 themes, including carbon cycle processes and large-scale climate patterns, to be addressed by a variety of disciplines. Almost 300 courses are, or can be, held in English for the benefit of international exchange students, although no complete undergraduate programs are taught in English. As elsewhere in Sweden, there are no tuition fees for home or international students. Lund has a long history of welcoming international students and the university has the largest number of international students in Sweden. Student social life centres on the 13 'Nations', which the university describes as 'somewhere between a student union and a social club'. They are spread across the city, each with their own character, offering food, drink, a place to party, live music and accommodation.

Famous alumni include Nobel laureates Manne Siegbahn, (physics 1924), Bertil Ohlin, (economics 1977), Sune Bergstrom, (medicine 1982), and Arvid Carlsson, (medicine 2000), Swedish prime ministers Tage Erlander and Ingvar Carlsson, and tennis icon Björn Borg.

Lisa Leick, from Texas, who studied physical chemistry, initially found it difficult to adjust to a teaching style that emphasizes group work. But she found staff and students supportive. She said: "All the structured social events coordinated by the Nations made it really easy to integrate quickly into the culture and also provided an opportunity to take a break from thinking about university work."

89 (96) University of California, Davis
Founded 1905   www.ucdavis.edu

Arts & humanities	168
Engineering & IT	107
Life sciences & biomedicine	28
Natural sciences	95
Social sciences	163
Academic survey position	80
Employer survey position	284
Student faculty ratio	13.1:1
International faculty	5.8%
Undergraduates	22,872
Postgraduates	5,914
International students	4.9%
Research strength (Scopus) papers	24,384
Research strength (Scopus) citations	154,237
Impact (citations per paper)	6

Halfway between San Francisco and Lake Tahoe, this picturesque branch of the University of California (UC) system is in a small city of 64,000 people, so progressive it dug an underpass so as not to disturb migration patterns of toads that were getting squashed on a newly constructed highway. UC Davis boasts a department of viticulture and enology that helped build California's wine industry. In a pioneering model of interdisciplinary study, faculty specialize in chemistry, genetics, microbiology, engineering, horticulture, biochemistry, plant physiology, and sensory science. Together they choose varieties best suited to California growing conditions. Residents and members of the university community share a gleaming centre for the performing arts given by the Mondavi wine family and in 2008 the US$73 million Robert Mondavi Institute of Wine and Food Sciences opened. Agriculture is a mainstay of this school, and has been since it was first established as a state training farm, not incorporated as a university until 1959. Some US$418 million a year in research is conducted here, 12th among US public universities and up 85 per cent in just five years. UC Davis leads the nation in the number of undergraduate and doctoral degrees conferred in the biological sciences. It has nearly 100 faculty engaged in research in renewable energy, alternative vehicle fuels, and lighting technology. It has one of only two US centres authorized by the National Institutes of Health to develop medical therapies using human stem cells.

Undergraduates live and study on the largest campus of the UC system, so big it has its own airport and fire department. Students get around on bicycles and in vintage double-decker buses. UC Davis is the only UC school with colleges of law, medicine, education, management, and veterinary medicine, all of them highly rated. It is about to add a school of nursing in Sacramento.

Prominent alumni include US treasurer Anna Escobedo Cabral, UNICEF head Ann Veneman, Bechtel CEO Riley Bechtel, author Anthony Swofford (Jarhead), Kirin Brewing Company CEO Koichiro Aramaki, and Frederick Murphy, co-discoverer of the Ebola virus.

Fernando Mardones came from Chile to take a masters degree in preventative veterinary medicine and now works as an epidemiologist while his wife completes the same program. They were attracted to the university by the quality of the program and facilities and the prestige of the faculty. They also quickly grew to like the city. "It's a very natural environment," he said. "There is a lot of green space. Everyone is biking. No one smokes. It's a very special place to live."

90 (85=) Case Western Reserve University
Founded 1826   www.case.edu

Arts & humanities	294
Engineering & IT	149
Life sciences & biomedicine	76
Natural sciences	252
Social sciences	239
Academic survey position	186
Employer survey position	309
Student faculty ratio	6:1
International faculty	2.9%
Undergraduates	4,066
Postgraduates	4,274
International students	11.1%
Research strength (Scopus) papers	10,454
Research strength (Scopus) citations	77,634
Impact (citations per paper)	7

Firmly rooted in the sciences, Case Western Reserve University was created by the merger 40 years ago of two adjacent universities, one of them an institute of technology. Half the undergraduates specialize in engineering and the sciences, and three-quarters go on to earn advanced degrees. A recent expansion included a US$110 million research building to house 700 people studying cancer, genetic epidemiology, and other subjects, and another building to accommodate work in fuel-cell technology and structural biology. Now the renovation of many science laboratories has doubled the student capacity in areas such as biology. The university has also built up its faculty, expanding it by 20 per cent and bringing the student-faculty ratio down. Case Western Reserve's Seminar Approach to General Education and Scholarship program requires undergraduates to take personalized classes of no more than 17 students.

Case Western Reserve scientists conducted research determining the atomic weight of oxygen, proved the nonexistence of ether, developed simulated milk formula for infants, and detected neutrinos created by cosmic ray collisions with the atmosphere. One of those scientists, Albert Michelson, laid part of the foundation for Einstein's special theory of relativity, becoming the first American to win a Nobel prize in the sciences. Faculty and alumni have received 15 Nobel prizes. Case Western Reserve is 14th among private universities in America in government funding for research, receiving a combined US$400 million annually from the government along with other sources, much of it channelled to its highly rated medical school. Along with engineering, it is also particularly highly regarded for its programs in biomedical engineering and management. It offers an unusual masters degree in business administration focused on sustainable development.

Case Western Reserve alumni include the first female rear admiral in the US Navy, the first woman director of the US Centers for Disease Control, Craigslist founder Craig Newmark, former Ecuadorian president Alfredo Palacio, US presidential candidate Dennis Kucinich, several congressmen, author Richard North Patterson, and physicist Lawrence Krauss, author of the book The Physics of Star Trek.

Case Western Reserve feels dynamic and energetic, said Sumitha Nair, a doctoral candidate from India studying biomedical engineering. "We have new faculty and there has been a lot of construction, with much better space now than we had when I first got here. The program is very good here at Case, and very broad." One downside is the weather in the midwestern city of Cleveland. "I guess I have come to like it more now than when I first came here, but I'm from the southernmost state in India, with a tropical climate," she said. "I had never seen snow before in my life. I have seen a lot now."

91= (100) University of Helsinki
Founded 1640   www.helsinki.fi/university/

Arts & humanities 52
Engineering & IT.. 144
Life sciences & biomedicine 71
Natural sciences 72
Social sciences 68

Academic survey position 64
Employer survey position 301

Student faculty ratio 10.8:1
International faculty 14.4%
Undergraduates 12,044*
Postgraduates 21,995*
International students 3.3%

Research strength (Scopus) papers.................. 16,634
Research strength (Scopus) citations............. 124,269
Impact (citations per paper).................................... 7

The University of Helsinki is the oldest and largest in Finland, originally established in Turku, the then capital. It transferred to the new capital, Helsinki, in 1928. The university is in the midst of a two-year strategy focusing on research and internationalization. It is one of the founding members of the élite League of European Research Universities (LERU). The library, which is Finland's national library, has been improved by a new learning centre for students and staff. There are 11 faculties and 20 independent research institutes. Helsinki fared well in comparison with other European universities in an international research evaluation conducted in 2005 that gave high scores to two thirds of its 75 research units (five independent institutes and 70 faculty departments). At present, there are no tuition fees for foreign students, irrespective of their country of origin. However, with an average acceptance level of 23 per cent, it is not easy to gain a place. Many foreign students come through the European Union's Erasmus program. There are also reciprocal arrangements with leading universities elsewhere in the world, including the University of California, Berkeley, University of Tokyo, Moscow State University and the University of Toronto. The university is aiming to double the number of foreign undergraduate and doctoral students by 2009 and has launched 30 additional masters programs in English. Dedicated services aimed at foreign students such as language courses, cultural guidance and career guidance are also being improved and extended. Russia, Estonia, China, Germany, the UK and the US top the list of countries of origin for foreign students, among almost 100 different nationalities currently represented.

Well-known alumni include Jorma Ollila, until recently chief executive of Nokia, and Linus Torvalds, developer of the Linux software system. Seven out of ten Finnish presidents studied at Helsinki University, as did three Nobel prize winners.

Martha Vera, a Mexican student, enrolled on a communication masters in the Faculty of Social Sciences, said: "I chose the University of Helsinki specifically because of its status, despite the fact that everybody I met in Helsinki told me it is very hard to get in. My study program has met my expectations although it is hard work. The main drawback is that relevant and important information is often in Finnish and not accessible to a first-year degree student with a basic knowledge of the language. We get information about the practicalities of everyday life but not about how to book exams, for instance. At masters level, the compulsory Finnish language course has excellent tutors, though."

91= (93=) Université de Montréal
Founded 1878   www.umontreal.ca

Arts & humanities	59
Engineering & IT	87
Life sciences & biomedicine	60
Natural sciences	91
Social sciences	70
Academic survey position	58
Employer survey position	352
Student faculty ratio	14.5:1
International faculty	27.3%
Undergraduates	17,459
Postgraduates	7,329
International students	16.8%
Research strength (Scopus) papers	10,806
Research strength (Scopus) citations	65,721
Impact (citations per paper)	6

Université de Montréal is the largest university in Quebec and second largest in Canada. The French language university is one of Canada's major research centres. It has two affiliated schools, the École Polytechnique, an engineering school, and HEC Montréal, its business faculty, along with a network of affiliated hospitals. Université de Montréal is also the institution with the highest proportion of students in graduate studies in Canada, and the only Canadian university that covers all the health science disciplines. It is one of the few non-American universities sponsored by the Bill and Melinda Gates Foundation, which has given US$15 million for a major project to improve population and health capacity in French-speaking Sub-Saharan Africa. The university displayed its sporting prowess with students representing Canada in the Beijing Olympics in synchronized swimming, cycling, soccer, diving, swimming and wrestling. Among the Université de Montréal's innovative centres are BRAMS (Brains, Music and Sound), which combines neuroscience and music, and the Institute for Research in Immunology and Cancer. The university has researchers working in leading-edge disciplines such as pharmacogenomics, which combines the fields of drugs, genomics and cardiology, and nanotechnology. It also has centres specializing in areas as diverse as aerospace manufacturing and poultry research.

Some of its more famous alumni include UN High Commissioner for Human Rights, Louise Arbour, Oscar-winning filmmaker Denys Arcand, former Canadian prime minister Pierre Trudeau and the president of the International Criminal Court, Philippe Kirsch.

Brian Crane, a 34-year-old PhD candidate in comparative literature from Florida has lived in various parts of the continent but says he chose Montréal "to study in French at a world-class university in a North American city close to where I'll build my career." The university has "a strong international community and ties to both North America and Europe," he said, while Montréal is a world city on a human-scale. "Anything you learn in the classroom you can live in the cafés, festivals and business milieus." Studying abroad can be complicated and overwhelming," he said. "Like most large universities, Université de Montréal can seem bureaucratic when registering or paying fees, especially when you are doing it in a second language. Five minutes in the supportive international student office, with its helpful staff, usually works it out." While he finds departments and services to be first-rate, the buildings are less good. "The old buildings look impressive perched on the side of Mount Royal, but get inside and they can seem cramped and uncomfortable. The ongoing renovations are welcome."

93= (128) Hebrew University of Jerusalem
Founded 1918   **www.huji.ac.il**

Arts & humanities	41
Engineering & IT	209
Life sciences & biomedicine	58
Natural sciences	70
Social sciences	49
Academic survey position	56
Employer survey position	4
Student faculty ratio	14.8:1
International faculty	21.3%
Undergraduates	11,148
Postgraduates	6,255
International students	6.6%
Research strength (Scopus) papers	11,183
Research strength (Scopus) citations	67,022
Impact (citations per paper)	6

The dream of establishing a 'University of the Jewish People in the Land of Israel' was an integral part of the early Zionist vision, but it took seven years after the foundation stone was laid for the Hebrew University of Jerusalem to open. The first board of governors was chaired by Dr Chaim Weizmann, the founding father of the university, and included such luminaries as Albert Einstein and Sigmund Freud. The War of Independence in 1948 left the Mount Scopus campus cut off from Israeli, West Jerusalem, and alternative facilities were found throughout the city. Eventually, a new main campus was built at Givat Ram in the heart of Jerusalem, which now contains the scientific departments and the university's main library, which is also the Jewish National Library. Its collections of Hebraica and Judaica are the largest in the world. A health sciences campus was added in southwest Jerusalem, in partnership with the Hadassah Medical Organization, and there is an agricultural faculty at Rehovot, 20km south of Tel Aviv. Mount Scopus, in east Jerusalem, has again been the main home of the Hebrew University since 1981, acquiring new buildings as the institution has grown. The campus, which has a panoramic view of the city, has been revamped in recent years to allow access for the disabled. A state-of-the-art sports complex has also opened. Nearly 40 per cent of all civilian scientific research in Israel is conducted at the Hebrew University, which also enrols 30 per cent of the country's doctoral candidates. The university is home to 100 subject-related and interdisciplinary research centres, with particular strengths in biotechnology and computer science, astrophysics and cancer research, microbiology and genetic engineering. Research is also strong in the humanities, including Jewish studies, social sciences and law.

The Hebrew University's Rothberg International School offers a broad selection of courses taught in English and some in French, Spanish, Russian, and Hebrew. Seven MA degrees are also conducted in English. Students do not have to be Jewish and can live on campus in the new Scopus Student Village, within walking distance of the RIS, or arrange living accommodation off-campus.

Six recent Nobel prize winners have been Hebrew University graduates or researchers. Daniel Kahneman was the 2002 laureate for economics. In 2004, three graduates of the university, Aaron Ciechanover, David Gross and Avram Hershko took the chemistry prize, while Robert Aumann won the prize for economics in 2005. Famous alumni include three presidents of Israel: Ephraim Katzir, Yitzhak Navon and Moshe Katsav, and three prime ministers: Ehud Barak, Ariel Sharon and Ehud Olmert.

93= (65=) Ludwig-Maximilians-Universität München
Founded 1472   www.uni-muenchen.de

Arts & humanities	60
Engineering & IT	204
Life sciences & biomedicine	91
Natural sciences	48
Social sciences	99
Academic survey position	79
Employer survey position	290
Student faculty ratio	9:1
International faculty	14.3%
Undergraduates	40,379*
Postgraduates	4,565*
International students	15.6%
Research strength (Scopus) papers	19,315
Research strength (Scopus) citations	126,286
Impact (citations per paper)	7

Selected to become one of Germany's first three 'elite' universities, the Ludwig-Maximilians-Universität (LMU) in Munich will share a fund of €175 million that is designed to propel the country's top institutions up the global higher education rankings. Long recognized as one of the strongest research universities in Germany, it is also one of the largest and most internationally minded. Rector Bernd Huber says students from across the world travel to Munich because of its unique academic diversity that covers all areas including humanities, cultural studies, law, economics, sociology, medicine and the sciences. The university is involved in 26 collaborative research centres funded by the German Research Foundation (DFG), hosting 14 of them, and attracts external funding of more than €100 million a year from both national and international sources. A centre for advanced studies has been set up to promote and support interdisciplinary and international exchange. The LMU was not always situated in the Bavarian capital. When Duke Ludwig the Wealthy of Bavaria-Landshut founded it with a Papal concession, it was called the Ingolstadt University. It was relocated to Landshut in 1800 by Prince Elector Max IV Joseph of Bavaria, changing its name to the Ludwig-Maximilians-Universität two years later, in honour of two noblemen. Only in 1826 did the university finally move to the larger city of Munich. The main building has been in use since 1840. There are now 150 degree programs offered in numerous combinations.

Thirteen Nobel prize winners are associated with the university including Wilhelm Conrad Röntgen, who in 1895 discovered the X-ray, and Konrad Lorenz, who won the prize for medicine in 1973 for his discoveries in individual and social behaviour patterns. Interestingly all of the Nobel laureates who studied or taught at the LMU won prizes for the sciences, reinforcing its reputation as a leader in this area.

Before coming from Beijing to study German and business administration, Qi Meimei, a 26-year-old undergraduate, had received glowing reports of the LMU and Munich from friends, and she has not been disappointed. She particularly welcomes the opportunity to attend lectures outside her own faculty and to choose from a wide range of optional courses in addition to her mandatory basic courses. "The academic standards of the University are set very high," she said. "As most courses are in German, I would recommend that international students learn the language well. Students are not spoon-fed at the LMU: they are expected to use their own initiative and actively participate in classes. Munich is therefore not the right choice for passive students."

95 (132=) Korea Advanced Institute of Science & Technology
Founded 1971   www.kaist.edu

Engineering & IT	34
Life sciences & biomedicine	134
Natural sciences	46
Social sciences	299
Academic survey position	110
Employer survey position	239
Student faculty ratio	10:1
International faculty	13.2%
Undergraduates	2,948
Postgraduates	3,864
International students	7.4%
Research strength (Scopus) papers	9,790
Research strength (Scopus) citations	31,768
Impact (citations per paper)	3

The president of Korea's Advanced Institute of Science and Technology (KAIST), Nam Pyo Suh, is a Korean who has spent most of his life in the US and was head of mechanical engineering at the Massachusetts Institute of Technology (MIT) before returning to Korea, and KAIST's campus at Daejeon in the centre of the country. His ambition is to see KAIST become the MIT of Korea. KAIST was set up as a specialist graduate school, with a specific political remit to improve the quality of Korean science, technology and innovation. It began teaching undergraduates in 1986. Its special status has allowed it to avoid some of the heavy central control that the Korean government exerts on other universities. Undergraduates admitted to KAIST's four-year program do not have to choose their main subject definitively, which again allows more flexibility than is usual in the Korean education system. They will find a full spread of engineering and IT subjects on offer, plus biological and physical sciences and the mandatory business school. But there is no medical school and culture and the arts are present only on a small scale. KAIST is the place to be if you want a management or technology job in Korea's high-technology sector, which these days runs far deeper and wider than Samsung and LG. If you are not a Korean, be aware that you will be in a minority, although KAIST is good at recruiting international staff.

KAIST's list of distinguished alumni reflects its role as the academic arm of Korean high tech. Korea's first astronaut, So-Yeon Yi, did her PhD there. She now works at the Korean Aerospace Research Institute, one of a number of national research centres close to KAIST. Other graduates include Min Whoa Lee, chief executive of the Korea Technology Transfer Center, O Hyun Kwon, president of Large Scale Integration (of electronic devices) at Samsung, and Sam Soo Pyo, chief executive of the Korean arm of US database colossus Oracle.

Vasu Sampath from India, a fourth-year PhD chemistry student, said, "I have been studying at KAIST for six years. The department offers excellent facilities to perform research at an advanced level. I live in an on-campus apartment, which has good facilities such as air-conditioning and heating. KAIST has recently opened a well-equipped international kitchen, which allows me to meet many international students. There are certain drawbacks, such as lab meetings conducted in Korean, and it would be better if KAIST focused attention on organizing some cultural programs for improving the relationship not only with Koreans but also among foreign students. But overall I am glad to be a student at KAIST."

96 (110) University of Virginia
Founded 1819   www.virginia.edu

Arts & humanities	107
Engineering & IT	191
Life sciences & biomedicine	127
Natural sciences	269
Social sciences	111
Academic survey position	142
Employer survey position	56
Student faculty ratio	9.9:1
International faculty	3.9%
Undergraduates	14,534
Postgraduates	7,214
International students	7.8%
Research strength (Scopus) papers	15,347
Research strength (Scopus) citations	108,311
Impact (citations per paper)	7

With unusual autonomy, a campus so beautiful it's a UNESCO world heritage site, and a pedigree that includes three US presidents as founders and early leaders, the University of Virginia (UVA) is the most prestigious public university in America. It is considered among the 'public ivies', a comparison with the most elite private universities, but with a considerably lower tuition price that attracts Ivy League-quality students. UVA is in Charlottesville, one of America's best university towns and ranked among the most livable cities in the country. Former US president Thomas Jefferson founded the university, calling it 'the hobby of my old age.' Jefferson personally designed the campus.' The Grounds' are laid out around a rotunda modeled on the Pantheon in Rome flanked by red-brick columned 'pavilions', with classrooms and living quarters for faculty members, many recruited from top schools in Europe, all surrounding a rolling green lawn. Jefferson, a secularist, rejected the sectarian nature of universities at the time, banning the teaching of theology and making Virginia the first to teach such disciplines as philosophy, astronomy, botany, and political science. Its school of engineering and applied science was America's first university-affiliated engineering school. The university has been best known for teaching the humanities, although it has a well-regarded medical school and hospital system. UVA, is trying to boost science and engineering by raising US$3 billion by 2011, nearly a third of it for laboratories and other science, engineering, and medical research facilities. Like almost all American states, Virginia has steadily reduced financial support for its flagship university; taxpayers now underwrite barely eight per cent of the university's budget, an unusually low proportion. But in relying more on private than public funding, UVA has also demanded, and received, an extraordinary amount of autonomy, calling itself a 'privately financed public university', that can determine its own fate rather than being hemmed in by political considerations.

The university's alumni have included Javier Solano, former US ambassador to the UK William Farish, ex CEOs of AT&T, Yahoo, MasterCard, Marriott, and Pepsi, and Walter Reed, who discovered a vaccine for yellow fever. Robert F and Edward Kennedy went to law school here. Former president Woodrow Wilson attended, but did not graduate.

Iberedem Ekure, a third-year electrical engineering student from Nigeria, chose UVA because of its high ranking. "I already had a relative at the school and UVA looked beautiful in pictures (as it is in reality). I am completely satisfied with my choice as I have been able to explore so many avenues I never even thought of, learning a great amount along the way."

97 (77=) University of Pittsburgh
Founded 1787   www.pitt.edu

Arts & humanities 87
Engineering & IT.. 194
Life sciences & biomedicine 126
Social sciences 211

Academic survey position 169
Employer survey position 317

Student faculty ratio 6:1
International faculty 10.9%
Undergraduates 16,177
Postgraduates 7,822
International students 7.0%

Research strength (Scopus) papers.................. 23,406
Research strength (Scopus) citations 187,180
Impact (citations per paper)..................................... 8

One of America's oldest universities, the University of Pittsburgh was founded in 1787 in a log cabin on, what was then, the American frontier, well before many white people lived that far west. Since then, the university has continued pushing boundaries. The polio vaccine was developed there. A 'Pitt' researcher was the first to identify the chemical structure of Vitamin C. It was at Pitt that the world's first double-transplant operation was performed. The university is still at the cutting edge: it operates one of the fastest non-military supercomputers in the world, for example. The number of applicants for places has doubled since the millennium, sending the quality of incoming freshmen soaring. A US$500 million fund-raising campaign has proved so successful that administrators doubled the goal to US$1 billion and then doubled it again to add faculty and increase student financial aid, among other things. The university has vastly expanded its campus, including a new state-of-the-art stadium it shares with the Pittsburgh Steelers professional football team. It has spent US$19 million on the local Palace Inn Hotel, where it plans to build a new hospital on the 16-acre site.

Pitt was quick to carve out a particular niche for itself after the September 11, 2001 terrorist attacks by making global security a research priority, concentrating research on its Center for National Preparedness and Matthew B Ridgway Center for International Security, named after a Korean War-era American general. Faculty and students specializing in public and international affairs, public health, law, medicine, and information sciences are researching such topics as bioterrorism and cyber security. Pitt lured the Center for Biosecurity away from Johns Hopkins University to be part of this effort. And researchers are already developing a system to provide quick detection of disease outbreaks by sounding an alert when there are spikes in hospital emergency visits related to a specific complaint. Pitt's international students come mainly from China, India, South Korea, Taiwan, and Turkey. The university offers an unusual 'Certificate in Global Studies' for students who can select from concentrations including global health, international conflict and conflict resolution, and sustainable development.

Alumni include Gene Kelly, authors John Irving and August Wilson, Jaguar Cars Managing Director Bibiana Boerio, and Orient Overseas Container Line founder and owner Dong Haoyun.

Justin Chalker, a graduate who went on to Oxford to study organic chemistry on a Rhodes scholarship, chose Pitt because, he said, "they give you the freedom to pursue any interest you might have. If you're a motivated undergraduate, you're treated like a graduate student. Yet while I was focused on science for my degree, I was also able to take a lot of excellent liberal arts courses."

98 (117=) University of California, Santa Barbara
Founded 1909   www.ucsb.edu

Arts & humanities	169
Engineering & IT	62
Life sciences & biomedicine	79
Natural sciences	24
Social sciences	152
Academic survey position	61
Employer survey position	260
Student faculty ratio	21.5:1
International faculty	10.0%
Undergraduates	18,112
Postgraduates	2,906
International students	3.6%
Research strength (Scopus) papers	11,227
Research strength (Scopus) citations	80,042
Impact (citations per paper)	7

Based on cliffs overlooking the Pacific Ocean, the University of California, Santa Barbara (UCSB) is one of few universities in the US with its own beach. The campus, bordered on three sides by the Pacific Ocean, has miles of coastline as well as its own man-made lagoon. There are numerous walking and cycle paths across campus, around the lagoon and along the beach. Founded as an independent teachers' college, UCSB is the fourth-oldest general education campus in the California system. It has become an internationally renowned centre for teaching and research, distinguished for its interdisciplinary programs. Undergraduate majors and graduate programs are organized through three colleges: Letters and Science, Engineering, and Creative Studies. The College of Creative Studies offers students an alternative approach to education by allowing them to pursue advanced, independent work in the arts, mathematics, and sciences. The university is also home to the graduate school of education and the Bren school of environmental science and management.

UCSB is an international multicultural community. One in six graduate students is from abroad and there are more than 700 visiting international scholars each year. Santa Barbara also has a reputation for political activism, which dates back to anti-Vietnam War protests in the late 1960s and early 1970s. UCSB is home to 11 national centres and institutes, including eight that are sponsored by the National Science Foundation. Many of the older campus buildings are being replaced with newer, more modern facilities.The newly constructed Donald Bren Hall has been named the 'greenest' building in California and the second greenest building in the US. Research support from external sources has been breaking all records, growing by 22 per cent over the past two years.

Famous UCSB alumni include actors Michael Douglas, Barbara Rush and Benjamin Bratt, Giondomenico Picco, assistant secretary general of the United Nations, Prince Faisal Fahad of Saudi Arabia, Bob Ballard, chief scientist on the team that discovered the Titanic, and sculptor Richard Serra. UCSB has also had five Nobel prize winners: Finn E Kydland, (economics 2004), David J Gross, (physics 2004), Alan J Heeger, (chemistry 2000), Herbert Kroemer, (physics 2000), and Walter Kohn, (chemistry 1998).

Jing Sun, from Beijing, chose UCSB for her PhD in education for its academic reputation and the prospect of more financial assistance than she would receive at a private university. She has been satisfied on both counts. "In addition, UCSB has the most beautiful campus I've ever seen," she said. "It is a great school to pursue your study and Santa Barbara is a great place to live as well."

99= (77=) Purdue University
Founded 1869 **www.purdue.edu**

Arts & humanities	211
Engineering & IT	33
Life sciences & biomedicine	69
Natural sciences	67
Social sciences	140
Academic survey position	75
Employer survey position	107
Student faculty ratio	15.1:1
International faculty	17.5%
Undergraduates	31,002
Postgraduates	6,549
International students	12.5%
Research strength (Scopus) papers	18,493
Research strength (Scopus) citations	78,828
Impact (citations per paper)	4

In late 2001, when other US universities were reining in spending and enrolments, in the slowdown that followed the terrorist attacks of that year, Purdue made a strategic decision to do the opposite. The campus of the midwestern school, about an hour from Indianapolis and two hours from Chicago, so vast it has two golf courses and one of America's only university-owned airports, erupted in a flurry of new construction. Purdue went on an US$800 million building spree, adding, among other things, a bioscience centre and a nanotechnology centre that was recognized as one of the nation's best almost as soon as it opened. A US$126 million interdisciplinary research area called Discovery Park was established and Purdue hired 300 new faculty in five years, many of them women and minorities. Faculty salaries were raised, class sizes lowered, and the proportion of classes taught by faculty rather than by graduate teaching assistants was increased. The university still plans to increase graduate enrolment and graduate assistant stipends.

Purdue's College of Technology is the largest producer of engineering technology undergraduate degrees among US public institutions. Its divisions of industrial, nuclear, and aeronautical and astronautical engineering are particularly highly ranked. Its analytical chemistry, hospitality and tourism, and undergraduate landscape and architecture design programs are also at the top of their fields. In collaboration with Indianapolis universities, Purdue is creating the Indiana Consortium for Research in Energy Systems and Policy. Purdue was the first university in the US to establish a department of computer science, in 1962. Under its Engineering Projects in Community Service program, undergraduates use engineering and technology to solve problems for community service and educational organizations. And the university's Online Writing Lab (**owl.english.purdue.edu**) answers grammar and punctuation problems for more than 20 million users annually.

Purdue has turned out 22 American astronauts including Neil Armstrong, the first man to walk on the moon, and Gene Cernan, the last, more than any non-military US institution apart from MIT.

Himabindu Pucha had some apprehension about going to school in West Lafayette, Indiana: "the location does work against it, but you can't have it all," she said. She is now a doctoral student and has done a research internship at Intel, as well as being named one of 19 recipients of a US$10,000 national award recognizing outstanding women in engineering. Purdue leads the nation in the number of women engineering graduates. "I was a little bit scared about the social environment," she said. "I didn't know how I would fit in. But Purdue has so many grad students and they come from so many places that I feel perfectly comfortable here."

99= (88=) University of Southampton
Founded 1862   www.soton.ac.uk

Arts & humanities	229
Engineering & IT	96
Life sciences & biomedicine	190
Natural sciences	160
Social sciences	229
Academic survey position	166
Employer survey position	65
Student faculty ratio	9.9:1
International faculty	29.6%
Undergraduates	14,873
Postgraduates	6,599
International students	19.7%
Research strength (Scopus) papers	12,892
Research strength (Scopus) citations	70,388
Impact (citations per paper)	5

Having expanded considerably in recent years, Southampton University has been trying to capitalize on its status as one of the world's top 100. Its website has an introduction to the university in 21 languages and it has students of more than 100 nationalities. A member of the Russell Group of leading UK research universities, Southampton also belongs to the Worldwide Universities Network of 16 research-led institutions in Europe, North America, Australia and China. The proportion of income derived from research at Southampton is among the highest in Britain. Southampton is a pleasant, if architecturally undistinguished city, on the south coast of England, little more than an hour's travelling time from London. The university's location has also encouraged strong links with Europe. The main Highfield campus, in a leafy location two miles from the city centre, has been the focus of recent development. A Centre for Banking, Finance and Sustainable Development opened in 2008 and a new student services centre provides learning support and other advisory facilities, backed up on line for students in other areas of the university. The Waterside Campus, in the city's dock area, houses the National Oceanography Centre, a £49 million joint project with the Natural Environment Research Council, considered Europe's finest. Art courses are based in Winchester, 12 miles north of Southampton. Social and sports facilities have recently been expanded and upgraded, with the addition of an indoor sports complex and swimming pool. International students are guaranteed a place in the university's residential accommodation.

John Denham, the UK's first Secretary of State for Innovation, Universities and Skills, was president of the students' union. Lord Plant of Highfield was Professor of European Political Thought before becoming Master of St Catherine's College, Oxford. Singer/songwriter Brian Eno studied art at Winchester.

Jose Beltran, a Mexican postgraduate studying environmental management and modelling, said: "This is my first experience overseas, and I'm glad that I came to Southampton. I find it has better weather than I expected and the university has a friendly and secure environment, with staff willing to help you, an excellent academic level, and approachable professors. In the masters course on which I am enrolled, I have the opportunity to live with 27 students from all over the world, and I mean 'to live with' because we live in the student halls, sharing the same building and even the kitchen in small groups of seven people. This unique experience creates the opportunity to learn beyond the lectures, to appreciate different cultures and to build friendships for the future."

Our students come from over 120 different countries. And go on to do a million different things.

Griffith University is one of Australia's most prestigious universities.

During the past 33 years, more than 100,000 graduates from over 120 countries have passed through our doors.

Spread over five campuses located in the Brisbane and Gold Coast region in Queensland, Griffith is highly regarded by overseas students thanks to its exceptional teaching staff and challenging academic programs.

Griffith students are perfectly placed to make the most of everything Australia has to offer academically, culturally and geographically.

Find out what Griffith could do for you, visit www.griffith.edu.au

QUEENSLAND
Brisbane
Gold Coast

Sydney

GRIFFITH UNIVERSITY

Gold Coast - Logan - Mt Gravatt - Nathan - South Bank

CRICOS 00233E GRI0622

2

What subject, what program?

This chapter helps you to identify and understand the subjects to study and is packed with fresh ideas about different disciplines and the career directions they can take you in. The following pages include worldwide rankings according to the THE-QS World University Rankings 2008 of the 100 best institutions in the five major academic areas: social sciences, arts and humanities, science, biomedicine and technology. (All charts are copyright: QS Quacquarelli Symonds 2009.)

Social sciences	139
Arts and humanities	145
Science	151
Biomedicine	156
Technology	161

People don't just go to university. They go to study dentistry, forestry or history; electronics, astronomy or art. Finding the right program is vital to the enjoyment of your university experience and future career. You may know which of these subjects is for you. If so, this chapter will help you to think where you might study it. If you don't know what you want to study, you might find some ideas here. Either way, you will need to seek detailed advice on specific disciplines and universities and how subjects are taught at different institutions. Teaching methods and class sizes can vary greatly in all subjects.

You will need to look at the other chapters of this book for more on important issues such as how to finance your studies and the realities of study abroad. University prospectuses and websites are the right place to find detailed subject-specific information. A searchable course listing for every university featured in this chapter is available on **www.topuniversities.com**. You should also consult other specialist sources such as subject associations, professional societies and research institute websites to get a fuller picture. Remember, it is often not easy to find the right subject to study. Even if you are already at university, it can be possible to change direction. Don't hesitate to approach your university to find out what options are available.

Studying the social sciences

If you are a prospective undergraduate, there are two sorts of social science to think about. One includes the subjects you encountered at school, such as sociology, economics and education. The other encompasses all those the teachers never told you about, such as science policy and population studies. While the arts and humanities are mainly about individual achievement, the social sciences are about group behaviour. They answer questions such as why people decide to commit crime, or whether higher taxes make people work harder or work less hard. This means that the social sciences are needed if we are to understand the rapid social change that characterizes modern societies. The obvious example is climate change. If we are going to do something about it, we will need engineers to produce new types of cars, power stations and the rest. But much of the technology we need to cut energy use already exists. Social science can tell us why householders do not insulate their homes, and help develop the marketing messages that might help persuade them to do so.

While every society is distinctive, the social sciences are becoming more globalized as they adopt similar methodologies. In recent years, the European Social Survey has been set up to gather consistent data on 28 European countries. Because they answer important questions about society, the social sciences are the avenue to many interesting and rewarding jobs and careers. In recent years, the 'big' rewards have been in MBAs and other business degrees. Now, employers in the public and non-profit sectors also value them, as well as business. If your ambitions lie in this direction, it is worth thinking whether you need a business qualification from an institution of recognized world standing, or one that will cost a lot less and fit better with a local employer. QS, has a wealth of valuable information on MBAs at **www.topmba.com**. Bear in mind that many business courses are taught in specialist graduate institutions, so some of the places you might want to consider do not appear in the subject rankings in this chapter, which are intended to measure the performance of large, general universities.

As well as business behaviour, the social sciences also analyze the performance of societies as a whole, and include politics and government. These are obvious subjects, along with law, for anyone planning a career as a politician. But they are also of value if you plan on a less visible career in public service. A qualification in government could just give you the extra wisdom you need to propel yourself into the higher ranks of the public sector instead of spending decades at a lower level. Economics is perhaps the ultimate career-propelling social science, and is also one of the oldest. Economics is the course of choice for leading lights such as journalists, politicians and top civil servants. In a less visible way, most big companies, even those far from the financial sector, employ economists, who are often powerful in strategy formation.

The social sciences fascinate students, academics and policymakers alike because, at their best, they produce evidence-based truths about society and how to change it. But this means that these are difficult subjects. To tackle many of them properly you will need to know about statistics, research design and the like, as well as the subject matter you are studying. A high level of confidence with mathematics will be essential. You could do this from first degree level, but many specific social science topics such as medical sociology, population studies or technology policy are taught mainly as postgraduate subjects. Many social science courses have demanding entry qualifications. Top students are willing to pay big fees and travel long distances to get to the right institutions, such as the Harvard Kennedy School of Government (HKS) or London School of Economics (LSE).

Our table of the top social science institutions worldwide shows that there is room at the top. Harvard is regarded as best in the world by some distance. After all, it has the world's most prestigious business school, as well as HKS. Its west coast rival Berkeley is some way behind, and after Berkeley there is a big gap before Stanford, LSE and other major UK and

US universities. This represents the biggest lead held by Harvard in any of the discipline areas. Note, too, that despite the parade of big, old, English-language universities that dominate this table, Denmark, China, Japan, South Korea and others have institutions, which peer reviewers think are producing worthwhile scholarship. Many nations have a capital city university which either, like Tokyo, supplies government with its top thinkers, or which houses the nation's main policy-producing think-tank.

Finally, teacher training is the original business of many of the world's universities and education is still the biggest department in many universities, at least in terms of student numbers. On that measure, it is certainly the biggest social science. While many students cross borders to study education, it is worth making sure that the course you plan to take will be accepted by the education ministry back home as a valid qualification. Some countries insist that secondary school teachers have a first degree followed by specialist training; others do not. Despite research evidence that primary and preschool education are the key to life achievement, the qualifications expected for teachers of younger children are lower in many parts of the world. It is often said that some people know from an early age that they want to be teachers, while others, know from an equally early age that they do not. In between is a group who may consider the idea. If you are one such, the current economic climate may help your decision. Teachers are one group you never see mentioned in news stories about job cuts.

Top 100 in social sciences

Rank	Institution	Country	Score	Citations per paper
1	HARVARD University	US	100.0	4.6
2	University of California, BERKELEY	US	91.6	3.4
3	STANFORD University	US	82.6	4.9
4	London School of Economics and Political Science (LSE)	UK	82.1	2.6
5	University of CAMBRIDGE	UK	81.8	3.1
6	University of OXFORD	UK	80.8	3.4
7	YALE University	US	80.5	4.3
8	University of CHICAGO	US	79.2	4.0
9	PRINCETON University	US	76.8	4.9
10	MASSACHUSETTS Institute of Technology (MIT)	US	76.1	4.5
11	COLUMBIA University	US	75.2	4.3
12	University of BRITISH COLUMBIA	CA	72.0	3.4
13	University of CALIFORNIA, Los Angeles (UCLA)	US	71.5	4.7
14=	AUSTRALIAN National University	AU	71.4	2.4
14=	McGILL University	CA	71.4	3.5
16	University of TORONTO	CA	71.0	3.5
17	CORNELL University	US	64.6	3.5
18	National University of SINGAPORE	SG	61.9	2.4
19	University of MELBOURNE	AU	61.7	2.6
20	University of MICHIGAN	US	60.9	4.2
21	University of TOKYO	JP	59.9	1.8
22	University of PENNSYLVANIA	US	58.4	4.2
23	NEW YORK University (NYU)	US	58.2	3.8

Rank	Institution	Country	Score	Citations per paper
24	PEKING University	CN	57.8	2.2
25	MONASH University	AU	57.6	2.0
26	DUKE University	US	53.2	5.1
27	University of SYDNEY	AU	51.4	2.3
28	University of NEW SOUTH WALES	AU	50.9	3.0
29	NORTHWESTERN University	US	50.6	3.6
30	University of AUCKLAND	NZ	49.7	2.5
31=	University of COPENHAGEN	DK	48.8	2.6
31=	UCL (University College London)	UK	48.8	4.1
33	SEOUL National University	KR	47.9	2.5
34	University of HONG KONG	HK	47.5	2.3
35=	CARNEGIE MELLON University	US	47.2	4.8
35=	University of WARWICK	UK	47.2	2.7
37	Université Catholique de LOUVAIN (UCL)	BE	46.2	2.7
38	University of CALIFORNIA, San Diego	US	45.9	5.1
39	University of QUEENSLAND	AU	45.7	2.8
40	University of WISCONSIN-Madison	US	45.4	3.9
41	JOHNS HOPKINS University	US	45.1	4.3
42	KYOTO University	JP	44.8	1.8
43	University of AMSTERDAM	NL	44.7	3.6
44	TSINGHUA University	CN	44.1	1.5
45	Katholieke Universiteit LEUVEN	BE	43.7	3.0
46	BOSTON University	US	43.5	4.0
47	GEORGETOWN University	US	42.9	2.4
48	KING'S College London	UK	42.4	5.7
49	Hebrew University of JERUSALEM	IR	42.3	2.4
50	MAASTRICHT University	NL	42.2	3.7
51=	FUDAN University	CN	41.7	1.7
51=	ERASMUS University Rotterdam	NL	41.7	3.2
53	YORK University	CA	41.6	2.4
54=	University of VIENNA	AT	41.0	2.9
54=	University of EDINBURGH	UK	41.0	3.3
56=	TEL AVIV University	IR	40.9	2.9
56=	QUEEN'S University	CA	40.9	2.7
58	LEIDEN University	NL	40.8	3.4
59=	University of ILLINOIS	US	40.7	3.3
59=	TRINITY College Dublin	IE	40.7	2.1
61	University of WESTERN ONTARIO	CA	40.6	3.2
62=	Freie Universität BERLIN	DE	40.1	2.9
62=	STOCKHOLM School of Economics	SE	40.1	3.6

Top 100 in social sciences continued

Rank	Institution	Country	Score	Citations per paper
64	SIMON FRASER University	CA	40.0	2.4
65	BROWN University	US	39.5	4.5
66=	CHINESE University of Hong Kong	HK	39.3	2.4
66=	University of MANCHESTER	UK	39.3	3.3
68	University of HELSINKI	FI	38.8	3.4
69	HONG KONG University of Science & Technology	HK	38.6	3.4
70	Université de MONTRÉAL	CA	38.5	3.0
71	University of MINNESOTA	US	38.1	3.8
72	CHULALONGKORN University	TH	37.8	1.8
73	PENNSYLVANIA STATE University	US	37.7	2.9
74	National TAIWAN University	TW	37.6	1.9
75=	University College DUBLIN	IE	37.5	1.6
75=	Università Commerciale Luigi BOCCONI	IT	37.5	2.7
77	LUND University	SE	37.4	2.4
78=	CALIFORNIA Institute of Technology (Caltech)	US	37.0	3.4
78=	Université Paris Sorbonne (PARIS IV)	FR	37.0	0.6
80	UPPSALA University	SE	36.9	3.2
81	Universitat POMPEU FABRA	ES	36.6	2.6
82	University of DELHI	IN	36.5	1.5
83=	WASEDA University	JP	36.4	1.2
83=	University of TOULOUSE I - Sciences Sociales	FR	36.4	1.7
85	IMPERIAL College London	UK	36.2	3.6
86=	University of TEXAS at Austin	US	36.1	3.5
86=	OHIO STATE University	US	36.1	3.4
86=	Université PARIS I Panthéon Sorbonne	FR	36.1	1.2
89	NANYANG Technological University	SG	35.9	1.7
90	University of BOLOGNA	IT	35.8	2.3
91=	UTRECHT University	NL	35.7	3.8
91=	HUMBOLDT-Universität zu Berlin	DE	35.7	2.4
91=	JAWAHARLAL NEHRU University	IN	35.7	0.8
94=	McMASTER University	CA	35.1	3.6
94=	University of AARHUS	DK	35.1	2.7
96	Universidad Autónoma de BARCELONA	ES	34.8	2.0
97	University of LANCASTER	UK	34.4	3.2
98	University of OTAGO	NZ	34.3	3.1
99	Ludwig-Maximilians-Universität MÜNCHEN (LMU)	DE	33.6	3.1
100	VICTORIA University of Wellington	NZ	33.2	2.0

 university

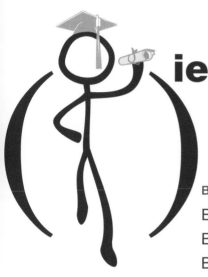 ie

Maximize your
future potential.

BACHELOR DEGREES (Taught in English or Spanish)

Bachelor in Architecture

Bachelor in Communication

Bachelor in Business Administration (BBA)

Bachelor in Tourism Management*

Bachelor of Laws (LLB)

Bachelor in Art History

Bachelor in Biology

Bachelor in Psychology

*Only offered in English

IE University extends the IE Business School education model to its Bachelor degrees. With us you will discover a completely different way of learning. International and contemporary, **where business management, technology and humanities are integrated** into a curriculum that combines practical training, both in the classroom and online.

IE University offers scholarship programs for all of its degrees.

Learn more at an upcoming events in your city.

University · Campus de Santa Cruz La Real · Cardenal Zúñiga, 12 · 40003 Segovia. Spain · T. +34 921 412 410 · **e-mail: university@ie.edu**

www.ie.edu/university

Studying the arts and humanities

If you have opened this book, you may be contemplating crossing an ocean, or at least an international frontier, to further your higher education. If your aim is an MBA, or a PhD in some high-tech discipline, you may well be aiming for an institution with international standing where you will get an education whose quality is recognized around the world. If you study engineering at MIT, you will end up with a qualification whose worth is understood across the planet. Things are not quite the same in the arts and humanities. A discovery in chemistry, which is made in France, is also a discovery for chemists in Brazil. The same is true in medicine, and even to some extent in economics and other social sciences. But despite everything we know about globalization, each nation has its own culture, and that means that the arts and humanities are not global in the sense of the other subjects we look at in these pages.

It can also be a little tricky to define the arts and humanities. We probably know what the arts are. They range from visual art to theatre, music of all types, film and TV. The humanities are harder to nail down. But they certainly include languages, history, archaeology (even though many archaeologists work more or less like scientists), literature, theology and many other big subjects. Some topics such as law and anthropology may be counted as social sciences in some countries and as humanities in others. In the past, it might have been forgivable to regard the arts and humanities as a sort of social luxury. Real economic activity was about hitting pieces of metal with hammers, and the arts were something that society, or rich patrons, paid for from the profits. But take the UK today, for example, where only about 13 per cent of the economy is accounted for by manufacturing. Other industries are bigger, including finance, public services, and the arts. Publishing, the TV and theatre create jobs. And think of the last time you went to the cinema. You almost certainly left before the credits had finished rolling, because of the sheer number of people it takes to make a movie.

The table of the top arts and humanities universities worldwide does not include citations data, because many academics in these areas do not publish journal articles in the same way as their colleagues in other disciplines. But the peer review data shows that big, old institutions in the English-speaking world have the most academic prestige. Peking University, in 23rd place, is the first on the list not to work wholly, or mainly, in English. It is followed by leading German and French institutions, with the University of Tokyo not far behind. The reason for this dominance by English-speaking institutions seems to be that academics around the world feel the need to know what is happening in English-based culture. Russian scholars may argue that Tolstoy gave as much as Shakespeare to the world of literature, but they are in a minority. Most arts academics know what is going on in English and in their own culture, unless they are English-based. So there are always going to be more people who know about English culture than Italian or French, however mighty the artistic achievements of these nations. And to study these languages and cultures, you need to go to the places where they are spoken and lived.

While much of the world's higher education is going over to English language provision, language learning must, by definition, be an exception. The same applies to history. Here there are two issues: one is that the key documents may well not be in English, and the other is that, despite immense progress in recent years, they may not be fully available online. Often the historian must make his or her way to a former colonial power to investigate today's developing world. To see the grand record of Spain's involvement in Latin America, the Archive of the Americas, you must go to Seville in Spain. And to read the equivalent record of British involvement in India, you must head for London, where the British Library has now absorbed the papers of the Raj and its predecessor, the East India Company. It encompasses millions of documents in English and many other languages.

The arts and humanities also embrace a vast range of more practical courses, which lead to a complete range of careers. Some, such as librarianship, are studied by tens of thousands of people around the world each year and lead to solid, if not spectacularly rewarded, jobs: a good option if you want a professional challenge that comes with above average job security. Today's librarians love books, but their jobs now tend to involve providing information in the form of digital media to professionals in universities, companies, government departments and other corners of the knowledge economy. Applicants for librarianship courses often have language and literature qualifications, and take a one-year masters course.

If you have the artistic temperament, but also like the idea of a profession, there is architecture. Perhaps the most prestigious humanities topic, with a real mission to meet the human need for shelter. In any country in the world, architecture courses are highly sought-after. They have high fees, they take a long time, and they involve a lot of learning about materials, structures and other aspects of engineering, as well as an artistic imagination. Those architects who achieve high recognition can become strikingly well paid, but not all corners of the arts and humanities produce wealth for their practitioners.

The overall lesson is, that as well as a massive set of subjects, the arts and humanities encompass a great variety of career options. Many arts academics perform, maybe in music or the theatre, as well as teaching and doing research. Some such lives as a professional in the arts and humanities may be less financially rewarding than other options discussed in these pages. Many musicians and linguists have portfolio careers in which they combine teaching and practice. However, research on musicians' plural careers, carried out at the Institute of Education in London, shows that they are often exceptionally satisfying.

Top 100 in the arts and humanities

Rank	Institution	Country	Score
1	HARVARD University	US	100.0
2	University of California, BERKELEY	US	93.1
3	University of OXFORD	UK	91.3
4	University of CAMBRIDGE	UK	89.1
5	YALE University	US	86.2
6	PRINCETON University	US	81.8
7	COLUMBIA University	US	81.7
8	STANFORD University	US	80.3
9	University of CHICAGO	US	79.3
10	University of CALIFORNIA, Los Angeles (UCLA)	US	77.3
11	University of TORONTO	CA	74.3
12	AUSTRALIAN National University	AU	74.0
13	McGILL University	CA	70.8
14	CORNELL University	US	67.2
15	NEW YORK University (NYU)	US	64.2
16	University of MELBOURNE	AU	62.8
17	University of SYDNEY	AU	62.6
18	University of BRITISH COLUMBIA	CA	61.9
19	University of MICHIGAN	US	61.5
20	MASSACHUSETTS Institute of Technology (MIT)	US	60.5

Rank	Institution	Country	Score
21	DUKE University	US	58.4
22	JOHNS HOPKINS University	US	57.1
23	PEKING University	CN	56.4
24	Freie Universität BERLIN	DE	55.2
25	Université Paris Sorbonne (PARIS IV)	FR	55.0
26	University of EDINBURGH	UK	54.8
27	BROWN University	US	54.3
28	University of TOKYO	JP	54.1
29	UCL (University College London)	UK	53.6
30	National University of SINGAPORE	SG	53.1
31	London School of Economics and Political Science (LSE)	UK	52.9
32	TRINITY College Dublin	IE	52.8
33	MONASH University	AU	52.5
34	École Normale Supérieure, PARIS	FR	51.3
35	LEIDEN University	NL	51.0
36	University of AMSTERDAM	NL	50.7
37	KYOTO University	JP	50.4
38	KING'S College London	UK	50.1
39	University of AUCKLAND	NZ	49.7
40	University of PENNSYLVANIA	US	49.4
41	Hebrew University of JERUSALEM	IR	48.1
42	Katholieke Universiteit LEUVEN	BE	47.8
43	RUTGERS, The State University of New Jersey	US	47.4
44	University of VIENNA	AU	47.1
45	University of TEXAS at Austin	US	46.3
46	University of HONG KONG	HK	45.7
47	UPPSALA University	SE	45.6
48	HEIDELBERG Universität	DE	45.4
49	BOSTON University	US	45.2
50	HUMBOLDT-Universität zu Berlin	DE	44.9
51	University of NEW SOUTH WALES	AU	44.7
52	University of HELSINKI	FI	44.4
53	INDIANA University Bloomington	US	44.2
54	Università degli Studi di ROMA - La Sapienza	IT	43.9
55	University of BOLOGNA	IT	43.8
56=	University of WISCONSIN-Madison	US	42.5
56=	WASEDA University	JP	42.5
58	University of COPENHAGEN	DK	42.4
59	Université de MONTRÉAL	CA	42.3
60=	Ludwig-Maximilians-Universität MÜNCHEN (LMU)	DE	42.1
60=	Université Catholique de LOUVAIN (UCL)	BE	42.1

Top 100 in the arts and humanities continued

Rank	Institution	Country	Score
60=	School of Oriental and African Studies, University of LONDON	UK	42.1
63	GEORGETOWN University	US	41.4
64	MACQUARIE University	AU	41.0
65	UTRECHT University	NL	40.9
66	University of MANCHESTER	UK	40.7
67	University of QUEENSLAND	AU	40.4
68	Université PARIS I Panthéon Sorbonne	FR	40.0
69	Universität FREIBURG	DE	39.2
70	YORK University	CA	39.0
71	University of ST ANDREWS	UK	38.8
72	Eberhard Karls Universität TÜBINGEN	DE	38.7
73	University College DUBLIN	IE	38.6
74	City University of NEW YORK	US	38.5
75	University of WARWICK	UK	38.4
76	SEOUL National University	KR	38.1
77	University of LEEDS	UK	37.6
78	University Complutense MADRID	ES	37.4
79	Ateneo de MANILA University	PH	37.3
80	TEL AVIV University	IR	37.1
81	University of OTAGO	NZ	36.8
82=	University of NOTRE DAME	US	36.6
82=	University of the PHILIPPINES	PH	36.6
84	University of CALIFORNIA, Irvine	US	36.4
85	TSINGHUA University	CN	36.0
86	LA TROBE University	AU	35.9
87	University of PITTSBURGH	US	35.7
88	University of ALBERTA	CA	35.5
89	FUDAN University	CN	35.4
90	University of BRISTOL	UK	35.3
91=	STONY BROOK University	US	35.1
91=	University of BASEL	CH	35.1
93	University of CALIFORNIA, San Diego	US	35.0
94	University of BARCELONA	ES	34.6
95	Universität GÖTTINGEN	DE	34.5
96	LUND University	SE	34.4
97=	University of GENEVA	CH	33.9
97=	Universidad Nacional Autónoma de México (UNAM)	MX	33.9
97=	VICTORIA University of Wellington	NZ	33.9
100	University of AARHUS	DK	33.8

Best
of both worlds

Trinity College is the only Irish university to rank in the top 100 world universities (49th) and amongst the top 50 European universities (13th) by the Times Higher Education - QS World University Rankings. Our excellent reputation for teaching and research of the highest quality puts the university at the forefront of higher education in Ireland and internationally.

With our atmospheric leafy quads, traditional cobbled squares and legendary libraries – including the Long Room containing the Book of Kells – it is the archetypal seat of learning.

Trinity is at the cutting edge of research, technology and innovation with our exciting new state-of-the–art nanoscience complex and Science Gallery. We also have an excellent new sports complex and an unrivalled position right in the heart of Ireland's vibrant capital city. When you are not studying, the social scene on and off campus is great.

So why not enjoy the best of both worlds at Trinity College Dublin?

To find out more please contact The International Office at: international@tcd.ie or checkout our website: www.tcd.ie/International

University of Dublin
Trinity College Dublin

أونيۏرسيتي تيکنولوݢي مارا
UNIVERSITI TEKNOLOGI MARA

Premier University of Choice in Malaysia

With 12 state campuses, 9 city campuses and 3 satellite campuses UiTM is Malaysia's largest University.

FACULTIES

SCIENCE & TECHNOLOGY :
- Faculty of Applied Sciences
- Faculty of Information Technology and Quantitative Sciences
- Faculty of Architecture, Planning and Surveying
- Faculty of Sports Science and Recreation
- Faculty of Health Sciences
- Faculty of Medicine
- Faculty of Pharmacy
- Faculty of Dentistry
- Faculty of Civil Engineering
- Faculty of Electrical Engineering
- Faculty of Mechanical Engineering
- Faculty of Chemical Engineering

SOCIAL SCIENCE & HUMANITIES :
- Faculty of Law
- Faculty of Administrative Science and Policy Studies
- Faculty of Communication and Media Studies
- Faculty of Art and Design
- Faculty of Music
- Faculty of Education
- Faculty of Artistic and Creative Technology

BUSINESS & MANAGEMENT :
- Faculty of Accountancy
- Faculty of Business Management
- Faculty of Hotel and Tourism Management
- Faculty of Information Management
- Faculty of Office Management and Technology

For further details on Postgraduate Programmes please visit our Institute of Graduate Studies website at www.ipsis.uitm.edu.my

ISO 9001:2000 Cert. No. KLR 0404089

www.uitm.edu.my

Studying science

According to Professor Steve Jones, a geneticist at University College London (UCL), you don't have to be especially clever to be a scientist: because science works by carrying out experiments which are designed to answer a specific question, it is a routine activity, which anyone of normal mental powers can accomplish. Despite Jones' many achievements in science, there is another view. In practice, even designing an experiment that really does answer the question you want it to, is incredibly difficult. Staying level with the subject you work in is tough, and is essential if you want to be asking the right questions in the first place. And most scientific fields are now so specialist that having big new ideas that will alter thinking in the subject is no task for simple minds. But Jones is right to point to the importance of the scientific method, which works by designing experiments to answer specific questions. It is a unique and highly productive way of working, developed during the seventeenth-century scientific revolution by Galileo and others. It has given us big ideas, such as relativity, and evolution by natural selection, and the technology that surrounds us today, from satellite television to hip transplants.

Science is now big business. The National Science Foundation in the US, one of the world's biggest science funders, spends US$6 billion a year, 20 per cent of the federal research funding going into US universities. The UK research councils are spending about £2.8 billion a year, about half on science. The European Commission's current framework program for research has a budget of more than €50 billion over seven years. This means that there are plenty of jobs for scientists, and unemployment is low. Many governments across the world recognize that qualified scientists are important to an advanced economy and put effort into getting people to study science. As a result, there may well be special scholarships or fee breaks available to study science or engineering that are not available to students in other areas.

The way into a scientific career is probably clearer than for almost any other category of employment that we discuss in this book: you have to go to university and get a science degree. Most of the subjects you can study are old-stagers in the university calendar. The big ones are chemistry, physics, mathematics and biology. But in recent years, many smaller subjects such as environmental science have grown rapidly, while options such as physics and chemistry have struggled to build numbers. Most notable has been the rise in the numbers studying forensic science, driven by the popularity of TV shows such as CSI and Silent Witness. If you really know that you want to be an astronomer or a forester, you may as well go to university and study that subject. If you change your mind later, you will still have a scientific training that will impress employers. But for most people, a broader degree that keeps options open may be the best choice. If you study chemistry for your first degree, you can always become a forensic scientist later.

Biology is one area of science where course titles have changed in response to advancing knowledge. Our awareness that life is really one big system has led to subjects such as botany or zoology becoming less common as single subjects for a whole degree. This means that you should look closely at course structures to make sure you can specialize in the area that interests you in the second or later years. Watch out for subject name changes made in the interests of course marketing: 'molecular science' is in fact chemistry: still a fascinating and vital science. Note, too, that not all sciences are taught in science departments. Materials science is a fast-changing field because of the demand for new materials for renewable energy and other emerging priorities. But, because it has grown out of metallurgy, many universities put it in the engineering faculty. Agriculture is often in a department of its own and has perhaps the most unusual intake of any university subject, being dominated by the sons, and increasingly the daughters, of the previous generation of farmers.

Science is now generating new knowledge at a massive rate. Over a million articles are published each year in scientific journals, each one, at least in theory, containing new knowledge about some aspect of the universe. This means that in the modern age, you cannot learn enough in a bachelors degree course to become a scientist. You will need a higher degree, probably a doctorate, and for three reasons: one is to learn how to generate new experimental knowledge as well as finding out what other people have discovered; the second is to position yourself in a specific research field; the third is, simply, to get a qualification that proves you are a researcher. The PhD is often compared to a driving licence that shows the world that you are a capable researcher, and this is especially true in science.

Very few scientists are unemployed anywhere in the world. Many have academic careers, which can lead them into spin-off businesses, and other lucrative options that are not open to historians and linguists. In addition, many industries employ scientists, at an early stage, to carry out research and development, but often in senior positions later in their careers. Their numerical and analytical skills mean that many also work in public service.

This ranking table shows that big general universities, such as Berkeley and Cambridge, mix with specialist institutions such as Imperial College, London and the Massachusetts and California Institutes of Technology, at the top of the league of scientific world esteem. It is true that these universities have the big budgets and the top teams. But the private sector, in particular, may be less inclined to look only at graduates from these top universities when it hires scientists than it would be in other subject areas.

Top 100 in science

Rank	Institution	Country	Score	Citations per paper
1	MASSACHUSETTS Institute of Technology (MIT)	US	100.0	8.2
2	University of California, BERKELEY	US	99.5	8.5
3	University of CAMBRIDGE	UK	98.3	6.7
4	HARVARD University	US	96.1	10.1
5	University of OXFORD	UK	92.3	6.5
6	PRINCETON University	US	91.1	10.1
7	CALIFORNIA Institute of Technology (Caltech)	US	90.7	11.7
8	STANFORD University	US	88.0	7.8
9	University of TORONTO	CA	79.2	6.3
10	University of TOKYO	JP	77.2	5.3
11	CORNELL University	US	76.8	7.0
12	University of CHICAGO	US	75.2	12.1
13	KYOTO University	JP	74.4	5.0
14	IMPERIAL College London	UK	74.3	6.2
15	ETH Zurich (Swiss Federal Institute of Technology)	CH	73.7	6.4
16	PEKING University	CN	73.0	3.8
17	YALE University	US	72.1	8.1
18	University of CALIFORNIA, Los Angeles (UCLA)	US	72.0	8.7
19	École Normale Supérieure, PARIS	FR	68.5	6.2
20	University of BRITISH COLUMBIA	CA	67.8	7.4
21	AUSTRALIAN National University	AU	66.1	5.8

Rank	Institution	Country	Score	Citations per paper
22	McGILL University	CA	63.1	4.8
23	COLUMBIA University	US	62.5	8.5
24	University of CALIFORNIA, Santa Barbara	US	61.9	7.8
25	Université Pierre-et-Marie-Curie PARIS VI	FR	60.0	5.2
26	ÉCOLE POLYTECHNIQUE	FR	59.6	5.4
27	University of MELBOURNE	AU	58.7	5.7
28	TSINGHUA University	CN	57.1	2.3
29	Lomonosov MOSCOW STATE University	RU	56.6	2.2
30	University of CALIFORNIA, San Diego	US	55.6	6.2
31=	National University of SINGAPORE	SG	55.5	4.5
31=	SEOUL National University	KR	55.5	4.1
31=	TECHNION - Israel Institute of Technology	IR	55.5	4.1
34	University of TEXAS at Austin	US	54.9	6.5
35	University of MICHIGAN	US	54.8	6.6
36	University of ILLINOIS	US	53.4	6.3
37=	UTRECHT University	NL	52.4	5.5
37=	Università degli Studi di ROMA - La Sapienza	IT	52.4	3.8
39	University of NEW SOUTH WALES	AU	50.2	4.8
40=	OSAKA University	JP	49.5	4.2
40=	Technische Universität MÜNCHEN (TUM)	DE	49.5	6.1
42	University of WATERLOO	CA	48.9	3.9
43	HEIDELBERG Universität	DE	48.3	6.5
44	University of SYDNEY	AU	48.1	4.7
45	JOHNS HOPKINS University	US	48.0	9.1
46	Korea Adv Inst of Science & Technology (KAIST)	KR	47.4	3.6
47	University of PENNSYLVANIA	US	45.9	8.6
48	Ludwig-Maximilians-Universität MÜNCHEN (LMU)	DE	45.8	6.1
49	University of Science and Technology of CHINA	CN	45.5	3.6
50	National TAIWAN University	TW	45.1	3.6
51	University of ALBERTA	CA	44.9	5.3
52	Université Paris-Sud PARIS XI	FR	44.6	5.4
53=	MONASH University	AU	44.4	4.4
53=	NEW YORK University (NYU)	US	44.4	11.0
55	University of VIENNA	AT	44.2	4.9
56	University of WISCONSIN-Madison	US	43.9	6.5
57	TOKYO Institute of Technology	JP	43.5	4.2
58	University of QUEENSLAND	AU	43.4	4.7
59=	HONG KONG University of Science & Technology	HK	43.2	4.9
59=	PENNSYLVANIA STATE University	US	43.2	6.8
61=	TEL AVIV University	IR	43.1	5.2

Top 100 in science continued

Rank	Institution	Country	Score	Citations per paper
61=	GEORGIA Institute of Technology	US	43.1	6.0
63	FUDAN University	CN	42.3	3.1
64=	UPPSALA University	SE	42.1	5.3
64=	Universität GÖTTINGEN	DE	42.1	5.1
66	TRINITY College Dublin	IE	41.8	4.6
67	PURDUE University	US	41.7	5.1
68=	LEIDEN University	NL	41.5	6.0
68=	TOHOKU University	JP	41.5	4.3
70=	Hebrew University of JERUSALEM	IE	41.2	6.2
70=	STONY BROOK University	US	41.2	7.1
72=	University of HELSINKI	FI	41.0	6.1
72=	DELFT University of Technology	NL	41.0	4.4
74	LUND University	SE	40.9	6.3
75	University of COPENHAGEN	DK	40.7	5.8
76	Ecole Polytechnique Fédérale de LAUSANNE	CH	40.6	5.2
77=	Indian Institute of Technology Bombay (IITB)	IN	40.2	3.1
77=	CHALMERS University of Technology	SE	40.2	4.7
79	DUKE University	US	39.8	6.8
80	CARNEGIE MELLON University	US	39.6	9.0
81	SAINT-PETERSBURG State University	RU	39.4	2.1
82=	University of EDINBURGH	UK	39.2	7.3
82=	McMASTER University	CA	39.2	4.8
82=	Freie Universität BERLIN	DE	39.2	5.1
85=	University of WASHINGTON	US	39.0	8.3
85=	TEXAS A&M University	US	39.0	5.3
85=	University of WARWICK	UK	39.0	4.2
88	UCL (University College London)	UK	38.9	5.5
89	University of BRISTOL	UK	38.8	6.6
90	University of BARCELONA	ES	38.4	5.3
91	Université de MONTRÉAL	CA	38.3	5.5
92	University of AARHUS	DK	38.1	6.6
93=	Katholieke Universiteit LEUVEN	BE	38.0	4.6
93=	University of SÃO PAULO	BR	38.0	3.6
95	University of CALIFORNIA, Davis	US	37.9	6.0
96=	NANJING University	CN	37.7	2.7
96=	KTH, ROYAL Institute of Technology	SE	37.7	3.8
98	BOSTON University	US	37.2	7.1
99	Technische Universität BERLIN	DE	37.1	4.7
100	RUTGERS, The State University of New Jersey	US	37.0	6.1

香港城市大學
**City University
of Hong Kong**

*A University
Beyond the City*

City University of Hong Kong is proud of its comprehensive and international involvement in teaching, research and industry linkages through exchanges of academics and students, research collaboration, joint teaching and so on. Expanding collaborative and exchange partnerships with institutions outside Hong Kong forms a key part in the University's outreach endeavour.

http://www.cityu.edu.hk/elco

Studying biomedicine

Not long ago, biology was nice and simple: if things were green and stood still, they were studied in the botany department; if they ran away, they were zoology; if they were too small to see, they were microbiology; and, if they could speak, they were raw material for the medical school. Now we know better. We are aware that we share most of our genes with our near relations, which is no surprise given that we have only been biologically separate from them for a few hundred thousand years. More interesting, perhaps, are the many ways in which our bodies develop and work that are shared with animals far removed from us in evolutionary terms, even single-celled organisms. All this means that there is no longer a subject called medicine, which exists in isolation from the rest of science. Instead, the life sciences are more of a single unit, resting on a common appreciation of DNA and protein formation as the underlying way in which life reproduces and functions.

But, medicine is still a distinct area of the life sciences, because it involves our own species. This means that if you are planning a medical career, you will need to be able to deal with people. Nor is this a simple matter of developing a reassuring bedside manner. People vary wildly in their reaction to drugs and other treatments. Many experiments prove that the reality of the placebo effect, whereby people feel better after taking pills with no active ingredients, is completely real. And the continuing popularity of homoeopathy suggests that patients can feel the benefit from liquids, which do not contain a single molecule of any pharmaceutical. More importantly, medicine is different because it is the uniquely important science of human life. Biomedicine is the term for this nexus of medicine, biology, human behaviour and other subjects. Under its umbrella come a massive range of subjects, specialisms and careers, which can involve unparalleled personal rewards and some pretty impressive financial ones as well.

Medicine itself includes a wide range of specialities. To get involved in one of them, you will need a medical degree. In many countries, you can enter university from school to take one. But in the US, and some other important nations, you need to take a degree and then enter a medical school which teaches the subject as a graduate course. People who take this route typically read some biological subject at bachelor level, but it is not strictly necessary to do so.

While there are many medical specialisms, from oncology to childcare, you will have plenty of time at medical school to work out which appeals. But do be aware that medical courses take a long time, involve huge amounts of work, and incur some of the heftiest fees in higher education. Many students end their courses with so much debt that they are tempted, like the fictional doctor in the song by satirical writer Tom Lehrer, to 'specialize in diseases of the rich.'

If the dizzy heights of being a full-scale doctor or surgeon seem a little forbidding, or the time and cost of qualifying are unfeasible, the range of other medical specialisms has been expanding in recent years. There is growing demand for nurses, physiotherapists, dieticians and other professionals who can solve real problems without resorting to full-bore medical intervention. Indeed, modern medicine is now so complex that many practitioners rarely go near a sick person. Some, such as sports medicine specialists, treat people who are by definition fit and well. Others such as histologists look at samples, not people. More interesting perhaps is the convergence of technology and medicine. We are used to the idea that chemists, pharmacologists and other types of scientist develop drugs for medical trials and eventual use. But just think how much engineering is involved in modern medicine. Major multinationals make scanners that allow us to spot problems with any part of the body from the brain to the lungs. While many people working in medical instrumentation have backgrounds in mainstream engineering, there are also specialist medical engineering courses at graduate and undergraduate level.

When technology reaches the body itself, things can get even more exciting. Remember those science fiction tales where people can regrow lost limbs or withered organs? In November 2008, something close to this happened in Spain. A woman whose windpipe had been damaged by disease, got it replaced. Instead of doing a transplant from another person, the doctors took a windpipe from a deceased donor, washed every living cell out of it, and used the inert structure to grow a new one with the woman's own cells in it, avoiding all problems of rejection. This case proves that science, engineering and surgery are now combining in new ways. In future it could be heart valves or even brain cells that are made in the same way. And the Spanish-UK team that did the work shows that this is a lively, competitive and global field

The biomedicine table shows that modern biomedicine is expensive and calls for big budgets. Harvard is at the top, because of the power, wealth and status of Harvard Medical School; the next places are taken by British and other North American universities. Some, such as Caltech, have medical research but no medical school. Notable here, too, is the Karolinska Institute in Sweden, a first-class institution that also runs the Nobel prize for medicine. Another interesting entry at 17 is the National University of Singapore. The Singapore government has made biomedicine a key part of its innovation strategy. But note, too, that many major medical breakthroughs are not made at universities. The 2008 Nobel prize for medicine was given to three people who work in free-standing research institutions. In addition, the THE-QS World University Rankings only cover institutions which teach undergraduates, so the ranking does not list (say) Rockefeller University in New York, or other exclusively postgraduate institutions. As ever, you will need to use these tables as a starting point and then research further.

Top 100 in biomedicine

Rank	Institution	Country	Score	Citations per paper
1	HARVARD University	US	100.0	12.5
2	University of CAMBRIDGE	UK	87.1	10.4
3	JOHNS HOPKINS University	US	84.7	10.2
4	University of California, BERKELEY	US	83.7	10.4
5	University of OXFORD	UK	81.4	10.3
6	STANFORD University	US	80.3	11.4
7	YALE University	US	76.4	10.2
8	MASSACHUSETTS Institute of Technology (MIT)	US	75.7	14.3
9	University of CALIFORNIA, San Diego	US	69.4	11.2
10	McGILL University	CA	68.0	8.2
11=	IMPERIAL College London	UK	65.4	8.9
11=	University of CALIFORNIA, Los Angeles (UCLA)	US	65.4	9.8
13	University of TORONTO	CA	64.1	8.0
14	University of BRITISH COLUMBIA	CA	61.8	7.2
15	University of TOKYO	JP	60.5	6.9
16	CALIFORNIA Institute of Technology (Caltech)	US	59.5	13.7
17	National University of SINGAPORE	SG	58.7	5.6
18	CORNELL University	US	57.6	8.4
19	PEKING University	CN	56.9	3.2
20	COLUMBIA University	US	56.3	9.7
21	DUKE University	US	55.7	9.9

Top 100 in biomedicine continued

Rank	Institution	Country	Score	Citations per paper
22	PRINCETON University	US	54.4	11.0
23	KAROLINSKA Institute	SE	54.0	7.9
24	KYOTO University	JP	53.1	6.9
25	UCL (University College London)	UK	52.6	8.5
26	University of MELBOURNE	AU	52.3	6.3
27	University of SYDNEY	AU	51.9	5.9
28=	University of CALIFORNIA, Davis	US	51.4	7.0
28=	WASHINGTON University in St Louis	US	51.4	10.2
30	MONASH University	AU	50.4	6.0
31	University of MICHIGAN	US	49.6	9.4
32=	University of EDINBURGH	UK	48.9	8.5
32=	University of QUEENSLAND	AU	48.9	6.0
34	KING'S College London	UK	48.7	7.3
35	University of CHICAGO	US	48.4	9.5
36	OSAKA University	JP	47.5	8.2
37	AUSTRALIAN National University	AU	46.9	6.4
38	UPPSALA University	SE	45.6	8.1
39	University of HONG KONG	HK	45.0	7.3
40	SEOUL National University	KR	44.9	4.7
41	University of PENNSYLVANIA	US	44.8	9.4
42	University of AUCKLAND	NZ	43.9	5.8
43	BOSTON University	US	43.2	9.7
44	University of WASHINGTON	US	43.1	9.9
45	University of ALBERTA	CA	41.9	6.3
46	University of BRISTOL	UK	40.4	7.5
47	University of WISCONSIN-Madison	US	40.3	8.0
48	HEIDELBERG Universität	DE	40.0	7.4
49	FUDAN University	CN	39.0	2.7
50=	University of NEW SOUTH WALES	AU	38.2	6.4
50=	BROWN University	US	38.2	8.1
52	McMASTER University	CA	38.1	7.9
53=	NEW YORK University (NYU)	US	37.9	8.2
53=	EMORY University	US	37.9	10.0
55	VANDERBILT University	US	37.7	9.9
56	TSINGHUA University	CN	37.1	2.6
57	University of MANCHESTER	UK	36.8	7.2
58	Hebrew University of JERUSALEM	IR	36.7	6.5
59	University of COPENHAGEN	DK	36.1	7.6
60=	Université de MONTRÉAL	CA	36.0	7.0

Rank	Institution	Country	Score	Citations per paper
60=	University of VIENNA	AT	36.0	7.9
62	UTRECHT University	NL	35.3	7.4
63	University of NORTH CAROLINA	US	35.0	8.8
64=	CHINESE University of Hong Kong	HK	34.9	5.2
64=	Universidad Nacional Autónoma de México (UNAM)	MX	34.9	3.2
64=	University of CALIFORNIA, Irvine	US	34.9	8.9
67=	ETH Zurich (Swiss Federal Institute of Technology)	CH	34.7	8.8
67=	HONG KONG University of Science & Technology	HK	34.7	5.4
69	PURDUE University	US	34.5	5.6
70	University of OTAGO	NZ	34.2	5.2
71	University of HELSINKI	FI	33.9	8.1
72	NORTHWESTERN University	US	33.8	8.3
73	CARNEGIE MELLON University	US	33.7	5.6
74=	University of GLASGOW	UK	33.6	8.9
74=	LEIDEN University	NL	33.6	7.9
76	CASE WESTERN RESERVE University	US	33.0	8.7
77	Université Louis Pasteur STRASBOURG I	FR	32.6	7.1
78	NANYANG Technological University	SG	32.3	3.4
79	University of CALIFORNIA, Santa Barbara	US	32.2	7.7
80	University of AMSTERDAM	NL	32.1	7.6
81	University of WESTERN AUSTRALIA	AU	32.0	6.2
82=	SHANGHAI JIAO TONG University	CN	31.9	1.7
82=	University of ZURICH	CH	31.9	8.1
84=	National TAIWAN University	TW	31.8	4.4
84=	TEXAS A&M University	US	31.8	5.3
84=	Katholieke Universiteit LEUVEN	BE	31.8	7.0
84=	NANJING University	CN	31.8	3.1
84=	University of MINNESOTA	US	31.8	7.6
89	University of Science and Technology of CHINA	CN	31.4	3.5
90	DALHOUSIE University	CA	31.3	6.3
91	Ludwig-Maximilians-Universität MÜNCHEN (LMU)	DE	31.2	6.7
92	University of NOTTINGHAM	UK	31.1	6.0
93	Eberhard Karls Universität TÜBINGEN	DE	31.0	7.0
94	CARDIFF University	UK	30.8	5.2
95	University of DELHI	IN	30.6	3.6
96	INDIANA University Bloomington	US	30.2	6.9
97=	TRINITY College Dublin	IE	30.1	8.1
97=	BRANDEIS University	US	30.1	11.0
99=	University of BIRMINGHAM	UK	29.7	7.4
99=	ERASMUS University Rotterdam	NL	29.7	9.1

Studying technology

A hefty paradox underlies this area of university study. In many countries of the world, especially in Germany, Russia and East Asia, 'engineer' is a term of honour in the same league as being a doctor or a lawyer. But in the English-speaking world, engineering has less prestige. This is strange, because US and British inventors have always had leading roles in developing world-changing technology from the light bulb and the telephone to the internet and the World Wide Web. While engineering may seem to lack glamour, its more handsome twin 'technology' does not. Governments all over the world have seen how universities such as Stanford helped create Silicon Valley and, with it, major corporations and thousands of jobs. In an attempt to share in the next generation of this high-technology growth, they are encouraging technological universities to integrate into the regions in which they are located, in the hope that they will create new enterprises there. So you can expect the engineering course you might take to be more closely connected to end users than in the past.

One big choice you will have to face is whether to go for a traditional degree subject, probably involving the word 'engineering,' or for something with a newer feel such as nanotechnology or robotics. In articles about the key technologies of the 21st century, these two appear as major contenders along with various life-based technologies such as stem cells. New subjects come along all the time in technology. The old engineering standbys such as chemical, electrical, civil and mechanical engineering have been added to, over time, by electronics, IT, and design, whilst metallurgy has broadened into materials science, as polymers and other new types of material have come along. Even older and highly specialist fields change over time. Mining, nautical engineering, automotive engineering and agricultural engineering have all been altered by the IT revolution and new materials. The idea of going for something a little more fashionable may be a good one if you have a comparatively definite life plan. But if not, a subject such as electrical or mechanical engineering may be a better idea. For one thing, you need a degree whose title will still make sense in 30 years. By then, there may not be a subject called nanotechnology. Some forecasters think that in years to come, nanotechnology will just be the way in which engineers and scientists do their work.

You will also find that curricula across the technology field are changing in response to climate change and our growing awareness of the need for sustainability. It is engineers who will have to produce the fuel-sipping cars, the renewable energy sources and the flood defences we will need to get us through the coming decades. Another choice to be considered is whether to combine engineering with another subject. This could include languages: Japanese was in fashion a few years ago, but global change has made Chinese the contemporary favourite. Another option might be combing with management or business studies. If you want to see the world, languages might well be a good option, but there is a risk of diluting your primary qualification if you take this route.

One problem with engineering subjects in general is the vast increase in the amount of knowledge in all areas of technology. Engineering courses are famously hard work, because of the amount of material you have to absorb and the number of projects you have to complete. These, by the way, will give you teamwork skills that you will need in later life. This means that an engineering degree may well take longer than other courses apart, of course, from medicine. But even when you have got through the degree, you still have work to do. Engineers take decisions that can kill people, so admission to the profession will require approval from some national organization. It's similar to being certified as a doctor: except medics make mistakes that kill people one at a time. A defective bridge, ship or aircraft can remove hundreds.

In engineering, a higher degree is only really needed if you plan to become an academic. Then the usual masters or PhD route is appropriate. But for many engineers, the usual career path is to get a job and continue taking professional qualifications while you work. This means that you get paid and can repay your debts instead of adding to them. But, heed one word of warning: research led by Professor Michael Eraut at the University of Sussex, UK, suggests that engineers can be a little under-challenged in their first jobs. While the team you belong to may be designing an IT system that is vital to national security, or a spacecraft that will go to Mars, your role will be a tiny one. Don't be afraid to push for more responsibility. This could be one reason why the MBA is a popular postgraduate qualification for engineers.

The technology ranking table shows that the Massachusetts Institute of Technology (MIT) is the world's top technology institution by some distance. Behind it come Berkeley, Caltech and Stanford, the big three of Californian technology. Cambridge University and Imperial College, London, represent the UK. Cambridge is the centre of a major UK technology cluster, while Imperial College is still carrying out the mission it was given in the 19th century, of pushing innovation in the UK and worldwide. Carnegie Mellon in Pittsburgh is a world leader in many futuristic areas such as robotics. Asia's emphasis on technology is captured by the high positions of Tokyo University, Tsinghua University in Beijing, and the National University of Singapore. This is one table where many specialist institutions from MIT on down show up well.

Top 100 in technology

Rank	Institution	Country	Score	Citations per paper
1	MASSACHUSETTS Institute of Technology (MIT)	US	100.0	4.5
2	University of California, BERKELEY	US	93.9	5.0
3	STANFORD University	US	85.3	4.5
4	CALIFORNIA Institute of Technology (Caltech)	US	81.6	4.9
5	University of CAMBRIDGE	UK	76.2	3.5
6	CARNEGIE MELLON University	US	71.6	3.4
7	IMPERIAL College London	UK	70.9	2.9
8	GEORGIA Institute of Technology	US	68.9	3.0
9	University of TOKYO	JP	67.4	2.1
10	University of TORONTO	CA	66.0	3.5
11	National University of SINGAPORE	SG	64.5	2.9
12	TSINGHUA University	CN	63.4	1.2
13	ETH Zurich (Swiss Federal Institute of Technology)	CH	63.1	3.6
14	University of OXFORD	UK	61.6	3.4
15	PRINCETON University	US	61.5	4.3
16	University of CALIFORNIA, Los Angeles (UCLA)	US	61.4	4.3
17	DELFT University of Technology	NL	60.4	2.5
18	McGILL University	CA	60.1	2.5
19	HARVARD University	US	59.6	5.2
20	University of ILLINOIS	US	58.4	3.1
21	TOKYO Institute of Technology	JP	57.0	2.1
22=	University of BRITISH COLUMBIA	CA	56.8	2.8
22=	KYOTO University	JP	56.8	2.1

Rank	Institution	Country	Score	Citations per paper
24=	CORNELL University	US	56.4	4.0
24=	HONG KONG University of Science & Technology	HK	56.4	2.8
26	NANYANG Technological University	SG	55.2	2.1
27	University of NEW SOUTH WALES	AU	54.7	2.2
28	University of MELBOURNE	AU	54.4	2.8
29	TECHNION Israel Institute of Technology	IR	54.1	2.7
30	University of WATERLOO	CA	53.9	2.1
31	ÉCOLE POLYTECHNIQUE	FR	52.6	2.6
32	University of TEXAS at Austin	US	52.0	3.2
33	PURDUE University	US	50.9	2.6
34	Korea Adv Inst of Science & Technology (KAIST)	KR	50.5	2.2
35	University of CALIFORNIA, San Diego	US	50.3	3.5
36=	AUSTRALIAN National University	AU	49.9	2.6
36=	Indian Institute of Technology Bombay (IITB)	IN	49.9	1.8
38=	University of MICHIGAN	US	49.2	3.5
38=	PEKING University	CN	49.2	1.7
40	Technische Universität MÜNCHEN (TUM)	DE	48.7	2.8
41	University of SYDNEY	AU	48.0	2.3
42	Indian Institute of Technology Delhi (IITD)	IN	47.7	1.7
43	SEOUL National University	KR	46.0	2.4
44	École Polytechnique Fédérale de LAUSANNE	CH	45.2	3.4
45	University of MANCHESTER	UK	44.8	2.7
46	University of ALBERTA	CA	44.6	2.5
47	MONASH University	AU	44.3	2.1
48	SHANGHAI JIAO TONG University	CN	43.8	1.1
49=	National TAIWAN University	TW	42.3	2.1
49=	OSAKA University	JP	42.3	1.9
49=	University of Science and Technology of CHINA	CN	42.3	1.6
49=	EINDHOVEN University of Technology	NL	42.3	2.9
53	TEXAS A&M University	US	41.8	2.3
54	KTH, ROYAL Institute of Technology	SE	41.5	2.5
55	CHALMERS University of Technology	SE	41.3	2.5
56=	University of AUCKLAND	NZ	40.8	2.1
56=	Katholieke Universiteit LEUVEN	BE	40.8	3.0
58	YALE University	US	40.7	4.0
59	Virginia Polytechnic Institute (VIRGINIA TECH)	US	40.4	2.3
60	University of EDINBURGH	UK	40.2	2.6
61	University of QUEENSLAND	AU	40.0	2.4
62	University of CALIFORNIA, Santa Barbara	US	39.8	4.6
63=	COLUMBIA University	US	39.5	3.7

Top 100 in technology continued

Rank	Institution	Country	Score	Citations per paper
63=	Politecnico di MILANO	IT	39.5	1.9
65	Technische Universität BERLIN	DE	39.3	2.1
66	RENSSELAER Polytechnic Institute	US	38.7	3.1
67	JOHNS HOPKINS University	US	38.5	4.3
68	Universität STUTTGART	DE	38.0	2.3
69	University of HONG KONG	HK	37.3	2.5
70=	R W Technische Hochschule AACHEN	DE	37.1	1.9
70=	Indian Institute of Technology Kanpur (IITK)	IN	37.1	1.9
72	Universität KARLSRUHE	DE	37.0	2.1
73	University of WISCONSIN-Madison	US	36.9	3.4
74=	CHINESE University of HONG KONG	HK	36.0	2.6
74=	Indian Institute of Technology Madras (IITM)	IN	36.0	1.6
76	VIENNA University of Technology	AT	35.9	2.1
77	Technical University of DENMARK	DK	35.8	3.3
78	University of PENNSYLVANIA	US	35.0	4.3
79=	PENNSYLVANIA STATE University	US	34.9	3.0
79=	McMASTER University	CA	34.9	2.9
81=	NORTHWESTERN University	US	34.6	4.0
81=	University of MARYLAND	US	34.6	3.2
83=	University of CHICAGO	US	34.5	4.9
83=	Indian Institute of Technology Kharagpur (IITKGP)	IN	34.5	1.7
85	University of WASHINGTON	US	34.3	4.9
86	CHULALONGKORN University	TH	34.0	1.9
87=	Université de MONTRÉAL	CA	33.9	2.6
87=	University of SOUTHERN CALIFORNIA	US	33.9	3.2
89	CITY University of HONG KONG	HK	33.7	2.9
90=	University of CALGARY	CA	33.5	1.6
90=	BANDUNG Institute of Technology	ID	33.5	0.9
92	FUDAN University	CN	33.2	1.7
93	BROWN University	US	33.1	4.4
94=	RMIT University	AU	33.0	1.5
94=	HELSINKI University of Technology TKK	FI	33.0	2.1
96=	UCL (University College London)	UK	32.8	3.2
96=	University of SOUTHAMPTON	UK	32.8	2.5
98=	University of BIRMINGHAM	UK	32.7	2.7
98=	TOHOKU University	JP	32.7	2.3
100	École Normale Supérieure, PARIS	FR	32.4	3.0

VYSOKÉ UČENÍ TECHNICKÉ V BRNĚ

110 1899 - 2009

BRNO UNIVERSITY OF TECHNOLOGY

aculties of

Architecture
Civil Engineering
Electrical Engeneering and
Communication
Faculty of business and Management
Fine Arts
Chemistry
Information Technology
Mechanical Engineering

Founding year:	1899
Type of institution:	public
Degree programmes:	Bachelor´s, Master´s, Doctoral
Tuition languages:	Czech, English
Total number of students:	22 479
International students:	1 853
Scholarships:	Yes, please contact lobpreis@ro.vutbr.cz for further details.
Range of tuition fees (in USD/year):	Regular study programmes are free. English taught programmes school fees range approx. from 1000 to 5000 USD/year
Admission successful rate:	Please see www.vutbr.cz for details on admission rate details.
Website:	www.vutbr.cz
Contact:	Antonínská 548/1, 601 90 Brno / vut@vutbr.cz / +420 54114 1111

With more than 22.000 students, the Brno University of Technology is one of the largest universities in the Czech Republic and the only technical university in the Czech Republic which covers the **whole spectrum of technical disciplines**. Its **8 faculties and Institute of Forensic Engineering** offer students 290 fields of study in the **Bachelor´s, Master´s and Doctoral (Ph.D.) study programmes.**

The VUT graduates are very successful in the industry, also thanks to very close cooperation between university and companies such as Siemens, ABB or IBM. According to survey of VUT concerning the graduates in 2006, 54% of students find their job before they graduate; the unemployment rate amongst graduates is only about 1%.

Student Residence Halls have a capacity to accommodate 6 800 students in rooms with internet access. VUT offers its students wide range of dining services (cafeterias, restaurants, pizzerias, snack bars) with modern catering system (cashless, no pre-ordering, online menus).

VUT also has the largest academic facility in the Czech Republic especially thanks to the newly-built multifunctional sport hall. Centre of Sports Activities offers 42 sport activities.

In 2006, VUT has received a prestigious certificate "Diploma Supplement Label". University has made numerous contacts with universities and other institutions around Europe, United States and also in Asia that enables its students to study in many countries abroad.

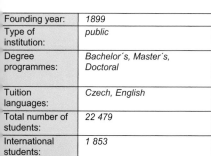

3

Study abroad

This chapter includes information and advice on what a period of international study could mean for your career and profiles the most popular current and upcoming study destinations worldwide, including information on universities and lifestyle. The chapter concludes with a list of institutions around the world that provide information to help you explore further your study abroad options.

An opportunity not to be missed

Studying abroad, whether for an exchange year or a full degree program, is an opportunity not to be missed. If it's for your undergraduate, graduate or even your postgraduate qualification, experiencing a different teaching style, a different culture and a different way of living will add to your education. Whether it's the challenge of asserting your independence or the knowledge that it can only be beneficial to your career that tempts you to consider studying abroad, you won't know what it's like until you try it. Higher education is a challenge in itself, but what happens when you add studying abroad to the experience? Moving out of home, and leaving the country: is the packing of bags, financial cost, and possible homesickness all worth it? As Rory, an English student who studied abroad in the US said: "I would advise anyone to take part in a study abroad program, because no matter how hard it was at times, it was an emotionally, culturally and ultimately a financially rewarding experience." And, Richard, an undergraduate student from New Zealand studying abroad in the US commented: "It's not often you get thrown into the cultural deep end. But from the moment you leave your comfort zone behind, and arrive in a new country to study abroad, you are set for one of the best experiences of your life." The world of higher education is an exciting one and as the THE-QS World University Rankings show, it's a truly global field. Make the most of your tertiary education years and add studying abroad to your experience.

In fact, speak to almost any student who has studied abroad and the chances are that by the end of the conversation you'll already be contemplating which destination to head off to yourself. Nadine studied for her undergraduate degree in Germany before heading to the Southern Hemisphere to pursue her masters 'down under' in Australia. "Staying in Australia for one and a half years and not seeing my family and friends was a challenge, but studying abroad enabled me to make friends from all over the world and I became more open-minded. Having to do everything in English from writing assignments to buying bus tickets was also a challenge, but it meant my English language skills improved and that has increased my ability to get jobs back home in Europe."

The world of higher education is becoming increasingly international and flexible due to this concept of studying abroad. Students are no longer confined to the university or higher education institution in their hometown, or even their country. Degrees can be taken in another continent altogether, in another language and in another higher education system. Statistics released from national and international agencies indicate that the popularity of international study continues to grow. Data from UNESCO and OECD confirms that the number of students pursuing education away from their home country has increased by 4.9 per cent, or an additional 127,336 in absolute numbers, on the previous data year, bringing the total to 2.73 million students. Since 2000, the number of students enrolled in international higher education has increased worldwide by 50 per cent, which reflects both the rapid expansion of higher education around the world and the sustained growth in demand for top quality graduates by international employers. Students can choose to study abroad for a semester, a year, or an entire degree gaining invaluable experience that will help them develop both personally and professionally.

Study abroad and your career

Studying abroad can certainly improve your employment prospects. An increased proficiency in English or another major language is just one of the many advantages. Add that to a developing awareness of different cultures, an increase in your own self-confidence, an extensive network of new colleagues and your new higher education qualification, and you'll have the edge that many employers are looking for. The overriding view from employers is that if you have an excellent academic track record, your nationality is no barrier to your future employment. In fact, if you can demonstrate a real passion to work in an international environment, bringing with you the qualification and skills you gained while studying abroad, you will very often be more attractive to employers than others around you.

International graduates are seen as huge assets by international employers in many sectors, from knowledge based industries like consulting and banking to global industries like healthcare, consumer products and automotive, as well as government, all seeking to establish a globally minded cadre of young administrators. Many international employers now focus on building relationships with universities and business schools to target the crème-de-la-crème of international graduates. The most straightforward source of entry for international students into companies is through internship programs. This allows employees the opportunity to view candidates at close hand, without having to complete all the formal visa requirements for full-time hiring.

Presenting your international skills

However, as a graduate in today's world of global mobility and opportunity, you will face competition from increasing numbers of other top graduates from around the world. Do not expect to simply walk into a great job just because you are qualified with a first degree, masters or PhD qualification. It is how you convey those skills and demonstrate your ability to apply them to the employment opportunities you are presented with that will see you succeed.

Of paramount importance is ensuring that you apply yourself and your skills in the most effective way, and knowing where, and how, to find the opportunities. It is also worth looking at what you expect in return and how you feel that international mobility will aid your career development. Also important, is how to convey your international experience as a valuable marketing tool for yourself. If an employer is torn between two like-for-like candidates, this could prove to be a deciding factor. On job applications and in interviews, it is important to point out that your choice to study abroad was a beneficial career decision and will add to your personal and occupational attributes. How did you decide upon your location? What skills have you learned that will help in your role? How have you grown on a personal level? And how did the placement tie in with your degree? Put simply, you need to prove that your study abroad experience has given you added value and wasn't just about fulfilling your backpacking dream. It is a common desire for many young people to want to travel, so it is important to stand out from the crowd and show what you have adopted and embraced from your time abroad.

International postgraduate study

The study abroad experience is not limited to undergraduate students. Those interested in pursuing their masters, PhD and MBA qualifications are also looking further afield than the institutions in their home countries. Data from the QS World Grad School Tour underlines how buoyant the interest in international masters and PhD study currently is, and the number of countries students are considering for their higher education.

Top ten most popular countries for masters or PhD study

Rank	Country	Interest (% preference)
1	US	80
2	UK	63
3	Canada	38
4	Australia	28
5	France	25
6	Spain	20
7	Singapore	16
8	Germany	16
9	Switzerland	15
10	Italy	13

Source & copyright: QS Research 2008

Additional research by QS into the MBA arena showed that in 2008, MBA applications were nearing record levels and competition for places was intense. Rose Martinelli of Chicago Graduate Business School says: "US applications have increased by over 100 per cent over the last three years, whilst international applications are also well up."

A growing trend

For employers around the world in any industry, success ultimately lies in the skill of their workforces. In a world, now international by nature, occupational and life skills can be accrued through international student mobility. The importance of this mobility as perceived by governments is also evident, with schemes such as the Abraham Lincoln Study Abroad Act of 2006 implemented by the US Senate, which calls for a national program to study abroad. The program will create fellowships and scholarships for individual students and establish partnerships with colleges and universities. The goal of the program is to create and sustain annual growth rates to achieve one million US students studying abroad, annually, by 2016. A report by the Institute of International Education showed that in 2008, more US students than ever before were studying abroad, a total of 241,791 up eight per cent from the previous year, and nearly 150 per cent more than a decade earlier.

Lauren Welch, head of advising for the US-UK Fulbright Commission in London says studying abroad adds weight to a student's future job prospects. "Employers are looking to graduates to have international experience either by studying or working abroad. Now there are many more opportunities to study and work abroad, or stay on and work afterwards." Welch also says that studying abroad gives you a great opportunity to be near worldwide centres which means some of the lecturers or tutors will have experience of these. "For instance, if you want to study finance, head for New York, London or Hong Kong, or if you want to study politics, Washington DC is a centre to aim for."

Country profiles

The following section looks at the ten most popular, overall, study abroad destinations (in alphabetical order): Australia, Canada, France, Germany, Japan, the Netherlands, the Nordic countries, Singapore, the UK and the US. Top Universities Guide also reviews three up and coming destinations to watch: New Zealand, South Korea and Switzerland.

The first section of each profile gives you a brief overview of the country itself. There's information for the adrenaline junkies, the arts' critics and the cuisine enthusiasts. We tell you whether to pack your sunhat or your raincoat and where some of the must-see places in that country are. We then look at the types of institutions in each country. What are the universities like? What institutions offer vocational training? What degree programs are available and how long do they take to complete? And perhaps most importantly, what are the entry requirements for each institution and what types of accommodation are available to you as an international student? We give an overview of fees, finance and the cost of living and outline some of the scholarships available (Chapter four goes into more detail of fees, finance and scholarships with a global perspective). Finally we give you a glimpse of student life: there are plenty of clubs and societies for international students to join. And we tell you about your opportunities to work while studying.

Ten most popular destinations

Australia	173
Canada	177
France	179
Germany	181
Japan	183
The Netherlands	187
The Nordic Countries	189
Singapore	193
UK	197
US	199

Three destinations to watch

New Zealand	203
South Korea	205
Switzerland	207

The right university can make a world of difference.

At the University of Melbourne we have a long history of leadership in research, innovation, teaching and learning.

Currently ranked No. 38 in the world and among the top ten Universities world-wide for the employability of our graduates,* the University has helped shape Melbourne and Australia's social, cultural and scientific life for over 150 years.

Our emphasis on innovation and critical thinking, world-recognised research success, and ongoing pursuit of new teaching methodologies keeps us at the forefront of higher education.

Become part of this tradition of leadership.

For further information visit:
www.futurestudents.unimelb.edu.au

Times Higher Education World University Rankings 2008

CRICOS: 00116K

dream large

THE UNIVERSITY OF
MELBOURNE

Study in Australia

Pros & cons

+ **Possibility of work and study**
+ **Reasonable costs of tuition and living**
+ **Good international reputation for degree quality**
- **Difficulty of gaining an entry visa**
- **High number of international students on some programs**

Why Australia?

Warm weather, beautiful beaches, national parks and, of course, those cuddly koalas: you can experience it all in a weekend, not to mention photographing the opera house, walking over the Harbour Bridge or cruising around Darling Harbour in Sydney. Australians have a love of the outdoors and with their welcoming hospitality it won't be long until you're treated to a real Aussie experience. Sometimes known as the world's seventh continent, Australia is a country of contrasts: from the barrenness of the outback, to the magic of the Blue Mountains, the underwater spectacle that is the Great Barrier Reef, to the spiritual experience attained by visiting Uluru, Ayers Rock. Cultures blend as much as the landscape in this country with city populations made up of a diverse mix of ethnicities including indigenous Aboriginal citizens, Greek, Italian, Vietnamese, Chinese and Filipino. For a study abroad experience of a lifetime, that will defy all your expectations, head 'down under'.

Six of the country's 41 universities appear in the top 50 of the 2008 THE-QS World University Rankings, the third highest number after the US and UK. Of the 41 universities, (38 are publicly funded and three private), 21 are ranked in the world's top 400.

Universities

The international reputation of Australia's tertiary education system is growing. The leading set of universities in Australia is known as 'The Group of Eight' and incorporates the major research institutions of the University of Adelaide, Australian National University, University of Melbourne, Monash University, University of New South Wales, University of Queensland, University of Sydney and the University of Western Australia. Australian higher education institutions comprise universities and government-funded technical and further education institutes (TAFE), which offer more vocationally-oriented courses for students pursuing a specific hands-on career. Bachelors degrees take three to four years to complete and masters degrees require a further one to two years of study. Certificates, diplomas and advanced diplomas offered in TAFE institutes usually need one or two years of study.

Australian institutions set their own entry requirements, but for most university programs, 12 years of education is the minimum standard. For those without an appropriate academic background, bridging qualifications are offered to enable students to reach the standard required for degree level programs. If a student's education has not been conducted in English, he/she will need to submit a recognized language qualification, the level of which will be set by the institution.

Additionally, for students with English as a second language, a sufficient level of proficiency is required. The IELTS™ test, the only one accepted by the Australian Department of Immigration and Citizenship (DIAC), is needed to gain a student visa and to meet minimum academic requirements. Each Australian university or institute of study has its own English language requirements, so students need to check the IELTS™ score required for their chosen course of study.

Fees, finance & cost of living

Tuition fees are set by individual universities and vary by faculty and individual program. On average, fees vary from AU$14,000 per year for an arts degree at a smaller university, to AU$50,000 per year for a medical degree at one of the country's most prestigious institutions. However, degree programs in the fields most popular for international students such as business, law and engineering, tend to range between AU$18,000 and AU$25,000 per year.

The Australian government offers a number of scholarships for those students wishing to study abroad but these are not available for international students undertaking English language training. Three scholarships are dedicated to international students from the Asia-Pacific and Middle East regions: Endeavour Awards, Australian Leadership Awards and Australian Development Scholarships, known as the Australian Scholarships, are awarded by the Australian Agency for International Development (AusAID) and the Department of Education, Employment and Workplace Relations (DEEWR): www.australianscholarships.gov.au. Individual education institutions have scholarships, which international students may apply for and other scholarships are offered by international and charitable organizations. These need to be applied for in the student's home country, not in Australia. For postgraduate students from Commonwealth countries looking to study abroad in Australia, the Association of Commonwealth Universities provides a guide to scholarships offered by governments, Rotary International, World Bank, World Health Organization, Asian Development Bank, United Nations, Rockefeller Foundation and other organizations: http://www.acu.ac.uk/home. A comprehensive database of Australian scholarships available to both domestic and international students can be found at: www.studyinaustralia.gov.au.

Students studying abroad in Australia will require approximately AU$12,500 per year to pay for books, accommodation, food, utility bills and entertainment. Cities can be expensive to live in, but there are good discounts for students. Medical care is not free in Australia and all students are expected to maintain an Overseas Student Health Cover (OSHC), an insurance policy that allows them to claim back the cost of their medical treatment from their individual health funds. Most institutions have medical care on campus, or can recommend a local doctor.

Student life

There is much to see and do in Australia from cheering on the boats in the annual Sydney to Hobart Yacht Race to dressing up in finery and having a punt on the famous Melbourne Cup horse race. Each Australian city has its unique atmosphere Brisbane and Perth are renowned for their beach culture and Melbourne for its artistic flair. Because of the size of the country, cheap travel between cities (via buses and trains) can take days, but you'll be able to prepare for your assignments on the way! International students are permitted to work a maximum of 20 hours a week during term time and full-time in vacations.

Before applying for work, students need a work permit from the local Department of Immigration, Multicultural and Indigenous Affairs (DIMIA) office. The most popular jobs are in the hospitality, catering and retail sectors.

The University of Newcastle, Australia is a progressive international university and one of Australia's leading research institutions.

We are ranked:

- 375th University in the world
  (Shanghai Jiao Tong University Academic Ranking 2008)
- 61st University in the Asia-Pacific
  (Shanghai Jiao Tong University Academic Ranking 2008)
- One of the world's top 100 Universities for engineering/
  technology and computer sciences
  (Shanghai Jiao Tong University rankings by field 2007)
- Australian top 10 for research funding and outcomes

Our student population is just over 28,500 including some 6,000 international students from more than 80 countries studying both on and offshore.

The university has five faculties: Business and Law; Education and Arts; Engineering and Built Environment; Health; Science and Information Technology.

Our graduates are highly regarded both in Australia and internationally. We have a first class International Foundation program that provides a nationally recognised pathway to undergraduate degree programs as well as a modern, fully equipped Language Centre. The centre is also an official test centre for the International English Language Testing System (IELTS). We also offer exciting and challenging Postgraduate coursework and research programs all of which are available either on-campus, by distance or online.

Our students enjoy outstanding facilities including well-stocked libraries, award winning buildings, a state-of-the-art sporting complex as well as shops and cafes all set within a natural bushland campus. We believe it is the perfect place in which to grow – academically, professionally and personally.

Visit our website:
www.international.newcastle.edu.au

or contact us:
international@newcastle,edu.au

A PLACE OF OPPORTUNITY

Canada's top university for what you care about most.

Changing the world.

You told us that the right university will help you make a difference. And you define that university by its overall quality of education, breadth of courses, academic reputation and quality of career preparation. Students give U of T top marks in all four areas. And if you ask professors in other countries about academic excellence, U of T is Canada's leader — one of only five universities worldwide that place in the top 16 across all academic fields.* In short, if you care about the world and you care about academic excellence, U of T is where you belong.

UNIVERSITY OF
TORONTO
www.utoronto.ca

CANADA'S ANSWERS TO THE WORLD'S QUESTIONS.

* Source: 2008 Times Higher Education Supplement.

Canada

Pros & cons

+ A huge variety of programs to meet every interest
+ Credentials recognized around the world
+ Opportunity to work during studies and after graduation
- A smaller cluster of universities than found in other countries
- Variation in the structure of degree programs between some provinces

Why Canada?

Whether it's the thrill of skiing down Whistler's slopes, the opportunity to savour the taste of maple syrup or an internationally recognized qualification that you're after, Canada has it all. A varied landscape covering the same size of Europe, six time zones in the one country and the potential to experience four seasons in one day, studying in Canada offers international students flexible degree programs, direct access to teaching professors and the chance to undertake research which accounts for more than one third of Canada's research efforts, the highest proportion in the G8 countries.

With 12 universities in the top 200 of the world and another eight in the top 400 of the THE-QS World University Rankings, students can experience a quality education in a country that, according to the United Nations, is one of the best places to live in the world.

Universities

Undergraduate degrees in Canada consist of three or four years of study, depending on the province and whether the degree is general or specialized. Honours degrees, or a baccalaureate program which indicates a higher level of academic achievement, may take an additional year to complete. Each university sets its entry standards and these tend to vary according to the program of study. Usually there will be a minimum academic average set and, in some instances, course pre-requisites for admission to the program (particularly in the sciences and engineering). Students who have not been educated in English will be expected to demonstrate their language ability through an IELTS™, MELAB or TOEFL® result. All Canadian institutions set application deadlines and recommend that students check and apply six to eight months before their intended start date. Some universities will offer January, May and September start dates although the typical academic year runs from September to April.

Most Canadian universities follow a trimester system with three sessions: fall, winter/spring and summer, the latter being optional for many students. Individual program courses can last one trimester, or the entire academic year, the level of credit being earned is adjusted accordingly. Assessment is based on a combination of mid-term examinations, term papers and class presentations. In addition to university options, students will find university colleges, institutes of technology and advanced learning, community colleges, and colleges of applied arts and technology, a number of which are able to grant degree-level qualifications, although many of the community colleges offer diplomas, certificates and associate degrees.

As one of the largest systems of higher education in the world, Canada has an extremely robust quality assurance and accreditation process ensuring that degree-level studies are recognized internationally. Most Canadian universities subscribe to the Association of Universities and Colleges of Canada principles of institutional quality assurance. Adherence to these principles is renewed every five years.

Fees, finance & cost of living

Tuition fees are set by each individual institution and vary between private and public institutions, and by subject area. Undergraduate programs range from C$10,000 to C$24,000 per year depending on the chosen location and program of study. Working as a student is also an option. Full-time students are permitted to work on campus without a work permit if they are enrolled at an appropriately recognized institution. Off campus, work is also available, to a maximum of 20 hours per week during the academic term and full-time during vacations, if certain requirements are fulfilled.

Furthermore, graduates of public post-secondary institutions, and degree programs at private institutions, may work in Canada, with a work permit for up to three years, depending on the length of their program of study. While the quality of education and living standards are among the highest in the world, the cost of living is fairly moderate, allowing students to stretch their budgets as far as possible. Accommodation is very often provided at a reasonable cost by universities in the first year of a program. In subsequent years, students seek private housing off-campus. Living costs vary across the country, but students are able to live reasonably well on approximately C$8,000 to C$10,000 per year. An education cost calculator at www.educationau-incanada.ca may help students prepare a budget.

Scholarships and other forms of financial aid are available to offset the costs of study in Canada. The best source of funds tends to be individual universities and colleges, many of whom offer scholarships. The Canadian government also funds a range of awards for graduate students including the C$50,000 Vanier Scholarships which provide financial support to domestic and international students pursuing doctoral programs at Canadian universities. (Candidates must be nominated by the university at which they will be pursuing their doctoral studies). A free service coordinates most national scholarship information and is available at www.educationau-incanada.ca and www.scholarships.gc.ca.

Student life

International students will enjoy all of the freedoms that protect Canadians: respect for human rights, equality and a stable and peaceful society. Access to medical care for students is dependant on the province of study. Alberta, British Columbia and Saskatchewan cover international students under their provincial health care plans. All other provinces require students to make their own arrangements and have sufficient private healthcare cover for the length of their studies. Most students spend between 15 and 20 hours a week in formal classes, and use free time to explore Canada's spectacular and varied scenery, or the vibrant city centres which offer music, dance, theatre, sports, and festivals all year round.

Study in France

Pros & cons
+ Large number of highly reputable universities
+ Many government grants for international students
+ Many bi-lingual French/English-based masters
- Most undergraduate courses in French only
- Post-study visa situation for employment
- Difficulty of gaining an entry visa

Why France?

More than 245,000 international students choose to study in France each year, and with the opportunities this country provides, it's easy to see why. In France you can live, breathe and taste the culture. It's a country for romantics, art lovers, food and wine connoisseurs; a country of history, architecture, intellect, passion and politics. If you want a study abroad experience that will tempt, challenge, educate and fulfil you, then France is the country. Imagine reading your text books in a Parisian patisserie sipping café au lait, or researching engineering techniques while marvelling at the Millau Bridge standing proud above the clouds. Outdoor enthusiasts can catch the Tour de France, ski the French Alps, or cycle through the Loire Valley. For those wishing to tempt their taste buds there's the boeuf of Burgundy, the crèpes of Brittany and the olives of Provence.

Whether it's cuisine, culture or haute couture that interests you, France will satisfy your curiosity, and 14 of France's universities are ranked in the top 400 in the world.

Universities

There are more than 3,000 institutions of higher education in France, including 87 public universities, 240 engineering schools and 230 business schools. Another 2,000 institutions offer tertiary qualifications in specialized vocational fields. The French higher education system is based on a common architecture of tertiary qualifications, LMD: licence (bachelor degree), masters, and PhD, embarked upon once a student has passed his or her baccalauréat (final exam). Foreign students currently in higher education in their home country can apply for admission to a comparable French institution, as long as they meet the entry requirements. (Further information on the LMD system can be found at www.topuniversities.com). There are two main types of tertiary education institution: 'universités', and 'les grandes écoles', which are uniquely French. Created in the early 19th century in parallel to the university system, they are extremely selective and offer education at a very high level. French engineering schools are internationally recognized and all 240 schools share common characteristics. This guarantees the quality of the engineering degree, which is at masters level and covers all areas of engineering science.

French business schools are also developing a name for themselves. Six of the top ten Masters in Management programs come from French-based business schools, according to Financial Times rankings. Further specialized institutions offer higher-level training in areas such as art, design, fashion, tourism, paramedical services and social services. There are three types of art schools: the écoles nationales supérieures d'art, which offer a national diploma after four or five years of study; schools for applied art, which are supervised by the Ministry of National Education; and schools of fine art by the Ministry of Culture, offering diplomas after three or five years of study. All have selective admission criteria.

There are also 20 architecture schools, overseen by the Ministry of Culture, offering the DPLG (Diplôme par le Gouvernement) architectural diploma, the only qualification in the field recognized for those working as architects in France. Studies last for six years in three cycles of two years each. CampusFrance, an agency responsible for promoting higher education, has information on more than 30,000 higher education courses in France. It also has everything a student considering studying abroad in France needs to know, from admission requirements to visa applications: (http://edufrance.fr/en/index.htm)

Fees, finance & cost of living

International students pay the same fees as domestic students at most universities and on most academic programs. In national universities, the state pays a very large part of each student's study expenses (about €10,000 per year), keeping admission fees relatively low. The French government, through the Ministry of Foreign Affairs, funds over 20,000 international students every year with two schemes. The first is scholarships offered jointly by the French government and the student's country of residence. The second enables French higher education institutions to enrol the best foreign students, while developing international university cooperation. The French Ministry of Education also offers grants to international students.

Since the introduction of the Euro, the costs of basic items like food and rent have increased, although this is not only in France. Cost of living indices suggest that Paris is about 15 per cent less expensive to live in than London. Other French cities are significantly less expensive. Student accommodation in France, especially in Paris, can be pricey and although it is good overall, the quality can vary on different campuses. University housing is in very short supply, even for French students, and most end up in private accommodation in the city. CROUS, the student social support service (which now comes under EduFrance), offers six types of student accommodation: rooms in university residences, renovated rooms, studios, small flats, low rent apartments (HLM) as well as accommodation in town. Student group health plans are available for international students to cover all, or part, of their medical bills not covered by the basic national system. To be eligible for the national student health plan, students must be under 28 and enrolled in a participating institution. Students 28 and older can obtain the special CMU health insurance.

Student life

Student services on campus are available to all students, although these can be limited due to the number of domestic students living at home. However, there is no shortage of French cultural activities to immerse yourself in, from cinema and dance clubs, to music and theatre. Sports fanatics will also feel at home on campus. The French government has invested heavily in providing excellent track, field and stadia for sports in all, except inner city universities, allowing plenty of opportunity to keep active between your studies. France can lure you in to study, but there is no easy way to stay on in this country of temptations after your program has finished. Internships are available but with a 20 per cent youth unemployment rate, there's a great deal of local competition for graduate jobs.

Study in Germany

Pros & cons

+ No, or low, tuition fees
+ Excellent academic reputation
+ Familiarity with international students
- Procedure for admission
- Still few English language programs

Why Germany?

Enjoying Christmas markets, exploring fairytale palaces, biking through forest trails or enjoying summer beer gardens: will there be any time to study in Germany? Home to more than 80 million people, Germany is a country extraordinarily rich in history, art, architecture, and music and a range of outdoor activities that will satisfy any urge to have a break from study. Surrounded by nine other European countries, Germany is a major player on the world stage. It's a country that encourages tourists to explore and discover its diverse people, culture and character, from the lively capital of Berlin, to the reserved Hanseatic cities of Hamburg, Bremen and Lübeck in the north, to colourful Bavaria in the south, or the historic eastern cities of Dresden and Leipzig. But only a third of Germany's population live in the big cities: 50 million live in small towns and another six million in villages. To fully experience Germany is to make time to go off the beaten track where you'll be constantly surprised by what you find.

Three German universities appear in the top 100 in the world and a further 31 are placed in the top 400.

Universities

With 300 institutions, Germany's higher education system, steeped in historical tradition, is one of the largest in Europe, and the most internationally recognized, as shown in the THE-QS 2008 World University Rankings. There are seven main types of higher education institution. The two most significant are university (Universität) and university of applied sciences (Fachhochschule). Universities offer programs in which research and study are very closely aligned, resulting in graduates gaining a firm grasp of the theoretical nature of their subject. The Fachhochschule offers students the opportunity to combine a basic level of academic knowledge with a more practical application relevant to the work environment. Other categories of institution include art and music colleges, church-sponsored universities, vocational universities in certain German states and private colleges. Universities offer different types of degree, many of which are unique to the German system. The Diplom, Magister Atium and Staatsexamen all represent qualifications that are currently available in many subject areas. In line with the Bologna Declaration, which came into effect in September 2007, the length it takes to study for a degree is now three to four years for a bachelors and an additional one or two for a masters. Many German students choose to complete their education with doctoral studies (Promotion).

The minimum entry requirement for study at a German university is the equivalent of the German Abitur, the local high school qualification, taken after 13 years of education. However, international students may also be required to take an admission assessment test (Feststellungsprüfung) that varies according to the type of institution. Students also have to demonstrate knowledge of German if the program of study they wish to pursue is taught in the local language. An increasing number of international programs are now being offered in English. Choosing to pursue higher education abroad is a major financial investment. Value for money is important and an official accreditation council implements standard procedures for all German tertiary institutions that wish to have government recognition and uses additional agencies to support and enforce this process.

Fees, finance & cost of living

One of the major attractions of studying in Germany is the almost universal support of all students by the state governments, meaning that there are very low tuition fees for international students. In most German states, tuition fees are now levied for local and international students alike at a rate of €1,000 per year. Students from outside of the EU must acquire a student visa. (See http://www.study-in-germany.de/english/1.120.40.html for exemptions). International students are required to take out public health insurance before they are permitted to register for their classes. This covers all medical expenses and costs less that €50 a month. Students over the age of 30 are not eligible for this cover and must obtain private health insurance.

In common with many European destinations, the cost of living is relatively high, though students are able to live economically on a monthly budget of €600 to €800 a month. Student fees also include some transport within the city of study. Because tuition fees are low, the need for financial aid and scholarships is greatly reduced. However, a range of awards exist that support students' living and study expenses. Many of these awards are offered by individual German states and are specific to the country of origin of the student applying for the award. A number of public and private organizations, as well as church groups, offer scholarships to students. Many focus on a student's talents, not only in the academic sense, but also in their social commitment. Democratic political parties in Germany have also recognized the value of international students to Germany and provide both financial aid and mentoring to outstanding students. The DAAD (German Academic Exchange Service) is an invaluable source of information on all aspects of study in Germany, including scholarships: www.daad.de

Student life

Most international students have the opportunity to live in accommodation organized by the university Studentenwerk (student office), which is either on campus or within a few minutes walk of the university. Other students organize their own flat share, known as Wohngemeinschaft (WG for short). This means the hub of student excitement tends to occur in the cities, where many student discounts are available for museums and galleries, theatres, and cinemas, the opera and some clubs and bars. Students can work without a permit while studying in Germany, although some from outside the EU are limited to 90 days or 180 half-days per year. Many universities have an office to help students find work, but as an international student, expect any spare time outside of study to be full of variety and opportunities to explore the country and culture and enjoy yourself.

Study in Japan

Pros & cons

+ **Reputation for academic excellence throughout Asia**
+ **Generous number of scholarships for international students**
+ **International student support**
- **High cost of tuition and living expenses**
- **Limited number of programs in English**
- **Lack of global reputation for undergraduate degrees**

Why Japan?

Thinking of studying in Japan? Start practising your chopstick technique, your karaoke voice and, most importantly, your Japanese. No matter how long you spend in Japan, this country's dynamic culture will envelop you. Ancient traditions stand side by side with modern technology and architecture. In the country where cherry blossom is celebrated, it's polite to slurp your soup. Because of Japan's varied geography and four distinct seasons, snow and beach holidays can be taken all year round Learning some Japanese is an important aspect of studying abroad in Japan. Most restaurant menus have photographs so you can see what you're ordering but, if all else fails, a vending machine will provide interim supplies. Japan is a country that will fascinate all students. There's so much more to it than miso soup, futon beds, and origami. Explore the festivals and folk art, high mountains and hot springs. Immerse yourself in Japanese culture; there's no other quite like it.

Ten Japanese universities appear in the top 200 of the 2008 THE-QS World University Rankings.

Universities

Japanese higher education is split into five types of institution: college of technology, professional training college (senmom gakko), junior college, college and university and graduate school. These institutions are either national, local, public, or private. There are over 700 universities in Japan, the majority of which are private. Undergraduate programs tend to last four years, with some six-year programs in dentistry, medicine and veterinary science. Almost all instruction is in Japanese. Junior colleges offer two-year diplomas, generally vocational in emphasis. At present, few of these programs are offered in English. Professional training colleges also provide for more vocational education, offering courses lasting between one and four years.

When applying for an undergraduate degree, students must be 18, have completed 12 years of education and have a recognized high school qualification. Students with only 11 years of schooling may enrol in one of the university preparatory courses. Each university has its own application procedure, the schedules of which are announced in June for programs beginning in April the following year. Some universities also have a September or October admissions procedure. Not all universities accept direct applications from international students. Details are available at www.jasso.go.jp (the Japan Student Services Organization). Students must also pass an entrance exam for Japanese universities. The Examination for Japanese University Admission for International Students (EJU) is administered by JASSO. Each university sets its own timetable. The exam is usually offered twice a year in June and November and includes: Japanese as a foreign language,

science (physics, chemistry, biology), Japan and the world, and mathematics. Students can choose to sit the exam in either Japanese or English. Additionally, some universities require non-native Japanese applicants to complete the Japanese Language Proficiency Test before admission is granted. This test is held worldwide in early December and tests vocabulary, grammar, reading and listening abilities. There is no interview or oral exam.

Fees, finance & cost of living

Japan is regarded as one of the most expensive countries in the world. However, the tuition fees for most institutions of higher education are very competitively priced. Universities, language institutes, junior colleges and professional training colleges all have different fees, which also depend on the subject area. The tuition fee is approximately 30 per cent higher for the first year of a program to cover admissions fees. Scholarships are available for international students, although they are less numerous in professional training colleges and language institutes. Scholarships are administered through the individual institutions and meet some, or all, of the tuition fees, plus an amount for living costs. Japanese government 'Monbukagakusho' scholarships provide up to JPY134,000 a month for potential undergraduate students. Additional funding is available from JASSO, local government, individual educational institutions, corporate bodies and private foundations. Students who have received superior scores on their EJU university entrance exam are eligible to receive an honours scholarship for privately financed international students.

Living expenses vary according to where you choose to study. Tokyo tends to be the most expensive city, although others are also quite costly. On average, students spend JPY130,800 per month on living expenses, including housing, study and entertainment. The majority goes towards accommodation and travel expenses (there are no student discounts on travel), whether in university halls of residence or private apartments. Food is cheap if you find the right places to go. Most international students, approximately 75 per cent, choose to live in private accommodation. However, because of the cost and demand for housing in Japan, students can find it difficult to find a place to live. University service centres and private accommodation bureaux can help in most cases. All students must enrol in the national health insurance system. Payments are made monthly and vary according to where students live. Under the scheme, students pay only 30 per cent of their medical expenses for treatment covered by the insurance.

Student life

Students must apply for their alien registration card within 90 days of arrival and carry it with them at all times. International students can work up to 28 hours a week in paid employment during term-time and a maximum of eight hours a day during vacations. They can also stay on in Japan to work after graduation but must have their immigration status changed. Each student is assigned an academic tutor, and sometimes a student tutor, to help him/her adapt to the different learning culture. The Cooperative Society (Co-op) on campus, a membership organization similar to a Students' Union, also provides support and services to students such as a travel agency, housing association, bookshop, food stores and restaurants. For students wishing to ring home while they study abroad, internet calls are the cheapest option.

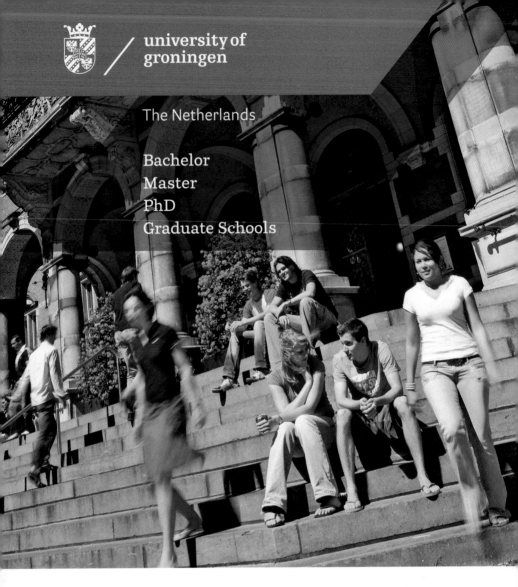

university of
groningen

The Netherlands

Bachelor
Master
PhD
Graduate Schools

Since its inception in 1614, the University of Groningen has enjoyed an international reputation as a dynamic and innovative centre of higher education offering high-quality teaching and research. Balanced study paths encourage students and researchers to develop their individual talents.

By joining forces and pooling resources with prestigious international partner universities and networks, the University of Groningen plays an important role in the exchange of knowledge.

Economics and Business

Humanities

Law

Behavioural and Social Sciences

Life Sciences

Science and Technology

Spatial Sciences

Study in the Netherlands

Pros & cons

+ Excellent value for money
+ Unique problem-based learning tradition
+ English language teaching
- Difficulty in remaining to work after studies
- Lack of international recognition of Dutch degrees

Why the Netherlands?

Did you know that reality-TV show Big Brother is a Dutch invention? That you can get from the north of the Netherlands to the south in just three hours? Or, that the Dutch consume 16.5kg of cheese per person each year? Boasting a relaxed and easygoing atmosphere for its 16 million multicultural citizens, the Netherlands offers a perfect student experience. The capital city of Amsterdam is home to Anne Frank's house, beautiful 17th century architecture, peaceful canals and some of the best museums and galleries in Europe. Bike through the tulips, take time out on one of the Frisian islands, tap your foot in time to the music at the North Sea Jazz Festival, the largest in the world, or relax at an eetcafe, one of the many affordable, small and popular pub-like eateries. It may only be a small country but the opportunities to learn and explore are endless.

The Netherlands is home to one of the highest moving universities in the 2008 THE-QS World University Rankings. VU University moved almost 150 places taking the number of Dutch universities in the top 250 to 12, including four in the top 100.

Universities

Dutch higher education programs have secured a reputation for high quality and well organized content. All programs are checked against a list of criteria to ensure consistent standards and in some cases Dutch programs are accredited by another country's national accreditation organization. The overall style of education in the Netherlands is known as Problem-Based Learning (PBL) and is regarded as one of the best approaches to higher education in the world today. There are two distinct types of higher education institution in the Netherlands: universities (universiteiten) and universities of professional education (hogescholen). Most programs are offered in English, making them very accessible for international students. The 14 government-approved universities, which currently cater for 200,000 students, focus on research and teaching from an academic point of view. Three of these universities specialize in engineering. The 42 government-approved universities of professional education prepare more than 350,000 students each year for the workplace. These institutions offer a range of qualifications, predominantly in agriculture, engineering and technology, economics and business administration, health care, fine and performing arts, education (teacher training) and social welfare. There are also 11 International Education Institutes, offering advanced courses exclusively in English for international students. These institutions focus on development-related subjects taught in small groups, of various nationalities.

Entry requirements are based on a student's qualifications, language skills, and any specifics of the chosen academic field of study. As a minimum, a student will have to have the equivalent of a Dutch VWO Diploma, awarded after 13 years of education. For students with 12 years of education, bridging courses are available. Because so many programs are available in English, students do not need to demonstrate language proficiency in Dutch, but they will be expected to show competence in English through an IELTS™ or TOEFL® exam. Applying to Dutch universities is straightforward, with application deadlines in April or May of the year in which studies commence.

Fees, finance & cost of living

Tuition fees at Dutch institutions are subsidized by the national government, and undergraduate fees vary by subject. Popular areas such as business, economics, law and management are more expensive than literature and history, with fees anywhere between €2,000 and €12,500 a year. There are few nationally organized undergraduate scholarships available, but a number of major schemes exist for postgraduate programs. Some undergraduate scholarships exist for students from specific countries around the world and these tend to be administered by local Netherlands Education Support Offices (NESO). Some individual universities organize, fund and award scholarships to international students. The online search facility offered by Grantfinder www.grantfinder.nl is helpful in locating scholarships.

The cost of living in the Netherlands is relatively expensive. Many students live on between €700 and €900 a month, with accommodation costs either in university or private residences accounting for between €300 and €450 of that budget. Student discounts and subsidized food costs at institutions can offset some of the expenses of being a student in the Netherlands. All international students need to have health insurance to obtain an entry visa into the Netherlands. If a student is under the age of 30, working part-time or staying longer than three years, the health cover situation alters. Details are available from each institution or at www.nuffic.nl. There are excellent infrastructure and travel links throughout the Netherlands. In cities and towns, many people use a bicycle to get around. For longer journeys trains, buses and planes provide reasonably priced fares all over the Netherlands and farther afield.

Student life

As a student in the Netherlands life will revolve around the town or city you are studying in, rather than your university campus. There are many student clubs and societies to join, well-equipped sports facilities and student discounts which allow you to visit museums and art galleries throughout the country. Students from outside the European Economic Area (EEA) are allowed to work while studying, although you must have a work permit and there are restrictions on what you can do. Students must choose to either work full-time during June, July and August, or part-time for a maximum ten hours per week throughout the year. Students who wish to can apply to stay for one year after their studies as a highly skilled migrant, which also gives you more time to explore this fabulous country.

Study in the Nordic Countries (Denmark, Finland, Iceland, Norway & Sweden)

Pros & cons

+ **High academic quality, strictly enforced and maintained**
+ **Many programs taught in English**
+ **Active social and cultural life**
- **High cost of living**
- **Some difficulty with residence permits**

Why the Nordic Region?

From Denmark's mix of modern cities, enchanting villages and sleepy islands, to Norway's Viking traditions, snowy plateaux and majestic fiords, each of the five countries that make up the Nordic region has its own unique character. Finland has the world's biggest smoke sauna and 200,000 reindeer. Sweden, the home of IKEA, has countryside perfect for outdoor adventure, and Iceland's scenery complete with lava, glaciers, and geysers will cater for everyone. However, despite their historical and geographical differences, these countries do have weather in common. There's no escaping the long hard snow-filled winters with little light, but you will enjoy the beautiful summers with endless hours of sunshine. If you study abroad in one of these countries you'll have the best of both worlds: bustling cities of Copenhagen (Denmark), Helsinki (Finland), Reykjavik (Iceland), Oslo (Norway) and Stockholm (Sweden) and the tranquil and peaceful natural environment. Whichever Nordic country you choose to study in, there'll be plenty to write home about.

Higher education in these countries is making its mark. Twenty-three universities appear in the top 400 of the 2008 Times Higher–QS World University Rankings, six of which are in the top 100. Sweden has the highest number of ranked universities with eight in the top 400. Finland follows closely with seven and Norway and Denmark each have four.

Universities

The higher education systems of the Nordic countries are all organized in a similar way. Each offers three or four-year bachelors degrees and one or two-year masters programs. They are largely state-dominated, with public rather than private institutions offering degree-level education. Universities tend to offer degree-level teaching while university colleges and vocational colleges offer diplomas and certificates in more applied and practical subjects. The smallest system is Iceland, where ten institutions offer degree and vocational education programs to 12,000 students, mostly in Icelandic. The other four much larger systems have universities and colleges teaching students from all over the world in either English or the local language. Norway has the most private investment in higher education, with 29 institutions holding either program or institutional accreditation from the government. Finland provides the largest number of English language programs in Europe outside the UK, within its parallel binary system of universities (offering more academic programs) and universities of applied sciences (where the more vocational and technical subjects are taught). Sweden and Denmark offer diverse systems of higher education, where vocational and academic programs are both readily available.

Entry requirements are also similar. Students must have a minimum of 12 years of education although in Denmark, Finland and Norway, 13 years is preferred. If a student's qualification is not sufficient to meet the required entry levels, he or she may complete a university preparatory course. In each of the five country systems, individual universities have their own application processes and deadlines.

Fees, finance & cost of living

One of the great advantages of higher education in the Nordic countries is that tuition fees are either reasonably priced or not yet in existence. Denmark charges market-rate tuition fees on a modest scale. Individual universities or colleges may charge a small administrative fee for every semester, but these amounts are not as high as the tuition fees of other European countries. However, the cost of living in these five countries is extremely high. University or private accommodation tends to be the largest single expenditure for students studying here. Scholarships are available for a number of the Nordic countries. Denmark offers several government schemes and supports a range of EU mobility programs. Norway administers a range of awards and scholarships through the Norwegian Centre for International Cooperation in Higher Education (SIU). A Quota Scheme also exists for 1,100 students every year from developing countries, Eastern Europe and Central Asia. Sweden and Iceland both offer scholarships to cover living costs through their national agencies, and in all countries certain universities and colleges offer awards for specific countries or academic subjects. Details can be found at individual institutions' websites.

Another element of life in the Nordic countries is the excellent welfare state, offering protection for all in society. Students from the European Economic Area (EEA) are covered for all medical care, including emergencies, by their own medical system. Other international students are covered by the local system in Denmark (after a period of six weeks), Finland (if you are a member of the Students' Union), Iceland (if your program of study is full-time),and in Norway and Sweden (if your program of study is longer than a year in length).

Student life

Universities and colleges in the big cities can offer more facilities than those in smaller centres. Common to all institutions is the customary range of academic, social and sporting clubs organized on or near campus by students, for students. Student Unions and Guilds also offer useful resources for students in terms of discounts and advice. Each county has an excellent transport network that allows students to explore not only their chosen place of study, but also the other Nordic countries located close by. Trains, long distance buses and an increasing number of budget airlines cater for students through various discounts, and a number of ferry companies enable you to enjoy very cheap travel between Finland and Sweden in particular. As an international student you can work in all five Nordic countries, although each has specific conditions that need to be satisfied in order for you to work legally. In most cases you can work 20 hours a week in term time and full-time during the vacation periods, depending on the status of your study visa or residence permit. During the rest of your spare time, make the most this spectacular region by train, boat or skis and explore!

WORLD ARTS TOUR

Asia's Festivals for Recruiting Students to Design Education and to the Creative and Performing Arts

Seoul • Hong Kong • Kuala Lumpur • Singapore

21 February – 3 March 2010

Extra features in 2010
Industrial Design
Product Design
Engineering Design

Book your participation now!
Contact us for details and visit us at www.qsworldarts.com

All Asia, Middle East and New Zealand
Mandy Mok
mm@qsnetwork.com

America, Canada and Europe
Peter MacDonald
peter@qsnetwork.com

Australia
Jason Newman
jason.newman@qsnetwork.com

Study in Singapore

Pros & cons

+ Increasing international reputation
+ Ability to work after graduation
+ Links with international universities
- Lack of global visibility for Singaporean qualifications
- Vast array of private colleges with unclear reputations
- Limited numbers of students from all world regions

Why Singapore?

Since shopping and eating are favourite activities of Singaporeans, studying abroad in Asia's cleanest and most highly organized society could be dangerous to both your bank balance and your waistline. But don't let that stop you from experiencing this country of diversity: Chinese, Malay, Indian and European cultures combine/co-exist to form an exciting environment. Singapore is one of the world's greatest financial and trade centres, and also one of the most strictly governed: locals and visitors can be fined for anything from not flushing public toilets to dropping chewing gum. The heat and humidity (the coolest temperature ever recorded is C19.5°) provide for long lazy evenings at street cafés, safaris through the world's first night zoo, or cruises past river banks lined with museums, theatres and concert halls. With an excellent transport system, superb infrastructure and reputation for safety, Singapore is one of the world's favoured destinations.

Two of its universities are in the top 200 of the 2008 THE-QS World University Rankings, but Singapore's top publicly-funded universities attract more applications from local and international students than there are places available.

Universities

The National University of Singapore, Nanyang Technological University and Singapore Management University, teach the entire range of academic subjects and all offer undergraduate degree qualifications, in addition to postgraduate and research programs. The country also has five polytechnics, offering two and three-year diplomas in many different subject areas, which focus on educating students in a more vocational way. And, tightly regulated by the Singaporean Ministry of Education,there are private institutions offering undergraduate and diploma programs. Several also teach qualifications with international curricula, such as for the Chartered Institute of Marketing and the Association of Chartered Certified Accountants. A further trend is the growth of offshore campuses. Universities in Australia, Finland, New Zealand, and the UK, and 16 further universities from Asia, Europe and the US have opened campuses in Singapore, providing a range of undergraduate programs. These international partnerships allow students to study for a fraction of the cost of travelling overseas for the same program.

Admission to both universities and polytechnics is dependent on individual program requirements. At both levels, students should have completed at least 12 years of education. For students wishing to study medicine or dentistry, an application requires grades to be presented rather than predicted. Application deadlines vary depending on the program of study and are made directly to the institution. Deadlines are either at the end of December in the year before a student commences study, or at the end of February in the year of study. Some programs also require students to complete a TOEFL®

or IELTS™ test if English is not their first language, so international students should check the admission requirements of the particular program for which they are applying .

Fees, finance & cost of living

Individual institutions set tuition fees at the undergraduate level. Fees at the three local universities tend to vary by academic subject but generally range between SG$20,000 and SG$24,000. Exceptional programs, such as those in the medical field, are priced much higher and students can expect to pay anything up to SG$80,000 a year for tuition fees. Singapore's five polytechnics offer a lower fee rate for their diploma programs, with annual costs of SG$12,160. The cost of living in Singapore is very reasonable. Students have access to both university and private accommodation. The former tends to be the better option as it provides a good introduction to society and is the most economical. Those who choose to live in private apartments will find Singapore expensive. Depending on the type of accommodation, students will need to budget between SG$750 and SG$1,500 a month. This estimate should cover transport, entertainment, health insurance and books.

All national and international students are free to apply to the Singaporean Ministry of Education for a tuition grant once they have been admitted to their program of choice. This scheme allows for a grant of between SG$14,000 and SG$16,000 for most programs to be paid against tuition fees. For programs such as medicine and music, the grant can be as high as SG$65,500 a year. However, international students are required to sign a bond in order to obtain a tuition grant, committing them to working in Singapore for three years after the completion of their university or polytechnic program. Scholarships and bursaries are also available from either the Ministry of Education or individual universities. Such schemes include the ASEAN Undergraduate Scholarships that provide for tuition costs, SG$3,500 annual living allowance and return travel between the recipient's country and Singapore; and the Singapore Technologies International Scholarships: www.moe. gov.sg. All institutions support their international student population through their International Student Services. The Overseas Students' Association also supports all international students over the age of 16. Students are recommended to have medical insurance while studying in Singapore: www.osa.org.sg.

Student life

Full -time students can work up to 16 hours a week during term time and full -time during vacations. However, in some cases a student's immigration status may prevent him or her from legally seeking employment. Details at www.mom.gov.sg. In between study commitments students can take time out in one of the 24-hour bowling alleys, on a mountain bike in East Coast Park, wakeboarding in the Kallang River, or swinging a round at one of Singapore's world famous, and very expensive, golf courses. With its green spaces and skyscrapers, designer stores and markets, there's arguably no other place quite like Singapore for experience as an international student.

Balancing Work And Studies Is Now Easy

Doors just don't open themselves. U21Global is your key to unlocking your true career potential. Take your career to new heights with our online **MBA** programme. Our courses are designed to foster both leadership and management skills, for whichever industry you're in.

Our flexible online programme means you can study anytime, anywhere – striking the perfect work-life balance. You can benefit from the power of networking and knowledge-sharing with professors and students from over 60 countries.

U21Global is internationally accredited and backed by 17 world-class universities. So you are assured of excellent support in achieving your future goals, whilst enjoying the present.

To find out more:
Call: +65 6410 1399 or email us at
campus@u21global.edu.sg

www.u21global.edu.sg/regional1

Affiliated Universities

Fudan University • Korea University • Lund University • National University of Singapore • Shanghai Jiao Tong University • Tecnológico De Monterrey • University College Dublin • University of Birmingham • University of Delhi • University of Edinburgh • University of Glasgow • University of Hong Kong • University of Melbourne • University of Nottingham • University of Queensland • University of Virginia • Waseda University

Study in the United Kingdom (UK)

Pros & cons

+ High number of top institutions appearing in the world's top 400
+ English language teaching
+ Variety of experiences inside and outside the classroom
- High cost of tuition and living expenses
- High numbers of international students on some programs

Why the UK?

Buckingham Palace, Big Ben, double-decker buses, steak and ale pies: the metropolis of London is home to some of the most famous sights and smells in the Northern Hemisphere. But there's more to this small island nation of 60 million people than its capital city. Made up of four distinct parts, England, Northern Ireland, Scotland and Wales, the UK is a treasure trove of history, architecture, culture and scenery. Explore centuries-old castles and palaces, marvel at the mystery of Stonehenge, walk, cycle or 4WD through the picturesque Lake District or the Scottish highlands, or brave the cold for a surf in the Irish Sea. Studying in the UK also puts you on the doorstep of Europe. The Eurostar will whisk you to European destinations in under two hours, plentiful cheap air travel allows you to escape the study books for the weekend, and there's never any shortage of live shows or concerts to go to. Studying abroad in the UK will give you an enriching education both inside and outside the classroom.

UK universities are regarded as being among the finest in the world, with 29 in the top 200 of the 2008 THE-QS World University Rankings and four in the top ten, showing that the UK higher education system is second only to that of the US.

Universities

There are more than 140 institutions in the UK offering undergraduate degrees to 1.6 million full-time students, 99,000 of whom are international students. Another 500 colleges offer educational programs of differing kinds. Comprehensive and multifaculty UK universities and colleges offer the full range of academic subject areas from accountancy to zoology. No separate institutions exist for subjects such as business, law and medicine at the undergraduate level, though some universities offer subject specializations such as the London School of Economics (social sciences), the School of Pharmacy (pharmaceutical sciences) and the Institute of Education (teacher training and education). Almost all universities in the UK are state-financed.

Universities and colleges offer five broad types of qualification. Colleges tend to teach for the Higher National Certificate (HNC), Higher National Diploma (HND), Foundation Degree and Diploma of Higher Education. All last between one and two years and are the equivalent of the early stages of a bachelors degree in a range of subjects, such as art and design, engineering, media, social studies and technology. Universities tend to teach three or four-year undergraduate degree programs that are more academic in nature and lead to a bachelors qualification. Degree programs that are four years in length tend to include a period in industry or commerce, or a period of study abroad, such as an exchange scheme in Europe or the US. Students must have completed 13 years of education prior to coming to the UK and have a local high school qualification equivalent to UK A-levels. Students without 13 years of education are able to apply to UK universities and colleges that offer foundation or bridging programs. Acceptable entry grades are entirely dependent on the individual university or college, all of which publish explicit entry standards. Applications are generally made through a central system administered by the Universities and Colleges Application Service (UCAS): www.ucas.ac.uk. Students who don't speak English as a first language should check with their chosen institution to see what test results or certificate they need to complete prior to making their application.

Fees, finance & cost of living

The UK is a relatively expensive country in which to study. The UK government allows universities to set their own tuition fees, which tend to vary according to the prestige of the university. At most universities in England, students from the UK and the European Union pay up to £3,000 a year for tuition. International students can expect to pay somewhere between £6,500 and £13,000 a year, depending on whether a program is classroom or laboratory based. Queen's University in Belfast, Northern Ireland is ranked 202 in the world. Since devolution in UK government, Scotland and Wales set some policy for higher education, including fees. Over 170,000 students from 100 different countries choose to study at one of Scotland's 21 universities and colleges, three of which are in the top 100 in the world. Students permanently resident in Scotland do not have to pay tuition fees. International students, including those from EU and EEA countries pay fees, but there is financial support available. Two Welsh universities are in the world's top 400, with Cardiff University at 133. Resident Welsh students pay considerably lower fees in Wales than at universities elsewhere in the UK and for international students there are scholarship opportunities. The British Council Wales website has information on such scholarships as well as advice on visa applications and opportunities to learn English in Wales.

Costs for accommodation, utilities and books are generally high, although there are regional differences. London and the southeast generally have a higher cost of living than other parts of the UK. However, as a student you will have access to discounts on all sorts of services such as movie theatres, museums, tourist attractions and travel. Students can expect to pay anywhere between £5,500 (outside of London and the southeast) and £7,500 a year for living costs. The UK transport system is well developed but can be expensive if you don't book well in advance. Train, bus and flight networks cover the entire country and allow you to travel easily and quickly, and discount schemes are available. Students also have access to free medical care if their program of study is over six months in length.

Scholarships are difficult to obtain in the UK at undergraduate level. There are no schemes administered by government organizations and only partial funding offered by individual universities and colleges. Most schemes require you to hold an offer of admission before seeking an application for financial aid. Relevant information is available on the international or undergraduate university admissions web pages for each tertiary institution, and chapter four gives more information on available scholarships.

Student life

The UK offers international students an experience of a lifetime. With its unique history and centuries of interaction with European neighbours, there is much to explore and understand. And with the high number of UK universities in the top 400 worldwide, students can be sure of a quality educational experience. Universities and colleges offer a range of services including clubs, sports facilities and special interest societies such as debating clubs, political and cultural groups, and performing arts such as choirs and amateur dramatics. All students are eligible to join the National Union of Students, an organization that campaigns for the rights of students. Students from the European Economic Area (EEA) can work freely in the UK; other international students can work up to 20 hours a week in term time and full-time during vacations.

Study in the US

Pros & cons

+ Many reputable private and public universities
+ Good campus support for international students
+ Scholarships/financial aid for international students
- Tough student visa requirements
- Post-study visa for employment difficult
- Relatively high tuition fees

Why the US?

Shopping in New York, snowboarding in Colorado, roller blading in California or riding roller coasters in Florida: there is plenty to experience while studying abroad in the US. With 50 states, each with its own unique character, landscape and people, the US is a country to be explored: from the Midwestern agricultural states to the Pacific Northwest, the natural wonder of the Grand Canyon to the technology of the Kennedy Space Centre. The US is a country of history, influence and power, change, innovation and design. As an international student you'll be able to marvel at the White House in Washington DC, explore the freedom trail of Boston, New England, or spend your time celebrity-spotting in glamorous Beverly Hills. There is the 4th of July celebration to be enjoyed, Thanksgiving turkeys to eat, and tricks or treats to be sampled at Halloween. To study in the US is to experience the academic achievements of one of the world's richest countries.

The US has the highest number of universities in the world's top 400, including six in the top ten of the 2008 THE-QS World University Rankings. Only four UK universities: Oxford and Cambridge, Imperial College and University College London (UCL), have challenged the supremacy of the US this year.

Universities

There are two types of university in the US. The Ivy League universities are independent and funded entirely by income from student fees, research awards and fundraising. These are private institutions, like 75 per cent of US universities. The remaining 25 per cent, state-funded universities, are much cheaper to attend and have 75 per cent of US students. State universities include some of the top ranked universities in the world such as UC Berkeley and the University of California. The US education system also works on a credit system, which enables students to change their majors without losing any time during their degree. This credit system also makes transferring between universities relatively straightforward.

Studying medicine or law in the US is different from the rest of the world. There are almost no undergraduate medical degrees (Northwestern University is one of the only exceptions), or undergraduate law degrees. Students interested in medicine must study another subject in their first degree, while at the same time preparing for their MCAT (nine hours of multiple choice testing) to gain entry to medical school. Students interested in law tend to study for a liberal arts degree, while having to pass the LSAT test to gain entry to law school. The US also has many of the world's best undergraduate business programs and MBAs. US universities publish general entry criteria on their websites. For prospective international students who achieve top ten per cent grades in their home country, the chances of gaining entry to the top ten per cent of US universities are high,

Advancing Knowledge.
Transforming Lives.

Michigan State University is among the largest and most comprehensive universities in the United States, with a tradition and reputation to match.

Recognized around the world as a top research university, MSU has been advancing knowledge and transforming lives through innovative teaching, research, and outreach for more than 150 years.

Today, MSU is a dynamic and diverse academic community and a leader in international engagement that is making a difference from Michigan to Malawi.

- One of the top 100 universities in the world

- A world leader in plant sciences and food security

- First in the U.S. for graduate programs in education

- Second in the U.S. for nuclear physics program

- One of the top five universities in the U.S. for environmental sustainability

- Top 10 for study abroad participation and international student enrollment among public universities in the U.S.

MICHIGAN STATE
UNIVERSITY

msu.edu

but there will be exceptions. Some country high school qualifications are considered more advanced than US equivalents. For example, UK A-level grades can count towards credit for many US degrees, potentially taking as much as 12 months off the length of the degree. Domestic applicants have to take the SAT exam. If SAT results are a long way short of the average, it is generally not worth applying.

Fees, finance & cost of living

The elite US universities are the most expensive in the world. At the same time, they can be a gateway to the most attractive employment market in the world, and provide value for money in terms of class time and good access to professors. An added attraction for international students is the huge number of scholarships and financial aid packages available at many well-funded private universities, making them open to even the most disadvantaged, but bright, students. University scholarships tend to be awarded on financial need and/or merit. Merit can encompass special talent in sports, performing arts, community service participation or extracurricular involvement as well as outstanding academic performance. Many scholarships are renewable over a student's four years of study providing specified academic standards or grades are maintained. Many US universities' financial aid departments ask for a statement of your family's financial situation. If they want you and they decide that your family can only contribute US$1,000 per year, then, that is all you will have to pay. Alternatively, they may have international student loan schemes.

Students whose families can afford the bills should be prepared for tuition and fees varying between US$3,500 and US$60,000 per academic year. As a guideline, average fees are about US$16,000 per year, which is usually based on a nine-month academic year from September to May. Books, travel and living costs need to be added. Costs vary by city, with New York, Boston and San Francisco among the most expensive. Fraternities ('frats') and sororities still form a fundamental part of student life, with private buildings where students can party and relax. They also offer alternative accommodation to university dorms. Students must provide proof of having purchased private health insurance as part of their application. This is relatively straightforward unless a student has a pre-existing condition such as diabetes, which can turn the process into a time-consuming and expensive exercise. The international department at US institutions can advise international students on insurance options.

Student life

American universities encourage students to work alongside their course. Employment offices provide paid work on campus, for which an international student visa will suffice. You will need to apply for a social security number, at which point you can take any campus job such as a teaching assistant or sports attendant. As part of your international visa, you are allowed one year of optional practical training (OPT), enabling you to work anywhere in the US, in consulting, banking, engineering or any other field. The year allocation can be used in batches during summer internships, or in full after your degree. Special interest and sports clubs also play a major part in the social scene at many universities. Since American students tend to move away from home to attend university, you'll have many opportunities to meet and travel with new friends.

Global Quality, Thai Touch

Host of 6th QS-APPLE in 2010

At Mahidol University, we are committed to constantly expand our facilities, strengthen our academic resources, and develop our research activities to world-class levels.

With our experience and expertise, we can help our students adapt and excel in this ever-changing knowledge-based economy.

- **Ranked as Top University in Thailand for Research and Teaching by Commission for Higher Education since 2005**
- **Thai university with most publications and citations in international journals over last 10 years**
- **Received Thailand's Prime Minister Export Award for Most Recognized Service in International Higher Education**
- **Numerous outstanding research awards and prestigious international awards**

www.mahidol.ac.th

MAHIDOL UNIVERSITY
Wisdom of the Land

Study in New Zealand

Pros & cons

+ No limit on the time students can spend studying
+ Can work 20 hours per week while studying
+ Two-year post-study working visa available
- High international student fees
- Distance from rest of world

Why New Zealand?

Surf, ski or snowboard in season walk through beautiful native bush, or try a bungy jump: you'll get your education inside and outside in New Zealand. Discover the richness of Maori culture, photograph a silver fern, gaze at the Southern Cross or bathe your feet in thermal hot pools: New Zealand will give you experiences you'll never forget.

Universities

There are eight universities in New Zealand, six of which feature in the top 400 of the 2008 THE-QS World University Rankings. They offer undergraduate degrees in a range of subjects from medicine to business, agriculture to law. A unique aspect of New Zealand education is the New Zealand specific case studies incorporated into a degree, yet providing an international outlook. Undergraduate degrees are three to four years of study; conjoint and specialist degrees can take up to five or six years. International students need a visa or permit to study. To gain entry, students must pass either the TOEFL® or IELTS™ English Language Proficiency Exams; the results required depend on the program of study.

Fees, finance & cost of living

The New Zealand government funds up to 28 fees scholarships each year for international undergraduate students. Individual universities each have a scholarships office with a list of awards open to both domestic and international students. There is no limit on the time students can spend studying in New Zealand, as long as they have a current visa. The Ministry of Education ensures all educational institutes abide by the Code of Practice of pastoral care of international students. Full-time students are permitted to work up to 20 hours per week. Upon completion of a degree, students may accept a job offer, which will allow them to obtain a working visa and stay for another two years. International students studying in New Zealand should budget NZ$20,000 a year in living expenses.

Student life

Most university towns in New Zealand are centred on the institution itself so students are an important part of these communities. Student associations organize orientation events for new and returning students, and many businesses, such as retail outlets and cinemas, offer cheap rates for students.

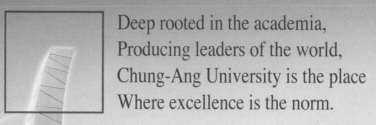

Deep rooted in the academia,
Producing leaders of the world,
Chung-Ang University is the place
Where excellence is the norm.

CHUNG·ANG UNIVERSITY, KOREA

Study in South Korea

Pros & cons

+ **Low cost of tuition**
+ **Courses in English**
+ **Opportunity to learn a new language**
- **Language barriers**
- **Political and religious association of institutions**

Why South Korea?

If you're tempted to try the spiciest dish in the world, then head to Korea. 'Pul t'ak', otherwise known as 'Fire Chicken' will be sure to test your taste buds. Korean cuisine is just one of the many unique experiences you'll encounter as an international student in this country rich in history, technology and culture.

Universities

Seven of Korea's 250 universities can be found in the top 400 of the 2008 THE-QS World University Rankings. The top three are known collectively as the SKY universities: Seoul National University, Korea University and Yonsei University. Korean institutions are recognized for their degrees in biotechnology, information technology and communications. Undergraduate degrees take four years to complete, masters degrees an additional two to three. There are two types of university in South Korea: national and private. National universities tend to have lower fees than private universities ranging from US$3,500 to US$6,000 per year. The academic year for undergraduate students begins in March and students are recommended to start the application process three to four months before the application deadline.

Fees, finance & cost of living

South Korea is less expensive to live and study in than many Western countries. Accommodation and food costs around US$300 each per month. Students studying in Korea on a D-2 visa can work up to 20 hours per week after one semester. There is no limit on the number of hours students can work during vacation. The Korea Foundation sponsors foreign students as does the South Korean Ministry of Education, Science & Technology, which maintains a scholarship program for foreign students. Individual universities also have scholarships available. Students must ensure they take out insurance to study in South Korea. Foreign students' insurance payments are reduced by 30 per cent and are paid every three months ahead of time.

Student life

University students are very active in clubs known as Tongari, the most popular being the traditional Korean drums. Take your hiking boots to South Korea: the landscape is mountainous. If you have the energy to visit one of the spectacular mountain temples, you'll be rewarded with a free vegetarian meal inside. Buses and subways are the cheapest form of transport in urban areas.

Università Cattolica del Sacro Cuore

5 campuses throughout Italy

over 42.000 students, 2.000 international

51 undergraduate and over 200 graduate
and post-graduate programs

over 130.000 alumni

www.ucsc

Study in Switzerland

Pros & cons

+ Moderate study fees
+ Scholarships available
+ Can work 15 hours per week while studying
- Tough entry regulations
- Language comprehension requirements

Why Switzerland?

Is there any better reason to study in Switzerland than being able to savour Swiss chocolate for a year? Situated in the heart of Europe, Switzerland is a small country renowned for its beautiful scenery, diversity of cultures and being able to ski right from your doorstep. Switzerland is also making its mark in the global higher education arena.

Universities

Two Swiss universities appear in the top 50 of the 2008 THE-QS World University Rankings, another one appears in the top 100 and a total of eight universities feature in the overall 400. There are two categories of tertiary education in Switzerland: universities of applied sciences, which offer professional training; and higher technical schools, which give students professional or vocational qualifications. A first degree requires three years of study in Switzerland and a masters, a further two. Many Swiss universities offer courses in English, but students do need a high level of language comprehension in German, French or Italian. Students must include a state-recognized Swiss maturity certificate or equivalent foreign certificate, as part of their application.

Fees, finance & cost of living

Most Swiss universities are publicly funded, making international study relatively affordable. The Swiss government, and some universities, also offer scholarships to international students. However, students must ensure they have sufficient funds to support themselves during their studies. International students may have up to 15 hours per week of paid employment. Accommodation is generally easy to find in Switzerland. There are some university student houses, but most students live in flat shares which are advertized on university notice boards or student websites such as www.students.ch and www.studisurf.ch. Don't expect flat shares to be furnished when you move in, and some won't even have light-bulbs! It is also obligatory for international students, staying longer than three months in Switzerland, to take out health insurance.

Student life

Studying abroad in Switzerland will be a unique and varied experience depending on which part of the multi-cultural country you are in. University student association membership (around CHF25 per semester) enables students to receive discounts around town and a train discount card offers free travel on train, bus or boat after 7pm for students under 25. Websites offer students discounted computer hardware and software, and discounted bank accounts and credit cards also exist for students.

Sources of information for study abroad*

Australia	IDP Education Australia www.idp.com
Austria	ÖAD Austrian Exchange Service www.oead.ac.at
Brazil	Study in Brazil www.studyinbrazil.org
Canada	Canadian Education Centre Network www.studycanada.ca
China	China Study Abroad www.chinastudyabroad.org
Denmark	CIRIUS Study in Denmark www.studyindenmark.dk
Finland	CIMO Centre for International Mobility www.studyinfinland.fi
France	Agence EduFrance www.edufrance.fr
Germany	DAAD German Academic Exchange Service www.daad.de
	The portal for students www.uni-pur.de
Greece	Study Abroad Greece www.studyabroadgreece.com
Hong Kong	Hong Kong Higher Education www.studyinhongkong.edu.hk
India	University Grants Commission www.ugc.ac.in
Iran	International Student Information System www.iran-student.com
Ireland	Education Ireland www.educationireland.ie
Italy	MIUR/CIMEA www.study-in-italy.it www.cimea.it
Japan	JASSO Japan Student Services Organization www.jasso.go.jp
Malaysia	Study Malaysia www.studymalaysia.com
Mexico	Secretaria De Educación Publica (SEP) www.sep.gob.mx
Netherlands	NUFFIC www.studyin.nl
New Zealand	Education New Zealand www.newzealandeducated.com
Norway	SIU www.studyinnorway.no
Russia	The School of Russian and Asian Studies www.sras.org
Singapore	Singapore Education www.singaporeedu.gov.sg
South Africa	Study South Africa www.studysa.co.za
South Korea	NIIED www.studyinkorea.co.kr
Spain	Eduespana www.eduespa.org
Sweden	The Swedish Institute www.studyinsweden.se
Switzerland	Studying in Switzerland www.switzerland.isyours.com
	Rectors' Conference of the Swiss Universities www.crus.ch
Taiwan	Ministry of Education www.studyintaiwan.org
Thailand	About Thailand Info www.aboutthailand.info/university.asp
Turkey	Study Turkey www.studyturkey.metu.edu.tr
UK	The British Council www.educationuk.org
US	Education USA www.educationusa.state.gov

General

Study Abroad (US based) www.studyabroaddirectory.com
Worldwide Classroom (US based) www.worldwide.edu
IIEPassport Study Abroad Directories (US based) www.iiepassport.org
Academic Programs International for US students www.academicintl.com
The Education Abroad Network (Australia& NZ based) www.educationabroadnetwork.org
American Institute For Foreign Study (AIFS) (US based) www.aifsabroad.com
Arabian Campus LLC - an academic service provider for the purpose of promoting accredited higher education programs and institutions within the Arabian region www.arabiancampus.com

*This compilation is copyright QS 2009

5th QS-APPLE

www.qsapple.org

**FIFTH QS ASIA PACIFIC PROFESSIONAL
LEADERS IN EDUCATION CONFERENCE
AND EXHIBITION**
**KUALA LUMPUR, MALAYSIA
24 - 26 NOVEMBER 2009**

The Prime Conference and Exhibition for Top International Educators in Asia, Europe, America and Australasia

helping to build world-class universities for Asia-Pacific communities through global partnership and collaboration

In partnership with

UNIVERSITY
OF MALAYA
KUALA LUMPUR
The leader in research and innovation.

UNIVERSITI
KEBANGSAAN
MALAYSIA
National University of Malaysia
Inspiring futures, nurturing possibilities.

6th QS-APPLE - Hosted by Mahidol University, Bangkok in November 2010

4

Fees, finance and scholarships

This chapter gives prospective students and parents an overview of study costs worldwide, and of finance and scholarships options. The first part of the chapter surveys the relative study and living costs around the world and lists the fees at the top 200 universities. The second part looks at financing your study, and surveys organizations offering scholarships in some of the more popular study destinations. There are great variations from country to country, between universities and within individual universities, depending on program. Average figures are used in the data tables, so further investigation is recommended in every case.

Studying at university is a major investment, one of the most important of your life. Having to study hard for several years and accumulate significant debt may seem like a bad bargain, but when you review the career options for today's top graduates, it becomes apparent that a good degree is almost priceless. Studying at a top university will have a positive impact on your future earnings potential and studying internationally can be even more highly regarded by top employers. With thousands of universities in the world and millions of students, it is little surprise that the availability and participation in higher education varies greatly worldwide, as do study and living costs. Today, smart students and parents can shop around the world to search out the best value, according to a career strategy. However, for any prospective student and his or her parents, it is important to know and fully understand the true costs of study at different institutions and their quality, in order to assess budgets, return on investment and, ultimately, make the best choice.

An end to free universities

The world of higher education is undergoing great change. Ron Perkinson of the International Finance Corporation (World Bank) described the "perfect storm of forces changing the shape of international education: increased importance of knowledge and credentials in the employment market, demographic increases in numbers of young people aged 18-24 around the world, reduced government funding and globalization." These forces are creating many changes, but the overwhelming change is that university education is no longer going to be free for the majority of people, even in their home countries. Most institutions today are either charging, or about to introduce charges for tuition. Private and public universities alike have passed on some of the study costs to their students for many years, but the implementation of full-cost tuition fees is now commonplace throughout Europe, Asia and North and Latin America. Across the world, a free university education is rapidly becoming a thing of the past. As a consequence, many young people are shopping overseas for the best deals; not necessarily the lowest overall cost, but the best price for a given quality. This calculation will vary according to the type of program that is chosen, the country of choice, the length of stay, as well as other factors that can be evaluated with the help of the THE-QS World University Rankings, which provide a guide to institutional quality and other indicators that should also be considered.

University study costs worldwide

Variations in study costs across the world may play a part in your choice of university, but these costs should always be considered alongside the quality of the university and course. The following table of average tuition costs by country, for domestic and international students for undergraduate and postgraduate programs, provides a quick basis for comparison. The data collected from the 500 universities listed in the directory (chapter six) at the back of this book forms the basis of these figures.

University fees in the US are the highest, on average, in the world. By contrast, a number of Scandinavian countries still charge no university fees, though this policy is under review and expectations are that most countries will introduce fees in the coming years. There are a number of other European countries where fees remain modest. The UK and Ireland are more expensive than European counterparts. The level of UK tuition fees for domestic students is dependent upon personal circumstances including family income. Nevertheless, the UK remains a very popular overseas study destination. According to AimHigher, the UK government-backed website for higher education, around 30,000 international students begin undergraduate courses each year in the UK, the vast majority of whom are full fee paying students.

Further research is recommended. There are many variations in the approach to tuition costs worldwide. Singapore, for example, has a unique arrangement. If a student is accepted for study, he or she will be eligible for a Ministry of Education grant if he or she signs a deed of covenant agreeing to work in Singapore for three years after graduation, reducing considerably the net cost of study.

Average annual university tuition costs by country US$

Country	Domestic		International	
	undergraduate	postgraduate	undergraduate	postgraduate
Argentina	3,773	5,373	3,773	5,373
Australia	12,918	12,445	17,515	18,025
Austria	1,038	865	1,604	1,604
Belgium	1,020	1,989	1,989	2,122
Canada	4,054	5,079	13,985	10,619
Chile	5,143	12,503	5,143	16,270
China	760	1,533	3,730	4,395
Czech Republic	0	0	11,620	11,075
Denmark	0	0	17,565	18,703
Finland	0	0	0	0
France	1,410	4,341	2,023	5,447
Germany	1,885	2,490	1,941	1,359
Hong Kong	5,910	10,880	9,740	12,822
Hungary	5,335	7,045	5,530	6,460
India	1,188	2,377	1,240	2,584
Indonesia	748	1,515	2,672	3,161
Ireland	7,124	5,925	22,001	17,410
Israel	2,513	3,118	5,793	9,398
Italy	2,510	2,419	2,530	3,199
Japan	5,683	5,696	5,683	5,696
Malaysia	594	2,066	1,828	3,316

Country	Domestic		International	
	undergraduate	postgraduate	undergraduate	postgraduate
Netherlands	2,864	3,672	7,479	12,698
New Zealand	3,324	4,547	14,877	15,350
Pakistan	1,583	1,013	4,783	2,943
Philippines	2,773	1,890	3,013	2,050
Poland	3,890	3,310	4,943	6,230
Portugal	1,450	7,980	1,450	7,980
Russia	2,950	2,908	3,150	3,300
Singapore	4,540	4,330	6,045	6,430
South Africa	2,118	1,750	6,420	4,583
South Korea	6,697	7,986	6,710	8,165
Spain	3,107	5,567	5,034	10,959
Sweden	0	0	0	0
Switzerland	1,216	1,140	1,276	1,166
Taiwan	1,681	1,508	1,966	1,520
Thailand	810	1,790	8,688	6,176
United Kingdom	5,505	9,077	19,684	22,505
United States	20,721	17,805	26,720	23,531

Copyright: QS Quacquarelli Symonds 2009

Note: Costs are calculated based on the average of the numbers supplied by or for institutions in each country, (exchange rates to US$ as at 01.05.08 www.oanda.com). An average has only been calculated where a minimum of two separate values are available for that country in that column. Any data updates will be published on www.topuniversities.com.

Tuition fees at the world's top 200 universities

The following data tables of average undergraduate and postgraduate fees for domestic and international students are intended to give outline guidance. You will need to research further and your study decision should always follow written confirmation of the tuition fees you will pay for the specific program you want to study.

In most countries, private universities charge higher fees than public universities. The top 200 universities in the THE-QS World University Rankings include private and public institutions, explaining some of the wide variation in fees, even within countries. Not surprisingly, many of the most expensive universities in the world are some of the top ranked US private institutions. Looking at these costs, together with the detailed information in the THE-QS World University Rankings data table (chapter six), the profiles of the top 100 universities worldwide (chapter one), and the subject rankings (chapter two), will help put them in perspective relative to the quality of the course and the institution. Tuition fees also often vary for different program types within universities, for example, many professional graduate degrees are more expensive than the averages quoted, while other courses are less expensive. The tuition fees in the table have been compiled (exchange rate to US$ as at 01.05.08) using many sources including published information, websites and telephone interviews. Where no clear information was available, a dash (-) appears. Any data updates will be published on www.topuniversities.com.

THE-QS Top 200 universities worldwide
Average annual tuition fees for domestic students US$

Rank	Institution	Undergraduate	Postgraduate
1	HARVARD University	31,460	31,460
2	YALE University	34,530	30,500
3	University of CAMBRIDGE	6,200	10,970
4	University of OXFORD	6,360	10,120
5	CALIFORNIA Institute of Technology (Caltech)	29,940	29,940
6	IMPERIAL College London	6,050	9,520
7	UCL (University College London)	6,200	11,670
8	University of CHICAGO	35,170	39,200
9	MASSACHUSETTS Institute of Technology (MIT)	34,990	34,990
10	COLUMBIA University	35,520	33,360
11	University of PENNSYLVANIA	-	29,390
12	PRINCETON University	34,290	35,440
13=	DUKE University	34,340	33,990
13=	JOHNS HOPKINS University	37,700	35,900
15	CORNELL University	34,600	30,000
16	AUSTRALIAN National University	6,360	14,290
17	STANFORD University	32,940	32,990
18	University of MICHIGAN	10,450	15,750
19	University of TOKYO	5,140	5,240
20	McGill University	3,300	2,490
21	CARNEGIE MELLON University	36,950	33,300
22	KING'S College London	6,200	10,410
23	University of EDINBURGH	3,500	11,170
24	ETH Zurich (Swiss Federal Institute of Technology)	1,260	1,260
25	KYOTO University	5,140	5,140
26	University of HONG KONG	6,670	21,820
27	BROWN University	35,580	35,580
28	École Normale Supérieure, PARIS	300	300
29	University of MANCHESTER	-	19,720
30	National University of SINGAPORE	4,400	-
30	University of CALIFORNIA, Los Angeles (UCLA)	-	-
32	University of BRISTOL	6,360	12,780
33	NORTHWESTERN University	35,060	35,060
34=	ÉCOLE POLYTECHNIQUE	-	8,560
34=	University of BRITISH COLUMBIA	4,080	3,810
36	University of California, BERKELEY	6,730	7,460
37	University of SYDNEY	19,270	14,150
38	University of MELBOURNE	20,030	-
39	HONG KONG University of Science & Technology	5,400	7,600

Rank	Institution	Undergraduate	Postgraduate
40	NEW YORK University (NYU)	33,270	27,340
41	University of TORONTO	5,400	6,760
42	CHINESE University of Hong Kong	5,400	5,400
43	University of QUEENSLAND	17,050	14,310
44	OSAKA University	5,140	5,140
45	University of NEW SOUTH WALES	20,500	15,200
46	BOSTON University	34,930	34,930
47	MONASH University	16,860	14,560
48	University of COPENHAGEN	0	0
49	TRINITY College Dublin	9,530	8,200
50=	Ecole Polytechnique Fédérale de LAUSANNE	1,190	750
50=	PEKING University	720	1,560
50=	SEOUL National University	6,560	7,920
53	University of AMSTERDAM	2,440	2,440
54	DARTMOUTH College	33,500	33,340
55	University of WISCONSIN-Madison	7,190	9,640
56	TSINGHUA University	780	-
57	HEIDELBERG Universität	1,560	1,560
58	University of CALIFORNIA, San Diego	8,060	10,080
59	University of WASHINGTON	6,390	9,420
60	WASHINGTON University in St Louis	35,520	35,520
61	TOKYO Institute of Technology	5,150	5,150
62	EMORY University	33,900	30,800
63	UPPSALA University	0	0
64	LEIDEN University	2,490	2,490
65	University of AUCKLAND	3,810	3,440
66	LONDON School of Economics and Political Science	6,200	28,270
67	UTRECHT University	2,440	2,440
68	University of GENEVA	950	950
69	University of WARWICK	5,920	28,740
70	University of TEXAS at Austin	7,670	5,740
71	University of ILLINOIS	6,980	6,740
72	Katholieke Universiteit LEUVEN	830	7,790
73	University of GLASGOW	3,420	6,740
74	University of ALBERTA	4,640	3,270
75	University of BIRMINGHAM	6,200	7,390
76	University of SHEFFIELD	6,200	14,390
77	NANYANG Technological University	4,680	4,330
78=	DELFT University of Technology	2,400	2,400
78=	Technische Universität MÜNCHEN (TUM)	1,560	1,560
78=	RICE University	29,960	26,600
81=	University of AARHUS	0	0

THE-QS Top 200 universities worldwide
Average annual tuition fees for domestic students US$ continued

Rank	Institution	Undergraduate	Postgraduate
81=	University of YORK	6,050	6,390
83=	University of ST ANDREWS	3,420	20,900
83=	GEORGIA Institute of Technology	5,640	6,440
83=	University of WESTERN AUSTRALIA	12,030	11,690
86	University of NOTTINGHAM	5,920	7,290
87	University of MINNESOTA	7,830	9,740
88	LUND University	0	0
89	University of CALIFORNIA, Davis	9,500	10,620
90	CASE WESTERN RESERVE University	34,450	31,000
91=	University of HELSINKI	0	0
91=	Université de MONTRÉAL	1,750	2,620
93=	Ludwig-Maximilians-Universität München (LMU)	230	230
93=	Hebrew University of JERUSALEM	2,450	3,330
95	KAIST Korea Adv Inst of Science & Technology	14,950	16,940
96	University of VIRGINIA	6,630	9,370
97	University of PITTSBURGH	12,110	14,880
98	University of CALIFORNIA, Santa Barbara	7,280	7,500
99=	University of SOUTHAMPTON	6,510	18,830
99=	PURDUE University	7,420	7,420
101	VANDERBILT University	34,410	1,430
102=	University of NORTH CAROLINA	2,250	2,600
102=	University of SOUTHERN CALIFORNIA	35,810	20,850
104	University of LEEDS	6,200	6,510
105	PENNSYLVANIA STATE University	-	16,650
106=	University of ZURICH	1,310	1,140
106=	University of ADELAIDE	5,990	4,520
108	University College DUBLIN	-	-
109	TECHNION Israel Institute of Technology	2,000	2,700
110	GEORGETOWN University	37,540	35,160
111	MAASTRICHT University	2,390	2,390
112	TOHOKU University	4,960	4,810
113	FUDAN University	-	1,280
114	TEL AVIV University	2,600	3,440
115	University of VIENNA	570	570
116	Université Catholique de LOUVAIN (UCL)	1,210	1,210
117=	McMASTER University	4,660	5,650
117=	QUEEN'S University	4,360	6,310
119	University of ROCHESTER	35,190	35,190
120	NAGOYA University	5,140	5,140

Rank	Institution	Undergraduate	Postgraduate
121	OHIO STATE University	8,410	9,700
122=	DURHAM University	-	-
122=	University of MARYLAND	8,010	440
124=	National TAIWAN University	870	890
124=	University of OTAGO	-	10,400
126	ERASMUS University Rotterdam	2,440	2,440
127	STONY BROOK University	-	8,600
128	EINDHOVEN University of Technology	2,390	2,390
129	University of WATERLOO	4,500	5,900
130	University of SUSSEX	6,200	8,480
131	University of BASEL	680	680
132	University of CALIFORNIA, Irvine	8,770	11,260
133=	CARDIFF University	6,360	6,250
133=	University of LIVERPOOL	6,200	6,510
133=	Technical University of DENMARK	0	0
136	University of GHENT	0	840
137=	Freie Universität BERLIN	-	-
137=	TEXAS A&M University	6,970	6,970
139	HUMBOLDT-Universität zu Berlin	-	280
140	École Normale Supérieure de LYON	260	330
141	University of Science and Technology of CHINA	-	3,800
142	WAGENINGEN University	-	2,440
143	NANJING University	-	900
144=	University of GRONINGEN	2,450	2,470
144=	SHANGHAI JIAO TONG University	-	1,400
146	University of ARIZONA	5,050	5,770
147=	Universität FREIBURG	780	780
147=	University of ARKANSAS	-	13,740
149	Université Pierre-et-Marie-Curie PARIS VI	260	420
150	Universidad Nacional Autónoma de México (UNAM)	-	-
151	RUTGERS, The State University of New Jersey	8,540	12,380
152	University of BATH	6,200	10,030
153	University of ABERDEEN	3,420	6,390
154	Indian Institute of Technology Delhi (IITD)	-	4,160
155=	Eberhard Karls Universität TÜBINGEN	1,560	1,560
155=	VU University AMSTERDAM	2,440	2,440
157	TUFTS University	35,840	35,050
158	KYUSHU University	5,120	5,210
159	University of WESTERN ONTARIO	4,520	5,410
160	QUEEN MARY, University of London	6,200	11,200
161	University of LAUSANNE	1,120	1,120
162=	CHALMERS University of Technology	0	0

THE-QS Top 200 universities worldwide
Average annual tuition fees for domestic students US$ continued

Rank	Institution	Undergraduate	Postgraduate
162=	NEWCASTLE University, NEWCASTLE Upon Tyne	6,200	8,030
164	SIMON FRASER University	4,620	6,270
165	University of FLORIDA	3,790	7,850
166=	Universität GÖTTINGEN	1,560	1,560
166=	CHULALONGKORN University	1,140	1,650
168	University of NOTRE DAME	29,070	28,970
169	Universität FRANKFURT am Main	2,340	400
170=	University of LANCASTER	6,200	6,630
170=	INDIANA University Bloomington	7,840	7,870
170=	University of CALGARY	4,510	4,680
173	KTH, ROYAL Institute of Technology	0	0
174	HOKKAIDO University	5,140	5,140
174=	Indian Institute of Technology Bombay (IITB)	2,700	5,000
174=	RENSSELAER Polytechnic Institute	37,990	38,820
177=	University of OSLO	0	110
177=	University of LEICESTER	6,060	-
179	University of CAPE TOWN	2,640	2,000
180=	University of COLORADO at Boulder	7,280	8,940
180=	WASEDA University	10,420	8,820
182	MACQUARIE University	14,320	17,380
183=	Université Libre de BRUXELLES (ULB)	1,210	1,210
183=	Lomonosov MOSCOW STATE University	-	-
185	BRANDEIS University	34,570	43,260
186=	University of BARCELONA	1,210	3,270
186=	University of CANTERBURY	3,420	3,420
188=	POHANG University of Science and Technology	5,400	6,570
188=	Technische Universität BERLIN	-	-
190	Universität STUTTGART	1,560	1,560
191	University of MASSACHUSETTS, Amherst	9,920	8,460
192=	University of BERN	1,260	1,260
192=	University of BOLOGNA	1,690	2,210
194	University of READING	6,200	6,200
195	University of ANTWERP	830	830
196	University of SÃO PAULO	-	-
197=	DALHOUSIE University	5,980	9,650
197=	University of BUENOS AIRES	-	-
199	KOBE University	4,730	3,920
200=	University of TWENTE	-	11,370
200=	University of ATHENS	-	-

Aim for Excellence

Asia's Leading Biomedical Research University

- ◎ International Health Program
- ◎ Molecular Medicine Program
- ◎ Bioinformatics Program
- ◎ Biophotonics
- ◎ Nursing
- ◎ Dentistry

Besides, we have a summer program on the Traditional Medicine, Taiwanese Culture and Art.

Asia

Taiwan

NATIONAL YANG-MING UNIVERSITY

Email: cia@ym.edu.tw
http://www.ym.edu.tw/cia

THE-QS Top 200 universities worldwide
Average annual tuition fees for international students US$

Rank	Institution	Undergraduate	Postgraduate
1	HARVARD University	31,460	31,460
2	YALE University	34,530	30,500
3	University of CAMBRIDGE	21,240	25,560
4	University of OXFORD	24,330	27,410
5	CALIFORNIA Institute of Technology (Caltech)	29,940	29,940
6	IMPERIAL College London	35,300	35,740
7	UCL (University College London)	26,890	27,840
8	University of CHICAGO	35,170	39,200
9	MASSACHUSETTS Institute of Technology (MIT)	34,990	34,990
10	COLUMBIA University	35,520	33,360
11	University of PENNSYLVANIA	35,920	-
12	PRINCETON University	34,290	35,440
13=	DUKE University	34,340	33,990
13=	JOHNS HOPKINS University	37,700	35,900
15	CORNELL University	34,600	32,800
16	AUSTRALIAN National University	16,700	18,880
17	STANFORD University	32,940	32,990
18	University of MICHIGAN	31,300	31,660
19	University of TOKYO	5,140	5,070
20	McGILL University	13,750	6,510
21	CARNEGIE MELLON University	36,950	33,300
22	KING'S College London	25,680	25,120
23	University of EDINBURGH	23,960	24,680
24	ETH Zurich (Swiss Federal Institute of Technology)	1,260	1,260
25	KYOTO University	5,140	5,140
26	University of HONG KONG	12,830	25,530
27	BROWN University	35,580	35,580
28	École Normale Supérieure, PARIS	300	300
29	University of MANCHESTER	20,700	31,800
30	National University of SINGAPORE	5,070	4,110
30	University of CALIFORNIA, Los Angeles (UCLA)	19,070	14,690
32	University of BRISTOL	25,830	26,200
33	NORTHWESTERN University	35,060	35,060
34=	ÉCOLE POLYTECHNIQUE	10,900	8,560
34=	University of BRITISH COLUMBIA	17,630	3,810
36	University of California, BERKELEY	23,830	22,400
37	University of SYDNEY	21,760	19,780
38	University of MELBOURNE	24,730	-
39	HONG KONG University of Science & Technology	8,910	7,600

THE-QS Top 200 universities worldwide
Average annual tuition fees for international students US$ continued

Rank	Institution	Undergraduate	Postgraduate
40	NEW YORK University (NYU)	33,270	27,340
41	University of TORONTO	18,920	14,690
42	CHINESE University of Hong Kong	10,270	5,400
43	University of QUEENSLAND	20,710	21,190
44	OSAKA University	5,140	5,140
45	University of NEW SOUTH WALES	20,500	18,850
46	BOSTON University	34,930	34,930
47	MONASH University	20,170	20,250
48	University of COPENHAGEN	16,600	16,600
49	TRINITY College Dublin	19,170	14,360
50=	Ecole Polytechnique Fédérale de LAUSANNE	1,190	750
50=	PEKING University	4,020	5,010
50=	SEOUL National University	6,560	7,890
53	University of AMSTERDAM	10,900	14,010
54	DARTMOUTH College	33,500	33,340
55	University of WISCONSIN-Madison	21,440	24,910
56	TSINGHUA University	4,360	-
57	HEIDELBERG Universität	1,560	1,560
58	University of CALIFORNIA, San Diego	20,020	14,690
59	University of WASHINGTON	22,130	21,460
60	WASHINGTON University in St Louis	35,520	35,520
61	TOKYO Institute of Technology	5,150	5,150
62	EMORY University	33,900	30,800
63	UPPSALA University	0	0
64	LEIDEN University	2,490	17,130
65	University of AUCKLAND	17,120	19,260
66	LONDON School of Economics and Political Science	24,370	31,670
67	UTRECHT University	10,150	16,220
68	University of GENEVA	950	950
69	University of WARWICK	26,020	32,680
70	University of TEXAS at Austin	24,540	14,070
71	University of ILLINOIS	18,250	16,980
72	Katholieke Universiteit LEUVEN	7,790	8,720
73	University of GLASGOW	20,510	22,080
74	University of ALBERTA	16,110	6,820
75	University of BIRMINGHAM	21,390	21,390
76	University of SHEFFIELD	22,650	32,510
77	NANYANG Technological University	7,020	8,750
78=	DELFT University of Technology	5,020	9,670

Rank	Institution	Undergraduate	Postgraduate
78=	Technische Universität MÜNCHEN (TUM)	1,560	1,560
78=	RICE University	29,960	26,600
81=	University of AARHUS	19,620	19,620
81=	University of YORK	18,040	18,040
83=	University of ST ANDREWS	21,590	23,660
83=	GEORGIA Institute of Technology	23,370	23,330
83=	University of WESTERN AUSTRALIA	20,500	21,590
86	University of NOTTINGHAM	16,720	17,200
87	University of MINNESOTA	18,470	16,840
88	LUND University	0	0
89	University of CALIFORNIA, Davis	30,110	25,620
90	CASE WESTERN RESERVE University	34,450	31,000
91=	University of HELSINKI	0	0
91=	Université de MONTRÉAL	11,760	15,840
93=	Ludwig-Maximilians-Universität München (LMU)	-	230
93=	Hebrew University of JERUSALEM	10,000	10,000
95	KAIST Korea Adv Inst of Science & Technology	14,950	16,940
96	University of VIRGINIA	25,640	19,130
97	University of PITTSBURGH	21,620	26,920
98	University of CALIFORNIA, Santa Barbara	25,960	22,460
99=	University of SOUTHAMPTON	30,330	-
99=	PURDUE University	22,220	22,220
101	VANDERBILT University	34,410	1,430
102=	University of NORTH CAROLINA	12,610	12,730
102=	University of SOUTHERN CALIFORNIA	35,810	20,850
104	University of LEEDS	20,840	19,090
105	PENNSYLVANIA STATE University	24,940	27,080
106=	University of ZURICH	1,500	1,060
106=	University of ADELAIDE	16,850	16,940
108	University College DUBLIN	-	-
109	TECHNION Israel Institute of Technology	2,500	3,380
110	GEORGETOWN University	37,540	35,160
111	MAASTRICHT University	12,460	17,910
112	TOHOKU University	2,470	2,460
113	FUDAN University	3,510	4,010
114	TEL AVIV University	7,770	20,560
115	University of VIENNA	570	570
116	Université Catholique de LOUVAIN (UCL)	1,210	1,210
117=	McMASTER University	13,260	13,890
117=	QUEEN'S University	14,420	10,140
119	University of ROCHESTER	35,190	35,190
120	NAGOYA University	5,140	5,140

THE-QS Top 200 universities worldwide
Average annual tuition fees for international students US$ continued

Rank	Institution	Undergraduate	Postgraduate
121	OHIO STATE University	21,020	23,860
122=	DURHAM University	16,630	19,220
122=	University of MARYLAND	21,350	960
124=	National TAIWAN University	870	890
124=	University of OTAGO	16,370	17,660
126	ERASMUS University Rotterdam	9,630	15,980
127	STONY BROOK University	12,880	12,620
128	EINDHOVEN University of Technology	7,930	13,170
129	University of WATERLOO	16,400	14,700
130	University of SUSSEX	22,410	22,410
131	University of BASEL	680	680
132	University of CALIFORNIA, Irvine	20,610	15,010
133=	CARDIFF University	20,510	19,200
133=	University of LIVERPOOL	22,970	22,970
133=	Technical University of DENMARK	21,900	21,900
136	University of GHENT	840	840
137=	Freie Universität BERLIN	-	-
137=	TEXAS A&M University	15,400	13,750
139	HUMBOLDT-Universität zu Berlin	-	280
140	École Normale Supérieure de LYON	260	330
141	University of Science and Technology of CHINA	2,870	3,580
142	WAGENINGEN University	-	12,850
143	NANJING University	-	-
144=	University of GRONINGEN	6,080	8,600
144=	SHANGHAI JIAO TONG University	-	-
146	University of ARIZONA	16,280	16,570
147=	Universität FREIBURG	780	780
147=	University of ARKANSAS	-	-
149	Université Pierre-et-Marie-Curie PARIS VI	260	420
150	Universidad Nacional Autónoma de México (UNAM)	480	1,000
151	RUTGERS, The State University of New Jersey	17,710	18,410
152	University of BATH	20,180	22,260
153	University of ABERDEEN	27,280	25,880
154	Indian Institute of Technology Delhi (IITD)	-	-
155=	Eberhard Karls Universität TÜBINGEN	1,560	1,560
155=	VU University AMSTERDAM	8,560	14,010
157	TUFTS University	35,840	35,050
158	KYUSHU University	3,000	4,670
159	University of WESTERN ONTARIO	13,550	12,050
160	QUEEN MARY, University of London	19,620	20,310

Rank	Institution	Undergraduate	Postgraduate
161	University of LAUSANNE	1,120	1,120
162=	CHALMERS University of Technology	0	0
162=	NEWCASTLE University, NEWCASTLE Upon Tyne	22,560	22,560
164	SIMON FRASER University	14,690	6,270
165	University of FLORIDA	21,400	23,730
166=	Universität GÖTTINGEN	1,560	1,560
166=	CHULALONGKORN University	11,130	9,540
168	University of NOTRE DAME	29,070	28,970
169	Universität FRANKFURT am Main	2,340	400
170=	University of LANCASTER	20,900	19,080
170=	INDIANA University Bloomington	22,320	21,270
170=	University of CALGARY	15,340	10,620
173	KTH, ROYAL Institute of Technology	0	0
174	HOKKAIDO University	5,140	5,140
174=	Indian Institute of Technology Bombay (IITB)	2,000	2,000
174=	RENSSELAER Polytechnic Institute	37,990	38,820
177=	University of OSLO	110	110
177=	University of LEICESTER	18,730	17,750
179	University of CAPE TOWN	5,790	3,680
180=	University of COLORADO at Boulder	26,760	24,140
180=	WASEDA University	10,420	8,820
182	MACQUARIE University	16,210	19,300
183=	Université Libre de BRUXELLES (ULB)	1,210	1,210
183=	Lomonosov MOSCOW STATE University	3,150	3,300
185	BRANDEIS University	34,570	34,570
186=	University of BARCELONA	1,210	3,270
186=	University of CANTERBURY	15,170	17,230
188=	POHANG University of Science and Technology	5,400	6,570
188=	Technische Universität BERLIN	-	-
190	Universität STUTTGART	1,560	1,560
191	University of MASSACHUSETTS, Amherst	20,500	12,970
192=	University of BERN	1,260	1,260
192=	University of BOLOGNA	1,690	2,210
194	University of READING	20,360	20,360
195	University of ANTWERP	830	830
196	University of SÃO PAULO	-	-
197=	DALHOUSIE University	13,170	17,140
197=	University of BUENOS AIRES	-	-
199	KOBE University	2,160	1,650
200=	University of TWENTE	3,110	3,890
200=	University of ATHENS	-	-

Living costs

In addition to tuition fees, you will need to consider a variety of additional costs. The living costs associated with moving out of the family home to study at university, and especially moving abroad, will form a large part of your expenditure. Costs include essentials such as accommodation, food, travel and books. At US institutions, these variables are often quoted as a single figure, so, it is very important that students or parents establish exactly which costs are included. Don't forget that you will also need to budget for extracurricular activity and travel, especially if you are studying overseas. And, remember that exchange rates will fluctuate and affect your budget.

So how can you find out about these costs of living? Where is the most expensive place to study? And where can you afford? There are numerous public sources and publications providing you with tables of the costs of living throughout the world, which tend to have slightly varied results, as differing criteria are used for each, but they generally present a similar 'big picture'. According to the most recent research by the Economist Intelligence Unit (EIU), Oslo maintains its place as the world's most expensive city: 1 Oslo, 2 Paris, 3 Copenhagen, 4 London, 5 Tokyo, 6= Reykjavik, 6= Zurich, 8 Osaka, 9= Frankfurt, 9= Helsinki. Other rankings have put Moscow or London at the top of the list. Websites such as www.citymayors.com provide this and much other data on living in cities worldwide.

This information can be a guide to the cost of study abroad, but actual costs will depend on your lifestyle and ability to budget. And, you are not just comparing like for like, as different cultures will encourage you to spend in different ways. Additionally, student environments usually have lower cost accommodation, restaurants, sports facilities and entertainment, than a city as a whole. Students are often eligible for concessions on transport and other items. Reading online blogs and real-life accounts can give a more real picture of the costs you may face. Some of the profiles of the top 100 universities (chapter one) and the country profiles (chapter three) give information on the student cost of living at different destinations. Local salary levels are likely to be commensurate with costs, some paid work could be a solution to supporting your time at university. Working part-time is becoming more of an accepted international trend for students, though it is important to establish in advance how much work is available, or permitted, according to local directives or visa restrictions.

Foreign currency influences

Among other ways to compare living costs, taking into account currency fluctuations, is the annual Big Mac Index, published by The Economist. This, in effect, measures the purchasing power parity (PPP) between currencies and the US$ and provides a basis for showing how changing market exchange rates affect similar goods (eg Big Mac hamburger) in different countries. As a general rule, the cost of living is higher where the US dollar is weak relative to the local currency and vice versa. In most of Asia living costs are historically low in dollar terms, with currencies being relatively undervalued against the dollar. Some of central and Eastern Europe also has had lower living costs in dollar terms. Latin America shows quite a substantial variation in its rating of countries. The UK has had a higher cost of living in dollar terms, and the European area, in particular Switzerland and Sweden. These values fluctuate greatly and websites such as www.oanda.com are sources of such information and other tools for understanding foreign currency fluctuations.

Broadly speaking, study in developed countries will be more costly than in developing countries. However, the reputation of universities tends to far outweigh tuition and living costs, as a factor when people make their study choices. Few students choose to move from developed countries to study in developing countries. By contrast, huge numbers of students from developing countries choose to study abroad. In spite of the higher study and living costs, they realize the importance of a high quality education and the recognition qualifications will carry for their future career. Indeed, the latest Education at a Glance published by the OECD, reports that tertiary students from sub-Saharan Africa are the most mobile in the world, while less than one per cent of US students studied overseas at the time of the research.

Costs will vary according to your destination country, the type and length of your program, what is included in the program cost, and costs that may include your passport, visa, airfare, medical costs, transportation, meals, books, insurance and accommodation, to name but a few. However, if you are planning to study abroad, do not let these facts deter you. You would encounter many of these costs at home, and the extra ones will generally be worth the outlay, especially with the level of financial aid available for international students and the fact that you will, more than likely, be well remunerated upon employment (see chapter three). The true cost of study will depend on many factors, and this value is just part of the overall package of studying at university.

Financing your education

All prospective students face university tuition fees and living expenses. Whether you are studying at home or abroad, securing and planning the finance of your university education can be a time consuming task. Different countries operate completely different funding arrangements with a distinction often being made between the levels of tuition fees domestic and international students pay. There are exceptions, depending on the country you wish to study in; for example, domestic and international students have access to at undergraduate, masters and PhD university programs free of charge in Finland, Norway and Sweden, while in the German public system of education students pay a maximum of €500 each semester.

The investment you choose to make in your university education, however, is exactly that: an investment. Although the cost of tuition fees and living expenses may seem high at the time of study, sufficient evidence exists to demonstrate that obtaining a degree has significant economic benefits over a working lifetime. Research by Universities UK indicates that the difference in earning power between those obtaining an undergraduate qualification and those leaving school with their high school qualifications can be as much as 25 per cent, or £160,000 over a working lifetime. Increased financial benefits accrue to those with masters and PhD degree, depending on the area of specialization and employment.

Loans, scholarships, bursaries and grants are available for prospective students to apply for to offset some or all of their university costs. At the end of this section, some advice is given on what scholarship and funding are available in each world region .

Student loans

Loans are an increasingly common way of funding university-level education for many students. They are generally offered by quasi-government organizations or commercial financial institutions, such as banks or specialized loan companies. It remains to be seen whether the current economic downturn will have an adverse affect on the willingness to loan money to students for education, but current indications are that loans will remain an important source of funding for all students. The US has long been the leader in government and private loan schemes for students at all levels of university education. The most comprehensive source of advice for loans and other forms of financial aid is www.fedmoney.org. In recent years, other commercial organizations have established themselves as significant providers of loans to national and, in some cases, international students studying in the US, including Nelnet www.nelnet.com, SallieMae www.salliemae.com and Access Group www.accessgroup.org. The majority of the loans granted from these organizations are contingent on parental guarantee, household income or other forms of security and attract a relatively low rates of interest over a lengthy repayment period. A number of loans, such as those under the Federal Stafford scheme, are underwritten and guaranteed by the federal government and are either subsidized for those students who are less well off, or not subsidized for all other students.

Throughout Europe, banks and government organizations are also involved in providing student loans for domestic and, depending on their circumstances, international students. The Student Loans Company in the UK administers loan schemes for tuition fees and maintenance grants for all UK and European Union students attending UK undergraduate programs to a maximum of £3,145 for tuition fees in 2009. Repayments are only made on the full loan amount after graduation and once your income exceeds a certain threshold, currently £15,000 per year. Loans are available for students intending to pursue their education overseas, although the terms of such loans tend to be very different from those for students wishing to study at home. Major local, and some international, banks generally offer such loans, depending on where you are resident, but they require significant guarantees. HSBC, Santander, Citibank, ABN AMRO and Barclays are amongst the few truly international banks that continue to provide education and career development loans for students wishing to study in other countries, while banks as diverse as The State Bank of India, The Bank of Baroda, The Bank of China, Nordea and Maybank in Malaysia provide some loan facilities for local students to pursue their education abroad.

SCHOLARSHIPS

QS, the career and education experts and organizers of the **QS World MBA Tour** and **World Grad School Tour**, provide access to a scholarship fund of a total of **US$1,600,000** to the attendees of its 2009 international fairs. The scholarships, from some of the world's leading business schools and universities as well as the annual **QS Community and Leadership Awards**, will benefit committed postgraduate students and business leaders of the future.

QS offers the QS Leadership Scholarship for MBA and Postgraduate Studies and the QS Community Scholarships for MBA and Postgraduate Studies.

Scholarships offered by partner universities and business schools include: **The Wharton School** Scholarship; **Chicago Booth School of Business** Scholarship; **IE Business School** Female Scholarship; **Vlerick Leuven Gent Management School** Scholarships; **Politecnico di Milano** Scholarships; **EMLYON Business School** Entrepreneurial Scholarship and **Cass Business School, London** Scholarships

In recent years, dozens of ambitious and talented professionals and brilliant students from **Bulgaria, Chile, China, France, Korea, India, Italy, Ukraine, USA** and several other countries have been awarded these scholarships.

For further information about the QS Scholarships visit: **www.topmba.com**

Scholarships

The following section surveys scholarships available around the world and funding opportunities for masters and PhD.

International scholarship organizations

A number of international scholarship and funding organizations exists to provide funding for international students. These organizations tend to be run on a charitable basis, although their individual missions and funding are varied, and they can focus their resources on specific countries, universities, or areas of study. Perhaps the most well known of these organizations is the Rotary Foundation which, since 1947, has supported nearly 38,000 students from 100 countries for part, or all, of their university education abroad. Three types of awards are available: Academic-Year Ambassadorial Scholarships, valued at US$23,000 valid for one year, and generally not intended for degree-awarding programs or unsupervised research; Multi-Year Ambassadorial Scholarships, valid for two years at an institution assigned by the Rotary Foundation Trustees and valued at US$11,500 for each year of study; and Cultural Ambassadorial Scholarships, for students wishing to participate in intensive language training or a cultural immersion program for between three and six months, with awards of between US$10,000 and US$15,000 depending on the period of study. All Rotary awards require recipients to participate in Rotary Foundation activities during and after their program of study, and each country's Rotary group operates a separate application process to any university application that may be required; www.rotary.org. Other international organizations are discussed in the following sections, depending on their specific focus.

University scholarships for international students

In recent years, more universities around the world have invested significant resources in scholarship funds for international students, including many of the institutions featured in this book. The competition to attract the most talented students is fierce, and the need is growing to offer scholarships that cover tuition fees, living expenses and other related costs in order to attract the best students. Individual universities set their own requirements, application methods, deadlines and other criteria. The amount of money available varies from institution to institution, and can include a full tuition fee and living expenses award, or may only be a much smaller bursary award to cover the cost of your books and learning materials. Scholarships can be awarded for one year, or the entire duration of your program, although the longer awards tend to depend on satisfactory academic progress in your degree. It is common for universities to offer scholarships for all levels of study, although some of the best institutions tend to offer more financial aid for masters and PhD students.

Details of the scholarships offered by individual universities are only available from them, which makes the task of gathering the relevant information, preparing the application material and meeting all the deadlines very labour intensive. Many universities link the application procedure for admission with their own scholarship schemes, making the process more straightforward. Most importantly, university scholarship deadlines tend to require as much, if not more, preparation and planning than the university application, because the competition for funding tends to be fierce. Each university will be able to advise very accurately on when the optimum time to submit a scholarship application is, but it is likely that you will need to submit all scholarship application materials at least nine months in advance.

Australia and New Zealand scholarships

An increasing number of awards offered by universities and government organizations are available for international students in Australia and New Zealand. A new initiative called 'Australian Scholarships' administers government and AusAID scholarships under three programs: the Australian Development Scholarships (for all levels of study), the Australian Leadership Awards Scholarships (masters and PhD) and Australian Endeavour Awards (masters and PhD). Funding generally covers tuition fees, living and other related expenses for international students; www.australianscholarships.gov.au.

The New Zealand government, through Education New Zealand, offer three types of scholarships for international students: LEARN fellowships (for PhD and research students), New Zealand International Undergraduate Fees Scholarships and New Zealand International Doctoral Research Scholarships. The undergraduate awards fund tuition fees, while the research awards additionally offer living, travel, books and other research costs; www.newzealandeducated.com.

UK scholarships

As the second most popular international degree-level study destination, the UK has a number of significant scholarship schemes. Most prominent are Chevening scholarships, which provide for 1,300 new graduate awards every year, with a further 200 fellowships available for international researchers. The scheme, funded by the UK's Foreign and Commonwealth Office, universities, the private sector and other government departments, mostly supports one-year masters degrees and selects only those students with a proven academic record, leadership potential and a commitment to return home to contribute to the socio-economic development of their own country. A new online application system has been launched for 2009/10 the details of which can be found at www.chevening.fco.gov.uk. Other government schemes include the Commonwealth Scholarship and Fellowship Plan (CSFP) and the Commonwealth Shared Scholarship Scheme, both of which offer funding for Commonwealth residents.

Other awards include the Asia Research Fellowship and Marshall scholarships. The latter support young American students of high ability to study for a degree in the UK. At least 40 scholars are selected each year to study either at graduate, or occasionally, undergraduate level in any field of study. Each scholarship is held for two years, renewable for a third in certain circumstances and covers tuition and living costs in addition to books and travel allowance; www.marshallscholarship.org.

General details of all scholarships offered for study in the UK are available on the British Council website, www.educationuk.org. Other awards and scholarships are available via individual university and college websites. Prestigious schemes include those offered by the London School of Economics (LSE), the University of Edinburgh and the Universities of Oxford and Cambridge.

European Union (EU) scholarships

Scholarships and funding opportunities for international students tend to come from a number of clearly defined sources such as the European Commission, national agencies and individual universities. The European Commission offers scholarships and mobility awards under a number of schemes, often directed at specific national groups of students. Mobility awards are available to fund the movement of students at all levels within Europe, and between countries as diverse as Australia, Canada, New Zealand, Korea, Japan and the US, while more mainstream scholarship schemes, such as Erasmus Mundus, offer international (non European) masters students tuition fees, and living costs awards of

€21,000 per year, for a maximum of two years. Such scholarships are only available at universities where an Erasmus Mundus masters program is in operation with one or more partners. Details are available at http://ec.europa.eu/education/programmes/mundus/ programme/back_en.html.

Each EU country has a national agency responsible for the international promotion of its higher education system. Such organizations also tend to administer scholarship schemes for international students at all levels, whether full degree programs or shorter periods of research or study abroad. Amongst the most prominent of these organizations are the German Academic Exchange Service (DAAD), the Netherlands Organization for International Cooperation in Higher Education (Nuffic), Campus France, the Swedish Institute and CIMO in Finland. Each has its own scholarship schemes and details are available on websites, many of which are listed at the end of chapter three. Germany's DAAD has a particularly helpful searchable scholarship database for university and national awards at: www.daad.de/deutschland/foerderung/stipendiendatenbank/00462. en.html. Many universities throughout Europe also have the resources to offer their own scholarships to support the most able international students. These awards are promoted and managed by the universities themselves and vary from country to country. Information is most commonly available directly from the universities.

US and Canada scholarships

Funding opportunities at universities in Canada and the US tend to be greater than in any other region of the world. Both public and private universities offer awards for local and international students at both undergraduate and graduate levels and encourage applications from students irrespective of their financial backgrounds. 'Needs blind' admission is one of the central facets of the admissions process throughout North America and allows for students to apply for degree programs and be assessed for financial aid independently of their family's resources, or their own. The majority of international students at US universities do, however, pay for their own tuition and living costs, although a significant minority receive some form of scholarship or financial aid from their university. According to the Institute of International Education, 25.9 per cent of international students in 2007/08 received some kind of financial aid from the universities they were enrolled at.

Government and other nationwide schemes are also available throughout North America. In Canada four major scholarships schemes are offered to international students, under which a number of additional schemes are administered. The Canadian Bureau of International Education (CBIE) is responsible for these awards and offers scholarships for all levels of university study; www.scholarships.gc.ca/noncanadians-en.html and www. destineducation.ca/intstdnt/awards-1_e.htm.

The Fulbright Commission offers approximately 1,800 new scholarships or study awards for international students wishing to pursue a period of study in the US. Program eligibility and selection is the responsibility of each individual overseas office or constituent award, administering the process separately from your university application. Each overseas country office manages different awards and so information must be sought at your local US embassy or Fulbright office. In India, for example, the United States India Educational Foundation (USEFI) manages seven different scholarship schemes under the Fulbright umbrella, all with different requirements and eligibility criteria; www.iie.org/fulbright.

The Bill & Melinda Gates Foundation provides scholarships, covering tuition and living costs, through the Gates Millennium Scholars scheme for US nationals or legal permanent residents who are of African American, American Indian, Asian Pacific Islander American or Hispanic American descent, attending university for the first term each Fall. Other scholarships are also available for very specific students, for example those undergraduate students attending the University of Washington. Full details are available at www. gatesfoundation.org/topics/Pages/scholarships.aspx. There are also a large number of corporate sponsored scholarship schemes for study in the US. For example, the Adobe Multi-National Scholarship Program, funded by Adobe Systems, provides scholarship awards to meritorious secondary school students attending a post-secondary degree program in business, design studies, education, engineering, graphic art, graphic design, mathematics or science and who need financial assistance to achieve their educational goals www.iiesf.org/new/programs/corporate.htm.

Asia scholarships

With ever more international students considering Asia as a destination for university study, more scholarship opportunities are emerging from governments, and universities intent on recruiting students to their programs. The opportunities for funding are very dynamic and so you should always refer to university websites and ministries of education for the latest news. Perhaps the most extensive of all scholarship schemes is that offered by the Japanese government through the Ministry of Education, Culture, Sports and Technology. The Monbukagakusho (MEXT) scholarships cover a range of study types including undergraduate, masters and PhD study, and include the cost of study, living and, in some cases, travel. Applications are administered through your local Japanese embassy or diplomatic mission. Other awards for study in Japan include those offered by the Japan Student Services Organization (JASSO) and a number of separate education and business foundations; www.jasso.go.jp/study_j/scholarships_e.html.

The Ministry of Education in Singapore offers a small number of scholarships for university study, most significantly the ASEAN scheme at the National University of Singapore and Nanyang Technological University. Universities automatically consider each successful applicant to an undergraduate program for the ASEAN scheme, if they are from another Asian country. Other awards are available for undergraduate and graduate programs of study, the details of which can be obtained from universities.

South Korea has invested significant resources into its official international scholarship schemes, a number of which support the separate efforts of the larger local universities. Awards are available mostly for masters and PhD study, but a small number of undergraduate scholarships are also available, although often tied to studies in the Korean language. The largest scheme is the Korean Government Scholarship Program administered by the Ministry of Education and Human Resources, which offers awards for masters and PhD students in addition to those seeking research and language training; www.studyinkorea.go.kr/english/niied_e.jsp.

The China Scholarship Council coordinates the majority of scholarships available for international students wishing to study in China. Applications are available annually and are coordinated by local Chinese embassies or other official bodies between January and April of the proposed year of study. The value of the scholarships vary, but generally include an exemption from tuition and other official fees, a living allowance or one-off payment, health insurance and the cost of one inter-city journey; http://en.csc.edu.cn.

Masters and PhD funding

Funding opportunities for graduate students tend to be more specific than for other levels of university study and can be linked to specific universities, areas of study, or particular countries. In this section we review some of the general forms of funding available to masters and PhD offered by organizations and foundations. Scholarships and funding arrangements available for graduate students wishing to study in specific countries are surveyed in the preceding section of this chapter.

The Ford Foundation, through its International Fellowship Program, operates one of the most innovative scholarships programs, intended to support masters and PhD students, and focuses on three broad areas: asset building and community development, knowledge, creativity and freedom, and peace and social justice. The program provides generous awards covering tuition fees, living costs and, in some cases, the costs associated with language or academic preparation and operates in countries throughout the world, with a current focus in Africa, Latin America, Central, East and South Asia and the Middle East. Applicants are judged on their commitment to support and develop their own communities and their proposed type and scope of graduate study. The International Fellowship Program is administered by local country partners, all of whom set their own application and selection deadlines; www.fordifp.net.

The Aga Khan Foundation provides graduate awards for students from developing countries who have no other means of funding their graduate studies. The Foundation prioritizes applications from prospective masters students, and also considers new PhD students. Applications are accepted from students resident in countries where the Aga Khan Foundation is active, including Bangladesh, Canada, India, Pakistan, Syria, France, the UK and the US. Awards are made on the basis of a 50 per cent grant and 50 per cent loan to cover tuition and living costs. Applications are made through regional offices, with an annual deadline of March 31; www.akdn.org/akf_scholarships.asp.

The Gates Cambridge Trust, established in 2000, offers approximately 100 graduate scholarships a year for citizens of all countries, except the UK, applying for masters or PhD studies at the University of Cambridge. A Gates Cambridge Scholarship covers the relevant tuition fees, all living costs (currently estimated as £12,250 per year), travel to the university, and a discretionary contribution towards the costs of supporting dependants at Cambridge. The application process operates in parallel to the graduate application process to the university itself; www.gatesscholar.org.

The World Bank administers two significant scholarship schemes for graduate students: the Robert S McNamara Fellowships (RSM Fellowships) are for PhD students undertaking research related to their thesis, and provides funding to a maximum of US$25,000 for a ten month period; the Joint Japan/World Bank Graduate Scholarship Program (JJ/WBGSP) offers scholarships for masters students in economics, health, education, agriculture, environment, natural resource management or other development-related subjects. The JJ/WBGSP scholarships require students to have an unconditional offer for an eligible masters program, and will pay all tuition, travel and living costs for successful applicants; www.worldbank.org/wbi/scholarships.

There are other graduate scholarship opportunities and other kinds of financial aid available to fund masters or PhD study. Some sources of funding are specific to an individual subject area or research initiative, but each of the universities that you are interested in applying to will be able to provide additional advice on the best sources of funding, or scholarships that previous students have been successful in winning.

When you want to go to graduate school and study abroad...

Take the tests that can *take you anywhere.*

The TOEFL® and GRE® tests

More Accepted

Choose from more than **8,000 colleges and universities worldwide.**

More Accessible

Take the exam at a location near you. Choose from **thousands of test centers** in Europe, Africa and the Middle East.

More Support

ETS provides **free** and **low-cost test preparation and practice** materials to help you succeed on exam day.

To learn more or to register for the GRE and TOEFL tests, visit:
www.ets.org/toptests/topuniversities

Listening. Learning. Leading

5

How to apply to university

This chapter reviews the elements you have to arrange and provide when applying to university, anywhere in the world. It offers tips and advice and gives you background on what admissions staff expect to see. Additional specific guidance relevant to undergraduate, graduate and research applications is provided, to help increase the chances of your application being successful.

Applying to your local university, or to an international institution, for any degree-level study should not be taken lightly. Our competitive world makes the process of university application extremely significant for those who wish to enter the best and most suitable university for their own abilities. Whether you choose to apply to one of the world's top universities in Europe, or a smaller college in Canada, Singapore or New Zealand, you will need to invest much time and effort in the application. Advice is available from various sources to make the process more manageable and to increase your chances of success. Teachers, lecturers, careers counsellors, parents and current students are potentially all able to provide you with tips. All provide a slightly different, but valuable, experience of the process and help you make the best of your application.

In some cases, applying to university can take more than a year and the thorough preparation of all of your application materials can take some time. Within the application process, there is never one single area that is more important than any other. Universities regard applications holistically and, as such, your preparation must be thorough and consistent to ensure that all of the elements are your very best efforts and reflect your highest standards.

Basic application materials

The content of application forms tends to be similar across all countries and levels of study. You need to provide your name, age, address, details of schooling, academic achievements, (including final exams, that have yet to provide results), and the program of study that you are interested in. These sections require precision and honesty and are regarded by admissions staff as the most basic information that qualifies your application for further consideration. Some institutions will offer you the opportunity to submit forms online, in which case the need to write legibly is no longer relevant. However, the care you take in completing the online forms and sending the correct documents is as important, whether your application is submitted by post, fax or all online. Admissions staff are continually frustrated by incorrectly spelt and poorly presented application materials. Remember, the basics of good and accurate presentation can have the important benefit of your application being taken seriously. In addition to the completion of a basic application form, all universities will require you to submit, either online or by post, a range of supporting materials, including any relevant test scores, copies of certificates, transcripts and mark sheets. These will form much of the supporting evidence for your application.

Statement of purpose and essays

All students intending to study at university will have heard countless stories about the importance of statement of purpose, or application essays, which cannot be underestimated. These are consistently the most misunderstood part of the application process and, as such, cause the greatest amount of concern. Irrespective of the country or university you wish to apply to, the opportunity to write about something at relative length is often the only chance you have to deviate from, what is essentially, a rather mundane and list-like process. In the US, Canada and throughout Asia, this piece of writing serves two main purposes: to demonstrate your command of the written word in English, and to give an insight into you as a person. Deciding what to include in this kind of essay is very difficult and requires a lengthy period of preparation before you submit it. Some universities expect you to demonstrate knowledge of their programs or reputation, while others want you to exhibit strong extracurricular interests to complement your academic record. Most universities publish an outline of what they expect so you can tailor your writing to their specific demands. If in any doubt, contact the admissions staff and ask exactly what they expect. Talking with current students, or alumni, may also help.

Universities view the importance of the application essay in quite unique ways. Some of the most competitive universities in Australia, the UK and the US, use this extended piece of writing as the defining element that separates applications from one another and ensures that some are accepted and others rejected. This certainly occurs in cases where many applications are received from students with very similar academic records, and the university has little alternative to other measures to select. Smaller institutions in Europe and the US, with limited student numbers and applications, also focus a great deal of their admissions effort on the assessment of the extended piece(s) of writing. Their emphasis is often on building a particular community or atmosphere on campus and, therefore, it is extremely important how different individuals might be able to contribute.

Your attitude and approach to writing one of these extended essays is important. Honesty is essential in all that you commit to paper. It is not uncommon for students to inflate their achievements or interests, only to have them questioned by a member of admissions staff via email or telephone, bringing their entire application into doubt. Your school or college advisor may be an excellent resource to help you develop a coherent argument. He or she may allow you to draft a number of versions so that the final result reflects not only your character but also your best effort. The shorter kind of essays, or personal statements, will expect you to balance concrete examples of your interest in the academic subject area you are applying for, with a demonstration that you have qualities outside the classroom that the university would benefit from. As a general rule, irrespective of the kind of essay expected, you should be able to feel confident that, once written, your friends would be able to both recognize you in it, and be interested in learning a little more!

References and letters of support

Depending on the system of education you are applying to, and the university, 'reference letters' or 'letters of support' are often requested to substantiate your academic record, what you have written about yourself and to help the university judge your potential to benefit from the program of study. Two main questions arise. Firstly, and in many ways most importantly, who writes your reference? Secondly, what should the references say about you as a person, as a student, or as someone with potential to complete a future program of study.

Choosing a referee is an extremely important task and one that may have a significant impact on the success or failure of your application. Referees must know you as a person, and as a student, and be able to write in support of your application in a very honest, open and direct manner. Most universities expect to receive references from teachers, tutors or counsellors, though in some situations, it will be relevant to ask your employer or someone that knows you in another context, such as an extracurricular activity. Most admissions staff will not examine who the person is, though they will note their relationship to you. Their main focus will be the content of the reference, so there are no particular advantages in asking well-known people to be your referees. Above all, those who write your references should know you well and be able to describe you in a way that reflects the best of your abilities and the qualities that make you unique. Comments on your academic and intellectual strengths are particularly important in applications to the more competitive universities.

The style in which a reference should be written is very much dependent on the university. Many US universities will provide a pro-forma sheet that allows referees to indicate your academic abilities in relation to those in your graduating class, for example. Others will allow a more free flowing approach, encouraging referees to express exactly what they feel about you as an applicant, and as a potential member of the university. In either case, guidelines are issued along with other application materials so that the people you choose to be your referees are fully aware of exactly what is expected. Your references will be important because they help give a flavour of you as an individual and separate you from other students with very similar entry qualifications. References that are written positively and informed with examples of your work, your activities, or a flavour of your character, are more likely to help your application be successful than those that are routine and simply list your attributes.

Interviews

Interviews are no longer as common as they once were. With more students studying abroad, many universities have recognized that it is often unreasonable to expect candidates to fly overseas for an interview, in addition to the potentially high tuition fees they will have to pay if accepted. Some institutions, however, continue to interview applicants because they believe it is the fairest way of selecting students. These institutions will expect you to be available for an interview. For international students, this means flying to the university itself, or you can sometimes meet former students or visiting admissions staff in, or nearer, your country.

The purpose of the interview is to make a final selection, based on the application materials you have already submitted. Interviews can focus on a number of areas, including the subject that you have applied for, your extracurricular interests, or the reasons behind wanting to come and study at that particular university. In an interview, an institution tends to be looking for a number of qualities in your answers. Firstly, they will be looking for a passion for, and knowledge of, your academic subject. Secondly, they will want to see that you have the ability to think independently and critically, and grasp any complex or new issues raised in the discussion. Thirdly, they will want to assess whether you are a good fit for their environment. Finally, they will want to assess your confidence and your all-round abilities. Preparing for an interview is not always easy and staff at the institution can guide you as to what they expect. If you are given the opportunity of an interview, be sure of the reasons for your application, your knowledge of the study subject, your own unique qualities, and what you might be able to bring to the university. Make sure that you have fully studied all sources of information such as university websites and talked to any relevant people you can, before your interview.

Deadlines and timing your application

Deadlines are really important and it is essential that you know when they are. In almost all countries, application deadlines exist for all, or certain categories of students. All institutions publish these dates at least one year in advance and make very clear to applicants the consequences of missing them. Deadlines really are the very last line past which you cannot move. Many institutions will not review your application at all, if it is received after the published date. This is a terrible situation, if all of the other elements of your application are very strong, and would normally qualify you for a place.

The timing of your application can have a significant impact on whether you are successful or not. In many of the very popular programs, the earlier you submit a completed application the better your chances of gaining a place, if you have met the minimum entry requirements. Similarly, at the most popular universities, programs fill up quickly and so applications received early can increase the chances of a positive decision. The process obviously varies from country to country, but, as a general rule, submitting your application early will be beneficial to you.

English language requirements

Most international students will need to submit the results of a test of their English language abilities. At present two tests of English language are most commonly accepted by universities and colleges, the TOEFL® and IELTS™, and these are available for prospective students to sit either online (in the case of TOEFL®) or at one of the many test centres worldwide each organization operates. Both tests require specific preparation and a fee is charged for registering and sitting the examinations.

The TOEFL® can be taken online (iBT), or more traditionally as the Paper-based Test (PBT) at locations all over the world. The two tests differ slightly, but provide universities with a very accurate view of prospective students' reading, listening, speaking and writing abilities. Taken over three hours, test scores can be sent directly to the universities and added to the other application material. More information, and how to practice online, is available at **www.ets.org/toefl**.

The IELTS™ test consists of four separate modules: listening, reading, writing and speaking, the first three of which must be taken on the same day. The total test time is two hours and 45 minutes, and candidates have a choice between general training and academic purposes in the reading and writing modules. All IELTS™ tests have to be undertaken at a recognized testing centre. Over one million people take the IELTS™ test each year. It is recognized by over 6,000 institutions worldwide, including over 2,000 universities and colleges in the US alone. IELTS™ is developed within Cambridge ESOL's Quality Control System which is based on over 90 years' experience of English language testing. More information is available at **www.ielts.org**.

Undergraduate applications

Applications for undergraduate degrees, known as bachelors degrees, vary from country to country and, on occasions, from university to university. At this level, applications tend to be confined to a number of similar elements, including the completion of a basic form, a statement of purpose or series of general essays, a maximum of two academic references and confirmation of examination results, depending on your system of education.

In recent years there has been a centralization of undergraduate application systems around the world, allowing students to apply through a single administrative body that liaises directly with chosen universities. For example, the UK's Universities and Colleges Admissions Service (UCAS) system is based on a single application form, allowing a student to apply for up to five courses at different universities. In Australia, the Universities Admissions Centre covering New South Wales and the Australia Capital Territory allows students to apply to a maximum of six courses at the same, or different universities. In each of these examples, applications are made online and must adhere to very strict deadlines. This also applies to a number of other systems operated in countries as diverse at Finland and the US.

Essays

It is common practice for universities to provide topics or questions for undergraduate applicants as a basis for the application essay(s). This enables admissions staff to learn about your personal qualities and the way in which you think and behave. Topics could be, for example, 'What was the defining moment of your childhood?' or, 'Describe how a failure in your life made you a better person.' Frequently, international students will not be asked for an interview and therefore this essay can serve the purpose of an 'interview on paper.' You need to work carefully on these essays and they can take a great deal of time. Many universities that favour this approach will ask you to write several essays, making the effort needed to make your application much greater than you might anticipate, and so you should make sure you leave enough time for it.

In some parts of the world, the approach is different. The UK, Australia, the Netherlands and other countries in Europe operate a more limited essay type format for their applicants. In the UK, for example, this is known as a 'personal statement' on the UCAS application form for which one page of A4 paper is allowed. The intention is to test whether the applicant is able to express him or herself succinctly, capturing the important aspects of his or her personality and interest in an academic subject. Few of these universities will interview you, so admissions staff will want to see a blend of what makes you unique and what kind of contribution you will make to your chosen program of study, or university.

Admissions staff receive so many applications from qualified students at undergraduate level that it is essential you set yourself apart through what you submit, to improve your chances of success. The essay or statement of purpose is one way to do this, but another is to ensure that all your extra-curricula activities are listed on your application form. Admissions staff look for applicants who are well-rounded and able to balance a range of responsibilities outside of the classroom; this may include voluntary work, sporting achievements or the commitment of a part-time job. You may not think your holiday job or performance in the debating society was that significant, but universities may view this completely differently.

When you apply for an undergraduate degree may be the first time you have ever had to think about many of these issues. It is therefore crucially important that you take your time and ensure that each of the separate elements of the application is completed to the best of your ability. Investing time now, to write your essay or talk through a university application with your referee, can make the difference between success and failure.

Masters applications

In common with all graduate degrees, including other qualifications such as graduate diplomas and certificates, an application to a masters program is something that is entirely individual in terms of both your own academic interests and the university to which you are applying. Although many elements of the application are similar to those at undergraduate level, the emphasis is different: most significant is the focus on the academic aspect. Admissions staff look for a more sophisticated and detailed academic knowledge. This can either be expressed through the relevance of your undergraduate subject focus, or any work or voluntary experience you can offer as background to your masters degree. Most universities will require you to submit a statement of purpose and will regard this as a major part of your application. This should detail your past achievements, mostly academic (although extra-curricula success can be useful if directly relevant to the program), your present research interests, your educational objectives, your career plan(s) and your reasons for choosing your field of study. A statement of purpose should generally not be longer than two pages.

An increasing number of universities will also require you to submit a sample of academic writing. This should either be your best work from your undergraduate degree, or a combination of shorter pieces edited together to form a 'portfolio' of your written work. This requirement tends to be important to the more competitive academic fields and those with a direct link to developing a research career.

Your choice of referees for your letters of recommendation is also more critical at masters level. Universities prefer to receive recommendations in the form that they specify and from referees that are most familiar with your academic work. Where your undergraduate degree was in a more general, or different academic area, your choice of referee should be confined to a member of staff in the most relevant academic discipline. If you have relevant work experience, or if you have left university more than five years ago, then a letter of recommendation from an employer can also be considered.

Tests

Masters degree applications also differ from undergraduate in the use of standardized tests. The GRE® (Graduate Record Examination®), GMAT® (the Graduate Management Admission Test®), and the LSAT (Law School Admission Test), are used by universities all over the world to judge the academic ability of applicants in combination with other elements of the application. Although these tests do not replace the content of an undergraduate degree, they are specifically used to ascertain the ability of individual candidates in particular areas relevant to masters study, irrespective of the results of a first degree. For example, the GRE® General Test is used to measure a candidates' verbal reasoning, quantitative reasoning, critical thinking and analytical writing skills, not related to any specific academic field of study. Such tests require significant preparation and can require up to six months of additional study in order to perform well. In the past, only US universities required these standardized test results, but it is increasingly common for universities and business schools the world over to require applicants to sit such tests.

Whether the masters program you are applying to is in Australia, France, Malaysia or the US, admissions staff will assess you based on academic performance in your first degree, any required standardized tests, the relevance of your first degree to the masters, any relevant experience you are able to demonstrate, and your desire to successfully complete the program. Your application will have to balance all of these different elements in order for it to be successful.

Phd applications

As the pinnacle of academic achievement, the PhD requires the most specific of all application approaches. While certain general requirements must still be completed including application form, proof of previous education, transcripts, and at least two letters of recommendation, the PhD application process is very different from both the bachelors and masters degree systems. Many universities specify a number of minimum criteria for admission to a PhD program related to your undergraduate or masters degree, a specific level of academic achievement, and the extent to which you can already demonstrate a subject specialization.

Research proposal

First and foremost, all PhD applications require a prospective student to submit a preliminary thesis or research proposal: a well written outline of the suggested area of study. This document should be an overview of the research you want to undertake and will give an indication that you have already invested a significant amount of time in the consideration of the subject. It should also demonstrate that you have sufficient academic background and training to undertake a research project of this type and that you are aware of the academic literature in your field and how your project relates to existing research. Different universities suggest different lengths for this submission (often ten to 15 typed pages). This proposal is not a definitive guide for your future course of study; it allows the university to assess the potential of your research project.

Academic supervisor

In tandem with the development of a research proposal, the location of a potential supervisor able to support your future PhD is an important part of the application process. Here, the PhD application departs significantly from other types of university applications: each PhD applicant is required to locate an academic supervisor for his or her future research project. This can be done in a number of ways, but is now most commonly achieved through the use of the internet. Each university website lists the academic expertise and research interests of its staff, either by department or faculty, or as a 'directory of experts' for the whole institution. Once you have located a member of staff whose research interests are similar or complimentary to yours, you should approach that person directly to see if they would be willing, or able, to supervise your proposed research topic.

You should only submit a formal application to the university of your choice after you have written your research proposal, and located a potential supervisor, or at least made contact. PhD programs are so specific that universities do not generally welcome speculative enquiries or applications. The emphasis is on you, as a prospective research student, to navigate these initial hurdles to ensure that the project that you wish to pursue is relevant and able to be adequately supported in the university of your choice. Deadlines for the submission of PhD applications tend to be more flexible than at other levels of university study. However, the same rule applies: the earlier a completed application is received, the better your chances. Some of the top international research universities will specify an application deadline for the submission of all material (mid-January is common), to ensure that funding decisions can be made to support the student's PhD.

6

Information and resources

This chapter includes all the information you need to begin your search for a top university worldwide. It starts with a look at the growing phenomenon of cross-border university rankings, in particular the THE-QS World University Rankings, including the full data table of the top 200 universities worldwide. This is followed by a presentation of the methodology used to compile the rankings and an international list of organizations providing data on education around the globe. The chapter concludes with a directory of the top 500 universities worldwide, which includes full contact details.

Global university rankings   244
Top 200 universities worldwide: full data tables   247
THE-QS World University Rankings: methodology   257
Worldwide sources of data on higher education   263
Directory: top 500 universities worldwide   267

Global university rankings

In 2008, Times Higher Education (THE) and QS published the THE-QS World University Rankings for the fifth time, (third time in this book). Millions of people have viewed them online, at www.timeshighereducation.co.uk and www.topuniversities.com, and debate within the academic community has been incessant. A UNESCO experts' group spent more than a year poring over the methodology and there have been several international conferences devoted to the ranking process.

The need for international comparisons is growing. The travelling scholar dates back to the Middle Ages, but never before have such numbers crossed national boundaries. UNESCO estimates there to be more than 132 million students, over three million of whom are studying abroad. More than half of this travelling band go to four countries: France, Germany, the UK and the US, which takes by far the largest share despite fluctuations in recent years. Australia, Canada and Japan are the other big destinations, and countries such as China have set their sights on joining them. The THE-QS World University Rankings illustrate why students choose to go to these countries. US universities have consistently occupied more than a third of the top 100 places. Famous US names, led all five years by Harvard University, take most of the top 20 places, but their grip is soon loosened down the table. European universities match the US contingent in the top 100, led by UK institutions, and Australasia is close behind.

Widespread excellence

The rankings have shown that excellence in higher education is distributed more widely than many in the West have presumed. The high standing of Australian universities in Asia, for example, has helped propel six of them into the top 50, while 20 different countries are represented in the top 100. Some nations have only one institution in the top 200, but it has become a matter of economic and cultural importance, as well as national pride, to compete at this level. In Germany, which has 11 universities in the top 200 but none in the top 50, the government has awarded several billion Euros of extra investment to a group of elite institutions to promote their world standing. The 2006 edition of the Organization for Economic Cooperation and Development's (OECD) annual Education at a Glance report even expressed concern that some countries might be both overexposed to the international market and nearing their capacity in some academic areas. More than a third of postgraduates at UK universities were from overseas, while foreign students accounted for 39 per cent of masters' places in Australia and 41 per cent of PhDs in Switzerland. This illustrates the international demand for higher education, and also the need for prospective applicants to do their homework. Large concentrations of foreign students, especially of a single nationality, can dilute the experience of working and living in another country.

Global trends

Global rankings of universities are six years old and are used by students, employers, research funders, governments, and universities themselves. Although still controversial, these have now been recognized by bodies such as the International Association of Universities (IAU) as a permanent fixture on the international academic scene. The IAU's journal wrote: "The strength of the market seems unavoidable and rankings are its most resonant indicator at the moment." Recently, the debate has intensified on how rankings should be compiled. Discussions have taken place on every continent and numerous research papers have been published. But few people deny that there is a need for international comparisons of some sort. The world's leading universities are no longer content to be recognized as pre-eminent in their own country. Higher education has become such a global enterprise that the best institutions are often more interested in comparing themselves with rivals thousands of miles away. In the UK, Manchester University, for example, set itself the target of breaking into the top 25 in the world; Bristol University wanted to be in the top 50 and achieved that. It is easy to see why universities want to be recognised on the world stage. Companies and governments mount global searches before placing research contracts, top academics frequently move continents to further their careers and students, too, are increasingly mobile, particularly at postgraduate level. For some students, a move abroad may be the only way to find top quality tuition and academic facilities in a particular subject. For others, to experience a different culture and a new way of thinking is valuable enough in itself.

A 'world class university'

Nevertheless, there is still no consensus about the value of university rankings. Some, such as Philip Altbach, Director of the Center for International Higher Education, Boston College, continue to insist that a world ranking of universities cannot be made. "Everyone wants a world class university. No country feels it can do without one," he wrote when the 2005 rankings were published. "The problem is that no one knows what a world class university is, and no one has figured out how to get one." In all probability, there never will be agreement on a single method of comparing universities worldwide. But there has been widespread support for the objectives set in compiling the THE-QS World University Rankings: to produce an up-to-date view of the strengths of the leading institutions as they impact on research and teaching, and giving credit for an international outlook. They reflect the qualities seen in almost all the universities recognized informally as international powerhouses, which are institutions rooted in research, but proud of their teaching prowess.

Richard Levin, president of Yale University, told Newsweek magazine: "In response to the same forces that have propelled the world economy, universities have become more self-consciously global: seeking students from around the world who represent the entire spectrum of cultures and values, sending their own students abroad to prepare them for global careers, offering courses of study that address the challenges of an interconnected world and collaborative research programs to advance science for the benefit of all humanity. Of the forces shaping higher education, none is more sweeping than the movement across borders."

However, there are many valuable universities that do not aspire to international status. They may serve their local communities, usually with an emphasis on teaching, rather than research, or they may be determinedly national institutions with an eye to knowledge transfer. The universities in the THE-QS World University Rankings (and other similar rankings) tend to judge themselves internationally on the power of their research, often as members of the growing number of global higher education networks, and they recruit students and staff from many parts of the world.

THE-QS World University Rankings 2008

The table of the top 200 universities worldwide, according to the THE-QS World University Rankings, begins on the following page. A discussion of the methodology behind these rankings begins on page 257 after the table.

WHICH AUSTRALIAN UNIVERSITY HAS A GLOBAL REPUTATION FOR INNOVATION?

Swinburne – the only Australian member of the European Consortium of Innovative Universities.

For over a hundred years, Swinburne has been at the forefront of innovation in both teaching and intellectual output. We may not be a large university, but what we lack in size we more than make up for in quality. With a clear focus on education quality, we provide an intimate learning experience rated as one of the best in Australia. And with over US$200 Million to be invested in research over the next four years, Swinburne's commitment to research excellence is unparalleled.

Question everything.

THE-QS World University Rankings 2008*

2008 rank	2007 rank	University	Country	Peer review	Recruiter review	Faculty/ students	Citations per faculty	International faculty	International students	Overall score
1	1	HARVARD University	US	100	100	96	100	87	81	100.0
2	2=	YALE University	US	100	100	100	98	89	71	99.8
3	2=	University of CAMBRIDGE	UK	100	100	99	89	98	95	99.5
4	2=	University of OXFORD	UK	100	100	100	85	96	96	98.9
5	7=	CALIFORNIA Institute of Technology (Caltech)	US	100	74	98	100	100	93	98.6
6	5	IMPERIAL College London	UK	99	100	100	83	98	100	98.4
7	9	UCL (University College London)	UK	96	99	100	89	96	100	98.1
8	7=	University of CHICAGO	US	100	99	98	91	78	83	98.0
9	10	MASSACHUSETTS Institute of Technology (MIT)	US	100	100	90	100	33	94	96.7
10	11	COLUMBIA University	US	100	99	98	94	29	89	96.3
11	14	University of PENNSYLVANIA	US	97	98	88	99	83	79	96.1
12	6	PRINCETON University	US	100	98	75	100	91	82	95.7
13=	13	DUKE University	US	97	98	100	94	30	66	94.4
13=	15	JOHNS HOPKINS University	US	99	78	100	100	30	68	94.4
15	20=	CORNELL University	US	100	99	90	96	28	76	94.3
16	16	AUSTRALIAN National University	AU	100	93	82	74	99	91	92.0
17	19	STANFORD University	US	100	100	67	100	26	87	91.2
18	38=	University of MICHIGAN	US	99	99	85	84	59	51	91.0
19	17	University of TOKYO	JP	100	94	98	78	27	40	90.0
20	12	McGILL University	CA	100	97	99	51	62	95	89.7
21	20=	CARNEGIE MELLON University	US	95	97	82	79	50	97	89.6
22	24	KING'S College London	UK	93	98	89	70	91	85	89.5
23	23	University of EDINBURGH	UK	96	99	82	70	91	82	89.3
24	42	ETH Zurich (Swiss Federal Institute of Technology)	CH	95	82	56	99	100	94	89.1
25	25	KYOTO University	JP	99	87	80	91	30	26	87.4

2008 rank	2007 rank	University	Country	Peer review	Recruiter review	Faculty/ students	Citations per faculty	International faculty	International students	Overall score
26	18	University of HONG KONG	HK	94	90	86	59	100	92	87.1
27	32	BROWN University	US	92	83	64	99	56	58	85.2
28	26	Ecole Normale Supérieure, PARIS	FR	93	72	68	99	29	69	84.8
29	30	University of MANCHESTER	UK	91	100	82	56	91	84	84.4
30=	41	University of CALIFORNIA, Los Angeles (UCLA)	US	100	98	48	100	23	36	84.3
30=	33=	National University of SINGAPORE	SG	100	98	39	75	100	100	84.3
32	37	University of BRISTOL	UK	83	99	82	74	85	74	84.1
33	29	NORTHWESTERN University	US	88	97	78	82	30	61	83.3
34=	33=	University of BRITISH COLUMBIA	CA	100	93	69	67	33	61	83.0
34=	28	ÉCOLE POLYTECHNIQUE	FR	80	96	100	58	62	93	83.0
36	22	University of California, BERKELEY	US	100	100	24	100	88	36	82.9
37	31	University of SYDNEY	AU	99	97	55	54	97	93	82.4
38	27	University of MELBOURNE	AU	100	100	59	56	54	96	82.3
39	53=	HONG KONG University of Science & Technology	HK	86	90	60	72	100	97	81.4
40	49	NEW YORK University (NYU)	US	96	96	83	54	28	56	81.3
41	45	University of TORONTO	CA	100	94	18	100	80	46	81.1
42	38=	CHINESE University of Hong Kong	HK	85	84	80	57	98	86	81.0
43	33=	University of QUEENSLAND	AU	95	97	49	63	100	78	80.7
44	46	OSAKA University	JP	90	69	93	70	25	28	80.1
45	44	University of NEW SOUTH WALES	AU	97	99	35	68	83	91	79.8
46	47	BOSTON University	US	91	85	66	73	26	59	79.1
47	43	MONASH University	AU	98	99	52	37	99	99	78.7
48	93=	University of COPENHAGEN	DK	88	59	100	45	67	69	78.5
49	53=	TRINITY College Dublin	IE	90	96	68	42	99	76	78.2
50=	117=	Ecole Polytechnique Fédérale de LAUSANNE	CH	63	71	93	77	100	100	78.1
50=	36	PEKING University	CN	100	97	84	34	27	36	78.1

2008 rank	2007 rank	University	Country	Peer review	Recruiter review	Faculty/students	Citations per faculty	International faculty	International students	Overall score
50=	51=	SEOUL National University	KR	97	65	87	54	23	37	78.1
53	48	University of AMSTERDAM	NL	88	77	80	61	73	32	78.0
54	71=	DARTMOUTH College	US	64	93	88	95	28	57	77.8
55	55=	University of WISCONSIN-Madison	US	93	79	48	89	31	36	77.7
56	40	TSINGHUA University	CN	97	90	94	31	23	24	77.0
57	60	HEIDELBERG Universität	DE	87	59	81	58	54	81	76.9
58	58	University of CALIFORNIA, San Diego	US	98	58	35	100	20	29	76.3
59	55=	University of WASHINGTON	US	84	54	62	99	25	36	75.8
60	161=	WASHINGTON University in St Louis	US	64	55	100	95	24	54	75.7
61	90=	TOKYO Institute of Technology	JP	77	76	70	87	25	45	75.3
62	74=	EMORY University	US	62	67	96	91	43	47	75.0
63	71=	UPPSALA University	SE	91	60	43	85	70	41	74.9
64	84	LEIDEN University	NL	87	61	35	97	74	41	74.8
65	50	University of AUCKLAND	NZ	95	94	36	42	94	99	74.5
66	59	LONDON School of Economics and Political Science (LSE)	UK	88	100	59	26	100	100	74.2
67	89	UTRECHT University	NL	89	66	62	72	45	24	74.0
68	105	University of GENEVA	CH	69	36	58	98	97	100	73.9
69	57	University of WARWICK	UK	83	100	60	38	92	97	73.8
70	51=	University of TEXAS at Austin	US	95	95	26	69	60	43	73.3
71	73	University of ILLINOIS	US	94	67	43	72	37	51	73.2
72	61	Katholieke Universiteit LEUVEN	BE	92	83	34	72	52	51	73.1
73	83	University of GLASGOW	UK	72	78	67	69	95	60	73.0
74	97=	University of ALBERTA	CA	91	48	56	55	92	64	72.9
75	65=	University of BIRMINGHAM	UK	73	94	57	65	82	72	72.3
76	68	University of SHEFFIELD	UK	69	97	68	60	81	72	72.2
77	69	NANYANG Technological University	SG	87	87	47	38	100	99	72.1

2008 rank	2007 rank	University	Country	Peer review	Recruiter review	Faculty/ students	Citations per faculty	International faculty	International students	Overall score
78=	63	DELFT University of Technology	NL	78	87	66	49	80	66	71.8
78=	67	Technische Universität MÜNCHEN (TUM)	DE	73	59	86	57	54	77	71.8
78=	92	RICE University	US	62	55	76	95	42	73	71.8
81=	114=	University of AARHUS	DK	76	38	72	74	67	58	71.5
81=	74=	University of YORK	UK	62	93	77	57	95	84	71.5
83=	97=	GEORGIA Institute of Technology	US	78	83	22	99	39	78	71.3
83=	76	University of ST ANDREWS	UK	59	95	74	62	92	99	71.3
83=	64	University of WESTERN AUSTRALIA	AU	72	88	52	65	92	83	71.3
86	70	University of NOTTINGHAM	UK	72	98	64	46	90	89	71.0
87	142=	University of MINNESOTA	US	79	54	38	94	72	33	70.2
88	106	LUND University	SE	82	68	45	68	68	52	70.0
89	96	University of CALIFORNIA, Davis	US	84	46	42	96	28	26	69.9
90	85=	CASE WESTERN RESERVE University	US	60	42	95	88	21	51	69.8
91=	100	University of HELSINKI	FI	88	43	55	71	51	21	69.6
91=	93=	Université de Montréal	CA	89	36	36	70	83	74	69.6
93=	128	Hebrew University of JERUSALEM	IR	89	25	35	89	70	33	69.5
93=	65=	Ludwig-Maximilians-Universität München (LMU)	DE	84	45	69	51	51	70	69.5
95	132=	KAIST - Korea Advanced Institute of Science & Technology	KR	76	53	61	79	48	36	69.3
96	110	University of VIRGINIA	US	66	93	61	82	24	38	69.2
97	77=	University of PITTSBURGH	US	62	40	95	79	42	34	69.1
98	117=	University of CALIFORNIA, Santa Barbara	US	88	50	21	99	39	22	68.8
99=	77=	PURDUE University	US	85	82	34	60	60	57	68.6
99=	80=	University of SOUTHAMPTON	UK	63	90	61	61	87	83	68.6
101	82	VANDERBILT University	US	53	84	100	60	57	45	68.5
102=	151=	University of NORTH CAROLINA	US	74	87	61	71	22	21	68.4
102=	119	University of SOUTHERN CALIFORNIA	US	65	73	49	80	71	88	68.4

2008 rank	2007 rank	University	Country	Peer review	Recruiter review	Faculty/ students	Citations per faculty	International faculty	International students	Overall score
104	80=	University of LEEDS	UK	72	98	57	50	71	64	68.3
105	90=	PENNSYLVANIA STATE University	US	78	79	39	81	35	36	68.2
106=	62	University of ADELAIDE	AU	72	89	39	61	87	95	68.1
106=	140=	University of ZURICH	CH	76	38	21	99	99	68	68.1
108	177=	University College DUBLIN	IE	72	91	67	33	95	82	68.0
109	231=	TECHNION - Israel Institute of Technology	IR	84	58	48	79	18	18	67.9
110	102=	GEORGETOWN University	US	69	94	65	62	26	52	67.6
111	111	MAASTRICHT University	NL	51	72	80	72	61	100	67.4
112	102=	TOHOKU University	JP	63	49	98	63	38	31	67.2
113	85=	FUDAN University	CN	89	91	49	39	31	32	67.1
114	151=	TEL AVIV University	IR	85	47	24	98	17	19	66.7
115	85=	University of VIENNA	AT	89	67	10	67	64	85	66.6
116	123	Université Catholique de LOUVAIN (UCL)	BE	85	63	19	74	49	73	66.4
117=	108	McMASTER University	CA	86	42	26	91	27	32	66.2
117=	88	QUEEN'S University	CA	77	82	45	55	79	34	66.2
119	95	University of ROCHESTER	US	53	33	100	67	63	71	66.1
120	112=	NAGOYA University	JP	62	58	84	71	26	32	65.9
121	120	OHIO STATE University	US	73	80	40	70	59	41	65.8
122=	109	DURHAM University	UK	60	99	50	65	84	62	65.4
122=	79	University of MARYLAND	US	68	56	55	78	48	39	65.4
124=	114=	University of OTAGO	NZ	73	75	36	53	100	88	65.3
124=	102=	National TAIWAN University	TW	87	73	40	54	31	25	65.3
126	163=	ERASMUS University Rotterdam	NL	58	98	46	81	57	50	65.2
127	224	STONY BROOK University	US	71	35	47	75	63	81	65.1
128	130=	EINDHOVEN University of Technology	NL	57	55	100	41	98	42	64.8
129	112=	University of WATERLOO	CA	86	69	18	62	60	54	64.6

2008 rank	2007 rank	University	Country	Peer review	Recruiter review	Faculty/ students	Citations per faculty	International faculty	International students	Overall score
130	121	University of SUSSEX	UK	60	54	51	72	92	79	64.1
131	114=	University of BASEL	CH	62	32	98	34	84	80	63.9
132	140=	University of CALIFORNIA, Irvine	US	80	30	30	94	24	29	63.8
133=	99	CARDIFF University	UK	61	89	66	39	71	77	63.4
133=	130=	Technical University of DENMARK	DK	45	42	99	63	90	56	63.4
133=	101	University of LIVERPOOL	UK	54	81	69	55	80	67	63.4
136	124	University of GHENT	BE	68	47	84	43	40	43	63.1
137=	146	Freie Universität BERLIN	DE	85	22	24	72	47	68	62.6
137=	122	TEXAS A&M University	US	77	74	23	73	34	40	62.6
139	126=	HUMBOLDT-Universität zu Berlin	DE	79	43	64	36	42	56	62.5
140	157	École Normale Supérieure de LYON	FR	41	57	100	68	47	56	62.4
141	155=	University of Science and Technology of CHINA	CN	76	67	56	56	19	13	62.3
142	148	WAGENINGEN University	NL	41	35	90	80	42	97	62.0
143	125	NANJING University	CN	76	68	66	33	54	18	61.9
144=	173=	University of GRONINGEN	NL	63	49	67	60	61	34	61.8
144=	163=	SHANGHAI JIAO TONG University	CN	75	83	69	28	34	20	61.8
146	134	University of ARIZONA	US	69	55	42	81	24	30	61.5
147=	149=	CITY University of HONG KONG	HK	68	58	44	54	100	43	61.2
147=	144	Universität FREIBURG	DE	64	30	91	42	26	67	61.2
149	132=	Université Pierre-et-Marie-Curie PARIS VI	FR	66	17	89	40	24	90	61.0
150	192=	Universidad Nacional Autónoma de México (UNAM)	MX	81	86	59	20	42	15	60.9
151	177=	RUTGERS, The State University of New Jersey	US	79	42	47	51	52	29	60.7
152	145	University of BATH	UK	49	98	46	55	92	93	60.4
153	137=	University of ABERDEEN	UK	44	71	78	51	91	80	60.3
154	307=	Indian Institute of Technology Delhi (IITD)	IN	64	84	69	47	16	14	60.1
155=	304=	VU University AMSTERDAM	NL	64	50	84	38	37	31	59.8

2008 rank	2007 rank	University	Country	Peer review	Recruiter review	Faculty/ students	Citations per faculty	International faculty	International students	Overall score
155=	142=	Eberhard Karls Universität TÜBINGEN	DE	61	30	71	58	55	51	59.8
157	159=	TUFTS University	US	40	64	62	95	37	49	59.6
158	136	KYUSHU University	JP	59	44	74	64	20	31	59.5
159	126=	University of WESTERN ONTARIO	CA	67	61	26	77	63	31	59.4
160	149=	QUEEN MARY, University of London	UK	55	66	77	23	96	92	59.1
161	217	University of LAUSANNE	CH	48	51	41	85	85	82	59.0
162=	197=	CHALMERS University of Technology	SE	64	48	40	70	42	60	58.7
162=	129	NEWCASTLE University, NEWCASTLE Upon Tyne	UK	40	88	68	55	82	79	58.7
164	139	SIMON FRASER University	CA	76	57	19	51	93	48	58.5
165	135	University of FLORIDA	US	65	56	37	73	33	34	58.4
166=	223	CHULALONGKORN University	TH	79	77	59	21	23	14	58.3
166=	168=	Universität GÖTTINGEN	DE	69	25	65	46	39	52	58.3
168	155=	University of NOTRE DAME	US	56	83	44	72	26	35	58.1
169	209=	Universität FRANKFURT am Main	DE	54	51	66	57	30	80	58.0
170=	166=	University of CALGARY	CA	70	52	41	63	24	29	57.9
170=	137=	INDIANA University Bloomington	US	70	70	27	58	49	45	57.9
170=	147	University of LANCASTER	UK	52	77	60	37	90	80	57.9
173	192=	KTH, ROYAL Institute of Technology	SE	59	58	47	46	70	98	57.8
174=	151=	HOKKAIDO University	JP	54	52	74	63	20	24	57.6
174=	269	Indian Institute of Technology Bombay (IITB)	IN	74	76	44	43	23	13	57.6
174=	191	RENSSELAER Polytechnic Institute	US	52	46	34	92	62	48	57.6
177=	185=	University of LEICESTER	UK	37	59	63	71	77	95	57.5
177=	188=	University of OSLO	NO	67	41	57	43	46	60	57.5
179	200=	University of CAPE TOWN	ZA	61	66	15	68	86	82	57.4
180=	107	University of COLORADO at Boulder	US	56	24	52	90	37	20	57.3
180=	180=	WASEDA University	JP	79	89	36	23	43	30	57.3

2008 rank	2007 rank	University	Country	Peer review	Recruiter review	Faculty/ students	Citations per faculty	International faculty	International students	Overall score
182	168=	MACQUARIE University	AU	65	87	18	41	88	100	57.1
183=	154	Université Libre de BRUXELLES (ULB)	BE	63	62	19	65	50	96	56.9
183=	231=	Lomonosov MOSCOW STATE University	RU	80	72	39	31	17	25	56.9
185	208	BRANDEIS University	US	54	34	47	80	28	74	56.8
186=	194	University of BARCELONA	ES	77	52	19	60	24	38	56.4
186=	188=	University of CANTERBURY	NZ	62	86	24	37	99	93	56.4
188=	203=	Technische Universität BERLIN	DE	62	50	46	39	71	85	56.1
188=	233	POHANG University of Science and Technology	KR	37	34	67	99	52	19	56.1
190	165	Universität STUTTGART	DE	52	58	77	28	46	89	55.9
191	175=	University of MASSACHUSETTS, Amherst	US	65	54	28	68	53	26	55.8
192=	214	University of BERN	CH	40	28	59	83	93	45	55.4
192=	173=	University of BOLOGNA	IT	81	69	21	40	26	28	55.4
194	180=	University of READING	UK	44	76	56	49	80	77	55.3
195	187	University of ANTWERP	BE	43	37	99	37	56	59	55.1
196	175=	University of SÃO PAULO	BR	77	61	38	32	34	19	55.0
197=	264=	University of BUENOS AIRES	AR	66	91	56	19	31	34	54.8
197=	221=	DALHOUSIE University	CA	59	26	43	69	61	40	54.8
199	197=	KOBE University	JP	57	61	71	36	24	30	54.5
200=	248=	University of ATHENS	GR	40	47	67	72	-	92	54.3
200=	185=	University of TWENTE	NL	52	48	57	51	68	50	54.3

254

THE-QS World University Rankings: methodology

Ben Sowter, head of research at QS, outlines what the THE-QS World University Rankings measure, and how

The real difficulty facing those who seek to rank universities worldwide is not how to define them, but where to find the data that will enable reliable comparisons. Different national systems collect the data that matter to them and in the form that suits their purpose. The limited number of measures in the THE-QS World University Rankings reflect just how few indicators there are that transfer across borders, and even they can present problems, as outlined below.

The main rankings table evaluates six key aspects of university activity using the most recent data available at the time of initial publication: 1. Peer review; 2. Citations per faculty (research quality); 3. Student faculty ratio (teaching quality); 4. Recruiter review (graduate employability); numbers of 5. International faculty, and, 6. International students (international outlook).

Understanding the ranking indicators

1. Peer review

Peer review is a measure of the average reputation for research of a given institution amongst academics in each of five broad subject areas. It is the method used to assess academic quality in universities all over the world and it has formed a part of US university league tables for many years. In the absence of more precise statistical data on activities such as teaching and more up-to-date comparisons of research, it has become the central element of the THE-QS World University Rankings. It is, after all, partially a matter of opinion, which are the best universities in the world. Who better to ask than the people who work in them?

QS operates an international survey of academics asking them to identify institutions they consider best for research in the subject area(s) they identify themselves as knowledgeable in. Respondents are sourced from previous survey respondents and third-party databases. 6,354 responses were considered for the 2008 rankings. Respondents are asked to identify the subject area(s) with which they have most familiarity from the following: arts and humanities, life sciences and biomedicine, natural sciences, social sciences, and engineering and IT. They are also asked to identify which of three large geographical areas: 1. Americas, 2. Europe, Middle East & Africa, 3. Asia Pacific, they have most awareness of. Respondents are asked to identify up to 30 institutions they consider excellent in each subject area they have selected, from a list of institutions in the region(s) they have selected. They are not asked to rank those institutions; performance is based on the number of occurrences of each institution's name. Responses are weighted by region and compiled into five separate peer reviews for each of the five subject areas which are combined with equal weighting to yield the final result. Respondents are not able to respond in favour of their own institution. An analysis of 2008 respondents is available at www.topuniversities.com.

The peer review is based on an average of about 20 responses from over 6,000 respondents, resulting in a statistical universe of over 120,000 data points to evaluate just over 600 institutions. Whilst being statistically robust, since it is a reputation survey, it is sensitive to certain bias. For example, big name universities and universities in the world's largest cities may perform beyond expectations and respondents may identify institutions as strong in fields they may not even have. The response is growing dramatically each year the rankings are carried out, so the influence of such bias will diminish. Although any evaluation of university research strength is likely to be skewed in favour of universities operating in widely spoken languages, the peer review is more resistant to this problem than citations' scores, resulting in many universities from non-English speaking countries performing more strongly in the peer review evaluation. In addition, the peer review reflects no bias between any of the five main subject areas, so if you are interested in arts, humanities or social sciences, which are, relatively, under-represented by citations, this measure reflects a more even balance.

2. Citations per faculty

Citations in leading academic journals are a conventional measure of institutional research strength and the most common source of international academic comparisons. Dividing these by the number of faculty staff, takes into account the size of the institution. Citation numbers come from Scopus™ www.scopus.com. Faculty numbers come either from central statistics bodies, (many of which are listed for reference at the end of this chapter), from the universities directly, from institutions' websites or, in a few unusual cases, from an extrapolated average. Scopus™ supplies QS with the latest five complete years of publication data with citation counts. QS maps all of the names from the rankings exercise into the Scopus™ data. In 2008, over 22,500 name variants for the 604 institutions considered for the rankings were found. It is expected that this number will further increase for 2009 as we invite institutions to help identify additional names. The faculty number used is total and not purely restricted to research faculty. While it would be ideal to factor research output purely by those involved in its production, this level of data has proved difficult to collect globally and may constitute a future enhancement to the methodology.

In general, the breakdown of faculty is reasonably consistent across the sample institutions, but there are exceptions where a given institution may have a particular concentration of either teaching or research faculty. These institutions may be at an advantage or disadvantage in any indicator involving faculty numbers. Institutions with strong medical schools are at a particular advantage since citations are a more prolific practice in science, and particularly in medical subject areas than in any other. Also, citations data yields a strong language bias towards English and a strong cultural bias towards countries where academics place a stronger emphasis on publication, little consolation to institutions that work in other languages and whose academics stand correspondingly less chance of building up a competitive body of citations. The US is the most profound beneficiary of these last two factors as it is, by far, the most significant nation in terms of the publication of academic research in English. Furthermore, the research culture in the US and the sheer volume of citations registered by US universities suggests that their academics also cite each others' work more regularly than is the case in most of Europe or Asia. There is no suggestion of corruption, merely of a difference in normal academic practice.

3. Student faculty ratio

This is the most universally available metric that indicates commitment to teaching. There is no globally available measurement of teaching quality. Most countries do not even attempt national comparisons. The nearest proxy, however imperfect, is the faculty student ratio. Despite the onward march of technology, there is no substitute in conventional universities for face-to-face contact. Students value small teaching groups and the opportunity to consult tutors. Both student and faculty numbers come either from central statistics bodies, from the universities directly, from institutions' websites or, in a few unusual cases, from an extrapolated average. Separate numbers are collected for undergraduate and postgraduate students from each institution. In most cases, the sum of the two is used. In a scenario where separate metrics are not available, total student numbers are requested. The lower the number for a student faculty ratio, the better; which makes its inclusion in an index, based on high scores, a challenge. So, for purposes of the ranking, the ratio is reversed, thus essentially evaluating the number of faculty per student.

In a similar way to the citations indicator, the faculty score used is total, without identifying and eliminating faculty not contributing to research. As a result, universities with typical faculty demographics may be at an advantage or disadvantage. While this may remain the best universally available indicator of commitment to teaching, it is a far from perfect measure of teaching quality. In fact, measuring teaching quality remains one of the greatest challenges for international rankings. If you are concerned about teaching quality in particular, it may be worth your while to refer to country-specific rankings, a list of which can be found at www.topuniversities.com. Speaking to staff and alumni of the institution, either through your personal network or at an education fair, is also highly recommended as a way to gauge teaching quality at a particular institution.

4. Recruiter review

Recruiter review is a measure of the quality of graduates from particular institutions, from the perspective of global employers. QS conducts an annual survey of global graduate employers. Prospective respondents are sourced from QS' comprehensive databases, from a selection of partner and other organizations. 2,359 responses were considered for the results in 2008.

The recruiter review is conducted along very similar lines to the peer review. There is no distinction between different subject areas and it is operated in a near identical way to a single subject area peer review. Regional weightings are still applied. The international respondents come from a very diverse range of businesses in terms of scope, sector, size and nature. No weighting is applied on the basis of the seniority of respondent, or the scope of their recruitment base. While the international spread of the responding sample is rapidly improving year-on-year, the response and, thus, the results still show some bias towards English speaking nations in 2008.

5. Number of international faculty

The ability of an institution to attract, retain and adequately compensate international faculty members could be considered a measure of quality. The proportion of international faculty also gives prospective students an impression of the diversity of an institution and, perhaps, some feeling for its progressiveness, in terms of globalization. All faculty and international faculty data is collected via the same means as discussed for the student faculty indicator. Raw scores are simply a proportion of the faculty that are international (ie hold a foreign passport). The higher the proportion, the higher the eventual score.

Very high international faculty numbers may not necessarily be a good thing; poor quality faculty may be forced to seek employment outside their home nation and a poor quality institution may find it difficult to attract faculty from its own country. Understanding the nature of an institution from an international perspective is of value, however, it is best considered only in the context of other indicators of quality. It is important to take a balanced and comprehensive view of this kind of aspect of an institution, one that extends far beyond the scope of these rankings. This book helps reveal the first steps.

6. Number of international students

The proportion of international students also gives prospective students an impression of the diversity of an institution and perhaps some indication of its commitment to international students and the ability to provide them with adequate academic and other support. All student and international student data is collected via the same means as discussed for the student faculty indicator. The raw scores are simply a proportion of the full time student body that is international. Exchange students are not currently included. The higher the proportion, the higher the eventual score. Very high international student numbers may not necessarily be a good thing: a poor quality institution may find it difficult to attract students from its own country and, thus, focus on the overseas market. More students are able to engage in full program study abroad, if those programs are taught in a language they understand. This gives institutions in English-speaking countries an advantage for both of these international indicators. In the future, including, separately, exchange students in this consideration may help add balance and may, perhaps, become feasible as institutions, year-on-year, furnish the exercise with more complete data.

Overall, it is not easy to measure international activity. Some universities have whole campuses overseas, others have numerous partnership programs and exchange schemes. But it is possible to be globally active and internationally minded without such formal initiatives. The proportions of international students and staff have been selected as the most universally applicable indicators, although both have been accorded a low weighting, so as not to overplay their importance.

Weightings

Weightings are applied to the data results as set out in the chart below. (All decisions regarding the allocation of weightings are the responsibility of Times Higher Education). Finally, the total scores were transformed to a scale where the top score was set at 100 with the remainder being a proportion of the top score.

THE-QS World University Rankings criteria/weights

Criterion	Indicator	Description	Weight
Research quality	1. Peer review	Composite score drawn from peer review (in five subject areas) 6,354 responses	40%
	2. Citations per faculty	Score based on research performance factored against the size of the research body	20%
Teaching quality	3. Student faculty ratio	Score based on student/ faculty ratio	20%
Graduate employability	4. Recruiter review	Score based on responses to recruiter survey 2,359 responses	10%
International outlook	5. International faculty	Score based on proportion of international faculty	5%
	6. International students	Score based on proportion of international students	5%

Z-scores: a balancing tool

A statistical technique called the z-transformation, (sometimes known as normal or standard scores), has been applied to each measure. This is a statistical way of ensuring that each measure contributes the intended amount to the overall score. (For the statistically minded, it involves subtracting the mean score from each individual score and then dividing by the standard deviation of the scores. The percentile ranks of the z-scores are then plotted using a standard normal distribution table). This adjustment to the methodology, initiated in 2007, adds to the reliability of the ranking by ensuring that high performers on a single indicator do not gain a disproportionate advantage, and brings the ranking into line with other similar assessments. The use of z-scores has already reduced year-on-year volatility in the ranking.

Prior to 2007, scores for each indicator were scaled against the top performer on that measure; the leading institution was awarded 100 and subsequent institutions' scores scaled against that maximum. Where there was a steep curve in the distribution of scores, universities at the head of lowly weighted indicators, such as the proportion of international students, could benefit by the equivalent of up to 50 places in the top-weighted peer review section. Applying z-scores effectively 'flattens' the curve, normalizing the scores throughout the ranking to iron out such ripple effects. The change has benefited universities that are strong across the board and also explains some of the larger falls since 2006. In 2007, London School of Economics, for example, lost the benefit of a large lead in the proportion of international students and the methodological change has had a similar effect on Macquarie University, Australia, which had a big lead on international faculty.

Further potential indicators of university quality

Academic opinion was already considered a vital element if the rankings were to paint the most current picture of international higher education, rather than reflecting past glories. Even citations inevitably credit universities for work, which may have been carried out several years previously; Nobel prizes, which form a substantial part of the global university rankings published by Shanghai Jiao Tong University, often relate to research done far in the past. The thousands of academics who take part in the peer review exercise conducted by QS for the THE-QS World University Rankings are judging universities in their own discipline, as they are today. By aggregating the views of subject experts, we avoid impressionistic judgments of overall quality and provide material for the separate faculty-level rankings.

Other possible indicators have been considered and, either discarded as impractical or, shelved until enough data can be collected to make them reliable sources of comparison. This was the case initially with the employers' survey, which was omitted from the first edition of the rankings, in 2004, because the sample was considered too small. Now that the pool of international employers is larger and more diverse, it is considered a valuable addition and one that will continue to grow in the years to come.

Among the other indicators considered for inclusion in the rankings have been various spending measures. Many domestic rankings measure the amount spent on libraries, for example, but it was decided that, even if genuinely comparable data could be collected, too great an advantage would be conferred upon wealthy nations for the results to be meaningful. Similar objections have been raised to the use of graduate employment rates: there is a danger of comparing economies rather than universities.

Entry standards provide another obvious area of comparison and one much used in national league tables. But while business schools have an international entry standard, most areas of university life do not. Much work has been done on the equivalence of different qualifications, but it is not yet clear how this can be incorporated into a system of rankings such as these. No doubt other measures will be developed such as the proportion of staff with PhDs, or the number of PhDs awarded by each university, but, despite frequent appeals for workable additions, no glaring omission has yet emerged.

Major universities are complex and while attempting to encapsulate their quality in a few simple measures, the process of ranking inevitably involves simplification. Many US state universities, for example, or the Indian Institutes of Technology have a number of campuses and centres, but it is often beyond data-gathering feasibility to distinguish adequately between them. If handled separately, fewer of them would appear in the rankings and in lower positions. The units analysed in the rankings relate to universities, as they exist in practice. For example, the various colleges of the universities of London and California, which have their own management structures and in some cases award their own degrees, are treated individually.

Conclusions

The position of an institution in the THE-QS World University Rankings is, clearly, not only influenced by its activities and performance in the last 12 months, but by reputation, effort and achievements over years and decades and, in some cases, centuries. There are many factors outside direct institutional control that may have influenced the current position of a university, such as language, politics, economics, and culture, for example. The ranking of the top 200 or 500 worldwide can provide an interesting basis for initiating your research into university choice. However, rankings do not replace the need for that research entirely, but simply, perhaps, help make it more incisive.

The tables of the THE-QS World University Rankings do not, for example, consider institutional strength in many specific fields. The university profiles of the top 100 universities worldwide, in chapter one, take a more in-depth look and highlight specific areas of excellence. For a student considering economics or marine engineering, for example, a more detailed analysis will be required by looking at the subject area rankings for science and technology in chapter two. There are certainly many institutions worldwide that offer real excellence in specific fields, but may not do so across an entire broad subject area and thus may not be revealed in these rankings.

The continuing research work involved in this ranking exercise is not exhaustive, nor is it, obviously, customised to any single person's specific quest for the right program or course. Your own personal university ranking, evolved according to your own personalized criteria, combined using your own weightings and only looking at institutions that meet your own search requirements would yield very different results. The THE-QS World University Rankings, this book, Top Universities Guide and www.topuniversities.com are designed to provide a good starting point for your journey. Visiting the websites of the institutions listed on the following pages is also a good starting point for your own further research on higher education in particular countries across the world.

Worldwide sources of data on higher education*

Australia
Department of Education, Science & Training www.dest.gov.au
Department of Education, Employment and Workplace Relations (DEEWR)
   www.deewr.gov.au
Australian Education International http://aei.dest.gov.au

Brazil
MEC - Ministry of Education Portal http://portal.mec.gov.br

Canada
Statistics Canada www.statcan.ca/english/edu/edstat.htm
Canada's Higher Education and Career Guide www.canadian-universities.net
Association of Universities and Colleges of Canada www.aucc.ca/search/search.php
Canadian Education Statistics Council www.cesc.ca
The University Presidents' Council of British Columbia www.tupc.bc.ca

China
National Bureau of Statistics of China www.stats.gov.cn
Ministry of Education of the People's Republic of China www.moe.edu.cn

Finland
Statistics Finland - Finland in Figures www.stat.fi/tup/suoluk/index_en.html
KOTA - statistical data on universities and fields of education http://kotaplus.csc.fi

France
Ministry of Education www.education.gouv.fr
INSEE - National Institute for Statistics and Economic Studies www.insee.fr
The French Official Statistics Portal www.statistique-publique.fr

Germany
Federal Statistical Office Germany www.destatis.de/e_home.htm
Bayerisches Landesamt für Statistik und Datenverarbeitung www.statistik.bayern.de
Regionaldatenbank Deutschland - GENESIS Online - Das statistische Informationssystem
des Bundes und der Länder https://www.regionalstatistik.de/genesis/online/logon

Greece
National Statistical Service of Greece www.statistics.gr
Ministry of National Education and Religious Affairs www.ypepth.gr

Hong Kong
Census and Statistics Department www.censtatd.gov.hk
Hong Kong SAR Government portal, GovHK www.gov.hk
University Grants Committee www.ugc.edu.hk
Education Bureau www.edb.gov.hk

India
Department of Higher Education in India www.education.nic.in
National University of Educational Planning and Administration www.nuepa.org
Government of India, Ministry of Statistics and Programme Implementation
   www.mospi.nic.in

Iran
Ministry of Science, Research and Technology www.msrt.ir

Ireland
Central Statistics Office www.cso.ie
Higher Education Authority www.hea.ie
Department of Education and Science www.education.ie

Israel
Central Bureau of Statistics www.cbs.gov.il/engindex.htm

Italy
Italian National Institute of Statistics www.istat.it/english
Ministero dell'Università e della ricerca http://statistica.miur.it

Japan
Statistics Bureau Ministry of Internal Affairs www.stat.go.jp
Ministry of Education www.mext.go.jp
Japan Student Services Organization www.jasso.go.jp

Malaysia
Department of Statistics Malaysia www.statistics.gov.my
Ministry of Higher Education (Institut Pengajian Tinggi Awam (IPTA)) www.mohe.gov.my
Ministry of Higher Education - Dept of Higher Education www.mohe.gov.my

Mexico
INEGI - Instituto Nacional de Estadistica Geografia e Informatica www.inegi.org.mx

The Netherlands
CBS - Central Bureau of Statistics - Statistics Netherlands www.cbs.nl

New Zealand
Ministry of Education New Zealand www.minedu.govt.nz

Norway
Statistics Norway www.ssb.no/en

Pakistan
Higher Education Commission (HEC) www.hec.gov.pk

Russia
Federal State Statistics Service www.gks.ru
The School of Russian and Asian Studies www.sras.org

Singapore
Statistics Singapore www.singstat.gov.sg

South Africa
Statistics South Africa www.statssa.gov.za
Education, Republic of South Africa www.education.gov.za

South Korea

Ministry of Education, Science and Technology http://english.mest.go.kr
KNSO - Korea National Statistical Office www.nso.go.kr/eng2006/emain/index.html
Korea Council for University Education www.kcue.or.kr

Spain

Instituto Nacional de Estadistica www.ine.es

Sweden

Swedish National Agency for Higher Education www.hsv.se
Statistics Sweden www.scb.se

Switzerland

CRUS - Rectors' Conference of the Swiss Universities www.crus.ch
Swiss Federal Statistical Office www.bfs.admin.ch

Turkey

Ministry of National Education www.meb.gov.tr

Thailand

Ministry of Education www.moe.go.th
Commission on Higher Education www.inter.mua.go.th

Taiwan

Ministry of Education - Republic of China (Taiwan) www.moe.gov.tw

US

National Center for Education Statistics www.nces.ed.gov
Common Data Set (CDS) example: http://cds.berkeley.edu

UK

Higher Education Statistics Agency www.hesa.ac.uk

The Leader In Research and Innovation
The Leader in Research and Innovation
The Leader in Research and Innovation
The Leader In Research and Innovation

The Leader in Research and Innovation

www.um.edu.my

innovation

UNIVERSITY
OF MALAYA

Directory: top 500 universities worldwide

The directory of the top 500 universities worldwide, according to the THE-QS World University Rankings 2008, begins on the next page. It gives you facts and contact details, including web addresses, to research all these institutions. Universities are listed alphabetically by country, from Argentina to Uruguay.

The world rank of each institution is given. Universities' strengths in the five main subject areas are also ranked (arts & humanities, engineering and IT, life sciences & biomedicine, natural sciences, and social sciences). The foundation year of each university is included, information on student faculty ratios, and the percentage of international faculty and students, together with overall student numbers. The data also reveals the academic survey position and employer survey position in the THE-QS World University Rankings 2008. Every university in this directory can also be found on www.topuniversities.com with electronic links to their websites and other details, including courses.

Note on the directory entries

The directory includes facts and figures on each institution, based on data provided as part of the research exercise behind the THE-QS World University Rankings 2008. This means that some entries are more comprehensive than others. Where possible, such gaps have been filled using publicly available sources.

While every effort has been made to ensure accuracy, collecting such a large amount of information from around the world always involves the risk of errors or omissions. This fact underlines the imperative of undertaking your own research in addition to this information, and the need for you to verify all data for your chosen course directly with the institution, before you take action based upon it. Any factual clarifications to the directory entries received by the publisher will be posted on www.topuniversities.com, as appropriate.

Argentina

Austral University

Founded 1977

C1063ABB Buenos Aires

www.austral.edu.ar

Academic survey position... 385
Employer survey position.... 126
Student faculty ratio 9.1:1
International faculty 5.3%
Undergraduates.............. 2,506
Postgraduates................... 424
International students 8.6%

World rank ...... 309= (401-500)
Subject area positions
Engineering & IT 297

University of Belgrano

Founded 1964

C1426DQG Buenos Aires

www.ub.edu.ar

Academic survey position... 385
Employer survey position.... 317
Student faculty ratio 9.4:1
International faculty 3.7%
International students 21.7%

World rank .401-500 (401-500)
Subject area positions
Engineering & IT 297

University of Buenos Aires

Founded 1821

1053 Buenos Aires

www.uba.ar

Academic survey position... 144
Employer survey position...... 63
Student faculty ratio 10.6:1
International faculty 6.9%
International students 7.0%

World rank .... 197= (264=)
Subject area positions
Arts & humanities 139
Engineering & IT 209
Life sciences & biomedicine 159
Natural sciences................ 145
Social sciences 158

Universidad Torcuato di Tella

Founded 1991

1428 Buenos Aires

www.utdt.edu

Academic survey position... 385
Employer survey position.... 134
Student faculty ratio 23.9:1
International faculty 26.2%
International students 10.9%

World rank .401-500 (401-500)
Subject area positions
Engineering & IT 297

Australia

University of Adelaide

Founded 1874

Adelaide
SA 5005

www.adelaide.edu.au

Academic survey position... 124
Employer survey position...... 70
Student faculty ratio 13.8:1
International faculty 29.6%
Undergraduates............ 12,170
Postgraduates................. 3,516
International students 26.0%

World rank .... 106= (62)
Subject area positions
Arts & humanities 146
Engineering & IT 167
Life sciences & biomedicine 139
Natural sciences................ 127
Social sciences 107

Australian National University

Founded 1946

Canberra
ACT 200

www.anu.edu.au

Academic survey position..... 17
Employer survey position...... 58
Student faculty ratio 7.6:1
International faculty 46.5%
Undergraduates.............. 7,532
Postgraduates................. 3,586
International students 23.3%

World rank 16 (16)
Subject area positions
Arts & humanities 12
Engineering & IT 36
Life sciences & biomedicine.. 37
Natural sciences................... 21
Social sciences 14

Australia continued

Curtin University of Technology

Founded 1987

Kent St Bentley
WA 6102

www.curtin.edu.au

Academic survey position... 240
Employer survey position...... 93
Student faculty ratio 16.5:1
International faculty.......61.9%
Undergraduates............ 24,240
Postgraduates................. 4,520
International students 43.4%

World rank 232 (235)
Subject area positions
Engineering & IT 186
Life sciences & biomedicine 232
Natural sciences................ 255
Social sciences 187

Deakin University

Founded 1974

Geelong
VIC 3217

www.deakin.edu.au

Academic survey position... 385
Employer survey position.... 184
Student faculty ratio 20:1
International faculty.......20.5%
Undergraduates............ 19,108
Postgraduates................. 3,939
International students 20.7%

World rank .... 396= (374=)
Subject area positions
Social sciences 258

Flinders University

Founded 1966

Adelaide
SA 5042

www.flinders.edu.au

Academic survey position... 385
Employer survey position.... 271
Student faculty ratio 6:1
International faculty.........4.5%
Undergraduates.............. 9,336
Postgraduates................. 2,179
International students 19.8%

World rank .... 273 (351=)
Subject area positions
Life sciences & biomedicine 278

Griffith University

Founded 1971

Brisbane
QLD 4111

www.griffith.edu.au

Academic survey position... 356
Employer survey position... 151
Student faculty ratio 21.9:1
International faculty.......37.2%
Undergraduates............ 21,771
Postgraduates................. 4,371
International students 23.1%

World rank .... 325= (309=)
Subject area positions
Social sciences 218

James Cook University

Founded 1970

Townsville
QLD 4811

www.jcu.edu.au

Academic survey position... 385
Employer survey position.... 340
Student faculty ratio 16.1:1
International faculty.........5.3%
Undergraduates............ 9,529*
Postgraduates............... 1,550*
International students 17.3%

World rank 401-500
Subject area positions
Engineering & IT 297

La Trobe University

Founded 1967

Melbourne
VIC 3086

www.latrobe.edu.au

Academic survey position... 210
Employer survey position.... 180
Student faculty ratio 19.6:1
International faculty.......32.6%
Undergraduates............ 17,276
Postgraduates................. 4,641
International students 20.7%

World rank .... 242= (205=)
Subject area positions
Arts & humanities 86
Life sciences & biomedicine 218
Natural sciences................ 290
Social sciences 180

Australia continued

Macquarie University

Founded 1964	Academic survey position... 147	World rank .... 182 (168=)
	Employer survey position...... 81	Subject area positions
North Ryde	Student faculty ratio 24.6:1	Arts & humanities 64
NSW 2109	International faculty 29.9%	Life sciences & biomedicine 196
	Undergraduates 15,351	Natural sciences 246
www.mq.edu.au	Postgraduates 6,056	Social sciences 122
	International students 36.6%	

University of Melbourne

Founded 1853	Academic survey position..... 21	World rank 38 (27)
	Employer survey position........ 9	Subject area positions
Parkville	Student faculty ratio 10.2:1	Arts & humanities 16
VIC 3010	International faculty 15.3%	Engineering & IT 28
	Undergraduates 25,589	Life sciences & biomedicine.. 26
www.unimelb.edu.au	Postgraduates 9,088	Natural sciences 27
	International students 27.1%	Social sciences 19

Monash University

Founded 1958	Academic survey position..... 28	World rank 47 (43)
	Employer survey position...... 15	Subject area positions
Clayton	Student faculty ratio 11.1:1	Arts & humanities 33
VIC 3800	International faculty 46.1%	Engineering & IT 47
	Undergraduates 32,865	Life sciences & biomedicine.. 30
www.monash.edu.au	Postgraduates 8,801	Natural sciences 53
	International students 34.5%	Social sciences 25

Murdoch University

Founded 1973	Academic survey position... 385	World rank 401-500
	Employer survey position.... 317	Subject area positions
Murdoch	Student faculty ratio 16:1	Engineering & IT 297
WA 6150	International faculty 3.5%	
	Undergraduates 8,593*	
www.murdoch.edu.au	Postgraduates 1,440*	
	International students 12.6%	

University of New South Wales

Founded 1949	Academic survey position..... 29	World rank 45 (44)
	Employer survey position...... 17	Subject area positions
Sydney	Student faculty ratio 14.8:1	Arts & humanities 51
NSW 2052	International faculty 27.2%	Engineering & IT 27
	Undergraduates 23,083	Life sciences & biomedicine.. 50
www.unsw.edu.au	Postgraduates 7,326	Natural sciences 39
	International students 23.2%	Social sciences 28

University of Newcastle

Founded 1965	Academic survey position... 297	World rank 286 (215)
	Employer survey position.... 147	Subject area positions
Callaghan	Student faculty ratio 17.3:1	Engineering & IT 222
NSW 2308	International faculty 20.8%	Life sciences & biomedicine 225
	Undergraduates 14,720	Social sciences 213
www.newcastle.edu.au	Postgraduates 2,897	
	International students 15.5%	

Australia continued

University of Queensland

Founded 1909

Brisbane
QLD 4072

www.uq.edu.au/
international

Academic survey position..... 41	World rank .... 43 (33=)
Employer survey position...... 38	Subject area positions
Student faculty ratio 11.7:1	Arts & humanities 67
International faculty.......49.6%	Engineering & IT 61
Undergraduates............ 22,573	Life sciences & biomedicine.. 32
Postgraduates................. 5,623	Natural sciences.................. 58
International students 18.1%	Social sciences 39

Queensland University of Technology

Founded 1908

Brisbane
QLD 4001

www.qut.edu.au

Academic survey position... 137	World rank .... 212 (195=)
Employer survey position...... 84	Subject area positions
Student faculty ratio 18.2:1	Arts & humanities 195
International faculty.......16.6%	Engineering & IT 101
Undergraduates............ 23,193	Life sciences & biomedicine 111
Postgraduates................. 4,188	Natural sciences................. 210
International students 13.6%	Social sciences 180

RMIT University

Founded 1887

Melbourne
VIC 3001

www.rmit.edu.au

Academic survey position... 183	World rank .... 206 (200=)
Employer survey position...... 60	Subject area positions
Student faculty ratio 19.2:1	Arts & humanities 149
International faculty.......52.8%	Engineering & IT 94
Undergraduates............ 27,420	Life sciences & biomedicine 196
Postgraduates................. 5,847	Social sciences 196
International students 47.1%	

University of South Australia

Founded 1991

Adelaide
SA 5001

www.unisa.edu.au

Academic survey position... 275	World rank .... 303= (291)
Employer survey position...... 89	Subject area positions
Student faculty ratio 23.1:1	Arts & humanities 160
International faculty.........5.4%	Social sciences 223
Undergraduates............ 18,642	
Postgraduates................. 4,689	
International students 32.8%	

Swinburne University of Technology

Founded 1908

Hawthorn
VIC 3122

www.swinburne.edu.au

Academic survey position... 385	World rank 401-500
Employer survey position.... 126	Subject area positions
Student faculty ratio 25.6:1	Engineering & IT 297
International faculty.......26.7%	
Undergraduates.............. 9,753	
Postgraduates................. 2,533	
International students 38.7%	

The University of Sydney

Founded 1850

Sydney
NSW 2006

www.usyd.edu.au

Academic survey position..... 26	World rank 37 (31)
Employer survey position...... 34	Subject area positions
Student faculty ratio 10.8:1	Arts & humanities 17
International faculty.......40.2%	Engineering & IT 41
Undergraduates............ 27,253	Life sciences & biomedicine.. 27
Postgraduates................. 9,142	Natural sciences.................. 44
International students 24.7%	Social sciences 27

Australia continued

University of Technology, Sydney

Founded 1988

Broadway
NSW 2007

www.uts.edu.au

Academic survey position... 235
Employer survey position...... 53
Student faculty ratio 19.7:1
International faculty.......46.7%
Undergraduates............ 17,417
Postgraduates................. 5,382
International students 26.1%

World rank .... 234 (259=)
Subject area positions
Arts & humanities 200
Engineering & IT 120
Life sciences & biomedicine 261
Social sciences 216

University of Tasmania

Founded 1890

Sandy Bay
TAS 7001

www.utas.edu.au

Academic survey position... 337
Employer survey position.... 216
Student faculty ratio 13.8:1
International faculty.......21.8%
Undergraduates............ 10,876
Postgraduates................. 1,875
International students 23.1%

World rank .... 291= (264=)
Subject area positions
Arts & humanities 193
Social sciences 288

The University of Western Australia

Founded 1911

Crawley
WA 6009

www.uwa.edu.au

Academic survey position... 121
Employer survey position...... 76
Student faculty ratio 11.2:1
International faculty.......33.2%
Undergraduates............ 12,554
Postgraduates................. 2,923
International students 19.8%

World rank .... 83= (64)
Subject area positions
Arts & humanities 128
Engineering & IT 147
Life sciences & biomedicine.. 81
Natural sciences................. 166
Social sciences 176

University of Wollongong

Founded 1951

Wollongong
NSW 2522

www.uow.edu.au

Academic survey position... 256
Employer survey position...... 91
Student faculty ratio 12.8:1
International faculty.......41.4%
Undergraduates............ 10,008
Postgraduates................. 3,217
International students 26.9%

World rank .... 207= (199)
Subject area positions
Arts & humanities 199
Engineering & IT 171
Life sciences & biomedicine 284
Social sciences 246

Austria

Karl-Franzens-Universiy Graz

Founded 1585

8010 Graz

www.uni-graz.at

Academic survey position... 241
Employer survey position.... 364
Student faculty ratio 21.8:1
International faculty.......11.9%
Undergraduates.......... 18,062*
Postgraduates.............. 2,830*
International students 9.3%

World rank .... 284= (279)
Subject area positions
Arts & humanities 217
Engineering & IT 246
Life sciences & biomedicine 259
Natural sciences................. 218
Social sciences 258

University of Innsbruck

Founded 1669

6020 Innsbruck

www.uibk.ac.at

Academic survey position... 268
Employer survey position.... 126
Student faculty ratio 27.9:1
International faculty.......22.0%
Undergraduates............. 11,766
Postgraduates................. 9,734
International students 29.2%

World rank .... 256= (225=)
Subject area positions
Arts & humanities 267
Natural sciences................. 168
Social sciences 278

272

Austria continued

Johannes Kepler University Linz

Founded 1966

4040 Linz

www.jku.at

Academic survey position... 363	World rank 401-500 (368)
Employer survey position.... 126	Subject area positions
Student faculty ratio 21.2:1	Engineering & IT 270
International faculty 18.4%	Natural sciences 192
International students 8.2%	

University of Vienna

Founded 1365

1010 Vienna

www.univie.ac.at

Academic survey position..... 57	World rank .... 115 (85=)
Employer survey position.... 163	Subject area positions
Student faculty ratio 42.4:1	Arts & humanities 44
International faculty 18.9%	Engineering & IT 217
Undergraduates............ 64,236	Life sciences & biomedicine.. 60
Postgraduates................. 7,018	Natural sciences 55
International students 20.6%	Social sciences 54

Vienna University of Technology

Founded 1815

1040 Vienna

www.tuwien.ac.at

Academic survey position... 253	World rank .... 244= (166=)
Employer survey position.... 268	Subject area positions
Student faculty ratio 12.5:1	Engineering & IT 76
International faculty 21.0%	Natural sciences 125
International students 19.7%	

Belgium

University of Antwerp

Founded 2003

2000 Antwerpen

www.ua.ac.be

Academic survey position... 288	World rank 195 (187)
Employer survey position.... 347	Subject area positions
Student faculty ratio 5.2:1	Arts & humanities 180
International faculty 16.0%	Social sciences 242
Undergraduates.............. 6,290	
Postgraduates................. 4,177	
International students 13.0%	

Vrije Universiteit Brussels (VUB)

Founded 1970

1050 Elsene

www.vub.ac.be

Academic survey position... 269	World rank .... 214= (229=)
Employer survey position.... 262	Subject area positions
Student faculty ratio 6.9:1	Arts & humanities 249
International faculty 2.2%	Engineering & IT 239
Undergraduates.............. 4,532	Life sciences & biomedicine 247
Postgraduates................. 3,487	Natural sciences 287
International students 9.9%	Social sciences 278

Université Libre de Bruxelles (ULB)

Founded 1834

1050 Bruxelles

www.ulb.ac.be

Academic survey position... 159	World rank .... 183= (154)
Employer survey position.... 181	Subject area positions
Student faculty ratio 23.3:1	Arts & humanities 154
International faculty 13.9%	Engineering & IT 221
Undergraduates............ 11,228	Life sciences & biomedicine 249
Postgraduates................. 8,787	Natural sciences 115
International students 27.6%	Social sciences 174

Belgium continued

University of Ghent

Founded 1817

9000 Ghent

www.ugent.be

Academic survey position... 134
Employer survey position.... 277
Student faculty ratio 7.3:1
International faculty 10.5%
Undergraduates 15,600
Postgraduates 13,653
International students 9.1%

World rank 136 (124)
Subject area positions
Arts & humanities 120
Engineering & IT 148
Life sciences & biomedicine 127
Natural sciences 156
Social sciences 205

Katholieke Universiteit Leuven

Founded 1425

3000 Leuven

www.kuleuven.ac.be

Academic survey position..... 47
Employer survey position.... 100
Student faculty ratio 15.1:1
International faculty 14.4%
Undergraduates 15,775
Postgraduates 13,827
International students 11.1%

World rank 72 (61)
Subject area positions
Arts & humanities 42
Engineering & IT 56
Life sciences & biomedicine.. 84
Natural sciences 93
Social sciences 45

University of Liège

Founded 1817

4000 Liège

www.ulg.ac.be

Academic survey position... 346
Employer survey position.... 347
Student faculty ratio 25:1
International faculty 6.0%
Undergraduates 8,505
Postgraduates 6,915
International students 19.1%

World rank .... 271= (262)
Subject area positions
Arts & humanities 278

Université Catholique de Louvain (UCL)

Founded 1425

1348 Louvain-la-Neuve

www.uclouvain.be

Academic survey position..... 77
Employer survey position.... 181
Student faculty ratio 23.6:1
International faculty 13.6%
Undergraduates 10,028
Postgraduates 10,508
International students 16.5%

World rank 116 (123)
Subject area positions
Arts & humanities 60
Engineering & IT 109
Life sciences & biomedicine 141
Natural sciences 133
Social sciences 37

Brazil

University of Campinas (Unicamp)

Founded 1966

Campinas
São Paulo 13083-970

www.unicamp.br

Academic survey position... 185
Employer survey position.... 392
Student faculty ratio 14.5:1
International faculty 10.4%
Undergraduates 15,219*
Postgraduates 1,779*
International students 1.5%

World rank .... 249 (177=)
Subject area positions
Arts & humanities 298
Engineering & IT 113
Life sciences & biomedicine 218
Natural sciences 124
Social sciences 258

Estadual Paulista University

Founded 1976

São Paulo 01419-901

www.unesp.br

Academic survey position... 385
Employer survey position.... 126
Student faculty ratio 12.6:1
International faculty 2.1%
International students 6%

World rank ...... 401-500 (501+)
Subject area positions
Life sciences & biomedicine 294

Brazil continued

Federal University of Rio de Janeiro

Founded 1920

Rio de Janeiro 21941-901

www.ufrj.br

Academic survey position... 199
Employer survey position.... 332
Student faculty ratio 18.8:1
International faculty.........6.4%
International students 0%

World rank .... 334= (338)
Subject area positions
Arts & humanities 287
Engineering & IT 114
Life sciences & biomedicine 185
Natural sciences................. 200
Social sciences 235

Catholic University of Rio de Janeiro

Founded 1941

Rio de Janeiro 22453-900

www.puc-rio.br

Academic survey position... 335
Employer survey position.... 326
Student faculty ratio 14.5:1
International faculty.........7.0%
Undergraduates.......... 10,576*
Postgraduates.............. 2,025*
International students 2.8%

World rank .401-500 (401-500)
Subject area positions
Engineering & IT 219
Social sciences 266

University of São Paulo

Founded 1934

São Paulo 05311-970

www.usp.br

Academic survey position... 102
Employer survey position.... 188
Student faculty ratio 13.9:1
International faculty.........8.0%
Undergraduates............ 48,762
Postgraduates.............. 21,296
International students 2.6%

World rank .... 196 (175=)
Subject area positions
Arts & humanities 122
Engineering & IT 105
Life sciences & biomedicine 114
Natural sciences................... 93
Social sciences 153

Canada

University of Alberta

Founded 1908

Edmonton
AB T6G 2M7

www.ualberta.ca

Academic survey position..... 50
Employer survey position.... 269
Student faculty ratio 10.6:1
International faculty.......33.7%
Undergraduates............ 29,178
Postgraduates................. 5,419
International students 14.1%

World rank .... 74 (97=)
Subject area positions
Arts & humanities 88
Engineering & IT 46
Life sciences & biomedicine.. 45
Natural sciences................... 51
Social sciences 113

University of British Columbia

Founded 1908

Vancouver
BC V6T 1Z4

www.ubc.ca

Academic survey position..... 13
Employer survey position...... 59
Student faculty ratio 9:1
International faculty.........7.8%
Undergraduates............ 30,851
Postgraduates................. 7,113
International students 13.5%

World rank .... 34= (33=)
Subject area positions
Arts & humanities 18
Engineering & IT 22
Life sciences & biomedicine.. 14
Natural sciences................... 20
Social sciences 12

University of Calgary

Founded 1966

Calgary
AB T2N 1N4

www.ucalgary.ca

Academic survey position... 127
Employer survey position.... 244
Student faculty ratio 13.3:1
International faculty.........3.9%
Undergraduates............ 18,005
Postgraduates................. 5,099
International students 5.7%

World rank .... 170= (166=)
Subject area positions
Arts & humanities 219
Engineering & IT 90
Life sciences & biomedicine 115
Natural sciences................. 150
Social sciences 169

Canada continued

Carleton University

Founded 1942

Ottawa
ON K1S 5B6

www.carleton.ca

Academic survey position...	283
Employer survey position....	126
Student faculty ratio	20:1
International faculty	11.4%
Undergraduates	17,299
Postgraduates	2,487
International students	16.8%

World rank .... 346 (345=)
Subject area positions
Arts & humanities 221
Engineering & IT 270
Social sciences 179

Concordia University

Founded 1974

Montreal
QC H3G 1M8

www.concordia.ca

Academic survey position...	255
Employer survey position....	383
Student faculty ratio	18.1:1
International faculty	6.1%
Undergraduates	19,350
Postgraduates	4,013
International students	11.1%

World rank .... 357= (383=)
Subject area positions
Arts & humanities 208
Engineering & IT 169
Social sciences 190

Dalhousie University

Founded 1818

Halifax
NS B3H 4R2

www.dal.ca

Academic survey position...	190
Employer survey position....	126
Student faculty ratio	12.8:1
International faculty	17.6%
Undergraduates	10,700
Postgraduates	3,040
International students	8.4%

World rank .... 197= (221=)
Subject area positions
Arts & humanities 267
Engineering & IT 287
Life sciences & biomedicine.. 90
Natural sciences 196
Social sciences 169

Laval University

Founded 1663

Québec
QC G1K 7P4

www.ulaval.ca

Academic survey position...	227
Employer survey position....	364
Student faculty ratio	24.2:1
International faculty	16.6%
Undergraduates	22,243
Postgraduates	6,630
International students	10.7%

World rank .... 268= (280)
Subject area positions
Arts & humanities 125
Engineering & IT 228
Natural sciences 270
Social sciences 177

University of Manitoba

Founded 1877

Winnipeg
MB R3T 2N2

www.umanitoba.ca

Academic survey position...	289
Employer survey position....	126
Student faculty ratio	13.7:1
International faculty	16.2%
Undergraduates	20,893
Postgraduates	2,673
International students	9.5%

World rank .... 307 (304=)
Subject area positions
Arts & humanities 290
Life sciences & biomedicine 224
Natural sciences 246

McGill University

Founded 1821

Montreal
QC H3A 2T5

www.mcgill.ca

Academic survey position.....	11
Employer survey position......	36
Student faculty ratio	4.8:1
International faculty	18.2%
Undergraduates	17,558*
Postgraduates	5,040*
International students	26.1%

World rank 20 (12)
Subject area positions
Arts & humanities 13
Engineering & IT 18
Life sciences & biomedicine.. 10
Natural sciences 22
Social sciences 14

Canada continued

McMaster University

Founded 1887

Hamilton
ON L8S 4L9

www.mcmaster.ca

Academic survey position..... 73	World rank .... 117= (108)
Employer survey position.... 309	Subject area positions
Student faculty ratio 18.3:1	Arts & humanities 117
International faculty 5.5%	Engineering & IT 79
Undergraduates............ 19,534	Life sciences & biomedicine.. 52
Postgraduates................. 2,611	Natural sciences.................. 82
International students 6.3%	Social sciences 94

University of Montréal

Founded 1878

Montréal
QC H3C 3J7

www.umontreal.ca

Academic survey position..... 58	World rank .... 91= (93=)
Employer survey position.... 352	Subject area positions
Student faculty ratio 14.5:1	Arts & humanities 59
International faculty 27.3%	Engineering & IT 87
Undergraduates............ 17,459	Life sciences & biomedicine.. 60
Postgraduates................. 7,329	Natural sciences.................. 91
International students 16.8%	Social sciences 70

University of Ottawa

Founded 1848

Ottawa
ON K1N 6N5

www.uottawa.ca

Academic survey position... 172	World rank .... 222 (227=)
Employer survey position.... 126	Subject area positions
Student faculty ratio 25.6:1	Arts & humanities 213
International faculty 30.5%	Engineering & IT 146
Undergraduates............ 27,268	Life sciences & biomedicine 255
Postgraduates................. 3,867	Natural sciences................ 180
International students 5.6%	Social sciences 119

University of Québec

Founded 1968

Québec
QC G1K 9H7

www.uquebec.ca

Academic survey position... 205	World rank .... 334= (336=)
Employer survey position.... 362	Subject area positions
Student faculty ratio 33.7:1	Arts & humanities 236
International faculty 16.7%	Engineering & IT 234
International students 10.4%	Life sciences & biomedicine 127
	Natural sciences................ 242
	Social sciences 192

Queen's University

Founded 1841

Kingston
ON K7L 3N6

www.queensu.ca

Academic survey position... 100	World rank .... 117= (88)
Employer survey position.... 108	Subject area positions
Student faculty ratio 12.4:1	Arts & humanities 116
International faculty 24.9%	Engineering & IT 152
Undergraduates............ 14,700	Life sciences & biomedicine 111
Postgraduates................. 3,617	Natural sciences................ 160
International students 6.9%	Social sciences 56

Simon Fraser University

Founded 1965

Burnaby
BC V5A 1S6

www.sfu.ca

Academic survey position... 109	World rank 164 (139)
Employer survey position.... 211	Subject area positions
Student faculty ratio 22.8:1	Arts & humanities 132
International faculty 34.6%	Engineering & IT 116
Undergraduates............ 17,181	Life sciences & biomedicine 155
Postgraduates................. 3,199	Natural sciences................ 165
International students 10.4%	Social sciences 64

Canada continued

University of Toronto

Founded 1827	Academic survey position 9	World rank 41 (45)
	Employer survey position 52	Subject area positions
Toronto	Student faculty ratio 24.2:1	Arts & humanities 11
ON M5S 1A1	International faculty 25.7%	Engineering & IT 10
	Undergraduates 46,778	Life sciences & biomedicine .. 13
www.utoronto.ca	Postgraduates 12,029	Natural sciences 9
	International students 9.8%	Social sciences 16

University of Victoria

Founded 1963	Academic survey position ... 244	World rank .... 244= (213)
	Employer survey position 299	Subject area positions
Victoria	Student faculty ratio 21.3:1	Arts & humanities 221
BC V8P 5C2	International faculty 21.2%	Natural sciences 260
	Undergraduates 12,840	Social sciences 163
www.uvic.ca	Postgraduates 2,190	
	International students 14.3%	

University of Waterloo

Founded 1957	Academic survey position 70	World rank .... 129 (112=)
	Employer survey position 153	Subject area positions
Waterloo	Student faculty ratio 23.7:1	Arts & humanities 239
ON N2L 3G1	International faculty 17.4%	Engineering & IT 30
	Undergraduates 20,300	Life sciences & biomedicine 133
www.uwaterloo.ca	Postgraduates 2,260	Natural sciences 42
	International students 11.7%	Social sciences 108

The University of Western Ontario

Founded 1878	Academic survey position ... 140	World rank .... 159 (126=)
	Employer survey position 189	Subject area positions
London	Student faculty ratio 18.3:1	Arts & humanities 163
ON N6A 5B8	International faculty 18.4%	Engineering & IT 182
	Undergraduates 18,870	Life sciences & biomedicine 170
www.uwo.ca	Postgraduates 3,449	Natural sciences 265
	International students 6.1%	Social sciences 61

York University

Founded 1959	Academic survey position ... 141	World rank .... 252 (248=)
	Employer survey position 147	Subject area positions
Toronto	Student faculty ratio 20.8:1	Arts & humanities 70
ON M3J 1P3	International faculty 14.7%	Engineering & IT 281
	Undergraduates 40,971	Natural sciences 263
www.yorku.ca	Postgraduates 3,853	Social sciences 53
	International students 5.4%	

Chile

Pontificia Universidad Católica de Chile

Founded 1888	Academic survey position ... 225	World rank .... 241 (239=)
	Employer survey position 88	Subject area positions
Santiago	Student faculty ratio 12.2:1	Arts & humanities 226
www.puc.cl	International faculty 4.8%	Engineering & IT 179
	Undergraduates 15,380*	Life sciences & biomedicine 210
	Postgraduates 5,290*	Natural sciences 252
	International students 9.0%	Social sciences 225

Chile continued
Universidad de Chile

Founded 1843	Academic survey position... 262	World rank .... 320= (312=)
	Employer survey position.... 214	Subject area positions
Santiago	Student faculty ratio 15.5:1	Arts & humanities 250
www.uchile.cl	International faculty 7.8%	Engineering & IT 178
	Postgraduates 5,579	Natural sciences 265
	International students 4.2%	Social sciences 282

China
University of Science and Technology of China

Founded 1958	Academic survey position... 108	World rank .... 141 (155=)
	Employer survey position.... 167	Subject area positions
Hefei	Student faculty ratio 10.7:1	Engineering & IT 49
AnHui 230026	International faculty 1.8%	Life sciences & biomedicine.. 89
www.ustc.edu.cn	Undergraduates 6,362*	Natural sciences 49
	Postgraduates 7,196*	
	International students 2%	

Fudan University

Founded 1905	Academic survey position..... 55	World rank .... 113 (85=)
	Employer survey position..... 61	Subject area positions
Shanghai 200433	Student faculty ratio 11.6:1	Arts & humanities 89
www.fudan.edu.cn	International faculty 7.0%	Engineering & IT 92
	Undergraduates 12,294*	Life sciences & biomedicine.. 49
	Postgraduates 10,893*	Natural sciences 63
	International students 6.3%	Social sciences 51

Nanjing University

Founded 1902	Academic survey position... 107	World rank 143 (125)
	Employer survey position.... 162	Subject area positions
Nanjing	Student faculty ratio 9.4:1	Arts & humanities 154
Jiangsu 210093	International faculty 15.2%	Engineering & IT 124
www.nju.edu.cn	Undergraduates 10,501*	Life sciences & biomedicine.. 84
	Postgraduates 10,032*	Natural sciences 96
	International students 2.0%	Social sciences 153

Peking University

Founded 1898	Academic survey position..... 19	World rank .... 50= (36)
	Employer survey position...... 35	Subject area positions
Beijing 100871	Student faculty ratio 7.4:1	Arts & humanities 23
www.pku.edu.cn	International faculty 5.3%	Engineering & IT 38
	Undergraduates 14,786	Life sciences & biomedicine.. 19
	Postgraduates 15,894	Natural sciences 16
	International students 7.5%	Social sciences 24

Shandong University

Founded 1901	Academic survey position... 325	World rank .401-500 (401-500)
	Employer survey position.... 375	Subject area positions
Jinan	Student faculty ratio 56.8:1	Life sciences & biomedicine 237
Shandong 250100	International faculty 8.9%	Natural sciences 270
www.sdu.edu.cn	Undergraduates 34,004*	
	Postgraduates 9,782*	
	International students 8.6%	

China continued

Shanghai Jiao Tong University

Founded 1896

Shanghai 200240

www.sjtu.edu.cn

Academic survey position... 111
Employer survey position.... 104
Student faculty ratio 8.9:1
International faculty 8.2%
Undergraduates 16,260*
Postgraduates 12,554*
International students 3.0%

World rank .... 144= (163=)
Subject area positions
Arts & humanities 263
Engineering & IT 48
Life sciences & biomedicine.. 82
Natural sciences 139
Social sciences 177

Southeast University

Founded 1902

Nanjing
Jiangsu 210096

www.seu.edu.cn

Academic survey position... 379
Employer survey position.... 126
Student faculty ratio 13.4:1
International faculty 2.5%
Undergraduates 13,595*
Postgraduates 9,621*
International students 1.2%

World rank .401-500 (401-500)
Subject area positions
Life sciences & biomedicine 179

Tianjin University

Founded 1895

Nankai
Tianjin 300072

www.tju.edu.cn

Academic survey position... 299
Employer survey position.... 312
Student faculty ratio 14.2:1
International faculty 2.9%
Undergraduates 12,955*
Postgraduates 8,732*
International students 2.8%

World rank 386 (324)
Subject area positions
Engineering & IT 222
Life sciences & biomedicine 162

Tongji University

Founded 1907

Shanghai 200092

www.tongji.edu.cn

Academic survey position... 305
Employer survey position.... 126
Student faculty ratio 12.8:1
International faculty 1.5%
Undergraduates 17,273*
Postgraduates 12,119*
International students 2.2%

World rank .401-500 (401-500)
Subject area positions
Engineering & IT 183
Life sciences & biomedicine 208

Tsinghua University

Founded 1911

Haidian
Beijing 100084

www.tsinghua.edu.cn

Academic survey position..... 31
Employer survey position...... 68
Student faculty ratio 6.1:1
International faculty 3.4%
Undergraduates 11,534*
Postgraduates 15,913*
International students 4.0%

World rank 56 (40)
Subject area positions
Arts & humanities 85
Engineering & IT 12
Life sciences & biomedicine.. 56
Natural sciences 28
Social sciences 44

Xi'an Jiaotong University

Founded 1896

Xi'an
Shanxi 710049

www.xjtu.edu.cn

Academic survey position... 359
Employer survey position.... 126
Student faculty ratio 12:1
International faculty 5.1%
Undergraduates 15,560*
Postgraduates 11,542*
International students 1.7%

World rank .401-500 (401-500)
Subject area positions
Engineering & IT 166
Life sciences & biomedicine 284

China continued

Zhejiang University

Founded 1897

Hangzhou
Zhejiang 310058

www.zju.edu.cn

Academic survey position... 164	World rank .... 229 (209=)
Employer survey position.... 126	Subject area positions
Student faculty ratio 9.6:1	Arts & humanities 232
International faculty.........4.4%	Engineering & IT 102
Undergraduates 19,021*	Life sciences & biomedicine 120
Postgraduates 14,748*	Natural sciences 189
International students 2.8%	Social sciences 262

Colombia

Universidad de Los Andes

Founded 1948

Bogotá

www.uniandes.edu.co

Academic survey position... 371	World rank .401-500 (401-500)
Employer survey position.... 216	Subject area positions
Student faculty ratio 19.1:1	Engineering & IT 273
International faculty.........8.2%	
Undergraduates 10,985	
Postgraduates 1,610	
International students 4%	

Czech Republic

Charles University

Founded 1348

116 36 Praha 1

www.cuni.cz

Academic survey position... 197	World rank 261 (290)
Employer survey position.... 126	Subject area positions
Student faculty ratio 11.7:1	Arts & humanities 149
International faculty.........6.6%	Engineering & IT 288
Undergraduates 6,646*	Life sciences & biomedicine 266
Postgraduates 31,619*	Natural sciences 116
International students 15.3%	Social sciences 253

Czech Technical University in Prague

Founded 1707

166 36 Prague

www.cvut.cz

Academic survey position... 385	World rank ......401-500 (501&)
Employer survey position.... 211	Subject area positions
Student faculty ratio 13.3:1	Engineering & IT 228
International faculty.........2.5%	
Undergraduates 14,307	
Postgraduates 8,734	
International students 10.0%	

Denmark

University of Aarhus

Founded 1928

8000 Aarhus C

www.au.dk

Academic survey position... 105	World rank .... 81= (114=)
Employer survey position.... 340	Subject area positions
Student faculty ratio 8.6:1	Arts & humanities 100
International faculty.......19.9%	Engineering & IT 230
Undergraduates 9,835	Life sciences & biomedicine 127
Postgraduates 7,676	Natural sciences 92
International students 12.8%	Social sciences 94

University of Copenhagen

Founded 1479

1017 Copenhagen K

www.ku.dk

Academic survey position..... 65	World rank .... 48 (93=)
Employer survey position.... 196	Subject area positions
Student faculty ratio 3.9:1	Arts & humanities 58
International faculty.......20.1%	Engineering & IT 281
Undergraduates 11,341	Life sciences & biomedicine.. 59
Postgraduates 8,911	Natural sciences 75
International students 15.4%	Social sciences 31

Denmark continued

Technical University of Denmark

Founded 1829

2800 Kgs. Lyngby

www.dtu.dk

Academic survey position... 277
Employer survey position.... 304
Student faculty ratio 4.9:1
International faculty 32.0%
Undergraduates 3,732
Postgraduates 3,331
International students 12.3%

World rank .... 133= (130=)
Subject area positions
Engineering & IT 77
Natural sciences 201

University of Southern Denmark

Founded 1998

5230 Odense M

www.sdu.dk

Academic survey position... 385
Employer survey position.... 126
Student faculty ratio 9.1:1
International faculty 16.6%
Undergraduates 5,857
Postgraduates 4,759
International students 13.5%

World rank 295 (317)
Subject area positions
Arts & humanities 285

Egypt

Cairo University

Founded 1908

Giza

www.cu.edu.eg

Academic survey position... 267
Employer survey position.... 332
Student faculty ratio 52.3:1
International faculty 5%
International students 1.0%

World rank ...... 401-500 (501+)
Subject area positions
Arts & humanities 234
Engineering & IT 220
Life sciences & biomedicine 271
Social sciences 273

Finland

University of Helsinki

Founded 1640

00014 Helsinki

www.helsinki.fi

Academic survey position..... 64
Employer survey position.... 301
Student faculty ratio 10.8:1
International faculty 14.4%
Undergraduates 12,044*
Postgraduates 21,995*
International students 3.3%

World rank .... 91= (100)
Subject area positions
Arts & humanities 52
Engineering & IT 144
Life sciences & biomedicine.. 71
Natural sciences 72
Social sciences 68

Helsinki University of Technology TKK

Founded 1849

2150 Espoo

www.tkk.fi

Academic survey position... 251
Employer survey position.... 304
Student faculty ratio 7.3:1
International faculty 18.1%
Undergraduates 3,200
Postgraduates 8,110
International students 8.7%

World rank 211 (170)
Subject area positions
Engineering & IT 94
Natural sciences 175
Social sciences 278

University of Jyväskylä

Founded 1934

40014 Jyväskylä

www.jyu.fi

Academic survey position... 362
Employer survey position.... 126
Student faculty ratio 10.3:1
International faculty 11.9%
Undergraduates 4,091*
Postgraduates 8,368*
International students 2.9%

World rank .... 391= (374=)
Subject area positions
Natural sciences 279

Finland continued

Kuopio University

Founded 1972

70211 Kuopio

www.uku.fi

Academic survey position... 385
Employer survey position.... 126
Student faculty ratio 7.5:1
International faculty 7.2%
Undergraduates 4,821*
Postgraduates 904*
International students 2.6%

World rank .... 313= (267=)
Subject area positions
Engineering & IT 297

University of Oulu

Founded 1958

90014 Oulun Yliopisto

www.oulu.fi

Academic survey position... 385
Employer survey position.... 126
Student faculty ratio 9.3:1
International faculty 2.4%
Undergraduates 3,058
Postgraduates 9,172*
International students 2.2%

World rank .... 372 (354=)
Subject area positions
Engineering & IT 233

University of Tampere

Founded 1925

33014 Tampereen yliopisto

www.uta.fi

Academic survey position... 285
Employer survey position.... 126
Student faculty ratio 12.1:1
International faculty 7.2%
Undergraduates 2,870
Postgraduates 10,035*
International students 3.3%

World rank .... 336 (319=)
Subject area positions
Arts & humanities 218
Engineering & IT 259
Social sciences 208

University of Turku

Founded 1920

20014 Turku

www.utu.fi

Academic survey position... 247
Employer survey position.... 370
Student faculty ratio 10.7:1
International faculty 12.5%
Undergraduates 5,417*
Postgraduates 8,840*
International students 1.8%

World rank .... 246= (237=)
Subject area positions
Arts & humanities 235
Life sciences & biomedicine 167
Natural sciences 287
Social sciences 214

France

École Polytechnique

Founded 1794

91128 Palaiseau

www.polytechnique.edu

Academic survey position..... 89
Employer survey position...... 44
Student faculty ratio 3.7:1
International faculty 18.2%
Undergraduates 1,000
Postgraduates 1,496
International students 24.9%

World rank .... 34= (28)
Subject area positions
Engineering & IT 31
Life sciences & biomedicine 278
Natural sciences 26
Social sciences 204

École Nationale des Ponts et Chaussées ENPC

Founded 1747

75343 Paris

www.enpc.fr

Academic survey position... 385
Employer survey position.... 186
Student faculty ratio 6.3:1
International faculty 8.1%
International students 4.8%

World rank 294 (401-500)
Subject area positions
Engineering & IT 214

France continued

École Normale Supérieure Lettres et Sciences Humaines (ENS LSH)

Founded 1880

69342 Lyon

www.ens-lsh.fr

Academic survey position... 394
Employer survey position.... 126
Student faculty ratio 5.1:1
International faculty 10.5%
Undergraduates 655*
Postgraduates 119*
International students 11.1%

World rank 293
Subject area positions
Arts & humanities 105
Social sciences 291

ESCP-EAP Paris

Founded 1819

75011 Paris

www.escp-eap.eu

Academic survey position... 385
Employer survey position...... 97
Student faculty ratio 27.6:1
International faculty 39.8%
Postgraduates 3,763*
International students 45.0%

World rank . 401-500 (401-500)
Subject area positions
Social sciences 265

Université Joseph-Fourier, Grenoble I

Founded 1339

38041 Grenoble

www.ujf-grenoble.fr

Academic survey position... 264
Employer survey position.... 332
Student faculty ratio 12.9:1
International faculty 6.6%
Undergraduates 10,417
Postgraduates 6,479
International students 13.1%

World rank 282 (275)
Subject area positions
Engineering & IT 152
Life sciences & biomedicine 234
Natural sciences 131

HEC School of Management

Founded 1881

78351 Jouy en Josas

www.hec.edu

Academic survey position... 385
Employer survey position...... 41
Student faculty ratio 29.6:1
International faculty 34.3%
Undergraduates 363
Postgraduates 2,653
International students 25.8%

World rank . 401-500 (401-500)
Subject area positions
Social sciences 128

Université des Sciences et Technologies de Lille (Lille I)

Founded 1562

59655 Villeneuve d'Ascq

www.univ-lille1.fr

Academic survey position... 385
Employer survey position.... 126
Student faculty ratio 12.5:1
International faculty 7.8%
International students 22.2%

World rank ...... 382= (401-500)
Subject area positions
Engineering & IT 243

École Normale Supérieure de Lyon

Founded 1987

69007 Lyon

www.ens-lyon.eu

Academic survey position... 300
Employer survey position.... 208
Student faculty ratio 2.9:1
International faculty 12.9%
Undergraduates 192
Postgraduates 755
International students 12.1%

World rank 140 (157)
Subject area positions
Engineering & IT 259
Natural sciences 139

France continued

Université Claude Bernard Lyon I

Founded 1971

69622 Villeurbanne

www.univ-lyon1.fr

Academic survey position... 385
Employer survey position.... 126
Student faculty ratio 18.3:1
International faculty 4.6%
International students 11.9%

World rank .401-500 (401-500)
Subject area positions
Natural sciences................ 285

University of Montpellier II - Sciences and Techniques of Languedoc

Founded 1970

34095 Montpellier

www.univ-montp2.fr

Academic survey position... 385
Employer survey position.... 126
Student faculty ratio 9.1:1
International faculty 3.5%
Undergraduates............ 4,541*
Postgraduates............... 4,355*
International students 16.1%

World rank .... 290 (301=)
Subject area positions
Life sciences & biomedicine 231
Natural sciences................ 239

University of Nancy I - Henri Poincaré

Founded 1970

54003 Nancy

www.uhp-nancy.fr

Academic survey position... 385
Employer survey position.... 126
Student faculty ratio 12.5:1
International faculty 6.4%
Undergraduates............ 7,842*
Postgraduates............... 6,833*
International students 11.9%

World rank ......401-500 (501+)
Subject area positions
Engineering & IT 297

École Normale Supérieure, Paris

Founded 1794

75230 Paris

www.ens.fr

Academic survey position..... 44
Employer survey position.... 139
Student faculty ratio 9:1
International faculty 6.3%
Undergraduates................. 434
Postgraduates................. 1,762
International students 15.4%

World rank 28 (26)
Subject area positions
Arts & humanities 34
Engineering & IT 100
Life sciences & biomedicine 136
Natural sciences................... 19
Social sciences 113

Sciences Po Paris

Founded 1872

75337 Paris

www.sciences-po.fr

Academic survey position... 340
Employer survey position.... 129
Student faculty ratio 5.8:1
International faculty 15.6%
Undergraduates.............. 2,896
Postgraduates................. 3,820
International students 38.0%

World rank .... 207= (227=)
Subject area positions
Social sciences 105

Université Paris I Panthéon Sorbonne

Founded 1258

75005 Paris

www.univ-paris1.fr

Academic survey position... 178
Employer survey position.... 248
Student faculty ratio 20.7:1
International faculty 6.5%
Undergraduates............ 19,527
Postgraduates.............. 14,771
International students 21.5%

World rank .... 288 (369=)
Subject area positions
Arts & humanities 68
Life sciences & biomedicine 289
Social sciences 86

France continued

Université Paris Sorbonne (Paris IV)

Founded 1200

75005 Paris

www.paris4.sorbonne.fr

Academic survey position... 104
Employer survey position.... 178
Student faculty ratio 28.6:1
International faculty 3.0%
International students 19.7%

World rank ....239= (295=)
Subject area positions
Arts & humanities 25
Engineering & IT 263
Life sciences & biomedicine 271
Natural sciences 175
Social sciences 78

Université Paris IX Dauphine

Founded 1968

75775 Paris

www.dauphine.fr

Academic survey position... 386
Employer survey position.... 242
Student faculty ratio 23:1
International faculty 8.1%
International students 25.4%

World rank .401-500 (401-500)
Subject area positions
Social sciences 232

Université Paris V Descartes

Founded 1971

75270 Paris

www.univ-paris5.fr

Academic survey position... 376
Employer survey position.... 126
Student faculty ratio 20.8:1
International faculty 11.0%
International students 17.2%

World rank 401-500 (391)
Subject area positions
Life sciences & biomedicine 284

Université Pierre-et-Marie-Curie Paris VI

Founded 1971

75005 Paris

www.upmc.fr

Academic survey position... 143
Employer survey position.... 126
Student faculty ratio 6.8:1
International faculty 4.2%
Undergraduates 14,511
Postgraduates 15,465
International students 22.9%

World rank .... 149 (132=)
Subject area positions
Engineering & IT 139
Life sciences & biomedicine 104
Natural sciences 25

Université Paris VII Denis Diderot

Founded 1971

75251 Paris

www.univ-paris-diderot.
fr

Academic survey position... 306
Employer survey position.... 126
Student faculty ratio 17.2:1
International faculty 8.1%
International students 17.2%

World rank ...... 362= (401-500)
Subject area positions
Arts & humanities 219
Natural sciences 179

Université Paris-Sud Paris XI

Founded 1970

91405 Orsay

www.u-psud.fr

Academic survey position... 279
Employer survey position.... 126
Student faculty ratio 11.2:1
International faculty 7.4%
Undergraduates 13,664*
Postgraduates 12,904*
International students 18.0%

World rank .... 266 (267=)
Subject area positions
Natural sciences 52

France continued

University of Rennes

Founded 1461

35065 Rennes

www.univ-rennes1.fr

Academic survey position... 385
Employer survey position.... 126
Student faculty ratio 14.2:1
International faculty........7.0%
Undergraduates............ 11,706
Postgraduates................. 9,249
International students 10.7%

World rank .401-500 (401-500)
Subject area positions
Engineering & IT 297

Université Louis Pasteur Strasbourg I

Founded 1567

67070 Strasbourg

www-ulp.u-strasbg.fr

Academic survey position... 222
Employer survey position.... 262
Student faculty ratio 17:1
International faculty.......11.6%
Undergraduates............ 9,974*
Postgraduates............... 8,002*
International students 19.8%

World rank .... 207= (184)
Subject area positions
Life sciences & biomedicine.. 77
Natural sciences................. 159

University of Toulouse III Paul Sabatier

Founded 1969

31062 Toulouse

www.ups-tlse.fr

Academic survey position... 396
Employer survey position.... 126
Student faculty ratio 18.6:1
International faculty.......12.2%
International students 17.2%

World rank ......401-500 (360=)
Subject area positions
Engineering & IT 263
Natural sciences................. 246

Germany

Rheinisch-Westfälische Technische Hochschule Aachen

Founded 1870

52062 Aachen

www.rwth-aachen.de

Academic survey position... 266
Employer survey position.... 214
Student faculty ratio 8:1
International faculty.......14.6%
Undergraduates............ 25,653
Postgraduates................. 5,023
International students 16.1%

World rank .... 216= (182)
Subject area positions
Engineering & IT 70
Natural sciences................. 151

Universität Bayreuth

Founded 1975

95440 Bayreuth

www.uni-bayreuth.de

Academic survey position... 385
Employer survey position.... 126
Student faculty ratio 8.7:1
International faculty.......11.8%
Undergraduates............ 9,012*
International students 8.0%

World rank .... 347= (297)
Subject area positions
Natural sciences................. 297

Freie Universität Berlin

Founded 1948

14195 Berlin

www.fu-berlin.de

Academic survey position..... 78
Employer survey position.... 126
Student faculty ratio 19.1:1
International faculty.......12.7%
Undergraduates............ 28,062
Postgraduates................. 5,711
International students 15.2%

World rank .... 137= (146)
Subject area positions
Arts & humanities 24
Engineering & IT 253
Life sciences & biomedicine 177
Natural sciences................... 82
Social sciences 62

Germany continued

Technische Universität Berlin

Founded 1770

10623 Berlin

www.tu-berlin.de

Academic survey position... 167
Employer survey position.... 256
Student faculty ratio 12.2:1
International faculty 21.6%
International students 20.7%

World rank .... 188= (203=)
Subject area positions
Engineering & IT 65
Life sciences & biomedicine 242
Natural sciences 99

Universität Bielefeld

Founded 1969

33615 Bielefeld

www.uni-bielefeld.de

Academic survey position... 252
Employer survey position.... 126
Student faculty ratio 23.7:1
International faculty 10.6%
Postgraduates 2,908*
International students 8.6%

World rank .... 328= (312=)
Subject area positions
Arts & humanities 213
Life sciences & biomedicine 289
Natural sciences 211
Social sciences 149

Ruhr-Universität Bochum

Founded 1962

44801 Bochum

www.ruhr-uni-bochum.
de

Academic survey position... 348
Employer survey position.... 395
Student faculty ratio 17:1
International faculty 12.6%
Undergraduates 27,459*
Postgraduates 5,078*
International students 12.1%

World rank .... 349= (333)
Subject area positions
Engineering & IT 288
Natural sciences 295

Rheinische Friedrich-Wilhelms-Universität Bonn

Founded 1818

53113 Bonn

www.uni-bonn.de

Academic survey position... 260
Employer survey position.... 126
Student faculty ratio 13.8:1
International faculty 10.1%
Undergraduates 24,671
Postgraduates 3,541
International students 14.4%

World rank .... 264= (276=)
Subject area positions
Arts & humanities 257
Natural sciences 118
Social sciences 197

Technische Universität Braunschweig

Founded 1745

38106 Braunschweig

www.tu-braunschweig.
de

Academic survey position... 385
Employer survey position.... 126
Student faculty ratio 12.1:1
International faculty 11.2%
International students 11.3%

World rank ...... 401-500 (383=)
Subject area positions
Engineering & IT 297

Universität Bremen

Founded 1971

28359 Bremen

www.uni-bremen.de

Academic survey position... 311
Employer survey position.... 126
Student faculty ratio 21.8:1
International faculty 11.3%
International students 15.4%

World rank .... 375 (364=)
Subject area positions
Engineering & IT 267
Social sciences 235

Germany continued

Technische Universität Darmstadt

Founded 1877

64289 Darmstadt

www.tu-darmstadt.de

Academic survey position... 344
Employer survey position.... 326
Student faculty ratio 8.9:1
International faculty.........9.8%
International students 20.4%

World rank .... 284= (239=)
Subject area positions
Engineering & IT 118
Natural sciences................ 229

Universität Dortmund

Founded 1968

44221 Dortmund

www.uni-dortmund.de

Academic survey position... 385
Employer survey position.... 126
Student faculty ratio 23.1:1
International faculty.......14.9%
Undergraduates 19,042*
Postgraduates............... 2,452*
International students 13.6%

World rank .401-500 (401-500)
Subject area positions
Engineering & IT 284

Technische Universität Dresden

Founded 1828

01069 Dresden

www.tu-dresden.de

Academic survey position... 314
Employer survey position.... 360
Student faculty ratio 8.2:1
International faculty.........9.9%
International students 10.7%

World rank .... 271= (243=)
Subject area positions
Engineering & IT 199
Life sciences & biomedicine 242
Natural sciences................ 297

Universität Düsseldorf

Founded 1966

40225 Düsseldorf

www.uni-duesseldorf.de

Academic survey position... 385
Employer survey position.... 126
Student faculty ratio 12:1
International faculty.........3.7%
International students 16.8%

World rank .... 303= (312=)
Subject area positions
Life sciences & biomedicine 218

Universität Duisburg-Essen

Founded 1972

45141 Essen

www.uni-duisburg-
essen.de

Academic survey position... 385
Employer survey position.... 126
Student faculty ratio 12.8:1
International faculty.......11.2%
Postgraduates............... 3,007*
International students 12.7%

World rank .401-500 (401-500)
Subject area positions
Engineering & IT 297

Universität Erlangen-Nürnberg

Founded 1742

91054 Erlangen

www.uni-erlangen.de

Academic survey position... 385
Employer survey position.... 126
Student faculty ratio 12.3:1
International faculty.......19.0%
Undergraduates............ 14,967
Postgraduates............... 11,402
International students 9.7%

World rank .... 320= (270=)
Subject area positions
Natural sciences................ 290

Germany continued

Universität Frankfurt am Main

Founded 1914

60054 Frankfurt am Main

www.uni-frankfurt.de

Academic survey position... 220	World rank .... 169 (209=)
Employer survey position.... 253	Subject area positions
Student faculty ratio 9.4:1	Arts & humanities 122
International faculty 6.4%	Life sciences & biomedicine 241
Undergraduates 20,062	Natural sciences 239
Postgraduates 2,420	Social sciences 167
International students 18.8%	

Universität Freiburg

Founded 1457

79085 Freiburg

www.uni-freiburg.de

Academic survey position... 156	World rank .... 147= (144)
Employer survey position.... 126	Subject area positions
Student faculty ratio 6.5:1	Arts & humanities 69
International faculty 5.0%	Life sciences & biomedicine 118
Postgraduates 2,242*	Natural sciences 204
International students 14.9%	Social sciences 205

Justus-Liebig-Universität Gießen

Founded 1607

35390 Gießen

www.uni-giessen.de

Academic survey position... 385	World rank .401-500 (401-500)
Employer survey position.... 126	Subject area positions
Student faculty ratio 15.8:1	Engineering & IT 297
International faculty 10.5%	
International students 7.9%	

Universität Göttingen

Founded 1737

37073 Göttingen

www.uni-goettingen.de

Academic survey position... 131	World rank .... 166= (168=)
Employer survey position.... 126	Subject area positions
Student faculty ratio 9.4:1	Arts & humanities 95
International faculty 10.2%	Engineering & IT 270
Undergraduates 20,829	Life sciences & biomedicine 124
Postgraduates 3,183	Natural sciences 64
International students 11.3%	

Martin-Luther-Universität Halle-Wittenberg

Founded 1817

06099 Halle

www.uni-halle.de

Academic survey position... 385	World rank ......401-500 (396=)
Employer survey position.... 126	Subject area positions
Student faculty ratio 11:1	Engineering & IT 297
International faculty 11.2%	
International students 8.0%	

Universität Hamburg

Founded 1919

20146 Hamburg

www.uni-hamburg.de

Academic survey position... 214	World rank .... 274= (216)
Employer survey position.... 126	Subject area positions
Student faculty ratio 11.7:1	Arts & humanities 245
International faculty 7.4%	Engineering & IT 247
International students 13.3%	Life sciences & biomedicine 208
	Natural sciences 138
	Social sciences 258

Germany continued

Leibniz Universität Hannover

Founded 1831

30167 Hannover

www.uni-hannover.de

Academic survey position... 397
Employer survey position.... 126
Student faculty ratio 38.3:1
International faculty.........4.8%
Undergraduates............ 20,374
Postgraduates................ 2,625
International students 17.0%

World rank ......401-500 (383=)
Subject area positions
Life sciences & biomedicine 270

Heidelberg Universität

Founded 1386

69117 Heidelberg

www.uni-heidelberg.de

Academic survey position..... 69
Employer survey position.... 198
Student faculty ratio 7.7:1
International faculty.......15.3%
Undergraduates............ 23,636
Postgraduates................ 3,105
International students 19.1%

World rank 57 (60)
Subject area positions
Arts & humanities 48
Engineering & IT 267
Life sciences & biomedicine.. 48
Natural sciences................... 43
Social sciences 108

Humboldt-Universität zu Berlin

Founded 1810

10099 Berlin

www.hu-berlin.de

Academic survey position..... 92
Employer survey position.... 299
Student faculty ratio 9.6:1
International faculty.......11.0%
Undergraduates............ 32,217
Postgraduates................ 3,684
International students 12.3%

World rank .... 139 (126=)
Subject area positions
Arts & humanities 50
Engineering & IT 284
Life sciences & biomedicine 125
Natural sciences................ 107
Social sciences 91

Universität Jena

Founded 1558

07740 Jena

www.uni-jena.de

Academic survey position... 385
Employer survey position.... 126
Student faculty ratio 10.5:1
International faculty.........4.7%
Undergraduates............ 17,469
Postgraduates................ 1,068
International students 5.2%

World rank .... 382= (316)
Subject area positions
Engineering & IT 297

Universität Karlsruhe

Founded 1825

76131 Karlsruhe

www.uni-karlsruhe.de

Academic survey position... 257
Employer survey position.... 269
Student faculty ratio 8.4:1
International faculty.......14.3%
Undergraduates............ 17,493
Postgraduates................ 1,000
International students 19.3%

World rank .... 207= (171=)
Subject area positions
Engineering & IT 72
Natural sciences................ 168

Christian-Albrechts-Universität zu Kiel

Founded 1665

24098 Kiel

www.uni-kiel.de

Academic survey position... 385
Employer survey position.... 126
Student faculty ratio 12.1:1
International faculty.......11.2%
Postgraduates.............. 1,947*
International students 8.3%

World rank ......401-500 (388=)
Subject area positions
Engineering & IT 297

Germany continued

Universität Köln (Cologne)

Founded 1388

50923 Köln

www.uni-koeln.de

Academic survey position... 284
Employer survey position.... 356
Student faculty ratio 22.2:1
International faculty 11.8%
International students 14.6%

World rank .... 318 (319=)
Subject area positions
Arts & humanities 170
Social sciences 202

Universität Konstanz

Founded 1966

78464 Konstanz

www.uni-konstanz.de

Academic survey position... 302
Employer survey position.... 126
Student faculty ratio 17.3:1
International faculty 13.9%
Undergraduates.............. 9,205
International students 8.8%

World rank .... 325= (311)
Subject area positions
Arts & humanities 140
Social sciences 273

Universität Leipzig

Founded 1409

04109 Leipzig

www.uni-leipzig.de

Academic survey position... 244
Employer survey position.... 126
Student faculty ratio 31.6:1
International faculty 6.9%
International students 8.3%

World rank .... 312 (292=)
Subject area positions
Arts & humanities 163
Life sciences & biomedicine 250
Natural sciences................ 187

Johannes Gutenberg Universität Mainz

Founded 1477

55122 Mainz

www.uni-mainz.de

Academic survey position... 385
Employer survey position.... 126
Student faculty ratio 17.9:1
International faculty 6.3%
International students 15.0%

World rank 332 (330)
Subject area positions
Natural sciences................ 199

Universität Mannheim

Founded 1907

68131 Mannheim

www.uni-mannheim.de

Academic survey position... 385
Employer survey position.... 293
Student faculty ratio 57.8:1
International faculty 4.0%
Undergraduates.............. 5,705
Postgraduates................. 6,161
International students 11.1%

World rank .... 349= (392)
Subject area positions
Social sciences 158

Universität Marburg

Founded 1527

35032 Marburg

www.uni-marburg.de

Academic survey position... 385
Employer survey position.... 126
Student faculty ratio 9.6:1
International faculty 11.3%
International students 11.0%

World rank .... 368= (341=)
Subject area positions
Engineering & IT 297

Germany continued

Technische Universität München

Founded 1868

80333 München

www.tu-muenchen.de

Academic survey position... 117
Employer survey position.... 195
Student faculty ratio 7.1:1
International faculty.......15.3%
Undergraduates............ 12,311
Postgraduates.............. 3,381*
International students 17.9%

World rank .... 78= (67)
Subject area positions
Engineering & IT 40
Life sciences & biomedicine 171
Natural sciences.................. 40

Universität Münster

Founded 1780

48149 Münster

www.uni-muenster.de

Academic survey position... 388
Employer survey position.... 126
Student faculty ratio 13:1
International faculty.......11.2%
International students 7.5%

World rank .... 398= (339=)
Subject area positions
Arts & humanities 273
Social sciences 293

Ludwig-Maximilians-Universität München

Founded 1472

80539 München

www.uni-muenchen.de

Academic survey position..... 79
Employer survey position.... 290
Student faculty ratio 9:1
International faculty.......14.3%
Undergraduates.......... 40,379*
Postgraduates.............. 4,565*
International students 15.6%

World rank ....93= (65=)
Subject area positions
Arts & humanities 60
Engineering & IT 204
Life sciences & biomedicine.. 91
Natural sciences.................. 48
Social sciences 99

Universität Regensburg

Founded 1962

93053 Regensburg

www.uni-regensburg.de

Academic survey position... 385
Employer survey position.... 126
Student faculty ratio 15.5:1
International faculty.......11.4%
International students 7.8%

World rank ...... 401-500 (378=)
Subject area positions
Engineering & IT 297

Universität des Saarlandes

Founded 1948

66041 Saarbrücken

www.uni-saarland.de

Academic survey position... 385
Employer survey position.... 126
Student faculty ratio 14:1
International faculty.......20.7%
International students 14.3%

World rank .... 357= (345=)
Subject area positions
Engineering & IT 297

Universität Stuttgart

Founded 1829

70049 Stuttgart

www.uni-stuttgart.de

Academic survey position... 231
Employer survey position.... 202
Student faculty ratio 8.1:1
International faculty.......12.6%
Undergraduates.............. 9,900
Postgraduates................ 9,300
International students 22.4%

World rank 190 (165)
Subject area positions
Engineering & IT 68
Life sciences & biomedicine 282
Natural sciences................. 168

Germany continued

Eberhard Karls Universität Tübingen

Founded 1477

72074 Tübingen

www.uni-tuebingen.de

Academic survey position... 181
Employer survey position.... 126
Student faculty ratio 8.8:1
International faculty 15.6%
Undergraduates 13,014
Postgraduates 9,832
International students 11.0%

World rank .... 155= (142=)
Subject area positions
Arts & humanities 72
Life sciences & biomedicine.. 93
Natural sciences 257
Social sciences 239

Universität Ulm

Founded 1967

89069 Ulm

www.uni-ulm.de

Academic survey position... 385
Employer survey position.... 126
Student faculty ratio 4:1
International faculty 10.1%
International students 11.0%

World rank .... 276= (263)
Subject area positions
Engineering & IT 297

Universität Würzburg

Founded 1402

97070 Würzburg

www.uni-wuerzburg.de

Academic survey position... 324
Employer survey position.... 126
Student faculty ratio 11.3:1
International faculty 11.6%
International students 8.2%

World rank .... 276= (270=)
Subject area positions
Arts & humanities 227
Life sciences & biomedicine 195

Greece

University of Athens

Founded 1837

10561 Athens

www.uoa.gr

Academic survey position... 306
Employer survey position.... 277
Student faculty ratio 9.2:1
International faculty 5.3%
International students 24.0%

World rank .... 200= (248=)
Subject area positions
Arts & humanities 186
Engineering & IT 263
Social sciences 267

National Technical University of Athens

Founded 1836

15780 Zografou

www.ntua.gr

Academic survey position... 385
Employer survey position.... 340
Student faculty ratio 16.5:1
International faculty 4%
International students 0%

World rank ......401-500 (356=)
Subject area positions
Engineering & IT 133

University of Crete

Founded 1973

71409 Heraklion

www.uoc.gr

Academic survey position... 390
Employer survey position.... 126
Student faculty ratio 19.4:1
International faculty 1.0%
Undergraduates 11,917
Postgraduates 2,083
International students 1.5%

World rank .401-500 (401-500)
Subject area positions
Engineering & IT 288

Greece continued

Aristotelian University of Thessaloniki

Founded 1925

541 24 Thessaloniki

www.auth.gr

Academic survey position... 320
Employer survey position.... 392
Student faculty ratio 47.3:1
International faculty 5.3%
International students 33.0%

World rank .401-500 (401-500)
Subject area positions
Arts & humanities 200
Engineering & IT 230

Hong Kong

The Chinese University of Hong Kong

Founded 1963

Shatin, N.T
Hong Kong SAR

www.cuhk.edu.hk

Academic survey position..... 74
Employer survey position...... 95
Student faculty ratio 7.8:1
International faculty 42.0%
Undergraduates............ 10,515
Postgraduates................. 3,175
International students 20.8%

World rank .... 42 (38=)
Subject area positions
Arts & humanities 111
Engineering & IT 74
Life sciences & biomedicine.. 64
Natural sciences................. 105
Social sciences 66

City University of Hong Kong

Founded 1984

Kowloon
Hong Kong SAR

www.cityu.edu.hk

Academic survey position... 136
Employer survey position.... 202
Student faculty ratio 12.6:1
International faculty 51.2%
Undergraduates.............. 9,780
Postgraduates................. 2,700
International students 9.1%

World rank .... 147= (149=)
Subject area positions
Arts & humanities 159
Engineering & IT 89
Life sciences & biomedicine 210
Natural sciences................. 224
Social sciences 103

University of Hong Kong

Founded 1911

Hong Kong SAR

www.hku.hk

Academic survey position..... 43
Employer survey position...... 65
Student faculty ratio 7.1:1
International faculty 57.9%
Undergraduates.............. 9,062
Postgraduates................. 6,836
International students 24.1%

World rank 26 (18)
Subject area positions
Arts & humanities 46
Engineering & IT 69
Life sciences & biomedicine.. 39
Natural sciences................. 103
Social sciences 34

Hong Kong University of Science & Technology

Founded 1991

Kowloon
Hong Kong SAR

www.ust.hk

Academic survey position..... 71
Employer survey position...... 67
Student faculty ratio 10.1:1
International faculty 68.1%
Undergraduates.............. 5,868
Postgraduates................. 2,546
International students 28.4%

World rank .... 39 (53=)
Subject area positions
Engineering & IT 24
Life sciences & biomedicine.. 67
Natural sciences................... 59
Social sciences 69

The Hong Kong Polytechnic University

Founded 1937

Kowloon
Hong Kong SAR

www.polyu.edu.hk

Academic survey position... 243
Employer survey position.... 251
Student faculty ratio 19.8:1
International faculty 57.3%
Undergraduates............ 11,641
Postgraduates................. 4,188
International students 19.2%

World rank .... 224= (256=)
Subject area positions
Arts & humanities 275
Engineering & IT 121
Life sciences & biomedicine 282
Social sciences 232

Hungary

Eötvös Loránd University

Founded 1635

Budapest

www.elte.hu

Academic survey position... 352	World rank ......401-500 (501&)
Employer survey position.... 378	Subject area positions
Student faculty ratio 16:1	Arts & humanities.............. 213
International faculty.........7.1%	Natural sciences................. 174
International students 4.1%	

India

University of Calcutta

Founded 1857

Kolkata
West Bengal 700073

www.caluniv.ac.in

Academic survey position... 202	World rank .401-500 (401-500)
Employer survey position.... 296	Subject area positions
Student faculty ratio 65.8:1	Arts & humanities.............. 196
International faculty.........5.3%	Engineering & IT 209
Undergraduates.......... 34,657*	Life sciences & biomedicine 234
Postgraduates............... 5,040*	Natural sciences................. 181
International students 8.6%	Social sciences 190

University of Delhi

Founded 1922

Delhi 110007

www.du.ac.in

Academic survey position... 116	World rank .... 274= (254)
Employer survey position.... 138	Subject area positions
Student faculty ratio 202.5:1	Arts & humanities.............. 135
International faculty.........1.1%	Engineering & IT 171
Undergraduates.......... 114,074	Life sciences & biomedicine.. 95
Postgraduates............... 18,543	Natural sciences................. 192
International students 1.1%	Social sciences 82

Indian Institute of Technology Bombay (IITB)

Founded 1958

Mumbai 400076

www.iitb.ac.in

Academic survey position... 112	World rank .... 174= (269)
Employer survey position.... 125	Subject area positions
Student faculty ratio 12.7:1	Engineering & IT 36
International faculty.........3.6%	Life sciences & biomedicine 175
Undergraduates.............. 2,036	Natural sciences................... 77
Postgraduates................. 3,221	Social sciences 253
International students 3%	

Indian Institute of Technology Delhi (IITD)

Founded 1961

New Delhi 110016

www.iitd.ernet.in

Academic survey position... 150	World rank .... 154 (307=)
Employer survey position...... 97	Subject area positions
Student faculty ratio 9:1	Engineering & IT 42
International faculty............2%	Life sciences & biomedicine 173
International students 5%	Natural sciences................. 119
	Social sciences 297

Indian Institute of Technology Kanpur (IITK)

Founded 1959

Kanpur
Uttar Pradesh 208016

www.iitk.ac.in

Academic survey position... 261	World rank ......242= (401-500)
Employer survey position.... 184	Subject area positions
Student faculty ratio 12.1:1	Engineering & IT 70
International faculty............6%	Natural sciences................ 218
Undergraduates.............. 2,288	
Postgraduates................. 1,522	
International students 2%	

India continued

Indian Institute of Technology Madras (IITM)

Founded 1959

Chennai 600 036

www.iitm.ac.in

Academic survey position... 274
Employer survey position.... 200
Student faculty ratio 11.4:1
International faculty.........5.3%
International students 8.6%

World rank ...... 303= (401-500)
Subject area positions
Engineering & IT 74
Natural sciences................. 173

Indian Institute of Technology Roorkee (IITR)

Founded 1847

Roorkee
Uttarakhand 247667

www.iitr.ernet.in

Academic survey position... 385
Employer survey position.... 238
Student faculty ratio 11.9:1
International faculty.........2.2%
Undergraduates.............. 2,292
Postgraduates................. 2,049
International students 1.2%

World rank .401-500 (401-500)
Subject area positions
Engineering & IT 191

University of Pune

Founded 1949

Pune
Maharashtra 411007

www.unipune.ernet.in

Academic survey position... 271
Employer survey position.... 277
Student faculty ratio 689.6:1
International faculty............3%
International students 3%

World rank .401-500 (401-500)
Subject area positions
Arts & humanities 294
Engineering & IT 179
Life sciences & biomedicine 261
Natural sciences................. 251

Indonesia

Bandung Institute of Technology

Founded 1959

Bandung 40116

www.itb.ac.id

Academic survey position... 197
Employer survey position.... 223
Student faculty ratio 15.1:1
International faculty............2%
Undergraduates............ 12,442
Postgraduates................. 3,242
International students 6%

World rank .... 315 (369=)
Subject area positions
Engineering & IT 90
Life sciences & biomedicine 210
Natural sciences................. 143

Universitas Gadjah Mada

Founded 1949

Bulaksumur
Yogyakarta 55281

www.ugm.ac.id

Academic survey position... 168
Employer survey position.... 254
Student faculty ratio 19:1
International faculty.........3.2%
Undergraduates............ 29,391
Postgraduates............... 13,953
International students 1.8%

World rank .... 316= (360=)
Subject area positions
Arts & humanities 178
Engineering & IT 234
Life sciences & biomedicine 106
Natural sciences................. 220
Social sciences 167

University of Indonesia

Founded 1851

Depok 16424

www.ui.ac.id

Academic survey position... 217
Employer survey position.... 183
Student faculty ratio 10.9:1
International faculty............8%
Undergraduates.......... 22,516*
Postgraduates............... 8,559*
International students 2%

World rank 287 (395)
Subject area positions
Arts & humanities 173
Engineering & IT 206
Life sciences & biomedicine 207
Social sciences 131

Iran

University of Tehran

Founded 1934

Tehran 1417614411

www.ut.ac.ir

Academic survey position... 287
Employer survey position.... 126
Student faculty ratio 14.6:1
International faculty 9%
Undergraduates 19,618
Postgraduates 19,740
International students 1.9%

World rank ......401-500 (501+)
Subject area positions
Engineering & IT 159
Natural sciences................ 229

Ireland

University College Cork

Founded 1845

Cork

www.ucc.ie

Academic survey position... 282
Employer survey position.... 111
Student faculty ratio 11.2:1
International faculty 33.1%
Undergraduates 11,150
Postgraduates 2,094
International students 12.7%

World rank .... 226 (286=)
Subject area positions
Arts & humanities 197
Engineering & IT 251

University College Dublin

Founded 1854

Dublin 4

www.ucd.ie

Academic survey position... 123
Employer survey position...... 62
Student faculty ratio 9.3:1
International faculty 36.7%
Undergraduates 13,547
Postgraduates 3,667
International students 19.5%

World rank .... 108 (177=)
Subject area positions
Arts & humanities 73
Engineering & IT 196
Life sciences & biomedicine 175
Natural sciences................ 238
Social sciences 75

Dublin City University

Founded 1975

Dublin 9

www.dcu.ie

Academic survey position... 385
Employer survey position.... 141
Student faculty ratio 12:1
International faculty 23.1%
Undergraduates 5,371
Postgraduates 1,860
International students 19.3%

World rank 302 (300)
Subject area positions
Engineering & IT 297

Dublin Institute of Technology

Founded 1978

Dublin 2

www.dit.ie

Academic survey position... 385
Employer survey position.... 174
Student faculty ratio 6.5:1
International faculty 4.7%
Undergraduates 12,687
International students 6.5%

World rank ....328= (351=)
Subject area positions
Engineering & IT 259

National University of Ireland, Galway

Founded 1845

Galway

www.nuigalway.ie

Academic survey position... 347
Employer survey position.... 219
Student faculty ratio 17.8:1
International faculty 22.0%
Undergraduates 9,112
Postgraduates 2,935
International students 15.8%

World rank ......368= (401-500)
Subject area positions
Life sciences & biomedicine 260

Ireland continued

University of Limerick

Founded 1972

Limerick

www.ul.ie

Academic survey position... 385	World rank ...... 394= (401-500)
Employer survey position.... 174	Subject area positions
Student faculty ratio 12.2:1	Engineering & IT 297
International faculty 29.8%	
Undergraduates 7,825	
Postgraduates 988	
International students 6.6%	

Trinity College Dublin

Founded 1592

Dublin 2

www.tcd.ie

Academic survey position..... 54	World rank .... 49 (53=)
Employer survey position...... 43	Subject area positions
Student faculty ratio 9:1	Arts & humanities 32
International faculty 46.5%	Engineering & IT 135
Undergraduates 9,852	Life sciences & biomedicine.. 97
Postgraduates 2,831	Natural sciences 66
International students 17.5%	Social sciences 59

Israel

Ben Gurion University of the Negev

Founded 1969

Be'er Sheva 84105

www.bgu.ac.il

Academic survey position... 228	World rank ....264= (286=)
Employer survey position.... 126	Subject area positions
Student faculty ratio 39.6:1	Arts & humanities 290
International faculty 3.4%	Engineering & IT 204
Undergraduates 10,666	Life sciences & biomedicine 162
Postgraduates 4,391	Natural sciences 241
International students 1.3%	Social sciences 218

Hebrew University of Jerusalem

Founded 1918

Jerusalem 91905

www.huji.ac.il

Academic survey position..... 56	World rank .... 93= (128)
Employer survey position.... 126	Subject area positions
Student faculty ratio 14.8:1	Arts & humanities 41
International faculty 21.3%	Engineering & IT 209
Undergraduates 11,148	Life sciences & biomedicine.. 58
Postgraduates 6,255	Natural sciences 70
International students 6.6%	Social sciences 49

Technion - Israel Institute of Technology

Founded 1924

Technion City Haifa 32000

www.technion.ac.il

Academic survey position..... 81	World rank .... 109 (231=)
Employer survey position.... 200	Subject area positions
Student faculty ratio 11.9:1	Arts & humanities 250
International faculty 1.2%	Engineering & IT 29
Undergraduates 8,706	Life sciences & biomedicine 142
Postgraduates 3,354	Natural sciences 31
International students 2.2%	Social sciences 293

Tel Aviv University

Founded 1956

Tel Aviv 69978

www.tau.ac.il

Academic survey position..... 76	World rank .... 114 (151=)
Employer survey position.... 277	Subject area positions
Student faculty ratio 19.1:1	Arts & humanities 80
International faculty 6%	Engineering & IT 127
Undergraduates 12,318	Life sciences & biomedicine 115
Postgraduates 6,902	Natural sciences 61
International students 2.7%	Social sciences 56

Italy

Università Commerciale Luigi Bocconi

Founded 1902

20136 Milano

www.unibocconi.eu

Academic survey position... 385
Employer survey position...... 42
Student faculty ratio 18.2:1
International faculty.........7.7%
Undergraduates.............. 8,208
Postgraduates................ 5,349
International students 9.9%

World rank .401-500 (401-500)
Subject area positions
Social sciences 75

University of Bologna

Founded 1088

40126 Bologna

www.unibo.it

Academic survey position..... 86
Employer survey position.... 153
Student faculty ratio 21.7:1
International faculty.........4.8%
Undergraduates............ 52,318
Postgraduates.............. 41,244
International students 5.4%

World rank .... 192= (173=)
Subject area positions
Arts & humanities 55
Engineering & IT 136
Life sciences & biomedicine 137
Natural sciences................. 134
Social sciences 90

University of Florence

Founded 1923

50121 Firenze

www.unifi.it

Academic survey position... 213
Employer survey position.... 126
Student faculty ratio 25.6:1
International faculty.........2.4%
Undergraduates............ 53,393
Postgraduates................ 9,218
International students 4.3%

World rank .... 349= (329)
Subject area positions
Arts & humanities 171
Natural sciences................ 156
Social sciences 171

Università Cattolica del Sacro Cuore (UCSC)

Founded 1921

20123 Milano

www.unicatt.it

Academic survey position... 385
Employer survey position.... 126
Student faculty ratio 9.9:1
International faculty.........1.2%
Undergraduates............ 26,516
Postgraduates.............. 16,005
International students 2.8%

World rank ......401-500 (501+)
Subject area positions
Arts & humanities 269

Politecnico di Milano

Founded 1863

20133 Milano

www.polimi.it

Academic survey position... 223
Employer survey position.... 111
Student faculty ratio 19.7:1
International faculty.........3.5%
Undergraduates............ 16,983
Postgraduates................ 9,820
International students 6.9%

World rank .... 291= (343=)
Subject area positions
Arts & humanities 288
Engineering & IT 63
Life sciences & biomedicine 271
Natural sciences................ 201

University of Naples - Federico II

Founded 1224

80125 Napoli

www.unina.it

Academic survey position... 338
Employer survey position.... 126
Student faculty ratio 57.8:1
International faculty.........2.2%
International students 8%

World rank ......398= (401-500)
Subject area positions
Arts & humanities 284

University of Padua

Founded 1222

35122 Padua

www.unipd.it

Academic survey position... 215
Employer survey position.... 395
Student faculty ratio 34.2:1
International faculty 4%
International students 0%

World rank .... 296= (312=)
Subject area positions
Arts & humanities 174
Engineering & IT 276
Life sciences & biomedicine 198
Natural sciences 163
Social sciences 291

Università degli Studi di Pavia

Founded 1361

27100 Pavia

www.unipv.eu

Academic survey position... 352
Employer survey position.... 126
Student faculty ratio 23.9:1
International faculty 6%
Undergraduates 22,087*
Postgraduates 3,203
International students 4.7%

World rank ...... 401-500 (388=)
Subject area positions
Arts & humanities 260
Engineering & IT 249

University of Pisa

Founded 1343

56126 Pisa

www.unipi.it

Academic survey position... 206
Employer survey position.... 126
Student faculty ratio 37:1
International faculty 2%
International students 2.2%

World rank 333 (325)
Subject area positions
Arts & humanities 183
Engineering & IT 168
Life sciences & biomedicine 247
Natural sciences 116

Università degli Studi di Roma - La Sapienza

Founded 1303

185 Roma

www.uniroma1.it

Academic survey position..... 72
Employer survey position.... 254
Student faculty ratio 32.6:1
International faculty 1.3%
Undergraduates 106,944*
Postgraduates 29,980
International students 4.2%

World rank 205 (183)
Subject area positions
Arts & humanities 54
Engineering & IT 118
Life sciences & biomedicine 184
Natural sciences 37
Social sciences 118

Università degli Studi di Roma - Tor Vergata

Founded 1982

173 Roma

web.uniroma2.it

Academic survey position... 385
Employer survey position.... 383
Student faculty ratio 31.2:1
International faculty 2.4%
Undergraduates 36,010
Postgraduates 9,664
International students 3.9%

World rank .401-500 (401-500)
Subject area positions
Natural sciences 213

University of Siena

Founded 1240

53100 Siena

www.unisi.it

Academic survey position... 385
Employer survey position.... 126
Student faculty ratio 29.3:1
International faculty 2.0%
International students 4.0%

World rank 401-500 (394)
Subject area positions
Social sciences 256

Italy continued

University of Trento

Founded 1962

38100 Trento

www.unitn.it

Academic survey position... 373	World rank . 401-500 (401-500)
Employer survey position.... 332	Subject area positions
Student faculty ratio 31.2:1	Engineering & IT 253
International faculty 5.1%	Natural sciences................ 228
Undergraduates.............. 9,529	Social sciences 299
Postgraduates 7,458	
International students 5.7%	

University of Trieste

Founded 1924

34127 Trieste

www.univ.trieste.it

Academic survey position... 313	World rank ...... 401-500 (374=)
Employer survey position.... 126	Subject area positions
Student faculty ratio 22.9:1	Arts & humanities 259
International faculty 1%	Natural sciences................. 185
International students 7.4%	

Japan

Chiba University

Founded 1901

Chiba-shi
Chiba 263-8522

www.chiba-u.ac.jp

Academic survey position... 343	World rank .... 298 (284=)
Employer survey position.... 317	Subject area positions
Student faculty ratio 13.7:1	Life sciences & biomedicine 157
International faculty 4.8%	
Undergraduates.......... 10,810*	
Postgraduates 3,546*	
International students 4.5%	

Gifu University

Founded 1949

Gifu 501-1193

www.gifu-u.ac.jp

Academic survey position... 385	World rank ...... 401-500 (345=)
Employer survey position.... 126	Subject area positions
Student faculty ratio 8.4:1	Engineering & IT 297
International faculty 1.8%	
Undergraduates.............. 6,013	
Postgraduates 1,713	
International students 4.4%	

Gunma University

Founded 1949

Maebashi
Gunma 371-8510

www.gunma-u.ac.jp

Academic survey position... 385	World rank .... 396= (331=)
Employer survey position.... 126	Subject area positions
Student faculty ratio 4.2:1	Engineering & IT 297
International faculty 4.8%	
Undergraduates.............. 5,184	
Postgraduates 1,408*	
International students 3.0%	

Hiroshima University

Founded 1949

Higashi-Hiroshima
Hiroshima 739-8511

www.hiroshima-u.ac.jp

Academic survey position... 280	World rank 267 (212)
Employer survey position.... 372	Subject area positions
Student faculty ratio 9.2:1	Engineering & IT 222
International faculty 2.5%	Natural sciences................ 229
Undergraduates............ 11,077	Social sciences 284
Postgraduates 4,533	
International students 4.1%	

Japan continued

Hitotsubashi University

Founded 1875

Tokyo 186-8601

www.hit-u.ac.jp

Academic survey position... 364
Employer survey position.... 149
Student faculty ratio 13.9:1
International faculty.........6.8%
Undergraduates.............. 4,465
Postgraduates................. 2,102
International students 9.5%

World rank ...... 378= (401-500)
Subject area positions
Arts & humanities 208
Social sciences 101

Hokkaido University

Founded 1876

Sapporo 060-0808

www.hokudai.ac.jp

Academic survey position... 218
Employer survey position.... 244
Student faculty ratio 8.5:1
International faculty.........2.1%
Undergraduates............ 11,734
Postgraduates................. 6,252
International students 4.0%

World rank .... 174= (151=)
Subject area positions
Engineering & IT 209
Life sciences & biomedicine 134
Natural sciences................. 147

Kanazawa University

Founded 1949

Kanazawa
Ishikawa 920-1192

www.kanazawa-u.ac.jp

Academic survey position... 385
Employer survey position.... 126
Student faculty ratio 11.2:1
International faculty.........4.8%
Undergraduates.............. 8,025
Postgraduates................. 2,294
International students 2.3%

World rank .401-500 (401-500)
Subject area positions
Engineering & IT 297

Keio University

Founded 1858

Tokyo 108-8345

www.keio.ac.jp

Academic survey position... 160
Employer survey position...... 93
Student faculty ratio 13.3:1
International faculty.........7.1%
Undergraduates............ 27,911
Postgraduates................. 4,394
International students 3.0%

World rank .... 214= (161=)
Subject area positions
Arts & humanities 186
Engineering & IT 162
Life sciences & biomedicine 165
Natural sciences................. 252
Social sciences 117

Kobe University

Founded 1949

Kobe
Hyogo 657-8501

www.kobe-u.ac.jp

Academic survey position... 200
Employer survey position.... 189
Student faculty ratio 8.7:1
International faculty.........4.1%
Undergraduates............ 11,866
Postgraduates................. 4,773
International students 5.8%

World rank .... 199 (197=)
Subject area positions
Engineering & IT 157
Life sciences & biomedicine 169
Natural sciences................. 208
Social sciences 133

Kumamoto University

Founded 1949

Kumamoto 860-8555

www.kumamoto-u.ac.jp

Academic survey position... 385
Employer survey position.... 126
Student faculty ratio 6.2:1
International faculty.........1.8%
Undergraduates.............. 8,032
Postgraduates................. 2,190
International students 2.0%

World rank .... 378= (386=)
Subject area positions
Engineering & IT 297

Japan continued

Kyoto University

Founded 1897

Kyoto 606-8501

www.kyoto-u.ac.jp

Academic survey position..... 22	World rank 25 (25)
Employer survey position...... 78	Subject area positions
Student faculty ratio 7.8:1	Arts & humanities 37
International faculty 6.5%	Engineering & IT 22
Undergraduates 13,235	Life sciences & biomedicine.. 24
Postgraduates 9,162	Natural sciences 13
International students 4.6%	Social sciences 42

Kyushu University

Founded 1911

Fukuoka 812-8581

www.kyushu-u.ac.jp

Academic survey position... 191	World rank 158 (136)
Employer survey position.... 293	Subject area positions
Student faculty ratio 8.4:1	Arts & humanities 180
International faculty 2.0%	Engineering & IT 171
Undergraduates 12,011	Life sciences & biomedicine 178
Postgraduates 7,186	Natural sciences 135
International students 6.2%	

Nagasaki University

Founded 1949

Nagasaki-shi 852-8521

www.nagasaki-u.ac.jp

Academic survey position... 385	World rank .... 362= (273=)
Employer survey position.... 126	Subject area positions
Student faculty ratio 8.3:1	Engineering & IT 297
International faculty 5.4%	
Undergraduates 7,717	
Postgraduates 1,482	
International students 3.1%	

Nagoya University

Founded 1871

Nagoya
Aichi Prefecture 464-8601

www.nagoya-u.ac.jp

Academic survey position... 174	World rank .... 120 (112=)
Employer survey position.... 205	Subject area positions
Student faculty ratio 7.4:1	Engineering & IT 122
International faculty 5.0%	Life sciences & biomedicine 190
Undergraduates 9,701	Natural sciences 111
Postgraduates 5,981	Social sciences 218
International students 6.5%	

Niigata University

Founded 1949

Niigata City 950-2181

www.niigata-u.ac.jp

Academic survey position... 385	World rank .401-500 (401-500)
Employer survey position.... 126	Subject area positions
Student faculty ratio 12.9:1	Engineering & IT 297
International faculty 4.1%	
Undergraduates 10,296*	
Postgraduates 2,106*	
International students 1.7%	

Okayama University

Founded 1870

Okayama 700-8530

www.okayama-u.ac.jp

Academic survey position... 385	World rank 401-500 (377)
Employer survey position.... 126	Subject area positions
Student faculty ratio 12:1	Engineering & IT 297
International faculty 2.3%	
Postgraduates 3,340*	
International students 3.4%	

Japan continued

Osaka University

Founded 1931

Osaka 565 - 0871

www.osaka-u.ac.jp

Academic survey position..... 53	World rank 44 (46)
Employer survey position.... 153	Subject area positions
Student faculty ratio 6.2:1	Arts & humanities 154
International faculty 4.4%	Engineering & IT 49
Undergraduates............ 16,204	Life sciences & biomedicine.. 36
Postgraduates................. 8,037	Natural sciences.................. 40
International students 5.4%	Social sciences 146

Osaka City University

Founded 1880

Osaka-shi 558-8585

www.osaka-cu.ac.jp

Academic survey position... 385	World rank ...... 401-500 (364=)
Employer survey position.... 126	Subject area positions
Student faculty ratio 15.2:1	Engineering & IT 297
International faculty 5.7%	
Undergraduates............ 7,197*	
Postgraduates............... 1,802*	
International students 2.7%	

Showa University

Founded 1928

Tokyo 142-8555

www.showa-u.ac.jp

Academic survey position... 385	World rank .... 359= (318)
Employer survey position.... 277	Subject area positions
Student faculty ratio 3.4:1	Engineering & IT 297
International faculty 2.9%	
Undergraduates............ 2,843*	
Postgraduates................. 456*	
International students 7%	

Tohoku University

Founded 1907

Sendai 980-8577

www.tohoku.ac.jp

Academic survey position... 162	World rank .... 112 (102=)
Employer survey position.... 267	Subject area positions
Student faculty ratio 5.3:1	Engineering & IT 98
International faculty 9.6%	Life sciences & biomedicine 180
Undergraduates............ 10,955	Natural sciences.................. 68
Postgraduates................. 7,109	
International students 6.2%	

Tokai University

Founded 1942

Hiratsuka
Kanagawa 259-1292

www.u-tokai.ac.jp

Academic survey position... 370	World rank .401-500 (401-500)
Employer survey position.... 126	Subject area positions
Student faculty ratio 17.4:1	Engineering & IT 226
International faculty 4.4%	
Undergraduates............ 28,784	
Postgraduates................. 1,504	
International students 1.1%	

University of Tokyo

Founded 1877

Tokyo 113-8654

www.u-tokyo.ac.jp

Academic survey position..... 14	World rank 19 (17)
Employer survey position...... 50	Subject area positions
Student faculty ratio 5.2:1	Arts & humanities 28
International faculty 5.4%	Engineering & IT 9
Undergraduates............ 14,085	Life sciences & biomedicine.. 10
Postgraduates............... 14,242	Natural sciences 10
International students 8.5%	Social sciences 21

Japan continued

Tokyo Institute of Technology

Founded 1881	Academic survey position..... 99	World rank .... 61 (90=)
	Employer survey position.... 123	Subject area positions
Tokyo 152-8550	Student faculty ratio 8.8:1	Arts & humanities 252
	International faculty.........4.6%	Engineering & IT 21
www.titech.ac.jp	Undergraduates.............. 4,911	Life sciences & biomedicine 229
	Postgraduates................. 5,014	Natural sciences................... 57
	International students 9.6%	

Tokyo Metropolitan University

Founded 1949	Academic survey position... 385	World rank .... 349= (335)
	Employer survey position.... 292	Subject area positions
Tokyo 192-0397	Student faculty ratio 12.5:1	Engineering & IT 297
	International faculty.........4.1%	
www.metro-u.ac.jp	Undergraduates............ 4,855*	
	Postgraduates............... 1,682*	
	International students 2.7%	

Tokyo University of Science (TUS)

Founded 1881	Academic survey position... 392	World rank .... 378= (364=)
	Employer survey position.... 340	Subject area positions
Tokyo 162-8601	Student faculty ratio 48.4:1	Engineering & IT 279
	International faculty.........5.3%	Life sciences & biomedicine 234
www.tus.ac.jp	International students 4%	Natural sciences................. 255

University of Tsukuba

Founded 1973	Academic survey position... 258	World rank .... 216= (209=)
	Employer survey position.... 290	Subject area positions
Tsukuba	Student faculty ratio 8.1:1	Engineering & IT 201
Ibaraki-ken 305-8577	International faculty.........4.1%	Life sciences & biomedicine 271
	Undergraduates............ 10,211	Natural sciences................. 143
www.tsukuba.ac.jp/	Postgraduates................. 6,373	Social sciences 293
	International students 7.2%	

Waseda University

Founded 1882	Academic survey position..... 91	World rank .... 180= (180=)
	Employer survey position...... 72	Subject area positions
Tokyo 169-8050	Student faculty ratio 14.6:1	Arts & humanities 56
	International faculty......11.6%	Engineering & IT 124
www.waseda.ac.jp	Undergraduates............ 37,800	Life sciences & biomedicine 160
	Postgraduates................. 9,826	Natural sciences................. 154
	International students 5.9%	Social sciences 83

Yokohama City University

Founded 1882	Academic survey position... 385	World rank ...... 362= (401-500)
	Employer survey position.... 126	Subject area positions
Yokohama 236-0027	Student faculty ratio 8.5:1	Engineering & IT 297
	International faculty.........3.0%	
www.yokohama-cu.ac.jp	Undergraduates............ 3,592*	
	Postgraduates................. 668*	
	International students 2.5%	

Japan continued

Yokohama National University

Founded 1949

Yokohama 240-8501

www.ynu.ac.jp

Academic survey position... 385
Employer survey position.... 256
Student faculty ratio 12.6:1
International faculty.........7.1%
Undergraduates.............. 7,894
Postgraduates................. 2,746
International students 7.0%

World rank .... 390 (354=)
Subject area positions
Engineering & IT 297

Korea, South

Chonbuk National University

Founded 1947

Jeonbuk 561156

www.chonbuk.ac.kr

Academic survey position... 385
Employer survey position.... 126
Student faculty ratio 10.4:1
International faculty.........5.1%
International students 3.5%

World rank .401-500 (401-500)
Subject area positions
Engineering & IT 297

Ewha Womans University

Founded 1886

Seoul 120-750

www.ewha.ac.kr

Academic survey position... 385
Employer survey position.... 387
Student faculty ratio 12:1
International faculty.........4.2%
Undergraduates............ 15,583
Postgraduates................. 5,400
International students 6.9%

World rank ......401-500 (501+)
Subject area positions
Engineering & IT 297

Hanyang University

Founded 1939

Seoul 133-791

www.hanyang.ac.kr

Academic survey position... 350
Employer survey position.... 395
Student faculty ratio 9:1
International faculty.........4.5%
Undergraduates.......... 24,483*
Postgraduates............... 7,315*
International students 2.6%

World rank 344 (401-500)
Subject area positions
Engineering & IT 297

KAIST - Korea Advanced Institute of Science & Technology

Founded 1971

Daejeon 305701

www.kaist.edu

Academic survey position... 110
Employer survey position.... 239
Student faculty ratio 10:1
International faculty.......13.2%
Undergraduates.............. 2,948
Postgraduates................. 3,864
International students 7.4%

World rank .... 95 (132=)
Subject area positions
Engineering & IT 34
Life sciences & biomedicine 134
Natural sciences................... 46
Social sciences 299

Korea University

Founded 1905

Seoul 136701

www.korea.edu

Academic survey position... 165
Employer survey position.... 312
Student faculty ratio 11.7:1
International faculty.........6.1%
Undergraduates............ 19,454
Postgraduates................. 7,479
International students 9.9%

World rank .... 236 (243=)
Subject area positions
Arts & humanities 166
Engineering & IT 202
Life sciences & biomedicine 154
Natural sciences................. 221
Social sciences 126

Korea, South continued

Kyung Hee University

Founded 1949

Seoul 130-701

www.kyunghee.ac.kr

Academic survey position... 385
Employer survey position.... 126
Student faculty ratio 12:1
International faculty 5.4%
Undergraduates 23,672
Postgraduates 2,672
International students 11.4%

World rank ......401-500 (501+)
Subject area positions
Engineering & IT 297

Pohang University of Science and Technology (POSTECH)

Founded 1986

Pohang 790-784

www.postech.ac.kr

Academic survey position... 334
Employer survey position.... 368
Student faculty ratio 9.3:1
International faculty 14.5%
Undergraduates 1,377
Postgraduates 1,565
International students 2.3%

World rank .... 188= (233)
Subject area positions
Engineering & IT 143
Natural sciences 163

Seoul National University

Founded 1946

Seoul 151 742

www.useoul.edu

Academic survey position..... 33
Employer survey position.... 173
Student faculty ratio 7:1
International faculty 3.6%
Undergraduates 14,476
Postgraduates 9,388
International students 7.6%

World rank ....50= (51=)
Subject area positions
Arts & humanities 76
Engineering & IT 43
Life sciences & biomedicine.. 40
Natural sciences 31
Social sciences 33

SungKyunKwan University

Founded 1398

Seoul 110-745

www.skku.edu

Academic survey position... 385
Employer survey position.... 126
Student faculty ratio 7.9:1
International faculty 5.7%
Undergraduates 18,703
Postgraduates 5,817
International students 11.7%

World rank .... 370= (380)
Subject area positions
Engineering & IT 297

Yonsei University

Founded 1885

Seoul 120-749

www.yonsei.ac.kr

Academic survey position... 194
Employer survey position.... 288
Student faculty ratio 7.5:1
International faculty 3.9%
Undergraduates 18,601
Postgraduates 10,516
International students 4.2%

World rank .... 203= (236)
Subject area positions
Arts & humanities 240
Engineering & IT 209
Life sciences & biomedicine 215
Natural sciences 188
Social sciences 129

Lebanon

American University of Beirut (AUB)

Founded 1866

Beirut 1107 2020

www.aub.edu.lb

Academic survey position... 385
Employer survey position.... 126
Student faculty ratio 10.3:1
International faculty 5.3%
Undergraduates 5,947
Postgraduates 872
International students 20.1%

World rank 401-500
Subject area positions
Engineering & IT 297

Malaysia

Universiti Malaya (UM)

Founded 1949

50603 Kuala Lumpur

www.um.edu.my

Academic survey position... 152
Employer survey position.... 149
Student faculty ratio 14.1:1
International faculty 18.4%
Undergraduates 18,051
Postgraduates 8,912
International students 9.9%

World rank .... 230= (246=)
Subject area positions
Arts & humanities 190
Engineering & IT 179
Life sciences & biomedicine 127
Natural sciences 197
Social sciences 137

Universiti Kebangsaan Malaysia (UKM)

Founded 1970

43600 Bangi

www.ukm.my

Academic survey position... 206
Employer survey position.... 293
Student faculty ratio 9.9:1
International faculty 20.2%
Undergraduates 18,684
Postgraduates 6,087
International students 4.5%

World rank .... 250 (309=)
Subject area positions
Arts & humanities 255
Engineering & IT 273
Life sciences & biomedicine 144
Natural sciences 201
Social sciences 155

Universiti Sains Malaysia (USM)

Founded 1962

11800 Penang

www.usm.my

Academic survey position... 229
Employer survey position.... 271
Student faculty ratio 15:1
International faculty 9.4%
Undergraduates 16,610
Postgraduates 4,417
International students 7.7%

World rank .... 313= (307=)
Subject area positions
Engineering & IT 239
Life sciences & biomedicine 123
Natural sciences 246
Social sciences 229

Universiti Putra Malaysia (UPM)

Founded 1931

43400 Serdang

www.upm.edu.my

Academic survey position... 263
Employer survey position.... 251
Student faculty ratio 12.2:1
International faculty 3.6%
Undergraduates 18,193
Postgraduates 6,246
International students 8.9%

World rank .... 320= (364=)
Subject area positions
Arts & humanities 260
Life sciences & biomedicine 213
Natural sciences 226
Social sciences 288

Universiti Teknologi Malaysia (UTM)

Founded 1915

81310 Skudai

www.utm.my

Academic survey position... 380
Employer survey position.... 158
Student faculty ratio 12.7:1
International faculty 15.9%
Undergraduates 19,833
Postgraduates 5,801
International students 11.8%

World rank 356 (401-500)
Subject area positions
Engineering & IT 295
Life sciences & biomedicine 244

Mexico

Instituto Tecnologico y de Estudios Superiores de Monterrey (ITESM)

Founded 1943

64849 Monterrey

www.itesm.mx

Academic survey position... 294
Employer survey position...... 38
Student faculty ratio 14.1:1
International faculty 3.5%
International students 3.9%

World rank ...... 328= (401-500)
Subject area positions
Engineering & IT 156
Social sciences 243

Mexico continued

Universidad Nacional Autónoma de México (UNAM)

Founded 1551	Academic survey position..... 87	World rank .... 150 (192=)
	Employer survey position...... 87	Subject area positions
4510 Ciudad de Mexico	Student faculty ratio 10.1:1	Arts & humanities 97
	International faculty 11.1%	Engineering & IT 107
www.unam.mx	Undergraduates 133,473	Life sciences & biomedicine.. 64
	Postgraduates 21,919	Natural sciences 107
	International students 1.2%	Social sciences 140

Netherlands

University of Amsterdam

Founded 1632	Academic survey position..... 63	World rank 53 (48)
	Employer survey position.... 121	Subject area positions
1012 WX Amsterdam	Student faculty ratio 7.8:1	Arts & humanities 36
	International faculty 22.4%	Engineering & IT 171
www.uva.nl	Undergraduates 15,883	Life sciences & biomedicine.. 80
	Postgraduates 9,280	Natural sciences 119
	International students 6.4%	Social sciences 43

VU University Amsterdam

Founded 1880	Academic survey position... 152	World rank .... 155= (304=)
	Employer survey position.... 258	Subject area positions
1081 HV Amsterdam	Student faculty ratio 7.4:1	Arts & humanities 154
	International faculty 9.4%	Engineering & IT 218
www.english.vu.nl	Undergraduates 13,150	Life sciences & biomedicine 120
	Postgraduates 6,826	Natural sciences 235
	International students 6.0%	Social sciences 124

Delft University of Technology

Founded 1842	Academic survey position..... 98	World rank .... 78= (63)
	Employer survey position...... 79	Subject area positions
2628 CN Delft	Student faculty ratio 9.3:1	Arts & humanities 203
	International faculty 25.8%	Engineering & IT 17
www.tudelft.nl	Undergraduates 9,453	Natural sciences 72
	Postgraduates 5,035	Social sciences 267
	International students 14.6%	

Eindhoven University of Technology

Founded 1956	Academic survey position... 203	World rank .... 128 (130=)
	Employer survey position.... 227	Subject area positions
5612 AZ Eindhoven	Student faculty ratio 4.3:1	Engineering & IT 49
	International faculty 43.3%	Natural sciences 154
w3.tm.tue.nl	Undergraduates 4,975*	
	Postgraduates 1,723*	
	International students 8.9%	

Erasmus University Rotterdam

Founded 1913	Academic survey position... 193	World rank .... 126 (163=)
	Employer survey position...... 31	Subject area positions
3000 DR Rotterdam	Student faculty ratio 12.2:1	Arts & humanities 188
	International faculty 16.2%	Life sciences & biomedicine.. 99
www.eur.nl	Undergraduates 17,103	Social sciences 51
	Postgraduates 9,574	
	International students 10.8%	

Netherlands continued

University of Groningen

Founded 1614

9700 AB Groningen

www.rug.nl

Academic survey position... 158
Employer survey position.... 264
Student faculty ratio 9.2:1
International faculty.......17.7%
Undergraduates............ 17,878
Postgraduates................. 5,183
International students 6.9%

World rank .... 144= (173=)
Subject area positions
Arts & humanities.............. 101
Life sciences & biomedicine 162
Natural sciences................ 182
Social sciences 143

Leiden University

Founded 1575

2300 RA Leiden

www.leiden.edu

Academic survey position..... 67
Employer survey position.... 186
Student faculty ratio 14.8:1
International faculty.......22.8%
Undergraduates............ 11,370
Postgraduates................. 5,260
International students 8.7%

World rank 64 (84)
Subject area positions
Arts & humanities................ 35
Engineering & IT 288
Life sciences & biomedicine.. 74
Natural sciences.................. 68
Social sciences 58

Maastricht University

Founded 1976

6211 LK Maastricht

www.unimaas.nl

Academic survey position... 239
Employer survey position.... 140
Student faculty ratio 7.8:1
International faculty.......17.9%
Undergraduates.............. 8,725
Postgraduates................. 3,304
International students 36.4%

World rank 111 (111)
Subject area positions
Life sciences & biomedicine 144
Social sciences 50

Radboud University Nijmegen

Founded 1923

6500 HC Nijmegen

www.ru.nl

Academic survey position... 327
Employer survey position.... 126
Student faculty ratio 8.1:1
International faculty.......23.3%
Undergraduates............ 13,054
Postgraduates................. 4,717
International students 7.0%

World rank .... 221 (195=)
Subject area positions
Arts & humanities.............. 281
Life sciences & biomedicine 198
Social sciences 288

University of Twente

Founded 1961

7522 NB Enschede

www.utwente.nl

Academic survey position... 234
Employer survey position.... 271
Student faculty ratio 10.5:1
International faculty.......20.4%
Undergraduates.............. 4,806
Postgraduates................. 3,671
International students 10.7%

World rank .... 200= (185=)
Subject area positions
Engineering & IT 117
Life sciences & biomedicine 296
Natural sciences................ 182
Social sciences 208

Utrecht University

Founded 1636

3508 TC Utrecht

www.uu.nl

Academic survey position..... 59
Employer survey position.... 169
Student faculty ratio 9.8:1
International faculty.......12.2%
Undergraduates............ 18,311
Postgraduates................. 9,802
International students 4.3%

World rank 67 (89)
Subject area positions
Arts & humanities................ 65
Engineering & IT 169
Life sciences & biomedicine.. 62
Natural sciences.................. 37
Social sciences 91

Netherlands continued

Wageningen University

Founded 1918

6700 HB Wageningen

www.wu.nl

Academic survey position...	303
Employer survey position....	357
Student faculty ratio	6.7:1
International faculty	10.9%
International students	28.5%

World rank	142 (148)
Subject area positions	
Engineering & IT	295
Life sciences & biomedicine	173
Natural sciences.................	216

New Zealand

University of Auckland

Founded 1883

Auckland 1142

www.auckland.ac.nz

Academic survey position.....	39
Employer survey position......	48
Student faculty ratio	14.6:1
International faculty	35.5%
Undergraduates............	23,052
Postgraduates.................	4,160
International students	33.2%

World rank	65 (50)
Subject area positions	
Arts & humanities	39
Engineering & IT	56
Life sciences & biomedicine..	42
Natural sciences.................	102
Social sciences	30

University of Canterbury

Founded 1873

Christchurch 8140

www.canterbury.ac.nz

Academic survey position...	169
Employer survey position......	86
Student faculty ratio	19.6:1
International faculty	44.9%
Undergraduates............	12,028
Postgraduates.................	1,706
International students	24.8%

World rank	186= (188=)
Subject area positions	
Arts & humanities	175
Engineering & IT	129
Natural sciences.................	160
Social sciences	135

Massey University

Founded 1927

Palmerston North
Private bag 11222

www.massey.ac.nz

Academic survey position...	276
Employer survey position....	230
Student faculty ratio	14.7:1
International faculty	37.3%
Undergraduates............	14,673
Postgraduates.................	4,362
International students	15.8%

World rank	283 (242)
Subject area positions	
Life sciences & biomedicine	244
Natural sciences.................	257
Social sciences	192

University of Otago

Founded 1869

Dunedin
P.O. Box 56

www.otago.ac.nz

Academic survey position...	118
Employer survey position....	129
Student faculty ratio	14.5:1
International faculty	65.0%
Undergraduates............	15,372
Postgraduates.................	2,853
International students	22.1%

World rank	124= (114=)
Subject area positions	
Arts & humanities	81
Life sciences & biomedicine..	70
Natural sciences.................	185
Social sciences	98

Victoria University of Wellington

Founded 1897

Wellington 6140

www.vuw.ac.nz

Academic survey position...	195
Employer survey position....	128
Student faculty ratio	20.8:1
International faculty	55.1%
Undergraduates............	14,428
Postgraduates.................	2,657
International students	24.0%

World rank	227= (234)
Subject area positions	
Arts & humanities	97
Natural sciences.................	276
Social sciences	100

New Zealand continued

University of Waikato

Founded 1964

Hamilton Private Bag 3105

www.waikato.ac.nz

Academic survey position... 395
Employer survey position.... 304
Student faculty ratio 16.4:1
International faculty.......29.7%
Undergraduates.............. 8,244
Postgraduates................. 1,826
International students 14.8%

World rank .... 378= (319=)
Subject area positions
Arts & humanities.............. 248
Social sciences 229

Norway

University of Bergen

Founded 1946

5020 Bergen

www.uib.no

Academic survey position... 236
Employer survey position.... 387
Student faculty ratio 16:1
International faculty.......25.2%
International students 11.0%

World rank .... 227= (225=)
Subject area positions
Arts & humanities.............. 140
Life sciences & biomedicine 266
Natural sciences................. 297
Social sciences 139

Norwegian University of Science and Technology

Founded 1996

7491 Trondheim

www.ntnu.no

Academic survey position... 322
Employer survey position.... 324
Student faculty ratio 18.1:1
International faculty.......26.7%
Undergraduates.......... 11,622*
Postgraduates............... 7,516*
International students 7.1%

World rank .... 328= (301=)
Subject area positions
Engineering & IT 144
Natural sciences................. 290

University of Oslo

Founded 1811

316 Oslo

www.uio.no

Academic survey position... 138
Employer survey position.... 314
Student faculty ratio 10.5:1
International faculty.......12.4%
Undergraduates.......... 17,645*
Postgraduates............... 9,433*
International students 13.1%

World rank .... 177= (188=)
Subject area positions
Arts & humanities.............. 120
Engineering & IT 183
Life sciences & biomedicine 187
Natural sciences................. 175
Social sciences 104

University of Tromso

Founded 1968

9037 Tromsø

www.uit.no

Academic survey position... 385
Employer survey position.... 126
Student faculty ratio 4.8:1
International faculty.......13.4%
International students 6.7%

World rank .... 320= (292=)
Subject area positions
Engineering & IT 297

Pakistan

University of Lahore

Founded 1999

Lahore

www.uol.edu.pk

Academic survey position... 368
Employer survey position.... 126
Student faculty ratio 11.3:1
International faculty.........1.8%
Undergraduates.............. 2,616
Postgraduates................... 585
International students 3.8%

World rank .401-500 (401-500)
Subject area positions
Engineering & IT 297

Pakistan continued

National University of Sciences and Technology (NUST), Pakistan

Founded 1991

Islamabad

www.nust.edu.pk

Academic survey position... 385
Employer survey position.... 329
Student faculty ratio 8.6:1
International faculty 2.5%
Undergraduates 4,930
Postgraduates 884
International students 1.8%

World rank ...... 376= (401-500)
Subject area positions
Life sciences & biomedicine 292

Peru

Pontificia Universidad Católica del Perú

Founded 1917

Lima 32

www.pucp.edu.pe

Academic survey position... 385
Employer survey position.... 242
Student faculty ratio 10.5:1
International faculty 0%
International students 1.7%

World rank .401-500 (401-500)
Subject area positions
Arts & humanities 275

Philippines

De La Salle University

Founded 1911

Manila 1004

www.dlsu.edu.ph

Academic survey position... 385
Employer survey position...... 92
Student faculty ratio 12.9:1
International faculty 6%
Undergraduates 11,450
Postgraduates 3,220
International students 4.4%

World rank ...... 401-500 (501+)
Subject area positions
Arts & humanities 260

Ateneo de Manila University

Founded 1859

Quezon City 1108

www.admu.edu.ph

Academic survey position... 155
Employer survey position.... 76
Student faculty ratio 16:1
International faculty 6.4%
Undergraduates 7,687
Postgraduates 2,069
International students 4.5%

World rank ...... 254= (401-500)
Subject area positions
Arts & humanities 79
Natural sciences 121
Social sciences 163

University of the Philippines

Founded 1908

Quezon City 1101

www.up.edu.ph

Academic survey position... 161
Employer survey position...... 82
Student faculty ratio 19.3:1
International faculty 4.0%
International students 5%

World rank .... 276= (398=)
Subject area positions
Arts & humanities 82
Life sciences & biomedicine 266
Natural sciences 153
Social sciences 143

University of Santo Tomas

Founded 1611

Manila 1008

www.ust.edu.ph

Academic survey position... 385
Employer survey position.... 117
Student faculty ratio 21.8:1
International faculty 1%
Undergraduates 30,809
Postgraduates 4,114
International students 1.6%

World rank ...... 401-500 (501+)
Subject area positions
Arts & humanities 188

Poland

Jagiellonian University

Founded 1364

31-007 Krakow

www.uj.edu.pl

Academic survey position... 254
Employer survey position.... 314
Student faculty ratio 10.5:1
International faculty.........2.0%
Undergraduates.............. 9,441
Postgraduates............... 27,844
International students 4.3%

World rank ....300= (331=)
Subject area positions
Arts & humanities.............. 117
Natural sciences................ 167

Warsaw University

Founded 1816

00-927 Warszawa

www.uw.edu.pl

Academic survey position... 237
Employer survey position.... 163
Student faculty ratio 23:1
International faculty.........3.1%
Undergraduates.......... 39,982*
Postgraduates............. 20,288*
International students 1.2%

World rank ....342= (345=)
Subject area positions
Arts & humanities.............. 140
Natural sciences................ 152
Social sciences 299

Warsaw University of Technology

Founded 1826

00-661 Warszawa

www.pw.edu.pl

Academic survey position... 388
Employer survey position.... 144
Student faculty ratio 12.6:1
International faculty............4%
International students 7%

World rank ......401-500 (371=)
Subject area positions
Engineering & IT 157

Portugal

University of Coimbra

Founded 1290

3004-531 Coimbra

www.uc.pt

Academic survey position... 242
Employer survey position.... 126
Student faculty ratio 17.2:1
International faculty.........4.2%
Undergraduates............ 11,831
Postgraduates................. 8,048
International students 3.2%

World rank ....387= (319=)
Subject area positions
Arts & humanities.............. 138
Engineering & IT 243
Life sciences & biomedicine 271
Natural sciences................ 281
Social sciences 284

Universidade Nova de Lisboa

Founded 1973

1099-085 Lisboa

www.unl.pt

Academic survey position... 345
Employer survey position.... 126
Student faculty ratio 12.6:1
International faculty.........8.3%
Undergraduates............ 12,175
Postgraduates................. 2,025
International students 9.4%

World rank ......401-500 (341=)
Subject area positions
Arts & humanities.............. 245

Universidade Catolica Portuguesa, Lisboa

Founded 1967

1649-023 Lisboa

www.ucp.pt

Academic survey position... 385
Employer survey position.... 126
Student faculty ratio 10.3:1
International faculty.........4.5%
International students 5.7%

World rank .401-500 (401-500)
Subject area positions
Engineering & IT 297

Russia

Lomonosov Moscow State University

Founded 1755

Moscow 119992

www.msu.ru

Academic survey position..... 88
Employer survey position.... 141
Student faculty ratio 13.6:1
International faculty 5%
Undergraduates 36,923*
Postgraduates 6,288*
International students 4.5%

World rank .... 183= (231=)
Subject area positions
Arts & humanities 166
Engineering & IT 104
Life sciences & biomedicine 132
Natural sciences 29
Social sciences 207

Novosibirsk State University

Founded 1959

Novosibirsk 630090

www.nsu.ru

Academic survey position... 321
Employer survey position.... 126
Student faculty ratio 13.2:1
International faculty 4.2%
International students 4.9%

World rank .401-500 (401-500)
Subject area positions
Engineering & IT 256
Natural sciences 172

Saint-Petersburg State University

Founded 1930

St.Petersburg 199034

www.spbu.ru

Academic survey position... 181
Employer survey position.... 223
Student faculty ratio 8.3:1
International faculty 4%
International students 0%

World rank ....224= (239=)
Subject area positions
Arts & humanities 191
Engineering & IT 186
Life sciences & biomedicine 237
Natural sciences 81
Social sciences 284

Tomsk State University

Founded 1888

Tomsk 634050

www.tsu.ru

Academic survey position... 385
Employer survey position.... 126
Student faculty ratio 5.9:1
International faculty 1%
International students 1%

World rank .401-500 (401-500)
Subject area positions
Engineering & IT 297

Saudi Arabia

King Fahd University of Petroleum & Minerals

Founded 1963

Dhahran 31261

www.kfupm.edu.sa

Academic survey position... 385
Employer survey position.... 126
Student faculty ratio 7.9:1
International faculty 67.3%
Undergraduates 6,523
Postgraduates 458
International students 10.4%

World rank .... 338=
Subject area positions
Engineering & IT 297

Singapore

Nanyang Technological University

Founded 1955

Singapore 639798

www.ntu.edu.sg

Academic survey position..... 68
Employer survey position...... 79
Student faculty ratio 12.1:1
International faculty 54.2%
Undergraduates 20,493
Postgraduates 5,270
International students 34.2%

World rank 77 (69)
Subject area positions
Arts & humanities 193
Engineering & IT 26
Life sciences & biomedicine.. 78
Natural sciences 110
Social sciences 89

Singapore continued

National University of Singapore (NUS)

Founded 1905

Singapore 119077

www.nus.edu.sg

Academic survey position..... 18
Employer survey position...... 26
Student faculty ratio 13.8:1
International faculty.......51.8%
Undergraduates............ 22,776
Postgraduates................. 5,196
International students 34.9%

World rank .... 30= (33=)
Subject area positions
Arts & humanities................ 30
Engineering & IT 11
Life sciences & biomedicine.. 17
Natural sciences.................. 31
Social sciences 18

Slovenia

University of Ljubljana

Founded 1919

Ljubljana 1000

www.uni-lj.si

Academic survey position... 338
Employer survey position.... 126
Student faculty ratio 11:1
International faculty.........3.9%
Undergraduates............ 39,775
Postgraduates................. 4,881
International students 2.1%

World rank .401-500 (401-500)
Subject area positions
Engineering & IT 288

South Africa

University of Cape Town

Founded 1829

Rondebosch 7701

www.uct.ac.za

Academic survey position... 180
Employer survey position.... 169
Student faculty ratio 28:1
International faculty.......28.9%
Undergraduates.......... 13,372*
Postgraduates............... 4,981*
International students 19.4%

World rank .... 179 (200=)
Subject area positions
Arts & humanities.............. 171
Engineering & IT 259
Life sciences & biomedicine 148
Natural sciences................. 182
Social sciences 151

University of KwaZulu-Natal

Founded 2004

Pinetown 3605

www.ukzn.ac.za

Academic survey position... 385
Employer survey position.... 126
Student faculty ratio 10:1
International faculty.......11.0%
Undergraduates............ 23,402
Postgraduates................. 5,106
International students 6.1%

World rank .401-500 (401-500)
Subject area positions
Engineering & IT 297

University of the Witwatersrand

Founded 1896

Johannesburg 2050

www.wits.ac.za

Academic survey position... 308
Employer survey position.... 235
Student faculty ratio 14.7:1
International faculty.......20.9%
Undergraduates............ 14,527
Postgraduates................. 3,407
International students 7.8%

World rank .... 319 (282=)
Subject area positions
Arts & humanities.............. 221
Social sciences 248

Spain

University of Barcelona

Founded 1450

8007 Barcelona

www.ub.edu

Academic survey position... 100
Employer survey position.... 240
Student faculty ratio 22.8:1
International faculty.........4.0%
Undergraduates............ 37,282
Postgraduates............... 11,664
International students 8.0%

World rank .... 186= (194)
Subject area positions
Arts & humanities................ 94
Engineering & IT 140
Life sciences & biomedicine 102
Natural sciences.................. 90
Social sciences 175

Spain continued

Universitat Autònoma de Barcelona

Founded 1968

8193 Barcelona

www.uab.es

Academic survey position... 149
Employer survey position.... 359
Student faculty ratio 18.1:1
International faculty 6.7%
Undergraduates 26,852*
International students 4.6%

World rank .... 256= (258)
Subject area positions
Arts & humanities 175
Engineering & IT 202
Life sciences & biomedicine 292
Natural sciences 135
Social sciences 96

Universidad Autónoma de Madrid

Founded 1968

28049 Madrid

www.uam.es

Academic survey position... 229
Employer survey position.... 264
Student faculty ratio 23.9:1
International faculty 7.1%
Undergraduates 26,827
Postgraduates 2,751
International students 5.2%

World rank .... 254= (306)
Subject area positions
Arts & humanities 281
Engineering & IT 297
Natural sciences 122
Social sciences 200

University Complutense Madrid

Founded 1293

28040 Madrid

www.ucm.es

Academic survey position... 138
Employer survey position.... 244
Student faculty ratio 9.1:1
International faculty 7.4%
International students 4.2%

World rank 306 (401-500)
Subject area positions
Arts & humanities 78
Engineering & IT 256
Life sciences & biomedicine 217
Natural sciences 158
Social sciences 133

University of Navarra

Founded 1952

31080 Pamplona

www.unav.es

Academic survey position... 385
Employer survey position.... 304
Student faculty ratio 12.5:1
International faculty 6.7%
Undergraduates 10,558
Postgraduates 4,312*
International students 14.4%

World rank ......401-500 (319=)
Subject area positions
Life sciences & biomedicine 237

Universitat Pompeu Fabra

Founded 1990

8002 Barcelona

www.upf.edu

Academic survey position... 328
Employer survey position.... 126
Student faculty ratio 13.1:1
International faculty 37.2%
Undergraduates 8,462
Postgraduates 1,197
International students 6.2%

World rank .... 342= (339=)
Subject area positions
Arts & humanities 242
Social sciences 81

University of Salamanca

Founded 1218

37008 Salamanca

www.usal.es

Academic survey position... 385
Employer survey position.... 126
Student faculty ratio 19.9:1
International faculty 7.4%
International students 12.6%

World rank .401-500 (401-500)
Subject area positions
Arts & humanities 205

Spain continued

Universitat de València

Founded 1499

46010 València

www.uv.es

Academic survey position... 330
Employer survey position.... 126
Student faculty ratio 25.1:1
International faculty.........1.6%
International students 5.8%

World rank 401-500 (393)
Subject area positions
Arts & humanities 206
Natural sciences................ 274

Sweden

Chalmers University of Technology

Founded 1829

412 96 Göteborg

www.chalmers.se

Academic survey position... 157
Employer survey position.... 271
Student faculty ratio 13.4:1
International faculty.......11.2%
Undergraduates.............. 1,413
Postgraduates................ 6,940
International students 13.2%

World rank .... 162= (197=)
Subject area positions
Engineering & IT 55
Natural sciences................ 77
Social sciences 267

University of Gothenburg

Founded 1891

405 30 Göteborg

www.gu.se

Academic survey position... 246
Employer survey position.... 362
Student faculty ratio 10.4:1
International faculty...........0%
Undergraduates............ 22,000
Postgraduates............... 2,246*
International students 7.8%

World rank .... 258= (276=)
Subject area positions
Arts & humanities 177
Natural sciences................ 244
Social sciences 184

Linköping University

Founded 1969

581 83 LINKÖPING

www.liu.se

Academic survey position... 391
Employer survey position.... 126
Student faculty ratio 13.9:1
International faculty...........0%
Undergraduates............ 17,200
Postgraduates.................... 807
International students 6.5%

World rank ......401-500 (371=)
Subject area positions
Engineering & IT 137

Lund University

Founded 1666

221 00 Lund

www.lu.se

Academic survey position..... 85
Employer survey position.... 160
Student faculty ratio 12.5:1
International faculty.......20.5%
Undergraduates............ 21,044
Postgraduates................ 5,703
International students 11.4%

World rank 88 (106)
Subject area positions
Arts & humanities 96
Engineering & IT 126
Life sciences & biomedicine 119
Natural sciences.................. 74
Social sciences 77

KTH, Royal Institute of Technology

Founded 1827

100 44 Stockholm

www.kth.se

Academic survey position... 188
Employer survey position.... 198
Student faculty ratio 12.1:1
International faculty.......21.2%
Undergraduates.............. 2,488
Postgraduates............... 11,335
International students 30.6%

World rank .... 173 (192=)
Subject area positions
Engineering & IT 54
Natural sciences.................. 96

Sweden continued

Stockholm University

Founded 1878

106 91 Stockholm

www.su.se

Academic survey position... 175
Employer survey position.... 330
Student faculty ratio 20.4:1
International faculty.......32.0%
Undergraduates............ 25,000
Postgraduates............... 1,532*
International students 4.1%

World rank ....239= (246=)
Subject area positions
Arts & humanities 109
Life sciences & biomedicine 171
Natural sciences................ 215
Social sciences 116

Stockholm School of Economics

Founded 1909

113 83 Stockholm

www.hhs.se

Academic survey position... 385
Employer survey position...... 63
Student faculty ratio 16.4:1
International faculty.......25.6%
International students 24.1%

World rank .... 280 (273=)
Subject area positions
Social sciences 62

Umeå University

Founded 1965

SE-901 87 Umeå

www.umu.se

Academic survey position... 399
Employer survey position.... 126
Student faculty ratio 11.4:1
International faculty.......26.4%
International students 10.4%

World rank 299 (299)
Subject area positions
Life sciences & biomedicine 198

Uppsala University

Founded 1477

751 05 Uppsala

www.uu.se

Academic survey position..... 52
Employer survey position.... 193
Student faculty ratio 12.9:1
International faculty.......21.1%
Undergraduates............ 16,797
Postgraduates................. 6,789
International students 8.6%

World rank .... 63 (71=)
Subject area positions
Arts & humanities 47
Engineering & IT 149
Life sciences & biomedicine.. 38
Natural sciences................... 64
Social sciences 80

Switzerland

University of Basel

Founded 1460

4003 Basel

www.unibas.ch

Academic survey position... 177
Employer survey position.... 387
Student faculty ratio 5.2:1
International faculty.......27.9%
Undergraduates.............. 6,911
Postgraduates................. 3,859
International students 18.8%

World rank .... 131 (114=)
Subject area positions
Arts & humanities 91
Life sciences & biomedicine 105
Natural sciences................. 229
Social sciences 221

University of Bern

Founded 1834

3012 Bern

www.unibe.ch

Academic survey position... 309
Employer survey position.... 126
Student faculty ratio 10.2:1
International faculty.......34.5%
Undergraduates.............. 6,594
Postgraduates................. 6,498
International students 9.5%

World rank .... 192= (214)
Subject area positions
Arts & humanities 242
Life sciences & biomedicine 296
Social sciences 276

Switzerland continued

ETH Zürich (Swiss Federal Institute of Technology)

Founded 1855

8092 Zürich

www.ethz.ch

Academic survey position..... 38
Employer survey position.... 106
Student faculty ratio 10.6:1
International faculty 54.7%
Undergraduates 7,161
Postgraduates 6,838
International students 25.9%

World rank 24 (42)
Subject area positions
Arts & humanities 202
Engineering & IT 13
Life sciences & biomedicine.. 67
Natural sciences 15
Social sciences 160

University of Geneva

Founded 1559

1211 Genève 4

www.unige.ch

Academic survey position... 129
Employer survey position.... 355
Student faculty ratio 10.4:1
International faculty 40.2%
Undergraduates 6,138
Postgraduates 4,378
International students 35.5%

World rank 68 (105)
Subject area positions
Arts & humanities 97
Engineering & IT 288
Life sciences & biomedicine 120
Natural sciences 130
Social sciences 146

Ecole Polytechnique Fédérale de Lausanne

Founded 1853

1015 Lausanne

www.epfl.ch

Academic survey position... 163
Employer survey position.... 145
Student faculty ratio 6.2:1
International faculty 63.2%
Undergraduates 3,238
Postgraduates 2,925
International students 41.5%

World rank .... 50= (117=)
Subject area positions
Engineering & IT 44
Natural sciences 76

University of Lausanne

Founded 1537

1015 Lausanne

www.unil.ch

Academic survey position... 259
Employer survey position.... 248
Student faculty ratio 13.3:1
International faculty 28.2%
Undergraduates 5,381
Postgraduates 5,185
International students 19.3%

World rank 161 (217)
Subject area positions
Arts & humanities 263
Engineering & IT 281
Life sciences & biomedicine 252
Natural sciences 282
Social sciences 183

University of St Gallen (HSG)

Founded 1898

9000 St Gallen

www.unisg.ch

Academic survey position... 385
Employer survey position...... 69
Student faculty ratio 19:1
International faculty 56.1%
Undergraduates 2,663*
Postgraduates 2,252*
International students 31.1%

World rank .... 325= (362=)
Subject area positions
Social sciences 125

University of Zürich

Founded 1833

8001 Zürich

www.uzh.ch

Academic survey position... 106
Employer survey position.... 340
Student faculty ratio 21.4:1
International faculty 48.0%
Undergraduates 7,405*
Postgraduates 16,826*
International students 15.3%

World rank .... 106= (140=)
Subject area positions
Arts & humanities 104
Engineering & IT 194
Life sciences & biomedicine.. 82
Natural sciences 113
Social sciences 105

Taiwan

National Central University

Founded 1962

Jhongli Taoyuan County 32001

www.ncu.edu.tw

Academic survey position... 381
Employer survey position.... 126
Student faculty ratio 15.5:1
International faculty 3.6%
Undergraduates 5,743
Postgraduates 5,045
International students 1.8%

World rank ......401-500 (398=)
Subject area positions
Natural sciences 276

National Cheng Kung University

Founded 1931

Tainan 70101

www.ncku.edu.tw

Academic survey position... 366
Employer survey position.... 288
Student faculty ratio 12:1
International faculty 4.7%
Undergraduates 10,476
Postgraduates 10,391
International students 3.4%

World rank .... 354= (336=)
Subject area positions
Engineering & IT 214

National Chiao Tung University

Founded 1896

Hsinchu 300

www.nctu.edu.tw

Academic survey position... 385
Employer survey position.... 332
Student faculty ratio 15.8:1
International faculty 2.5%
Undergraduates 5,009
Postgraduates 8,681
International students 3.2%

World rank .401-500 (401-500)
Subject area positions
Engineering & IT 206

National Sun Yat-sen University

Founded 1980

Kaohsiung 80424

www.nsysu.edu.tw

Academic survey position... 385
Employer survey position.... 126
Student faculty ratio 19.8:1
International faculty 9.0%
Undergraduates 4,120
Postgraduates 5,546
International students 2.4%

World rank .401-500 (401-500)
Subject area positions
Social sciences 263

National Taiwan University

Founded 1928

Taipei 10617

www.ntu.edu.tw

Academic survey position..... 66
Employer survey position.... 134
Student faculty ratio 13.6:1
International faculty 7.1%
Undergraduates 17,273
Postgraduates 15,029
International students 4.4%

World rank .... 124= (102=)
Subject area positions
Arts & humanities 152
Engineering & IT 49
Life sciences & biomedicine.. 84
Natural sciences 50
Social sciences 74

National Taiwan University of Science and Technology

Founded 1974

Taipei 106

www.ntust.edu.tw

Academic survey position... 385
Employer survey position.... 244
Student faculty ratio 14.6:1
International faculty 4.4%
Undergraduates 4,842
Postgraduates 3,408
International students 2.9%

World rank .401-500 (401-500)
Subject area positions
Engineering & IT 189
Life sciences & biomedicine 277

Taiwan continued

National Tsing Hua University

Founded 1955

Hsinchu 30013

www.nthu.edu.tw

Academic survey position... 247	World rank 281 (334)
Employer survey position.... 311	Subject area positions
Student faculty ratio 16.3:1	Engineering & IT 114
International faculty 7.3%	Natural sciences 139
Undergraduates 5,347	
Postgraduates 5,826	
International students 3.2%	

National Yang Ming University

Founded 1975

Taipei 112

www.ym.edu.tw

Academic survey position... 385	World rank 341 (401-500)
Employer survey position.... 126	Subject area positions
Student faculty ratio 4.7:1	Engineering & IT 297
International faculty 4.0%	
Undergraduates 1,836	
Postgraduates 2,196	
International students 3.5%	

Thailand

Chiang Mai University

Founded 1964

Chiang Mai 50200

www.chiangmai.ac.th

Academic survey position... 316	World rank .401-500 (401-500)
Employer survey position.... 364	Subject area positions
Student faculty ratio 16.1:1	Arts & humanities 270
International faculty 8.0%	Natural sciences 283
Undergraduates 24,422*	
Postgraduates 6,775*	
International students 6%	

Chulalongkorn University

Founded 1917

Bangkok 10330

www.chula.ac.th

Academic survey position..... 93	World rank .... 166= (223)
Employer survey position.... 121	Subject area positions
Student faculty ratio 10.2:1	Arts & humanities 119
International faculty 3.6%	Engineering & IT 86
Undergraduates 22,063	Life sciences & biomedicine 108
Postgraduates 13,538	Natural sciences 171
International students 8%	Social sciences 72

Kasetsart University

Founded 1943

Bangkok 10900

www.ku.ac.th

Academic survey position... 383	World rank ...... 400= (401-500)
Employer survey position.... 223	Subject area positions
Student faculty ratio 11.4:1	Life sciences & biomedicine 266
International faculty 9.0%	
International students 4%	

Mahidol University

Founded 1943

Nakhon Pathom Province 73170

www.mahidol.ac.th

Academic survey position... 278	World rank .... 251 (284=)
Employer survey position.... 202	Subject area positions
Student faculty ratio 7.5:1	Life sciences & biomedicine 113
International faculty 6.3%	Natural sciences 270
Undergraduates 15,771	
Postgraduates 8,770	
International students 2.5%	

Thailand continued

Thammasat University

Founded 1934

Bangkok 10200

www.tu.ac.th

Academic survey position... 340
Employer survey position.... 219
Student faculty ratio 12.9:1
International faculty 1.2%
International students 7%

World rank .401-500 (401-500)
Subject area positions
Arts & humanities 232
Social sciences 199

Turkey

Bilkent University

Founded 1984

Bilkent Ankara 6800

www.bilkent.edu.tr

Academic survey position... 315
Employer survey position.... 126
Student faculty ratio 11.7:1
International faculty 28.2%
International students 1.0%

World rank 374 (401-500)
Subject area positions
Arts & humanities 275
Engineering & IT 230
Natural sciences 285

Istanbul Technical University

Founded 1773

Maslak-Istanbul

www.itu.edu.tr

Academic survey position... 329
Employer survey position.... 392
Student faculty ratio 11.4:1
International faculty 12.5%
International students 0%

World rank .... 376= (390)
Subject area positions
Engineering & IT 133
Natural sciences 257

Istanbul University

Founded 1453

Eminonu-Istanbul

www.istanbul.edu.tr

Academic survey position... 342
Employer survey position.... 126
Student faculty ratio 11.7:1
International faculty 5%
International students 3.2%

World rank .401-500 (401-500)
Subject area positions
Arts & humanities 281
Social sciences 284

Koç University

Founded 1993

Istanbul 34450

www.ku.edu.tr

Academic survey position... 385
Employer survey position.... 332
Student faculty ratio 13.3:1
International faculty 29.1%
Undergraduates 3,146
Postgraduates 384
International students 1.0%

World rank 401-500
Subject area positions
Engineering & IT 297

Sabanci University

Founded 1994

Istanbul 34956

www.sabanciuniv.edu

Academic survey position... 385
Employer survey position.... 126
Student faculty ratio 13.7:1
International faculty 14.2%
Undergraduates 2,899
Postgraduates 577
International students 7%

World rank .401-500 (401-500)
Subject area positions
Engineering & IT 297

United Arab Emirates

United Arab Emirates University

Founded 1976

Al-Ain

www.uaeu.ac.ae

Academic survey position... 385	World rank 401-500
Employer survey position.... 126	Subject area positions
Student faculty ratio 11.4:1	Engineering & IT 297
International faculty 77.4%	
Undergraduates............ 12,130	
Postgraduates.................... 185	
International students 17.2%	

United Kingdom

University of Aberdeen

Founded 1495

Aberdeen AB24 3FX

www.abdn.ac.uk

Academic survey position... 286	World rank .... 153 (137=)
Employer survey position.... 141	Subject area positions
Student faculty ratio 8.1:1	Life sciences & biomedicine 155
International faculty 32.6%	Social sciences 273
Undergraduates.............. 8,944	
Postgraduates................. 2,209	
International students 18.7%	

Aberystwyth University

Founded 1872

Aberystwyth
Ceredigion SY23 2AX

www.aber.ac.uk/smba/
en

Academic survey position... 385	World rank .401-500 (401-500)
Employer survey position.... 126	Subject area positions
Student faculty ratio 15.7:1	Arts & humanities 230
International faculty 18.7%	
Undergraduates.............. 6,368	
Postgraduates................. 1,213	
International students 12.5%	

Aston University

Founded 1895

Birmingham B4 7ET

www.aston.ac.uk

Academic survey position... 385	World rank .... 316= (266)
Employer survey position.... 115	Subject area positions
Student faculty ratio 24.8:1	Engineering & IT 297
International faculty 28.5%	
Undergraduates.............. 6,803	
Postgraduates................. 1,117	
International students 16.2%	

Bangor University

Founded 1884

Bangor, Gwynedd LL57 2DG

www.bangor.ac.uk

Academic survey position... 385	World rank ...... 400= (401-500)
Employer survey position.... 126	Subject area positions
Student faculty ratio 13.2:1	Life sciences & biomedicine 254
International faculty 20.5%	
Undergraduates.............. 6,400	
Postgraduates................. 1,525	
International students 11.0%	

University of Bath

Founded 1966

Bath BA2 7AY

www.bath.ac.uk

Academic survey position... 249	World rank 152 (145)
Employer survey position...... 28	Subject area positions
Student faculty ratio 12.2:1	Arts & humanities 278
International faculty 33.4%	Engineering & IT 239
Undergraduates.............. 8,745	Life sciences & biomedicine 215
Postgraduates................. 2,498	Natural sciences................. 244
International students 24.9%	Social sciences 234

United Kingdom continued

University of Birmingham

Founded 1900

Birmingham B15 2TT

www.bham.ac.uk

Academic survey position... 115
Employer survey position...... 53
Student faculty ratio 10.5:1
International faculty 26.4%
Undergraduates 17,373
Postgraduates 6,338
International students 16.2%

World rank .... 75 (65=)
Subject area positions
Arts & humanities 134
Engineering & IT 98
Life sciences & biomedicine.. 99
Natural sciences 192
Social sciences 126

University of Bradford

Founded 1966

Bradford BD7 1DP

www.bradford.ac.uk

Academic survey position... 385
Employer survey position.... 297
Student faculty ratio 16.7:1
International faculty 25.7%
Undergraduates 7,934
Postgraduates 1,990
International students 27.4%

World rank .... 391= (349)
Subject area positions
Life sciences & biomedicine 278

University of Bristol

Founded 1876

Bristol BS8 1TH

www.bris.ac.uk

Academic survey position..... 83
Employer survey position...... 16
Student faculty ratio 7.6:1
International faculty 28.2%
Undergraduates 12,451
Postgraduates 3,674
International students 16.9%

World rank 32 (37)
Subject area positions
Arts & humanities 90
Engineering & IT 131
Life sciences & biomedicine.. 46
Natural sciences 89
Social sciences 150

Brunel University

Founded 1966

Middlesex
London UB8 3PH

www.brunel.ac.uk

Academic survey position... 384
Employer survey position.... 124
Student faculty ratio 14.7:1
International faculty 34.1%
Undergraduates 9,942
Postgraduates 2,797
International students 19.8%

World rank ....296= (292=)
Subject area positions
Engineering & IT 297

University of Cambridge

Founded 1209

Cambridge CB2 1TN

www.cam.ac.uk

Academic survey position....... 3
Employer survey position........ 1
Student faculty ratio 4.7:1
International faculty 41.4%
Undergraduates 12,300
Postgraduates 6,253
International students 26.7%

World rank .... 3 (2=)
Subject area positions
Arts & humanities 4
Engineering & IT 5
Life sciences & biomedicine.... 2
Natural sciences 3
Social sciences 5

Cardiff University

Founded 1883

Cardiff
Wales CF10 3XQ

www.cf.ac.uk

Academic survey position... 179
Employer survey position...... 70
Student faculty ratio 9.3:1
International faculty 21.7%
Undergraduates 16,632
Postgraduates 6,244
International students 17.9%

World rank .... 133= (99)
Subject area positions
Arts & humanities 158
Engineering & IT 214
Life sciences & biomedicine.. 94
Social sciences 163

United Kingdom continued

University of Dundee

Founded 1881

Dundee
Scotland DD1 4HN

www.dundee.ac.uk

Academic survey position... 318
Employer survey position.... 345
Student faculty ratio 9.4:1
International faculty 26.9%
Undergraduates.............. 9,479
Postgraduates................. 2,735
International students 13.7%

World rank .... 213 (171=)
Subject area positions
Life sciences & biomedicine 108

Durham University

Founded 1832

Durham
County Durham DH1 3HP

www.durham.ac.uk

Academic survey position... 187
Employer survey position...... 22
Student faculty ratio 11.5:1
International faculty 27.4%
Undergraduates............ 11,593
Postgraduates................. 2,687
International students 13.8%

World rank .... 122= (109)
Subject area positions
Arts & humanities 125
Life sciences & biomedicine 218
Natural sciences................. 189
Social sciences 148

University of East Anglia (UEA)

Founded 1963

Norwich
Norfolk NR4 7TJ

www.uea.ac.uk

Academic survey position... 385
Employer survey position.... 372
Student faculty ratio 10.6:1
International faculty 23.1%
Undergraduates.............. 7,644
Postgraduates................. 3,004
International students 19.0%

World rank .... 309= (356=)
Subject area positions
Arts & humanities 227

University of Edinburgh

Founded 1582

Edinburgh EH8 9YL

www.ed.ac.uk

Academic survey position..... 36
Employer survey position...... 19
Student faculty ratio 7.5:1
International faculty 32.6%
Undergraduates............ 15,764
Postgraduates................. 4,936
International students 19.3%

World rank 23 (23)
Subject area positions
Arts & humanities 26
Engineering & IT 60
Life sciences & biomedicine.. 32
Natural sciences................... 82
Social sciences 54

University of Essex

Founded 1965

Colchester
Essex CO4 3SQ

www.essex.ac.uk

Academic survey position... 298
Employer survey position.... 387
Student faculty ratio 11.2:1
International faculty 42.2%
Undergraduates.............. 5,532
Postgraduates................. 1,859
International students 33.4%

World rank .... 258= (272)
Subject area positions
Arts & humanities 263
Life sciences & biomedicine 296
Social sciences 123

University of Exeter

Founded 1955

Exeter
Devon EX4 4QJ

www.ex.ac.uk

Academic survey position... 316
Employer survey position.... 105
Student faculty ratio 12.9:1
International faculty 27.9%
Undergraduates.............. 9,152
Postgraduates................. 2,696
International students 15.3%

World rank .... 237= (220)
Subject area positions
Arts & humanities 163
Life sciences & biomedicine 289

United Kingdom continued

University of Glasgow

Founded 1451

Glasgow G12 8QQ

www.gla.ac.uk

Academic survey position... 124
Employer survey position.... 115
Student faculty ratio 9.2:1
International faculty 36.4%
Undergraduates 15,346
Postgraduates 3,947
International students 13.1%

World rank 73 (83)
Subject area positions
Arts & humanities 153
Engineering & IT 152
Life sciences & biomedicine.. 74
Natural sciences 145
Social sciences 180

Goldsmiths, University of London

Founded 1891

London SE14 6NW

www.goldsmiths.ac.uk

Academic survey position... 357
Employer survey position.... 126
Student faculty ratio 16.9:1
International faculty 25.1%
Undergraduates 4,215
Postgraduates 2,243
International students 21.7%

World rank ...... 394= (401-500)
Subject area positions
Arts & humanities 105
Social sciences 271

Heriot-Watt University

Founded 1821

Edinburgh EH14 4AS

www.hw.ac.uk

Academic survey position... 385
Employer survey position.... 352
Student faculty ratio 16.2:1
International faculty 31.9%
Undergraduates 5,107
Postgraduates 2,199
International students 30.9%

World rank ...... 401-500 (501+)
Subject area positions
Engineering & IT 297

University of Hull

Founded 1954

Hull HU6 7RX

www.hull.ac.uk

Academic survey position... 385
Employer survey position.... 126
Student faculty ratio 16.7:1
International faculty 22.0%
Undergraduates 12,309
Postgraduates 1,485
International students 13.9%

World rank . 401-500 (401-500)
Subject area positions
Engineering & IT 297

Imperial College London

Founded 1907

London SW7 2AZ

www3.imperial.ac.uk

Academic survey position..... 25
Employer survey position........ 5
Student faculty ratio 4.2:1
International faculty 41.9%
Undergraduates 8,205
Postgraduates 4,410
International students 39.6%

World rank 6 (5)
Subject area positions
Arts & humanities 208
Engineering & IT 7
Life sciences & biomedicine.. 11
Natural sciences 14
Social sciences 85

University of Kent

Founded 1965

Canterbury
Kent CT2 7NZ

www.kent.ac.uk/
international

Academic survey position... 385
Employer survey position.... 317
Student faculty ratio 14.6:1
International faculty 31.2%
Undergraduates 12,111
Postgraduates 1,513
International students 18.4%

World rank . 401-500 (401-500)
Subject area positions
Engineering & IT 297

United Kingdom continued

King's College London

Founded 1829

London WC2R 2LS

www.kcl.ac.uk

Academic survey position..... 46
Employer survey position...... 26
Student faculty ratio 6.8:1
International faculty 32.5%
Undergraduates 12,075
Postgraduates 5,114
International students 20.6%

World rank 22 (24)
Subject area positions
Arts & humanities 38
Engineering & IT 129
Life sciences & biomedicine.. 34
Natural sciences 107
Social sciences 48

Lancaster University

Founded 1964

Lancaster
Lancashire LA1 4YW

www.lancs.ac.uk

Academic survey position... 232
Employer survey position.... 120
Student faculty ratio 10.1:1
International faculty 31.7%
Undergraduates 8,317
Postgraduates 2,117
International students 18.8%

World rank .... 170= (147)
Subject area positions
Arts & humanities 133
Life sciences & biomedicine 271
Social sciences 97

University of Leeds

Founded 1831

Leeds LS2 9JT

www.leeds.ac.uk

Academic survey position... 120
Employer survey position...... 30
Student faculty ratio 10.5:1
International faculty 21.6%
Undergraduates 21,285
Postgraduates 4,942
International students 14.1%

World rank .... 104 (80=)
Subject area positions
Arts & humanities 77
Engineering & IT 138
Life sciences & biomedicine 157
Natural sciences 178
Social sciences 155

University of Leicester

Founded 1921

Leicester LE1 7RH

www.le.ac.uk

Academic survey position... 332
Employer survey position... 197
Student faculty ratio 9.6:1
International faculty 24.2%
Undergraduates 8,270
Postgraduates 3,452
International students 26.1%

World rank .... 177= (185=)
Subject area positions
Arts & humanities 242
Social sciences 251

University of Liverpool

Founded 1881

Liverpool L69 3BX

www.liv.ac.uk

Academic survey position... 221
Employer survey position.... 109
Student faculty ratio 9:1
International faculty 25.8%
Undergraduates 13,784
Postgraduates 2,683
International students 14.9%

World rank .... 133= (101)
Subject area positions
Arts & humanities 184
Engineering & IT 206
Life sciences & biomedicine 167
Natural sciences 243

London School of Economics and Political Science (LSE)

Founded 1895

London WC2A 2AE

www.lse.ac.uk

Academic survey position..... 60
Employer survey position........ 3
Student faculty ratio 10.2:1
International faculty 54.5%
Undergraduates 3,786
Postgraduates 4,446
International students 66.8%

World rank 66 (59)
Subject area positions
Arts & humanities 31
Life sciences & biomedicine 264
Natural sciences 265
Social sciences 4

United Kingdom continued

SOAS - School of Oriental and African Studies, University of London

Founded 1916

London WC1H 0XG

www.soas.ac.uk

Academic survey position... 301
Employer survey position.... 177
Student faculty ratio 11:1
International faculty 47.8%
Undergraduates.............. 2,352
Postgraduates................. 1,409
International students 50.3%

World rank .... 253 (243=)
Subject area positions
Arts & humanities 60
Social sciences 120

Loughborough University

Founded 1909

Leicestershire LE11 3TU

www.lboro.ac.uk

Academic survey position... 291
Employer survey position...... 73
Student faculty ratio 12.2:1
International faculty 28.8%
Undergraduates............ 10,523
Postgraduates................. 2,839
International students 19.1%

World rank .... 230= (237=)
Subject area positions
Engineering & IT 176
Life sciences & biomedicine 187
Social sciences 250

University of Manchester

Founded 1824

Manchester M13 9PL

www.manchester.ac.uk

Academic survey position..... 51
Employer survey position........ 7
Student faculty ratio 7.6:1
International faculty 32.7%
Undergraduates............ 23,029
Postgraduates................. 5,658
International students 20.1%

World rank 29 (30)
Subject area positions
Arts & humanities 66
Engineering & IT 45
Life sciences & biomedicine.. 57
Natural sciences................. 111
Social sciences 66

Newcastle University, Newcastle Upon Tyne

Founded 1963

Newcastle upon Tyne NE1 7RU

www.ncl.ac.uk

Academic survey position... 312
Employer survey position...... 75
Student faculty ratio 9.1:1
International faculty 26.6%
Undergraduates............ 13,687
Postgraduates................. 3,468
International students 18.5%

World rank .... 162= (129)
Subject area positions
Engineering & IT 266
Life sciences & biomedicine 213

University of Nottingham

Founded 1798

Nottingham NG7 2RD

www.nottingham.ac.uk

Academic survey position... 122
Employer survey position...... 24
Student faculty ratio 9.6:1
International faculty 31.8%
Undergraduates............ 20,725
Postgraduates................. 5,055
International students 22.4%

World rank 86 (70)
Subject area positions
Arts & humanities 128
Engineering & IT 140
Life sciences & biomedicine.. 92
Natural sciences................. 192
Social sciences 137

The Open University

Founded 1969

Milton Keynes MK7 6AA

www.open.ac.uk

Academic survey position... 292
Employer survey position.... 126
Student faculty ratio 24.5:1
International faculty 14.6%
Undergraduates............ 61,543
Postgraduates................. 4,684
International students 1%

World rank ......401-500 (501+)
Subject area positions
Arts & humanities 125
Social sciences 172

United Kingdom continued

University of Oxford

Founded 12th century

Oxford OX1 2JD

www.ox.ac.uk

Academic survey position....... 6	World rank .... 4 (2=)
Employer survey position........ 2	Subject area positions
Student faculty ratio 4.5:1	Arts & humanities 3
International faculty 38.1%	Engineering & IT 14
Undergraduates............ 12,173	Life sciences & biomedicine.... 5
Postgraduates................. 6,723	Natural sciences.................... 5
International students 27.8%	Social sciences 6

Queen Mary, University of London

Founded 1887

London E1 4NS

www.qmul.ac.uk

Academic survey position... 211	World rank .... 160 (149=)
Employer survey position.... 172	Subject area positions
Student faculty ratio 8.2:1	Arts & humanities 231
International faculty 38.7%	Engineering & IT 242
Undergraduates.............. 9,142	Life sciences & biomedicine 143
Postgraduates................. 2,388	Natural sciences................. 227
International students 23.9%	Social sciences 221

Queen's University of Belfast

Founded 1849

Belfast
Northern Ireland BT7 1NN

www.qub.ac.uk

Academic survey position... 293	World rank .... 202 (205=)
Employer survey position.... 102	Subject area positions
Student faculty ratio 10.3:1	Arts & humanities 245
International faculty 39.6%	Engineering & IT 279
Undergraduates............ 13,233	Natural sciences................. 270
Postgraduates................. 2,919	
International students 10.2%	

University of Reading

Founded 1892

Reading
Berkshire RG6 6AH

www.reading.ac.uk

Academic survey position... 280	World rank .... 194 (180=)
Employer survey position.... 126	Subject area positions
Student faculty ratio 10.7:1	Arts & humanities 206
International faculty 25.6%	Engineering & IT 277
Undergraduates.............. 8,969	Natural sciences................. 264
Postgraduates................. 2,694	
International students 17.6%	

Royal Holloway, University of London

Founded 1849

Egham
Surrey TW20 0EX

www.rhul.ac.uk

Academic survey position... 385	World rank 311 (401-500)
Employer survey position.... 126	Subject area positions
Student faculty ratio 12.1:1	Arts & humanities 184
International faculty 34.3%	
Undergraduates.............. 5,751	
Postgraduates................. 1,840	
International students 31.4%	

University of Sheffield

Founded 1897

Sheffield S10 2TN

www.shef.ac.uk

Academic survey position... 130	World rank 76 (68)
Employer survey position...... 38	Subject area positions
Student faculty ratio 9.1:1	Arts & humanities 140
International faculty 26.1%	Engineering & IT 122
Undergraduates............ 17,172	Life sciences & biomedicine 110
Postgraduates................. 4,517	Natural sciences................. 211
International students 16.3%	Social sciences 155

United Kingdom continued

University of Southampton

Founded 1862

Southampton SO17 1BJ

www.soton.ac.uk

Academic survey position... 166	World rank .... 99= (80=)
Employer survey position...... 65	Subject area positions
Student faculty ratio 9.9:1	Arts & humanities 229
International faculty 29.6%	Engineering & IT 96
Undergraduates............ 14,873	Life sciences & biomedicine 190
Postgraduates................. 6,599	Natural sciences................. 160
International students 19.7%	Social sciences 229

University of St Andrews

Founded 1413

St Andrews KY16 9AJ

www.st-andrews.ac.uk

Academic survey position... 192	World rank .... 83= (76)
Employer survey position...... 47	Subject area positions
Student faculty ratio 8.5:1	Arts & humanities 71
International faculty 33.1%	Life sciences & biomedicine 201
Undergraduates.............. 6,040	Natural sciences................. 246
Postgraduates................. 1,257	Social sciences 243
International students 31.4%	

University of Strathclyde

Founded 1796

Glasgow G1 1XQ

www.strath.ac.uk

Academic survey position... 333	World rank 270 (252)
Employer survey position...... 85	Subject area positions
Student faculty ratio 12.9:1	Engineering & IT 247
International faculty 30.0%	Social sciences 248
Undergraduates............ 11,836	
Postgraduates................. 4,879	
International students 11.5%	

University of Surrey

Founded 1891

Guildford
Surrey GU2 7XH

www.surrey.ac.uk

Academic survey position... 354	World rank 223 (190)
Employer survey position.... 119	Subject area positions
Student faculty ratio 10.7:1	Engineering & IT 222
International faculty 33.0%	Natural sciences................. 295
Undergraduates.............. 7,439	
Postgraduates................. 2,523	
International students 25.3%	

University of Sussex

Founded 1961

Falmer
East Sussex BN1 9RH

www.sussex.ac.uk

Academic survey position... 184	World rank 130 (121)
Employer survey position.... 235	Subject area positions
Student faculty ratio 11.3:1	Arts & humanities 109
International faculty 33.6%	Engineering & IT 256
Undergraduates.............. 7,423	Life sciences & biomedicine 229
Postgraduates................. 2,333	Natural sciences................. 290
International students 18.5%	Social sciences 102

Swansea University

Founded 1920

Swansea SA2 8PP

www.swan.ac.uk

Academic survey position... 385	World rank ...... 347= (401-500)
Employer survey position.... 248	Subject area positions
Student faculty ratio 12.3:1	Engineering & IT 297
International faculty 24.0%	
Undergraduates.............. 8,831	
Postgraduates................. 1,986	
International students 14.8%	

United Kingdom continued

UCL (University College London)

Founded 1826	Academic survey position..... 34	World rank 7 (9)
	Employer survey position...... 13	Subject area positions
London WC1E 6BT	Student faculty ratio 4.5:1	Arts & humanities 29
	International faculty 38.2%	Engineering & IT 96
www.ucl.ac.uk	Undergraduates............ 11,354	Life sciences & biomedicine.. 25
	Postgraduates................. 6,024	Natural sciences................... 88
	International students 37.7%	Social sciences 31

University of Warwick

Founded 1965	Academic survey position..... 84	World rank 69 (57)
	Employer survey position...... 11	Subject area positions
Coventry CV4 7AL	Student faculty ratio 10.1:1	Arts & humanities 75
	International faculty 33.2%	Engineering & IT 164
www2.warwick.ac.uk	Undergraduates............ 11,925	Life sciences & biomedicine 201
	Postgraduates................. 4,607	Natural sciences................... 85
	International students 28.0%	Social sciences 35

University of York

Founded 1963	Academic survey position... 172	World rank ....81= (74=)
	Employer survey position...... 55	Subject area positions
York YO10 5DD	Student faculty ratio 8.1:1	Arts & humanities 111
	International faculty 37.4%	Engineering & IT 253
www.york.ac.uk	Undergraduates.............. 7,762	Life sciences & biomedicine 150
	Postgraduates................. 2,385	Natural sciences................. 216
	International students 20.1%	Social sciences 187

United States of America

University of Alabama

Founded 1831	Academic survey position... 355	World rank ....354= (282=)
	Employer survey position.... 370	Subject area positions
Tuscaloosa	Student faculty ratio 11.6:1	Life sciences & biomedicine 250
AL 35487	International faculty 4.0%	Natural sciences................. 287
	Undergraduates............ 33,494	
www.ua.edu	Postgraduates................. 8,313	
	International students 4.3%	

University of Arizona

Founded 1885	Academic survey position... 133	World rank 146 (134)
	Employer survey position.... 229	Subject area positions
Tucson	Student faculty ratio 13.1:1	Arts & humanities 102
AZ 85721	International faculty 4.2%	Engineering & IT 185
	Undergraduates............ 26,509	Life sciences & biomedicine 190
www.arizona.edu	Postgraduates................. 6,601	Natural sciences................. 132
	International students 5.8%	Social sciences 143

Arizona State University

Founded 1885	Academic survey position... 189	World rank .... 260 (221=)
	Employer survey position.... 282	Subject area positions
Tempe	Student faculty ratio 21.4:1	Arts & humanities 256
AZ 85287	International faculty 6.6%	Engineering & IT 161
	Undergraduates............ 34,117	Life sciences & biomedicine 193
www.asu.edu	Postgraduates............... 7,600	Natural sciences................. 189
	International students 7.0%	Social sciences 160

United States of America continued

University of California, Berkeley

Founded 1868	Academic survey position....... 1	World rank 36 (22)
	Employer survey position...... 10	Subject area positions
Berkeley	Student faculty ratio 19.5:1	Arts & humanities 2
CA 94720	International faculty 30.4%	Engineering & IT 2
www.berkeley.edu	Undergraduates............ 24,121	Life sciences & biomedicine.... 4
	Postgraduates................. 9,652	Natural sciences 2
	International students 7.4%	Social sciences 2

Boston University

Founded 1839	Academic survey position..... 49	World rank 46 (47)
	Employer survey position...... 89	Subject area positions
Boston	Student faculty ratio 9.3:1	Arts & humanities 49
MA 02215	International faculty 5.1%	Engineering & IT 106
www.bu.edu	Undergraduates............ 17,715	Life sciences & biomedicine.. 43
	Postgraduates.............. 10,162	Natural sciences 98
	International students 13.0%	Social sciences 46

Boston College

Founded 1863	Academic survey position... 385	World rank 401-500
	Employer survey position.... 126	Subject area positions
Boston	Student faculty ratio 15.1:1	Engineering & IT 297
MA 02467	International faculty 7.9%	
www.bc.edu	Undergraduates.............. 9,584	
	Postgraduates................. 3,194	
	International students 5.0%	

Brandeis University

Founded 1948	Academic survey position... 219	World rank 185 (208)
	Employer survey position.... 375	Subject area positions
Waltham	Student faculty ratio 12:1	Arts & humanities 146
MA 02453	International faculty 5.8%	Life sciences & biomedicine.. 97
www.brandeis.edu	Undergraduates.............. 3,222	Natural sciences 222
	Postgraduates................. 1,709	Social sciences 276
	International students 16.8%	

Brigham Young University

Founded 1875	Academic survey position... 398	World rank .401-500 (401-500)
	Employer survey position.... 231	Subject area positions
Provo	Student faculty ratio 21.4:1	Life sciences & biomedicine 252
UT 84602	International faculty 0%	
www.byu.edu	Undergraduates............ 28,854	
	Postgraduates................. 2,396	
	International students 4.7%	

Brown University

Founded 1764	Academic survey position..... 48	World rank 27 (32)
	Employer survey position...... 99	Subject area positions
Providence	Student faculty ratio 9.6:1	Arts & humanities 27
RI 02912	International faculty 15.8%	Engineering & IT 93
www.brown.edu	Undergraduates.............. 5,863	Life sciences & biomedicine.. 50
	Postgraduates................. 2,093	Natural sciences 106
	International students 12.8%	Social sciences 65

United States of America continued

California Institute of Technology (Caltech)

Founded 1891

Pasadena
CA 91125

www.caltech.edu

Academic survey position..... 20
Employer survey position.... 133
Student faculty ratio 5.4:1
International faculty.......85.1%
Undergraduates................. 913
Postgraduates................. 1,220
International students 24.5%

World rank .... 5 (7=)
Subject area positions
Arts & humanities 213
Engineering & IT 4
Life sciences & biomedicine.. 16
Natural sciences.................... 7
Social sciences 78

University of California, Los Angeles (UCLA)

Founded 1919

Los Angeles
CA 90095

www.ucla.edu

Academic survey position..... 10
Employer survey position...... 29
Student faculty ratio 11.8:1
International faculty.........3.5%
Undergraduates............ 25,291
Postgraduates............... 11,367
International students 7.5%

World rank .... 30= (41)
Subject area positions
Arts & humanities 10
Engineering & IT 16
Life sciences & biomedicine.. 11
Natural sciences................... 18
Social sciences 13

University of California, San Diego

Founded 1960

La Jolla
CA 92093

www.ucsd.edu

Academic survey position..... 27
Employer survey position.... 206
Student faculty ratio 14.9:1
International faculty.........2.1%
Undergraduates............ 21,567
Postgraduates................. 4,843
International students 5.6%

World rank 58 (58)
Subject area positions
Arts & humanities 93
Engineering & IT 35
Life sciences & biomedicine.... 9
Natural sciences................... 30
Social sciences 38

University of California, Davis

Founded 1905

Davis
CA 95616

www.ucdavis.edu

Academic survey position..... 80
Employer survey position.... 284
Student faculty ratio 13.1:1
International faculty.........5.8%
Undergraduates............ 22,872
Postgraduates................. 5,914
International students 4.9%

World rank 89 (96)
Subject area positions
Arts & humanities 168
Engineering & IT 107
Life sciences & biomedicine.. 28
Natural sciences................... 95
Social sciences 163

University of California, Santa Barbara

Founded 1909

Santa Barbara
CA 93106-2070

www.ucsb.edu

Academic survey position..... 61
Employer survey position.... 260
Student faculty ratio 21.5:1
International faculty......10.0%
Undergraduates............ 18,112
Postgraduates................. 2,906
International students 3.6%

World rank .... 98 (117=)
Subject area positions
Arts & humanities 169
Engineering & IT 62
Life sciences & biomedicine.. 79
Natural sciences................... 24
Social sciences 152

University of California, Irvine

Founded 1965

Irvine
CA 92616-6050

www.uci.edu

Academic survey position..... 90
Employer survey position.... 126
Student faculty ratio 16.3:1
International faculty.........3.9%
Undergraduates............ 22,435
Postgraduates................. 4,486
International students 5.6%

World rank .... 132 (140=)
Subject area positions
Arts & humanities 84
Engineering & IT 131
Life sciences & biomedicine.. 64
Natural sciences................... 127
Social sciences 135

United States of America continued

University of California, Santa Cruz

Founded 1965

Santa Cruz
CA 95064

www.ucsc.edu

Academic survey position... 203
Employer survey position.... 126
Student faculty ratio 24.6:1
International faculty.........5.4%
Undergraduates............ 14,074
Postgraduates................. 1,355
International students 1.9%

World rank .... 235 (259=)
Subject area positions
Arts & humanities 148
Engineering & IT 273
Life sciences & biomedicine 149
Natural sciences................ 197
Social sciences 264

University of California, Riverside

Founded 1954

Riverside
CA 92521

www.ucr.edu

Academic survey position... 250
Employer survey position.... 126
Student faculty ratio 21.5:1
International faculty.........5.9%
Undergraduates............ 14,693
Postgraduates................. 2,155
International students 5.4%

World rank .... 262= (298)
Subject area positions
Arts & humanities 204
Life sciences & biomedicine 204
Natural sciences................ 235
Social sciences 278

Carnegie Mellon University

Founded 1900

Pittsburgh
PA 15213-3890

www.cmu.edu

Academic survey position..... 37
Employer survey position...... 33
Student faculty ratio 7.5:1
International faculty.......13.7%
Undergraduates.............. 5,674
Postgraduates................. 3,917
International students 28.0%

World rank .... 21 (20=)
Subject area positions
Arts & humanities 113
Engineering & IT 6
Life sciences & biomedicine.. 73
Natural sciences................... 80
Social sciences 35

Case Western Reserve University

Founded 1826

Cleveland
OH 44106

www.case.edu

Academic survey position... 186
Employer survey position.... 309
Student faculty ratio 6:1
International faculty.........2.9%
Undergraduates.............. 4,066
Postgraduates................. 4,274
International students 11.1%

World rank .... 90 (85=)
Subject area positions
Arts & humanities 294
Engineering & IT 149
Life sciences & biomedicine.. 76
Natural sciences................ 252
Social sciences 239

University of Chicago

Founded 1890

Chicago
IL 60637

www.uchicago.edu

Academic survey position..... 15
Employer survey position...... 18
Student faculty ratio 5.4:1
International faculty.......24.8%
Undergraduates.............. 4,880
Postgraduates................. 7,868
International students 19.9%

World rank .... 8 (7=)
Subject area positions
Arts & humanities 9
Engineering & IT 83
Life sciences & biomedicine.. 35
Natural sciences................... 12
Social sciences 8

University of Cincinnati

Founded 1819

Cincinnati
OH 45221

www.uc.edu

Academic survey position... 304
Employer survey position.... 368
Student faculty ratio 11.9:1
International faculty.........3.2%
Undergraduates............ 18,133
Postgraduates................. 6,505
International students 6.2%

World rank .... 268= (219)
Subject area positions
Arts & humanities 278
Life sciences & biomedicine 182

United States of America continued

University of Colorado at Boulder

Founded 1876

Boulder
CO 80309

www.colorado.edu

Academic survey position... 208
Employer survey position.... 126
Student faculty ratio 11.2:1
International faculty 9.3%
Undergraduates............ 24,755
Postgraduates................ 3,149
International students 3.0%

World rank .... 180= (107)
Subject area positions
Engineering & IT 149
Life sciences & biomedicine 150
Natural sciences................ 147
Social sciences 256

Colorado State University

Founded 1870

Fort Collins
CO 80523

www.colostate.edu

Academic survey position... 336
Employer survey position.... 126
Student faculty ratio 18.6:1
International faculty 8.1%
Undergraduates............ 20,129
Postgraduates................ 3,651
International students 0%

World rank 340 (326)
Subject area positions
Natural sciences................ 213

Columbia University

Founded 1754

New York
NY 10027-6902

www.columbia.edu

Academic survey position..... 16
Employer survey position...... 21
Student faculty ratio 5.3:1
International faculty 6.4%
Undergraduates.............. 6,728
Postgraduates............... 13,828
International students 22.5%

World rank 10 (11)
Subject area positions
Arts & humanities 7
Engineering & IT 63
Life sciences & biomedicine.. 20
Natural sciences.................. 23
Social sciences 11

University of Connecticut

Founded 1881

Storrs
CT 06269

www.uconn.edu

Academic survey position... 382
Employer survey position.... 126
Student faculty ratio 17.9:1
International faculty 5.7%
Undergraduates............ 15,859
Postgraduates................ 5,322
International students 6.0%

World rank .... 359= (328)
Subject area positions
Engineering & IT 297

Cornell University

Founded 1865

Ithaca
NY 14853

www.cornell.edu

Academic survey position..... 12
Employer survey position...... 14
Student faculty ratio 6.7:1
International faculty 5.8%
Undergraduates............ 13,500
Postgraduates................ 6,275
International students 17.4%

World rank .... 15 (20=)
Subject area positions
Arts & humanities 14
Engineering & IT 24
Life sciences & biomedicine.. 18
Natural sciences.................. 11
Social sciences 17

Dartmouth College

Founded 1769

Hanover
NH 03755

www.dartmouth.edu

Academic survey position... 151
Employer survey position...... 56
Student faculty ratio 6.9:1
International faculty 5.8%
Undergraduates.............. 4,127
Postgraduates................ 1,653
International students 12.6%

World rank .... 54 (71=)
Subject area positions
Arts & humanities 114
Engineering & IT 294
Life sciences & biomedicine 106
Natural sciences................ 275
Social sciences 108

United States of America continued

University of Delaware

Founded 1743

Newark
DE 19716

www.udel.edu

Academic survey position... 360
Employer survey position.... 126
Student faculty ratio 16.5:1
International faculty.........2.3%
Undergraduates............ 15,756
Postgraduates................. 2,811
International students 4.7%

World rank ....366= (343=)
Subject area positions
Engineering & IT 277

Drexel University

Founded 1891

Philadelphia
PA 19104

www.drexel.edu

Academic survey position... 385
Employer survey position.... 332
Student faculty ratio 11:1
International faculty.......10.4%
Undergraduates............ 11,453
Postgraduates................. 4,948
International students 7.9%

World rank ....338= (256=)
Subject area positions
Engineering & IT 284

Duke University

Founded 1838

Durham
NC 27708

www.duke.edu

Academic survey position..... 30
Employer survey position...... 23
Student faculty ratio 4.2:1
International faculty.........6.6%
Undergraduates.............. 6,372
Postgraduates................. 6,959
International students 14.6%

World rank .... 13= (13)
Subject area positions
Arts & humanities 21
Engineering & IT 111
Life sciences & biomedicine.. 21
Natural sciences................... 79
Social sciences 26

Emory University

Founded 1836

Atlanta
GA 30322

www.emory.edu

Academic survey position... 176
Employer survey position.... 166
Student faculty ratio 5.8:1
International faculty.......11.3%
Undergraduates.............. 6,667
Postgraduates................. 5,310
International students 10.2%

World rank .... 62 (74=)
Subject area positions
Arts & humanities 130
Life sciences & biomedicine.. 53
Natural sciences................. 262
Social sciences 253

University of Florida

Founded 1853

Gainesville
FL 32611

www.ufl.edu

Academic survey position... 145
Employer survey position.... 222
Student faculty ratio 14.2:1
International faculty.........7.8%
Undergraduates............ 33,376
Postgraduates.............. 13,762
International students 7.0%

World rank 165 (135)
Subject area positions
Arts & humanities 130
Engineering & IT 155
Life sciences & biomedicine 240
Natural sciences................. 122
Social sciences 223

Florida State University

Founded 1851

Tallahassee
FL 32306

www.fsu.edu

Academic survey position... 216
Employer survey position.... 326
Student faculty ratio 18.5:1
International faculty.......10.1%
Undergraduates............ 29,182
Postgraduates................. 6,796
International students 2.8%

World rank .... 300= (253)
Subject area positions
Arts & humanities 178
Life sciences & biomedicine 147
Natural sciences................. 204
Social sciences 252

United States of America continued

George Washington University

Founded 1821

Washington
DC 20052

www.gwu.edu

Academic survey position... 264
Employer survey position.... 159
Student faculty ratio 12.6:1
International faculty 9%
Undergraduates............ 10,003
Postgraduates................. 8,869
International students 7.6%

World rank ....246= (229=)
Subject area positions
Arts & humanities.............. 160
Life sciences & biomedicine 255
Social sciences 226

Georgetown University

Founded 1789

Washington
DC 20057

www.georgetown.edu

Academic survey position... 132
Employer survey position...... 49
Student faculty ratio 9.5:1
International faculty 4.9%
Undergraduates.............. 6,872
Postgraduates................. 6,669
International students 11.4%

World rank .... 110 (102=)
Subject area positions
Arts & humanities................ 63
Life sciences & biomedicine 153
Social sciences 47

Georgia Institute of Technology

Founded 1885

Atlanta
GA 30332

www.gatech.edu

Academic survey position..... 96
Employer survey position.... 102
Student faculty ratio 20.6:1
International faculty 9.9%
Undergraduates............ 12,008
Postgraduates................. 5,461
International students 18.2%

World rank ....83= (97=)
Subject area positions
Engineering & IT 8
Life sciences & biomedicine 264
Natural sciences.................. 61
Social sciences 282

University of Georgia

Founded 1785

Athens
GA 30602

www.uga.edu

Academic survey position... 348
Employer survey position.... 364
Student faculty ratio 15.6:1
International faculty 6%
Undergraduates............ 24,057
Postgraduates................. 6,738
International students 4.0%

World rank .... 361 (295=)
Subject area positions
Life sciences & biomedicine 296

Georgia State University

Founded 1913

Atlanta
GA 30302-3965

www.gsu.edu

Academic survey position... 385
Employer survey position.... 399
Student faculty ratio 20.1:1
International faculty 13.8%
Undergraduates............ 16,349
Postgraduates................. 5,326
International students 5.8%

World rank ......401-500 (396=)
Subject area positions
Engineering & IT 297

Harvard University

Founded 1636

Cambridge
MA 02138

www.harvard.edu

Academic survey position....... 2
Employer survey position........ 4
Student faculty ratio 5.7:1
International faculty 29.5%
Undergraduates.............. 8,044
Postgraduates.............. 13,528
International students 19.2%

World rank 1 (1)
Subject area positions
Arts & humanities.................. 1
Engineering & IT 19
Life sciences & biomedicine.... 1
Natural sciences..................... 4
Social sciences 1

United States of America continued

University of Hawaii

Founded 1908

Honolulu
HI 96822

www.uhm.hawaii.edu

Academic survey position... 295
Employer survey position.... 126
Student faculty ratio 9:1
International faculty 8.2%
Undergraduates............ 12,131
Postgraduates................ 4,098
International students 5.1%

World rank .... 262= (255)
Subject area positions
Arts & humanities 115
Social sciences 239

University of Houston

Founded 1927

Houston
TX 77004

www.uh.edu

Academic survey position... 385
Employer survey position.... 126
Student faculty ratio 25.5:1
International faculty 10.0%
Undergraduates............ 22,295
Postgraduates................ 5,507
International students 8.6%

World rank .401-500 (401-500)
Subject area positions
Life sciences & biomedicine 296

Howard University

Founded 1867

Washington
DC 20059

www.howard.edu

Academic survey position... 385
Employer survey position.... 189
Student faculty ratio 6.4:1
International faculty 0%
Undergraduates.............. 6,720
Postgraduates................ 2,762
International students 2.4%

World rank 345
Subject area positions
Engineering & IT 297

University of Illinois

Founded 1867

Chicago
IL 60680-5220

www.uillinois.edu

Academic survey position..... 42
Employer survey position.... 163
Student faculty ratio 12.9:1
International faculty 9.3%
Undergraduates............ 45,284
Postgraduates............... 17,658
International students 11.1%

World rank 71 (73)
Subject area positions
Arts & humanities 103
Engineering & IT 20
Life sciences & biomedicine 115
Natural sciences.................. 36
Social sciences 59

Illinois Institute of Technology

Founded 1890

Chicago
IL 60616

www.iit.edu

Academic survey position... 385
Employer survey position.... 126
Student faculty ratio 12.3:1
International faculty 17.1%
Undergraduates.............. 2,409
Postgraduates................ 3,632
International students 39.1%

World rank 401-500
Subject area positions
Engineering & IT 297

Indiana University Bloomington

Founded 1820

Bloomington
IN 47405-7000

www.indiana.edu

Academic survey position... 128
Employer survey position.... 151
Student faculty ratio 17.5:1
International faculty 13.6%
Undergraduates............ 29,325
Postgraduates................ 6,623
International students 9.7%

World rank .... 170= (137=)
Subject area positions
Arts & humanities 53
Life sciences & biomedicine.. 96
Natural sciences................. 208
Social sciences 160

United States of America continued

University of Iowa

Founded 1847

Iowa City
IA 52242-7700

www.uiowa.edu

Academic survey position... 271
Employer survey position.... 347
Student faculty ratio 12.1:1
International faculty 11.8%
Undergraduates 19,415
Postgraduates 5,995
International students 4.7%

World rank .... 219= (207)
Subject area positions
Arts & humanities 240
Life sciences & biomedicine 139
Social sciences 243

Iowa State University

Founded 1856

Ames
IA 50011-2011

www.iastate.edu

Academic survey position... 322
Employer survey position.... 126
Student faculty ratio 17.5:1
International faculty 22.1%
Undergraduates 20,121
Postgraduates 3,774
International students 8.0%

World rank .... 289 (276=)
Subject area positions
Engineering & IT 175
Life sciences & biomedicine 218
Natural sciences 278
Social sciences 299

Johns Hopkins University

Founded 1876

Baltimore
MD 21218-2688

www.jhu.edu

Academic survey position..... 24
Employer survey position.... 118
Student faculty ratio 3.9:1
International faculty 6.6%
Undergraduates 5,425
Postgraduates 8,915
International students 15.3%

World rank .... 13= (15)
Subject area positions
Arts & humanities 22
Engineering & IT 67
Life sciences & biomedicine.... 3
Natural sciences 45
Social sciences 41

University of Kansas

Founded 1865

Lawrence
KS 66045

www.ku.edu

Academic survey position... 372
Employer survey position.... 372
Student faculty ratio 12.1:1
International faculty 8.1%
Undergraduates 19,323
Postgraduates 5,398
International students 5.0%

World rank .... 349= (281)
Subject area positions
Life sciences & biomedicine 225

University of Kentucky

Founded 1865

Lexington
KY 40506

www.uky.edu

Academic survey position... 385
Employer survey position.... 126
Student faculty ratio 16.4:1
International faculty 5.5%
Undergraduates 17,443
Postgraduates 5,967
International students 4.7%

World rank ...... 401-500 (378=)
Subject area positions
Engineering & IT 297

Lehigh University

Founded 1865

Bethlehem
PA 18015

www3.lehigh.edu

Academic survey position... 385
Employer survey position.... 351
Student faculty ratio 12.7:1
International faculty 29.7%
Undergraduates 4,727
Postgraduates 1,296
International students 8.7%

World rank 401-500
Subject area positions
Engineering & IT 297

United States of America continued

Louisiana State University

Founded 1859

Baton Rouge
LA 70803

www.lsu.edu

Academic survey position... 385
Employer survey position.... 126
Student faculty ratio 18.7:1
International faculty 5.9%
Undergraduates 33,112
Postgraduates 4,352
International students 5.2%

World rank .401-500 (401-500)
Subject area positions
Life sciences & biomedicine 284

Loyola University Chicago

Founded 1870

Chicago
IL 60626

www.luc.edu

Academic survey position... 295
Employer survey position.... 126
Student faculty ratio 13.1:1
International faculty 1.8%
Undergraduates 9,428
Postgraduates 4,666
International students 2.7%

World rank .... 370= (350)
Subject area positions
Arts & humanities 160
Life sciences & biomedicine 244
Social sciences 214

University of Maryland

Founded 1856

College Park
MD 20742

www.umd.edu

Academic survey position... 135
Employer survey position.... 219
Student faculty ratio 10.8:1
International faculty 13.3%
Undergraduates 32,935
Postgraduates 9,484
International students 8.2%

World rank .... 122= (79)
Subject area positions
Arts & humanities 288
Engineering & IT 81
Life sciences & biomedicine 165
Natural sciences 104
Social sciences 187

Massachusetts Institute of Technology (MIT)

Founded 1861

Cambridge
MA 02139-4307

web.mit.edu

Academic survey position....... 5
Employer survey position........ 6
Student faculty ratio 6.6:1
International faculty 7.9%
Undergraduates 4,130
Postgraduates 5,851
International students 25.4%

World rank 9 (10)
Subject area positions
Arts & humanities 20
Engineering & IT 1
Life sciences & biomedicine.... 8
Natural sciences 1
Social sciences 10

University of Massachusetts, Amherst

Founded 1863

Amherst
MA 01003

www.umass.edu

Academic survey position... 145
Employer survey position.... 231
Student faculty ratio 17.4:1
International faculty 14.8%
Undergraduates 19,135
Postgraduates 3,313
International students 4.7%

World rank .... 191 (175=)
Subject area positions
Arts & humanities 191
Engineering & IT 102
Life sciences & biomedicine 137
Natural sciences 224
Social sciences 194

University of Miami

Founded 1925

Miami
FL 33124

www.miami.edu

Academic survey position... 385
Employer survey position.... 386
Student faculty ratio 8:1
International faculty 24.3%
Undergraduates 9,911
Postgraduates 4,711
International students 9.5%

World rank .... 237= (202)
Subject area positions
Engineering & IT 297

United States of America continued

University of Michigan

Founded 1817

Ann Arbor
MI 48109

www.umich.edu

Academic survey position..... 23
Employer survey position...... 19
Student faculty ratio 7.2:1
International faculty.......17.2%
Undergraduates............ 25,629
Postgraduates.............. 13,597
International students 11.1%

World rank .... 18 (38=)
Subject area positions
Arts & humanities 19
Engineering & IT 38
Life sciences & biomedicine.. 31
Natural sciences 35
Social sciences 20

Michigan State University

Founded 1855

East Lansing
MI 48824-0590

www.msu.edu

Academic survey position... 196
Employer survey position.... 169
Student faculty ratio 15.1:1
International faculty.......17.0%
Undergraduates............ 34,083
Postgraduates................. 8,222
International students 10.1%

World rank ....203= (159=)
Subject area positions
Engineering & IT 191
Life sciences & biomedicine 204
Natural sciences 127
Social sciences 129

University of Minnesota

Founded 1851

Minneapolis
MN 55455-0213

www.umn.edu

Academic survey position..... 95
Employer survey position.... 231
Student faculty ratio 13.9:1
International faculty.......21.8%
Undergraduates............ 28,825
Postgraduates............... 12,461
International students 6.7%

World rank .... 87 (142=)
Subject area positions
Arts & humanities 122
Engineering & IT 140
Life sciences & biomedicine.. 84
Natural sciences 137
Social sciences 71

University of Missouri

Founded 1839

Columbia
MO 65211

www.missouri.edu

Academic survey position... 385
Employer survey position.... 126
Student faculty ratio 9.2:1
International faculty.......11.7%
Undergraduates............ 35,547
Postgraduates............... 10,013
International students 4.7%

World rank ....:.. 389 (381=)
Subject area positions
Engineering & IT 297

University of New Mexico

Founded 1889

Albuquerque
NM 87131

www.unm.edu

Academic survey position... 373
Employer survey position.... 126
Student faculty ratio 10.1:1
International faculty.........7.0%
Undergraduates............ 16,447
Postgraduates................. 3,970
International students 3.2%

World rank .... 337 (358=)
Subject area positions
Engineering & IT 297

New York University (NYU)

Founded 1831

New York
NY 10012

www.nyu.edu

Academic survey position..... 35
Employer survey position...... 45
Student faculty ratio 7.5:1
International faculty.........5.6%
Undergraduates............ 20,385
Postgraduates............... 14,775
International students 12.3%

World rank 40 (49)
Subject area positions
Arts & humanities 15
Engineering & IT 243
Life sciences & biomedicine.. 53
Natural sciences 53
Social sciences 23

United States of America continued

City University of New York

Founded 1847	Academic survey position... 201
	Employer survey position.... 314
New York	Student faculty ratio 16.1:1
NY 10016-4309	International faculty 3.8%
	International students 7.7%
www.cuny.edu	

World rank .... 320= (358=)
Subject area positions
Arts & humanities 74
Life sciences & biomedicine 206
Natural sciences 229
Social sciences 237

University of North Carolina

Founded 1789	Academic survey position... 113
	Employer survey position...... 82
Chapel Hill	Student faculty ratio 9.9:1
NC 27599-2200	International faculty 3.2%
	Undergraduates 29,705
www.unc.edu	Postgraduates 10,062
	International students 3.3%

World rank .... 102= (151=)
Subject area positions
Arts & humanities 135
Engineering & IT 196
Life sciences & biomedicine.. 63
Natural sciences 139
Social sciences 112

North Carolina State University

Founded 1887	Academic survey position... 270
	Employer survey position.... 211
Raleigh	Student faculty ratio 15.4:1
NC 27695	International faculty 4.7%
	Undergraduates 21,864
www.ncsu.edu	Postgraduates 5,396
	International students 7.0%

World rank .... 219= (248=)
Subject area positions
Engineering & IT 186
Life sciences & biomedicine 225
Natural sciences 204

Northeastern University

Founded 1898	Academic survey position... 385
	Employer survey position.... 317
Boston	Student faculty ratio 17.9:1
MA 2115	International faculty 2.7%
	Undergraduates 16,214
www.northeastern.edu	Postgraduates 4,683
	International students 9.6%

World rank ...... 401-500 (386=)
Subject area positions
Engineering & IT 297

Northwestern University

Founded 1851	Academic survey position..... 62
	Employer survey position...... 37
Evanston	Student faculty ratio 8:1
IL 60208	International faculty 6.7%
	Undergraduates 8,574
www.northwestern.edu	Postgraduates 8,282
	International students 13.4%

World rank 33 (29)
Subject area positions
Arts & humanities 108
Engineering & IT 81
Life sciences & biomedicine.. 72
Natural sciences 114
Social sciences 29

University of Notre Dame

Founded 1842	Academic survey position... 209
	Employer survey position.... 100
Notre Dame	Student faculty ratio 12.6:1
IN 46556	International faculty 5.1%
	Undergraduates 8,363
www.nd.edu	Postgraduates 3,287
	International students 7.1%

World rank .... 168 (155=)
Subject area positions
Arts & humanities 82
Engineering & IT 251
Life sciences & biomedicine 294
Social sciences 200

United States of America continued

Ohio State University

Founded 1870

Columbus
OH 43210

www.osu.edu

Academic survey position... 114
Employer survey position.... 110
Student faculty ratio 13.6:1
International faculty 16.9%
Undergraduates............ 36,880
Postgraduates............... 11,359
International students 8.8%

World rank 121 (120)
Subject area positions
Arts & humanities 263
Engineering & IT 111
Life sciences & biomedicine 146
Natural sciences 101
Social sciences 86

University of Oklahoma

Founded 1890

Norman
OK 73019-0390

www.ou.edu

Academic survey position... 385
Employer survey position.... 126
Student faculty ratio 15.4:1
International faculty 10.1%
Undergraduates............ 17,834
Postgraduates................. 3,817
International students 4.8%

World rank .... 382= (373)
Subject area positions
Engineering & IT 297

University of Oregon

Founded 1876

Eugene
OR 97403-1226

www.uoregon.edu

Academic survey position... 326
Employer survey position.... 126
Student faculty ratio 16.2:1
International faculty 9.7%
Undergraduates............ 15,609
Postgraduates................. 3,159
International students 6.1%

World rank .... 373 (351=)
Subject area positions
Life sciences & biomedicine 150

University of Pennsylvania

Founded 1740

Philadelphia
PA 19104

www.upenn.edu

Academic survey position..... 32
Employer survey position...... 24
Student faculty ratio 6.9:1
International faculty 27.3%
Undergraduates............ 10,734
Postgraduates............... 10,550
International students 18.4%

World rank 11 (14)
Subject area positions
Arts & humanities 40
Engineering & IT 78
Life sciences & biomedicine.. 41
Natural sciences................... 47
Social sciences 22

Pennsylvania State University

Founded 1855

University Park
PA 16802

www.psu.edu

Academic survey position..... 97
Employer survey position.... 114
Student faculty ratio 13.7:1
International faculty 8.5%
Undergraduates............ 35,903
Postgraduates................. 5,785
International students 7.5%

World rank .... 105 (90=)
Subject area positions
Arts & humanities 238
Engineering & IT 79
Life sciences & biomedicine 180
Natural sciences................... 59
Social sciences 73

University of Pittsburgh

Founded 1787

Pittsburgh
PA 15260

www.pitt.edu

Academic survey position... 169
Employer survey position.... 317
Student faculty ratio 6:1
International faculty 10.9%
Undergraduates............ 16,177
Postgraduates................. 7,822
International students 7.0%

World rank .... 97 (77=)
Subject area positions
Arts & humanities 87
Engineering & IT 194
Life sciences & biomedicine 126
Social sciences 211

United States of America continued

Princeton University

Founded 1746	Academic survey position....... 7	World rank 12 (6)
	Employer survey position...... 31	Subject area positions
Princeton	Student faculty ratio 8.3:1	Arts & humanities 6
NJ 08544	International faculty.......32.5%	Engineering & IT 15
	Undergraduates.............. 4,845	Life sciences & biomedicine.. 22
www.princeton.edu	Postgraduates................. 2,416	Natural sciences.................... 6
	International students 19.4%	Social sciences 9

Purdue University

Founded 1869	Academic survey position..... 75	World rank ....99= (77=)
	Employer survey position.... 107	Subject area positions
West Lafayette	Student faculty ratio 15.1:1	Arts & humanities 211
IN 47907-1080	International faculty.......17.5%	Engineering & IT 33
	Undergraduates............ 31,002	Life sciences & biomedicine.. 69
www.purdue.edu	Postgraduates................. 6,549	Natural sciences.................. 67
	International students 12.5%	Social sciences 140

Rensselaer Polytechnic Institute

Founded 1824	Academic survey position... 233	World rank .... 174= (191)
	Employer survey position.... 287	Subject area positions
Troy	Student faculty ratio 15:1	Arts & humanities 290
NY 12180	International faculty.......18.2%	Engineering & IT 66
	Undergraduates.............. 5,146	Natural sciences................. 222
www.rpi.edu	Postgraduates................. 1,190	
	International students 10.4%	

Rice University

Founded 1891	Academic survey position... 169	World rank .... 78= (92)
	Employer survey position.... 227	Subject area positions
Houston	Student faculty ratio 8.2:1	Arts & humanities 272
TX 77005-1827	International faculty.......11.2%	Engineering & IT 110
	Undergraduates.............. 2,996	Life sciences & biomedicine 201
www.rice.edu	Postgraduates................. 2,082	Natural sciences................. 125
	International students 16.6%	Social sciences 226

University of Rochester

Founded 1850	Academic survey position... 225	World rank 119 (95)
	Employer survey position.... 383	Subject area positions
Rochester	Student faculty ratio 3.2:1	Arts & humanities 273
NY 14627	International faculty.......18.5%	Engineering & IT 250
	Undergraduates.............. 4,936	Life sciences & biomedicine 183
www.rochester.edu	Postgraduates................. 3,338	Natural sciences................. 229
	International students 15.9%	Social sciences 172

Rutgers, The State University of New Jersey

Founded 1766	Academic survey position..... 93	World rank .... 151 (177=)
	Employer survey position.... 304	Subject area positions
New Brunswick	Student faculty ratio 12.1:1	Arts & humanities 43
NJ 08901-8530	International faculty.......14.5%	Engineering & IT 159
	Undergraduates............ 31,230	Life sciences & biomedicine 225
www.rutgers.edu	Postgraduates................. 7,650	Natural sciences............... 100
	International students 5.5%	Social sciences 120

United States of America continued

Smith College

Founded 1871

Northampton
MA 01063

www.smith.edu

Academic survey position... 385
Employer survey position.... 146
Student faculty ratio 11.6:1
International faculty.........4.3%
Undergraduates.............. 2,651
Postgraduates................... 452
International students 6.3%

World rank .401-500 (401-500)
Subject area positions
Engineering & IT 297

University of South Carolina

Founded 1801

Columbia
SC 29208

www.sc.edu

Academic survey position... 385
Employer survey position.... 206
Student faculty ratio 14:1
International faculty.........6.9%
Undergraduates............. 17,774
Postgraduates................. 5,963
International students 3.6%

World rank .... 391= (362=)
Subject area positions
Engineering & IT 297

University of Southern California

Founded 1880

Los Angeles
CA 90089

www.usc.edu

Academic survey position... 148
Employer survey position.... 134
Student faculty ratio 11.7:1
International faculty.......21.6%
Undergraduates............. 15,917
Postgraduates............... 14,636
International students 21.9%

World rank .... 102= (119)
Subject area positions
Arts & humanities 135
Engineering & IT 87
Life sciences & biomedicine 187
Natural sciences................ 279
Social sciences 184

Stanford University

Founded 1891

Stanford
CA 94305-3020

www.stanford.edu

Academic survey position....... 4
Employer survey position........ 8
Student faculty ratio 9.2:1
International faculty.........4.9%
Undergraduates.............. 6,543
Postgraduates................. 9,565
International students 21.5%

World rank 17 (19)
Subject area positions
Arts & humanities 8
Engineering & IT 3
Life sciences & biomedicine.... 6
Natural sciences..................... 8
Social sciences 3

Stony Brook University

Founded 1957

Stony Brook
NY 11794

www.sunysb.edu/

Academic survey position... 126
Employer survey position.... 357
Student faculty ratio 12:1
International faculty.......18.4%
Undergraduates............. 14,734
Postgraduates................. 5,665
International students 19.1%

World rank 127 (224)
Subject area positions
Arts & humanities 91
Engineering & IT 189
Life sciences & biomedicine 185
Natural sciences.................. 70
Social sciences 208

Syracuse University

Founded 1870

Syracuse
NY 13244

www.syr.edu

Academic survey position... 385
Employer survey position.... 126
Student faculty ratio 14.9:1
International faculty.........4.0%
Undergraduates............. 12,728
Postgraduates................. 4,578
International students 10.6%

World rank 401-500
Subject area positions
Arts & humanities 285

United States of America continued

Temple University

Founded 1884

Philadelphia
PA 19122

www.temple.edu

Academic survey position... 361
Employer survey position.... 126
Student faculty ratio 13.1:1
International faculty 3.9%
Undergraduates............ 23,372
Postgraduates................. 6,322
International students 4.0%

World rank .401-500 (401-500)
Subject area positions
Life sciences & biomedicine 232
Social sciences 202

University of Tennessee

Founded 1794

Tennessee
TN 37996

www.utk.edu

Academic survey position... 385
Employer survey position.... 258
Student faculty ratio 11.4:1
International faculty 5.8%
Undergraduates............ 20,385
Postgraduates................. 7,067
International students 3.8%

World rank 308 (289)
Subject area positions
Engineering & IT 297

University of Texas at Austin

Founded 1827

Austin
TX 78712

www.utexas.edu

Academic survey position..... 40
Employer survey position...... 46
Student faculty ratio 18.2:1
International faculty 17.5%
Undergraduates............ 35,560
Postgraduates.............. 11,562
International students 9.2%

World rank .... 70 (51=)
Subject area positions
Arts & humanities 45
Engineering & IT 32
Life sciences & biomedicine 101
Natural sciences................... 34
Social sciences 86

Texas A&M University

Founded 1871

College Station
TX 77843

www.tamu.edu

Academic survey position... 103
Employer survey position.... 132
Student faculty ratio 19.6:1
International faculty 8.1%
Undergraduates............ 35,449
Postgraduates................. 7,860
International students 8.4%

World rank .... 137= (122)
Subject area positions
Arts & humanities 294
Engineering & IT 53
Life sciences & biomedicine.. 84
Natural sciences................... 85
Social sciences 184

Tufts University

Founded 1852

Medford
MA 02155

www.tufts.edu

Academic survey position... 309
Employer survey position.... 178
Student faculty ratio 9.8:1
International faculty 9.4%
Undergraduates.............. 4,997
Postgraduates................. 4,044
International students 10.7%

World rank .... 157 (159=)
Subject area positions
Arts & humanities 252
Life sciences & biomedicine 160
Social sciences 271

Tulane University

Founded 1834

New Orleans
LA 70118

www.tulane.edu

Academic survey position... 385
Employer survey position.... 160
Student faculty ratio 7.5:1
International faculty 0%
Undergraduates.............. 5,562
Postgraduates................. 3,459
International students 7.2%

World rank 233 (218)
Subject area positions
Life sciences & biomedicine 278

United States of America continued

University of Utah

Founded 1850

Salt Lake City
UT 84112

www.utah.edu

Academic survey position... 378
Employer survey position.... 126
Student faculty ratio 8.5:1
International faculty 16.7%
Undergraduates 16,817
Postgraduates 5,493
International students 6.2%

World rank .... 246= (261)
Subject area positions
Natural sciences 268

Vanderbilt University

Founded 1873

Nashville
TN 37240

www.vanderbilt.edu

Academic survey position... 224
Employer survey position...... 95
Student faculty ratio 3.7:1
International faculty 16.5%
Undergraduates 6,486
Postgraduates 4,930
International students 9.6%

World rank 101 (82)
Subject area positions
Life sciences & biomedicine.. 55
Social sciences 197

University of Vermont

Founded 1791

Burlington
VT 05405

www.uvm.edu

Academic survey position... 385
Employer survey position.... 126
Student faculty ratio 9.6:1
International faculty 5.0%
Undergraduates 9,701
Postgraduates 1,255
International students 1.8%

World rank 401-500
Subject area positions
Engineering & IT 297

University of Virginia

Founded 1819

Charlottesville
VA 22904-4132

www.virginia.edu

Academic survey position... 142
Employer survey position...... 56
Student faculty ratio 9.9:1
International faculty 3.9%
Undergraduates 14,534
Postgraduates 7,214
International students 7.8%

World rank 96 (110)
Subject area positions
Arts & humanities 107
Engineering & IT 191
Life sciences & biomedicine 127
Natural sciences 269
Social sciences 111

Virginia Commonwealth University

Founded 1838

Richmond,
VA 23284-2527

www.vcu.edu

Academic survey position... 385
Employer survey position.... 126
Student faculty ratio 11.8:1
International faculty 2.2%
Undergraduates 18,990
Postgraduates 6,439
International students 4.9%

World rank . 401-500 (401-500)
Subject area positions
Engineering & IT 297

Virginia Polytechnic Institute (Virginia Tech)

Founded 1872

Blacksburg
VA 24061

www.vt.edu

Academic survey position... 273
Employer survey position.... 193
Student faculty ratio 13.4:1
International faculty 13.3%
Undergraduates 22,684
Postgraduates 5,231
International students 7.3%

World rank .... 276= (248=)
Subject area positions
Engineering & IT 59

Wake Forest University

Founded 1834

Winston-Salem
NC 27106

www.wfu.edu

Academic survey position... 385
Employer survey position.... 156
Student faculty ratio 4.6:1
International faculty 8%
Undergraduates.............. 4,371
Postgraduates................ 2,314
International students 3.8%

World rank .... 218 (203=)
Subject area positions
Engineering & IT 297

University of Washington

Founded 1861

Seattle
WA 98195

www.washington.edu

Academic survey position..... 82
Employer survey position.... 231
Student faculty ratio 9.8:1
International faculty 4.4%
Undergraduates............ 26,622
Postgraduates............... 10,065
International students 7.5%

World rank .... 59 (55=)
Subject area positions
Arts & humanities 182
Engineering & IT 85
Life sciences & biomedicine.. 44
Natural sciences................... 85
Social sciences 113

Washington University in St Louis

Founded 1853

St Louis
MO 63130-4899

www.wustl.edu

Academic survey position... 152
Employer survey position.... 223
Student faculty ratio 4.5:1
International faculty 4.0%
Undergraduates.............. 6,512
Postgraduates................ 5,285
International students 11.8%

World rank .... 60 (161=)
Subject area positions
Arts & humanities 236
Life sciences & biomedicine.. 28
Natural sciences................ 283
Social sciences 226

Washington State University

Founded 1890

Pullman
WA 99164-1067

www.wsu.edu

Academic survey position... 385
Employer survey position.... 381
Student faculty ratio 11.2:1
International faculty 13.2%
Undergraduates............ 18,309
Postgraduates................ 3,269
International students 5.1%

World rank .... 365 (286=)
Subject area positions
Engineering & IT 297
Life sciences & biomedicine 261

College of William & Mary

Founded 1693

Williamsburg
VA 23187-8795

www.wm.edu

Academic survey position... 385
Employer survey position.... 208
Student faculty ratio 10.9:1
International faculty 5.3%
Undergraduates.............. 5,683
Postgraduates................ 1,695
International students 3.9%

World rank .... 382= (303)
Subject area positions
Engineering & IT 297

University of Wisconsin-Madison

Founded 1848

Madison
WI 53706

www.wisc.edu

Academic survey position..... 45
Employer survey position.... 113
Student faculty ratio 11.9:1
International faculty 6.8%
Undergraduates............ 28,341
Postgraduates............... 10,043
International students 7.3%

World rank .... 55 (55=)
Subject area positions
Arts & humanities 56
Engineering & IT 73
Life sciences & biomedicine.. 47
Natural sciences................... 56
Social sciences 40

United States of America continued

Yale University

Founded 1701

New Haven
CT 06520

www.yale.edu

Academic survey position....... 8
Employer survey position...... 12
Student faculty ratio 3.9:1
International faculty.......31.0%
Undergraduates.............. 5,296
Postgraduates................. 6,037
International students 15.9%

World rank .... 2 (2=)
Subject area positions
Arts & humanities 5
Engineering & IT 58
Life sciences & biomedicine.... 7
Natural sciences 17
Social sciences 7

Yeshiva University

Founded 1886

New York
NY 10033

www.yu.edu

Academic survey position... 385
Employer survey position.... 126
Student faculty ratio 5.4:1
International faculty.........5.6%
Undergraduates.............. 2,946
Postgraduates................. 2,904
International students 2.2%

World rank .... 366= (381=)
Subject area positions
Engineering & IT 297

Uruguay

Universidad ORT Uruguay

Founded 1942

Montevideo 11100

www.ort.edu.uy

Academic survey position... 385
Employer survey position.... 297
Student faculty ratio 5.6:1
International faculty.........8.5%
Undergraduates.............. 2,347
Postgraduates.................... 145
International students 1.7%

World rank ...... 387= (401-500)
Subject area positions
Engineering & IT 297

Engine of Korea

Hanyang University

 Hanyang University

Office of International Cooperation
Address: 345 Wangshimli-gil,
Seongdong-gu, Seoul 133-791 Korea
Tel : +822-2-2220-0045
Fax : +822-2-2281-1784
Email : kingswy@hanyang.ac.kr
Website : http://www.hanyang.ac.kr

Index

The following pages contain three indexes: universities (p353), topics (p360) advertisers (p362). Top Universities Guide is a reference work and many chapters contain information listed in an index-like way. For example, the sources of worldwide study information on page 209, and the international higher education data sources on pages 263-265. These entries are not duplicated in the following three indexes. Neither are topics such as individual countries. Please refer carefully to the table of contents on page nine which will clearly point you in the direction of all listings.

Index of universities

This index lists the universities to be found in main parts of this book: the THE-QS World University Rankings 2008 top 200 list and the profiles of the world's top hundred (shown in bold) in chapter one; the top 100 universities in social sciences, arts & humanities, science, biomedicine and technology featured in chapter two; the full data table of the THE-QS World University Rankings 2008 top 200 in chapter six and the top 500 to be found in the Directory in chapter six (also shown in bold). Scattered references to individual universities throughout the editorial and the data pages in chapter four of the fees of the top 200 are not indexed here. Many universities have very complicated names, and it is not always clear which part of the name should lead the alphabetical listing position. The priority has been to try to list universities alphabetically in the index in such a way that they might easily be found.

Abbreviations

Abbreviations have been used for reasons of space and clarity: University (or its equivalent in other languages) has been omitted or left as 'U' when it belongs in the centre of a name or is an integral part of it (eg University College London UCL). Commonly occurring words such as Technology, Institute, School etc, or their equivalents in other languages, have been abbreviated Tech, Inst, Sch etc.

A

Aachen Rheinisch-Westf Tech 164, **287**
Aarhus 21, 142,148, 154, **115**, 250, **281**
Aberdeen 22, 252, **325**
Aberystwyth **325**
Adelaide 22, 251, **268**
Alabama **333**
Alberta 21, **108**, 148, 153, 158, 163, 249, **275**
American Beirut AUB **308**
Amsterdam 21, **87**, 141,147,159, 259, **447**
Antwerp 22, 254 **273**
Arizona 22, 252, **333**
Arizona State **333**
Aston **325**
Ateneo de Manila 148, **314**
Athens 22,254, **294**

Athens Nat Tech U **294**
Auckland 21, **99**, 141, 147, 158, 163, 249, **312**
Austral **268**
Australian National 21, **50**, 140, 146, 152, 158, 163, 247, **268**
Autónoma de Barcelona 22, 142, 148, 154, 254, **318**
Autónoma de Madrid **318**

B

Bandung Inst of Tech 164, **297**
Basel 22, 148, 252, **320**
Bath 22, 252, **325**
Bayreuth **287**
Belgrano **268**
Ben Gurion U Negev **299**

353

Bergen **313**
Bern 22,254, **320**
Bielefeld **288**
Bilkent **324**
Birmingham 21, **109**, 159, 164, 249, **326**
Bocconi Luigi U Comm 142, **300**
Bologna 22, 142, 147, 254, **300**
Boston 21, **80**, 141,147,154,158, 248, **334**
Boston College **334**
Brandeis 22, 159, 254, **334**
Bradford **326**
Brigham Young **334**
Bristol 21, **66**, 148, 154, 158, 248, **326**
British Columbia 21, **68**, 140, 146, 152, 157,
    162, 248, **275**
Brunel **326**
Bonn Rheinisch Friedr-Wilhelms **288**
Bremen **288**
Brown 21, **61**, 142, 147, 158, 164, 248, **334**
Buenos Aires 22, 254, **268**

C

Cairo **282**
Calcutta **296**
Calgary 22, 164, 253, **275**
California Berkeley 21, **70**, 140, 146, 152,
    157, 162, 248, **334**
California Davis 21, **123**, 154, 158, 250, **335**
California Inst of Tech Caltech 21, **39**, 142,
    152, 157, 162, 248, **335**
California Irvine 22, 148, 159, 252, **335**
California Los Angeles UCLA 21, **64**, 140, 146,
    152, 157, 162, 247, **335**
California Riverside **336**
California San Diego 21, **92**, 141, 148, 153,
    157, 163, 249, **335**
California Santa Barbara 21, **132**, 153, 159,
    163, 250, **335**
California Santa Cruz **336**
Cambridge 21, **37**, 140, 146, 152, 157, 162,
    247, **326**
Canterbury (NZ) 22, 254, **312**
Cape Town 22, 253, **317**
Cardiff 22, 159, 252, **326**
Carleton **276**
Carnegie Mellon 21, **55**, 141, 154, 159, 162,
    247, **336**
Case Western Reserve 21, **124**, 159, 250, **336**
Catolica Portuguesa **315**
Chalmers U of Tech 22, 154, 163, 253, **319**

Charles Prague **281**
Chiang Mai **323**
Chiba **302**
Chicago 21, **42**, 140, 146, 152, 158, 164, 247,
    336
Chile **279**
Chile Pontificia U Católica **278**
China U Sci & Tech 22, 153, 159, 163, 259,
    279
Chinese U Hong Kong 21, **76**, 142, 159, 164,
    248, **295**
Chonbuk National **307**
Christian-Albrechts Kiel **291**
Chulalongkorn 22, 253, **323**
Cinncinnati **336**
City U Hong Kong 22, 164, 252, **295**
City U New York 148, **344**
Claude Bernard Lyon I **285**
Coimbra **315**
Colorado 22, 57, 79, 253, **337**
Colorado State **337**
Columbia 21, **44**, 140, 146, 153, 157, 163,
    247, **337**
Complutense Madrid 148, **318**
Concordia **276**
Connecticut **337**
Copenhagen 21, **82**, 141, 147, 154, 158, 248,
    281
Cornell 21, **49**, 140, 146, 152, 157, 163, 247,
    337
Crete **294**
Curtin U of Tech **269**
Czech Technical U Prague **281**

D

Dalhousie 22, 159, 254, **276**
Dartmouth College 21, **88**, 249, **337**
Dauphine Paris IX **286**
Deakin **269**
De La Salle **314**
Delaware **338**
Delft U Tech 21, **112**, 154, 162, 250, **310**
Delhi 142, 159, **296**
Denis Diderot Paris VII **286**
Denmark Tech 22, 164, 252, **282**
Descartes Paris V **286**
Dortmund **289**
Drexel **338**
Dublin City **298**
Dublin Inst of Tech **298**

Duisburg-Essen **289**
Duke 21, **47**, 141, 147, 154, 157, 247, **338**
Dundee **327**
Durham 22, 251, **327**
Düsseldorf **289**

E

East Anglia UEA **327**
École Nat Ponts et Chausées **283**
École Norm Supérieure Lyon 22, 252, **284**
École Norm Sup Lettres et Sc Hum Lyon **284**
École Norm Supérieure Paris 21, **62**, 147, 152, 164, 248, **285**
École Polytechnique 21, **69**, 153, 163, 248, **283**
Ecole Poly Féd de Lausanne 21, **84**, 154, 163, 248, **321**
Edinburgh 21, **57**, 141, 147, 154, 158, 163, 247, **327**
Eindhoven U Tech 22, 163, 251, **310**
Emory 21, **96**, 158, 249, **338**
Eötvös Loránd **296**
Erasmus 22, 141, 159, 251, **310**
Erlangen-Nürnberg **289**
ESCP-EAP **284**
Essex **327**
Estadual Paulista **274**
ETH Zurich 21, **58**, 152, 159, 162, 247, **321**
Ewha Womans **307**
Exeter **327**

F

Flinders **269**
Florence **300**
Florida 22, 253, **338**
Florida State **338**
Frankfurt am Main 22, 253, **290**
Freiburg 22, 252, 148, **290**
Freie U Berlin 22, 141, 147, 154, 252, **287**
Fudan 22, 141, 148, 154, 158, 164, 251, **279**

G

Gadjah Mada **297**
Geneva 21, **102**, 148, 249, **321**
Georgetown 22, 141, 148, 251, **339**
George Washington **339**
Georgia **339**

Georgia Inst of Tech 21, **117**, 154, 162, 250, **339**
Georgia State **339**
Ghent 22, 252, **274**
Gifu **302**
Glasgow 21, **107**, 159, 249, **328**
Göteborg **319**
Göttingen 22, 148, 154, 253, **290**
Goldsmiths U of London **328**
Griffith **269**
Groningen 22, 252, **311**
Gunma **302**

H

Hamburg **290**
Hanyang **307**
Harvard 21, **35**, 140, 146, 152, 157, 162, 247, **339**
Hawaii **340**
HEC Sch of Management **284**
Heidelberg 21, **91**, 147, 153, 158, 249, **291**
Helsinki 21, **125**, 142, 147, 154, 159, 164, 250, **282**
Helsinki U Tech **282**
Heriot-Watt **328**
Hiroshima **302**
Hitotsubashi **303**
Hokkaido 22, 253, **303**
Hong Kong 21, **60**, 141, 147, 158, 164, 248, **295**
Hong Kong Polytechnic **295**
Hong Kong U Sci & Tech 21, **73**, 142, 153, 159, 163, 248, **295**
Houston **340**
Hull **328**
Humboldt U zu Berlin 22, 142, 147, 252, **291**

I

Illinois 21, **105**, 141, 153, 162, 249, **340**
Imperial College 21, **40**, 142, 152, 157, 162, 247, **328**
Indiana Bloomington 22, 147, 159, 253, **340**
Indian Inst of Tech Bombay IITB 22, 154, 163, 253, **296**
Indian Inst of Tech Delhi IITD 22, 163, 252, **296**
Indian Inst of Tech Kanpur IITK 164, **296**
Indian Inst of Tech Kharagpur IITKGP 164
Indian Inst of Tech Madras IITM 164, **297**

Indian Inst of Tech Roorkee **297**
Indonesia **297**
Innsbruck **272**
Iowa **341**
Iowa State **341**
Istanbul **324**
Istanbul Tech **324**

J

Jawaharlal Nehru **142**
Jagiellonian **315**
James Cook **269**
Jerusalem Hebrew U 21, **127**, 141, 147, 154,
 158, 250, **299**
Johannes-Gutenberg Mainz **292**
Johannes Kepler U Linz **273**
Johns Hopkins 21, **48**, 141, 147, 153, 157,
 164, 247, **341**
Joseph-Fourier Grenoble I **284**
Justus-Liebig Gießen **290**
Jyväskylä **282**

K

Kanazawa **303**
Kansas **341**
Karl-Franzens-U Graz **272**
Karlsruhe 164, **291**
Kasetsart **323**
Karolinska Institute 158
Kebbangsaan Malaysia UKM **309**
Keio **303**
Kent **328**
Kentucky **341**
King Fahd Petr. & Min **316**
King's College 21, **56**, 141, 147, 158,
 247,**329**
Kobe 22, 254, **303**
Köln (Cologne) **292**
Konstanz **292**
Korea **307**
Korea Adv Inst of Sc & Tech KAIST 21, **129**,
 153, 163, 250, **307**
KTH Royal Inst Tech Sweden 22, 154, 163,
 253, **319**
Kumamoto **303**
Kuopio **283**
Kyoto 21, **59**, 141, 147, 152, 158, 162, 247,
 304
Kyushu 22, 253, **304**

L

Lahore **313**
Lancaster 22, 142, 253, **329**
La Trobe 148, **269**
Lausanne 22,253, **321**
Laval **276**
Leeds 22, 148, 251, **329**
Lehigh **341**
Leibniz Hannover **291**
Leicester 22, 253, **329**
Leiden 21, **98**, 141, 147, 154, 159, 249, **311**
Leipzig **292**
Leuven Katholieke U 21,**106**, 141, 147, 154,
 159, 163, 249, **274**
Libre de Bruxelles 22, 254, **273**
Liège **274**
Lille U des Sci et Tech Lille I **284**
Limerick **299**
Linköping **319**
Liverpool 22, 252, **329**
Lomonosov Moscow State 22,153, 254, **316**
London Sch of Economics (LSE) 21, **100**, 140,
 147, 249, **329**
Los Andes **281**
Loughborough **330**
Louisiana State **342**
Louis Pasteur Strasbourg I 159, **287**
Louvain U Catholique de (UCL) 22, 141, 147,
 251, **274**
Loyola U Chicago **342**
Ludwig-Maximillians-U München (LMU) 21,
 128, 142, 147, 153, 159, 250, **293**
Lund 21, **122**, 142, 148, 154, 250, **319**

M

Maastricht 22, 141, 251, **311**
Macquarie 22, 148, 254, **270**
Mahidol **323**
Malaya UM **309**
Manchester 21, **63**, 142, 148, 158, 163, 248,
 330
Manitoba **276**
M-Luther Halle-Wittenberg **290**
Mannheim **292**
Marburg **292**
Maryland 22, 164, 251, **342**
Massachusetts Amherst 22, 254, **342**
Massachusetts Inst of Tech MIT 21, **43**, 140,
 146, 152, 157, 162, 247, **342**

Massey **312**
McGill 21, **54**, 140, 146, 153, 157, 162, 247, **276**
McMaster 22, 142, 154, 158, 164, 251, **277**
Melbourne 21, **72**, 140, 146, 153, 158, 163, 248, **270**
Miami **342**
Michigan **52**, 140, 146, 153, 158, 163, 247, **343**
Michigan State **343**
Milano Politecnico 164, **300**
Minnesota 21, **121**, 142, 159, 247, **343**
Missouri **343**
Monash 21, **81**, 141, 147, 153, 158, 163, 248, **270**
Montpellier II Sci et Tech Languedoc **285**
Montréal 21, **126**, 142, 147, 154, 158, 164, 250, **277**
Münster **293**
Murdoch **270**

N

Nagasaki **304**
Nagoya 22, 251, **304**
Nancy I Henri Poincaré **285**
Nanjing 22, 154, 159, 252, **279**
Nanyang Technological 21, **111**, 142, 159, 163, 249, **316**
Naples Federico II **300**
Nat Central Taiwan **322**
Nat Cheng Kung **322**
Nat Chiao Tung **322**
Nat Sun Yat-Sen **322**
Nat Tsing Hua **323**
Nat U of Ireland Galway **298**
Nat U Sci & Tech NUST (PAK) **314**
Nat U Singapore NUS 21, **65**, 140, 147, 153, 157, 162, 248, **316**
Nat Yang Ming **323**
Navarra **318**
Newcastle (AUS) **270**
Newcastle (UK) 22, 253, **330**
New Mexico **343**
New South Wales 21, **79**, 141, 147, 153, 158, 163, 248, **270**
New York NYU 21, **74**, 140, 146, 153, 158, 248, **343**
Niigata **304**
Nijmegen Radboud U **311**
North Carolina 22, 159, 250, **344**

North Carolina State **344**
Northeastern **344**
Northwestern 21, **67**, 141, 159, 164, 248, **344**
Norwegian U Sci & Tech **313**
Notre Dame 22, 148, 253, **344**
Nottingham 21, **120**, 159, 250, **330**
Nova de Lisboa **315**
Novosibirsk State **316**

O

Ohio State 22, 142, 251, **345**
Okayama **304**
Oklahoma **345**
Open, The **330**
Oregon **345**
ORT Uruguay **351**
Osaka 21, **78**, 153, 158, 163, 248, **305**
Osaka City **305**
Oslo 22, 253, **313**
Otago 22, 142, 148, 159, 251, **312**
Oulu **283**
Ottawa **277**
Oxford 21, **38**, 140, 146, 152, 157, 162, 247, **331**

P

Padua **301**
Panthéon Sorbonne Paris I 142, 148, **285**
Paris Sorbonne Paris IV 142, 147, **286**
Paris-Sud Paris XI 153, **286**
Paul Sabbatier Toulouse III **287**
Pavia **301**
Peking 21, **85**, 141, 147, 152, 157, 163, 248, **345**
Pennsylvania 21, **45**, 140, 147, 153, 158, 164, 247, **345**
Pennsylvania State 22, 142, 153, 164, 251, **499**
Peru Pontificia U Católica **314**
Philippines 148, **314**
Pierre & Marie Curie Paris VI 22,153, 252, **286**
Pisa **301**
Pittsburgh 21, **131**, 148, 250, **345**
Pohang U Sci & Tech 222, 254, **308**
Pompeu Fabra 142, **318**
Princeton 21, **46**, 140, 146, 152, 158, 162, 247, **346**
Pune **297**

Purdue 22, **133**, 154, 159, 163, 250 **346**
Putra Malaysia UPM **309**

Q

Quebec **277**
Queen Mary (UK) 22, 253, **331**
Queen's (Canada) 22, 141, 251, **277**
Queen's Belfast **331**
Queensland 21, **77**, 141, 148, 153, 158, 163, 248, **271**
Queensland U of Tech **271**

R

Reading 22, 254, **331**
Regensburg **293**
Rennes **287**
Rensselaer Polytech Inst 22, 164, 253, **346**
Rice 21, **114**, 250, **346**
Rio de Janeiro Fed U **275**
Rio de Janeiro Pontífica U Católica **275**
RMIT 164, **271**
Rochester 22, 251, **346**
Roma La Sapienza 147, 153, **301**
Roma Tor Vergata **301**
Royal Holloway **331**
Ruhr U Bochum **288**
Rutgers State New Jersey 22, 147, 154, 252, **346**

S

Saarland **293**
Sabanci **324**
St Andrews 21, **118**, 148, 250, **332**
St Gallen (HSG) **321**
Sains Malaysia USM **309**
Saint Petersburg State 154, **316**
Salamanca **318**
São Paulo 22, 154, 254, **275**
SOAS Sch Oriental & African Studies 148, **330**
Sciences Po **285**
Seoul National 21, **86**, 141, 148, 153, 158, 163, 249, **308**
Shandong **279**
Shanghai Jiao Tong 22, 159, 163, 252, **280**
Sheffield 221, **110**, 249, **479**
Showa **305**
Siena **301**
Simon Fraser 22, 142, 253, **277**

Smith College **347**
Southeast **280**
Southampton 22, **134**, 164, 250, **332**
South Australia **271**
South Carolina **347**
Southern California 22, 164, 250, **347**
Southern Denmark **282**
Stanford 21, **51**, 140, 146, 152, 157, 162, 247, **347**
Stockholm **320**
Stockholm Sch Economics 141, **320**
Stony Brook 22, 148, 154, 251, **347**
Strathclyde **332**
Stuttgart 22, 164, 254, **293**
Sung Kyun Kwan **308**
Surrey **332**
Sussex 22, 252, **332**
Swansea **332**
Swinburne U of Technology **271**
Sydney 21, **71**, 141, 146, 153, 158, 163, 248, **271**
Sydney U Technology **272**
Syracuse **347**

T

Tasmania **272**
Taiwan National 22, 142, 153, 159, 163, 251, **322**
Taiwan Nat Sci & Tech **322**
Tampere **283**
Tech U Berlin 22, 154, 164, 254, **288**
Tech U Braunschweig **288**
Tech U Darmstadt **289**
Tech U Dresden **289**
Tech U München (TUM) 21, **113**, 153, 163, 250, **293**
Technion Israel Inst of Tech 22, 153, 163, 251, **299**
Tecnologico de Monterrey ITESM **309**
Tehran **298**
Teknologi Malaysia UTM **309**
Tel Aviv 22, 141, 148, 153, 251, **299**
Temple **348**
Tennessee **348**
Texas A&M 22, 154, 159, 163, 252, **348**
Texas at Austin 21, 104, 142, 147, 153, 163, 249, **348**
Thammasat **324**
Thessaloniki Aristotelian U **295**
Tianjin **280**

Tohoku 22, 154, 164, 251, **305**
Tokai **305**
Tokyo 21, **53**, 140, 147, 152, 157, 162, 247, **305**
Tokyo Institute of Tech 21, **95**, 153, 162, 249, **306**
Tokyo Metropolitan **306**
Tokyo Science (TUS) **306**
Tomsk **316**
Tongji **280**
Torcuato di Tella **268**
Toronto 21, **75**, 140, 146, 152, 157, 162, 248, **278**
Toulouse I Sci Soc **325**
Trento **302**
Trieste **302**
Trinity College Dublin 21, **83**, 141, 147, 154, 159, 248, **299**
Tromso **313**
Tsingua 21, **90**, 141, 148, 153, 158, 162, 249, **280**
Tsukuba **306**
Tübingen, Eberhard Karls 22, 148, 159 , 253, **294**
Tufts 22, 28, 59, 253, **348**
Tulane **348**
Turku **283**
Twente 22, 254, **311**

U

UCSC U Cattolica dell Sacre Cuore **300**
Ulm **294**
U Campinas Unicamp **274**
University College Cork **298**
University College Dublin 22, 142, 148, 251, **298**
University College London UCL 21, **41**, 141, 147, 154, 158, 164 , 247, **333**
Umeå **320**
UNAM México 22, 148, 159, 252, **310**
United Arab Emirates **325**
Uppsala 21, **97**, 142, 148, 153, 159, 249, **320**
Utah **349**
Utrecht 21, **101**, 142, 148, 153, 159, 249, **311**

V

Valencia **319**
Vanderbilt 22, 158, 250, **349**
Victoria (CAN) **278**

Victoria Wellington (NZ) 142, 148, **312**
Vienna 22, 159, 251, **273**
Vienna U Tech 141, 147, 153, 164, **273**
Virginia 21, **130**, 250, **349**
Virginia Commonwealth **349**
Virginia (Poly)Tech 163, **349**
Vrije U Amsterdam 22, 252, **310**
Vrije U Brussels **273**

W

Wageningen 22, 252, **312**
Waikato **313**
Wake Forest **350**
Warsaw **315**
Warsaw U of Tech **315**
Warwick 21, **103**, 141, 148, 154, 249, **333**
Waseda 22, 142, 147, 253, **306**
Washington 21, **93**, 154, 158, 164, 249, **350**
Washington U in St Louis 21, **93**, 158, 249, **350**
Washington State **350**
Waterloo (CAN) 22, 153, 163, 251, **278**
Western Australia 21, **119**, 159, 250, **272**
Western Ontario 22, 253, **278**
WHU Otto Besiheim Koblenz **415**
William & Mary **350**
Wisconsin Madison **89**, 141, 147, 153, 158, 164,249, **350**
Wollongong **272**
Würzburg **294**

X

Xi'an Jiaotong **280**

Y

Yale 21, **36**, 140, 146, 152, 157, 163, 247, **351**
Yeshiva **351**
Yokohama City **306**
Yokohama National **307**
Yonsei **308**
York (CAN) 141, 148, **278**
York (UK) 21, 116, 250, **333**

Z

Zhejiang **281**
Zurich 22, 159, 251, **321**

Index of topics

This non-exhaustive, index of topics gives pointers to some of the subjects and organizations in the editorial chapters of this book, not obvious from the contents listing on page nine.

For information on specific countries and associated study organizations, please refer to chapter three, in particular.

For details of scholarship giving organizations worldwide, please refer to the country sections in chapter three and the special section on scholarships in chapter four.

For sources of information on higher education worldwide, please refer to the table in chapter six.

The content of the profiles of the THE-QS World University Rankings top 100 have not been separately indexed.

A

Abraham Lincoln Study Abroad Act 169
academic peer review 257
Agriculture 151, 161
AimHigher 212
alumni 25, 35- 34
archeology 145
Archive of the Americas 145
architecture 145
arts and humanities **145-148**
ASEAN Scholarships 194
astronomy 151
automotive 161, 168

B

banking/financial services 168, 169
biology 151, 156
biomedicine & life sciences) **156-159**
Bologna Accord 29, 181
botany 151, 156
British Library 145
business school 25, 168, 240
business studies 161

C

career 26, 29, 146, 168
Chartered Institute of Marketing 193
chemistry 145, 151
citations 258
climate change 139, 161

consulting 68

D

DAAD German Academic Exchange Service 182
DIAC 173
dietician 156

E

economics 139
education fair 25
EJU 183
engineering and IT 145, 151, **161-164**
environmental science 151
European Social Survey 139

F

film 145
forensic science 151
forestry 151
Fulbright Foundation 160
funding study **227-233**

G

government studies 139
GMAT® 240
GRE® 240

H

histology 156
higher education data sources worldwide
263-265
history 145, 152
homeopathy 156

I

IBT 238
IELTS™ 173, 177, 187, 193, 203, 238
Institute of Education 146
Institute of International Education 169
international skills 168
internship 168
interviews 237
Ivy League 199

J

JASSO Japan Student Services
Organization 183
journalism 139

L

languages 18, 145,
law 145
librarianship 146
life sciences and biomedicine 18, 19, 88, 307
313, 316
linguistics 152
living costs 226
LSAT 240

M

manufacturing 145
masters 17, 25, 26, 29, 161, 167, 168, 169,
181, 189, 233, 240
materials science 151, 161
mathematics 139, 151
MBA 139, 162, 169
medical engineering 156
medical school 156
medical sociology 139
medicine 145, 156, 161
metallurgy 151, 161
microbiology 156

molecular science 151
music 146

N

nanotechnology 161
National Science Foundation 151
nursing 156

O

OECD 18, 167
oncology 156

P

peer review 257
pharma/healthcare 156
PhD 17, 25, 26, 30, 152, 161, 168, 169, 181,
223, 240
politics 139, 169
physics 151
physiotherapy 156
population studies 139
Procter & Gamble P&G 34, 35
professional services 32-34
public service 139
publishing 145

Q

QS World Grad School Tour 25, 169
QS World MBA Tour 25

R

rankings methodology 257-262
robotics 161, 162

S

Scopus™ 258
scholarships 229-232
science (natural sciences) 151-154
Silicon Valley 161
social sciences 139-142
sports medicine 156
stem cells 161
study abroad 167-209
study abroad information sources 209

T

teaching 140, 146
technology (engineering & IT) **161-164**
television 145
theatre 146
theology 145
THE-QS World University Rankings 2008 **244-62**
- top 200 21, 247
TOEFL® 77, 187, 193, 203, 238

U

UCAS 98, 239
UNESCO 167
Universities Admissions Centre UAC 337
university application **235-241**
university tuition fees **211-225**

W

World Bank 211

Z

zoology 151, 156

Index of advertisers

Top Universities Guide is very grateful for the support from its sponsors and advertisers

A

Australian National University 11

B

Bandung Institute of Technology 160
Bruno University of Technology 165

C

Chung-Ang University 204

D

Dubai International Academic City 7

E

ETS GRE® 234
ETS TOEFL® 16

G

Griffith University 135
University of Groningen 186

H

Hanyang University 352
Hitotsubashi University 184
University of Hong Kong
    Inside back cover
City University of Hong Kong
    Inside front cover & 155
Hong Kong Polytechnic University 8
HKUST Hong Kong University of
    Science & Technology 12

I

IELTS™ 24
Inha University 219
Instituto de Empresa 143

K

KAIST Korea Advanced Institute of
  Science and Technology 20
Khon Kaen University 255
King Fahd University of Petroleum & Minerals
  31
King's College 196
Kyung Hee University 136

M

Mahidol University 202
University of Melbourne 172
Michigan State University 200

N

Nanyang Technological University NTU
  Front cover flap
National Yang-Ming University 220
National University of Singapore
  – Business School 192
University of Newcastle (AUS) 175
University of New South Wales 2
Tisch School of the Arts, New York University
  (NYU) 144

P

Pohang University of Science and Technology -
POSTECH 138

Q

QS APPLE 210
QS Global Workplace 171
QS World Grad School Tour 28
QS Scholarships 228
QS Showcase 366
QS WorldARTS 191
QS WorldCLASS 364
University of Queensland 27

S

Università Cattolica del Sacro Cuore 206
Scopus™ 256
Swinburne University of Technology 246

T

Tecnológico de Monterrey 166
TopUniversities.com 208
TopUniversities Fairs 32
University of Toronto 176
Trinity College Dublin 149

U

UiTM Universiti Teknologi MARA 150
UKM Universiti Kebangsaan
  Malaysia Back cover flap
UM University of Malaya 1 & 266
UPM Universiti Putra Malaysia 242
UTM Universiti Teknologi Malaya 23
UNITEN Universiti Tenaga Nasional 368
Universitas 21 Global 195

Y

Yonsei University Bookmark & 5

World *Class*

Classroom for Leaders of Asia's Schools

THE - QS World
University Rankings

Boost your university's global recognition!

Exclusive two-day/three-night seminar and social networking for university executive heads and senior planners

As part of its continuing efforts to help university leaders understand the **THE–QS World University Rankings** and propel their institutions towards global recognition, QS Asia takes you through a highly exclusive annual series of top-level lifestyle seminars at some of Asia's most exciting destinations - Singapore 2008, Bali 2009 and Langkawi 2010.

Network and discuss high-end university strategies with not just your Asian peers but also other key industry players and top personnel of major employers in a relaxed and hospitable atmosphere that includes sports and leisure activities.

An extremely elite congregation meant only for key decision makers and senior level management, consideration of a sponsorship opportunity would be most valuable for your institution in increasing its brand visibility and awareness.

For further details, please contact us or visit **www.qsworldclass.com** for more information

QS ASIA QUACQUARELLI SYMONDS PTE LTD
Tel: +65 6457 4822 Email: enquiries@qs-asia.com

Notes

SHOWCASE

An exclusive top-level showcase of the workings of Asia's best universities

From the producers
of THE-QS World
University Rankings

> ▶ Top Asian university leaders present the best of their institutions to their peers across the world, conveying their aspiration to make a key contribution to the advance of global higher education standards.

Sustained economic growth in Asia over the last twenty years has helped propel many of its universities into the top tier of world education. The advent of global ranking of universities has ensured that this status now achieves international visibility. Capitalising on their historically high standards of higher education, these institutions now have a tale to tell to their peers in America, Europe and Australasia.

To be published annually from April 2010 onwards - in high quality print and online - QS WorldClass SHOWCASE will offer an exclusive top-level showcase of the workings of Asia's best universities.

OBJECTIVES
- To increase the awareness of Asian universities at top level among the best higher education institutions in America, Europe and Australasia.
- To provide a platform upon which leading Asian educationalists and industry leaders can share their achievements, strategies and philosophies with their worldwide counterparts.
- To examine the methodologies used in university rankings and relate them to the advancement of global higher education standards.

CONTENTS OF QS WorldClass SHOWCASE
- Exclusive interviews with presidents of top Asian universities
- Exclusive interviews with Asian education ministers
- Feature interview with a global celebrity who passionately advocates the benefits of education
- Feature interviews with leaders of major Asian corporations
- Tables of the QS Asian University Rankings with commentary
- Tables of THE-QS World University Rankings with commentary

DISTRIBUTION
The printed edition of QS WorldClass SHOWCASE will be presented free of charge to each of the two top executive heads (e.g. president and provost) of the following:
- Top 500 Universities as featured in the THE-QS World University Rankings
- Top 200 Universities as featured in the QS Asian University Rankings
- China's 106 "Project 211" Universities
- Top 20 Indian Universities
- Top 20 Middle East Universities
- Key embassies worldwide
- Top 200 Asian Corporations ranked by THE-QS World University Rankings under "Recruiter's Review"

ONLINE
QS WorldClass SHOWCASE online edition hosted at www.qsworldclass.com, may be freely accessed via web browsers. It will be publicised by emails sent to the QS-APPLE (www.qsapple.org) world wide academic community comprising some 63,000 senior faculty and administrators in over 60 countries. Search engine optimisation expertise will be applied during the editing of the texts to ensure that the pages will appear high in Google and other searches.

For more information, please contact **Mandy Mok** at +65 9841 9121 or mm@qsnetwork.com

Notes

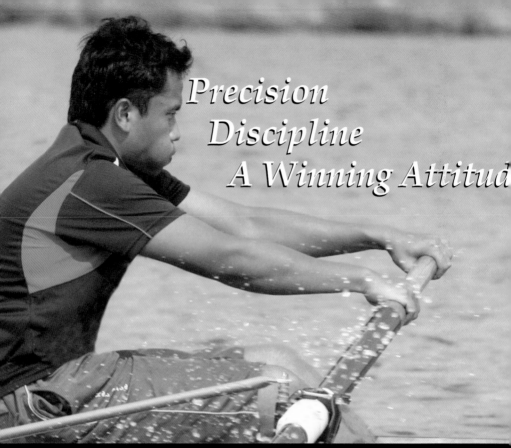

Precision
Discipline
A Winning Attitud

The Hallmark of a University Education - UNITEN

Recognized worldwide for outstanding achievements in **Research, Innovation** and **Academic Excellence**

www.uniten.edu.n

UNIVERSITI TENAGA NASIONAL
(398494K)

UNITEN GENERATES PROFESSIONALS

Putrajaya Cam
43009 Kajang, Selangor, Mal
Tel: +60-3-8921 2020 / Fax: +60-3-8928
crm@uniten.ed